Y0-DBV-117

J J W

Spirituality of the Premonstratensians

CISTERCIAN STUDIES SERIES: NUMBER TWO HUNDRED FORTY-TWO

Premonstratensian Texts and Studies, 2

François Petit, O. Praem.

Spirituality of the Premonstratensians

The Twelfth and Thirteenth Centuries

Translated by
Victor Szczurek, O. Praem.

Edited with a Foreword by
Carol Neel

α

Cistercian Publications
www.cistercianpublications.org

LITURGICAL PRESS
Collegeville, Minnesota
www.litpress.org

A Cistercian Publications title published by Liturgical Press

Cistercian Publications
Editorial Offices
Abbey of Gethsemani
3642 Monks Road
Trappist, Kentucky 40051
www.cistercianpublications.org

Originally published as:
François Petit, *La spiritualité des Prémontés aux XIIe et XIIIe siècles*
© Librairie Philosophique J. Vrin, Paris 1947
http: www.vrin.fr

© 2011 by Order of Saint Benedict, Collegeville, Minnesota. All rights reserved. No part of this book may be reproduced in any form, by print,
microfilm, microfiche, mechanical recording, photocopying, translation,
or by any other means, known or yet unknown, for any purpose except
brief quotations in reviews, without the previous written permission of
Liturgical Press, Saint John's Abbey, P.O. Box 7500, Collegeville, Minnesota
56321-7500. Printed in the United States of America.

1	2	3	4	5	6	7	8	9

Library of Congress Cataloging-in-Publication Data

Petit, François, O. Praem.
    [Spiritualité des prémontrés au XIIe et XIIIe siécles. English]
    Spirituality of the Premonstratensians : the twelfth and thirteenth
centuries / François Petit ; translated by Victor Szczurek ; edited with
a foreword by Carol Neel.
        p. cm. — (Cistercian studies series ; no. 242)
        (Premonstratensian texts and studies ; 2)
    Includes index.
    ISBN 978-0-87907-242-1 — ISBN 978-0-87907-795-2 (e-book)
    1. Premonstratensians—Spiritual life—History. 2. Monastic and
religious life—History—Middle Ages, 600–1500. I. Neel, Carol.
II. Title.
BX3903.P3 2010
271'.19—dc22

                                                    2010031507

Contents

Foreword

The present volume undertakes a task rarely embraced by contemporary scholarship in historical and religious studies—to render in English a distinguished, much-cited European work of the mid-twentieth century. The magisterial stature of this 1947 study of the religious culture and spiritual practice of the medieval Premonstratensians by François Petit, O. Praem., *La Spiritualité des Prémontrés*, has elicited this unusual and demanding enterprise.[1] The inherent interest in this book's material, the continuing vitality of the author's perspective, and the influence of his work on subsequent scholarship alike testify to its potential usefulness for the wider audience excluded by the limited availability of the French original, long since out of print. Like Herbert Grundmann's *Religiöse Bewegungen*, a work of some twelve years before Petit's likewise recently made available to a wide English-speaking readership as *Religious Movements in the Middle Ages*, Petit's essay is at once robust history, essential historiography, and still-fresh discussion of some of the most important aspects of medieval religious culture.[2] At the same time, its evocation of historical spiritual patterns

---

[1] François Petit, *La Spiritualité des Prémontrés aux XIIe et XIIIe siècles*, Études de théologie et d'histoire de la spiritualité 10 (Paris: J. Vrin, 1947).

[2] Herbert Grundmann, *Religious Movements in the Middle Ages: The Historical Links between Heresy, the Mendicant Orders, and the Women's Religious Movement in the Twelfth and Thirteenth Century, with the Historical Foundations of German Mysticism*, trans. Steven Rowan (Notre Dame, IN: University of Notre Dame Press, 1995). This work was first published as *Religiöse Bewegungen im Mittelalter: Untersuchungen über die geschichtlichen Zusammenhänge zwischen der Ketzerei, den Bettelorden und der religiösen*

presents twenty-first-century readers with an engaging, enriching alterity to their own understanding.

Petit's work on the development of the spirituality of the Order of Prémontré remains the only monograph in any European language on this major aspect of the medieval reformation. The Premonstratensian or Norbertine Order—founded by the ascetic preacher Norbert of Xanten in 1121 ~~in Burgundy~~ and often called by medievals and moderns alike "white canons" after their distinctive dress—spread across Europe and into the Holy Land in the course of the twelfth century, then worldwide in modernity. Professional scholarship on this order's origins and efflorescence has nonetheless been disproportionately scant.[3] Petit's synoptic interpretation of Premonstratensian sources and his generous inclusion of lengthy quotations from them have ironically, in their respective persuasiveness and abundance, discouraged scholars of the next few generations from undertaking further study of the literature, historical figures, and spiritual practices he addresses. This was surely not Petit's intent. Indeed the present translation aims to build on recent efforts in this series and elsewhere to redress the dearth of studies of the medieval white canons, inviting others to continue Petit's investigations. The present English version thus represents this early twentieth-century author's synoptic exploration of the spirituality of the early canons in Norbert's filiation for those with specialist interest in this religious order. Because Petit is everywhere concerned to set Premonstratensian religious culture in the wide context of the medieval Church, moreover, this translation also offers his work to the many more readers interested in medieval history generally and in the development of Christian thought through the centuries.

Central to Petit's employment of the history of Western religious orders is his description of the white canons, clergy living a common religious life according to the Rule of Saint Augustine on the

---

Frauenbewegung im 12. und 13. Jahrhundert und über die geschichtlichen Grundlagen der deutschen Mystik: Anhang, Neue Beiträge zur Geschite der religiösen Bewegungen im Mittelalter (Hildesheim: Olms, 1935).

[3] For basic bibliography on Norbert of Xanten and his early followers, see Theodore J. Antry and Carol Neel, trans., *Norbert and Early Norbertine Spirituality*, CWS (New York: Paulist Press, 2007), 243–45, nn 1–8.

Norbertine model, as the necessary interstitial development between the monastic communities of the early Middle Ages and the mendicant movements of the thirteenth century.[4] While this satisfying framework for understanding the medieval proliferation of varieties of religious life is now widely accepted, Petit's formulation adds rich detail from the writings and practices of the canons of the early centuries. His work is thus path-breaking and at the same time determinative of much later scholarship on historical spirituality. Indeed, Grundmann's mightily influential work is itself shaped by analogous commitment to a wide view of European piety and practice through the lens of a distinctive charism, along the lines of argument that shape Petit's thesis on Premonstratensian influence.[5]

At the time of Petit's writing during the Second World War for the volume published shortly thereafter, "spirituality" was a category of human experience relegated to the fringes of scholarly consideration. Devotional works considered spiritual practices, texts, and traditions—indeed some might be scholarly—but in general the imaginative and interior lives of individuals were not considered appropriate material for the historian's craft. Conversely, works on historical spirituality from the earlier twentieth century rarely achieved scholarly integrity with respect to source usage, awareness of historical contexts, and solidity of argument. The great originality and utility of Grundmann's work—the first major historical survey of the devotional lives and ascetic practices of ordinary folk, especially women—was to recast interpretation of agency in medieval European religious life to acknowledge the influence of lay and feminine voices. Similarly, the power in Petit's study of the Premonstratensians of the early centuries is its demonstration of the articulateness and originality of the collective voice of an order, as he acknowledges, generally unconcerned with formal canonization or eminence of office, instead shaping the laity's spiritual lives through ritual observance and the modeling of locally honored saints.[6] Neither intellectual history narrowly speaking nor precisely social

[4] Petit, esp. 33–34, 267.
[5] Robert E. Lerner, intro to Grundmann, *Religious Movements*, esp. 5.
[6] Petit, for instance 91, 102.

history, scholarship on the history of spirituality such as Grundmann's and Petit's, focused rather on the nexus of theology and
devotion, remained for decades, except for a few outstanding works,
marginalized in the professional study of the European past. In the
later twentieth century, however, attention to spirituality has
emerged as among the most exciting, illuminating, and productive
aspects of historical research. Petit's work has experienced new life
in the context of works such as André Vauchez's study of European
sanctity across centuries (*La sainteté en Occident*) and Caroline
Bynum's attention to the incarnational piety and ascetic behaviors
of medieval women (*Holy Feast and Holy Fast*).[7]

Among an abundant recent literature valorizing the kinds of
texts from which Petit reconstructed the shape and essence of the
medieval Order of Prémontré, several elements have emerged as
closely related to his objectives in *Spirituality of the Premonstratensians* and generally affirmative of his sense of the importance of the
white canons and other twelfth-century Augustinians to the transformation of European religious life in their period. Among these,
the works of Christopher Brooke, Giles Constable, and Rachel
Fulton require special mention here for the ways in which they
mirror and develop arguments toward which Petit pointed. Brief
attention to these scholars' works here will at once demonstrate
the ongoing vigor of *Spirituality of the Premonstratensians* and invite
readers' attention to further scholarship in its tradition. Brooke's
general framework for the development of the medieval reform is
enshrined in his essential survey, *Age of the Cloister*. Like Petit,
Brooke takes the Premonstratensians as the most radically innovative of the twelfth-century reform movements.[8] Constable's more
detailed study of the twelfth-century orders, depending in part on
Philip of Harvengt, a Premonstratensian author pivotal in Petit's

----

[7] André Vauchez, *La sainteté en occident au derniers siècles de moyen age: d'après les
procès de canonisation et les documents hagiographiques* (Rome: École française de Rome,
1981); Caroline Walker Bynum, *Holy Feast and Holy Fast: The Religious Significance
of Food to Medieval Women* (Berkeley: University of California Press, 1987).

[8] Christopher Brooke, *The Age of the Cloister: The Story of Monastic Life in the
Middle Ages* (Mahwah, NJ: HiddenSpring, 2003). See especially Brooke's chapter,
"St. Norbert and St. Francis" (217–32) in which he calls Norbert "[t]he most original
exponent of apostolic life in the twelfth century" (217).

analysis, takes exegesis of the story of Mary and Martha as key to differences among the twelfth-century charisms.[9] Fulton's treatment of the affective character of twelfth-century religious life—arguably the most important and persuasive work in English on medieval spirituality in the past two decades—again focuses on Philip of Harvengt as the most adventuresome element in the period's rapidly developing cult of the Virgin; her work is explicitly indebted to Petit's extraordinarily broad reading and sensitive response to the medieval sources.[10]

Despite its profound value for scholars and readers of the current generation, Petit's work poses some difficulties in translation. This version, rather than obscuring his work's difference from more recent and English-speaking conventions, embraces his distinctively generational and Francophone traits as central to his perspective and essential to his work's historiographical importance. Despite its proximity to the most thoughtful and compelling of recent interpretations of medieval religious life, *Spirituality of the Premonstratensians* is very much a work of the French mid-century. The author's style is discursive, frequently conversational, sometimes intimate—written in a tone unknown to more recent academic publications and generally alien to the more reserved English manner of scholarly expression. Petit's deep familiarity with the great corpus of medieval texts from the order also leads him to reference sources less meticulously than readers here, schooled in Anglo-Germanic tradition, may expect.

At the same time, Petit reveals his own allegiances and opinions about the past in a way professional historians and medievalists working in religious studies—even more recent spiritual authors—generally now eschew. He argues, for example, not only on behalf of the Premonstratensians but also of the mendicants, especially the Dominicans, that the Augustinian pattern of religious life adopted by Prémontré and the Preachers responded to the spiritual

---

[9] Giles Constable, *Three Studies in Medieval Religious and Social Thought: The Interpretation of Mary and Martha, The Idea of the Imitation of Christ, The Orders of Society* (Cambridge: Cambridge University Press, 1995), esp. 44–92, esp. 71–72.

[10] Rachel Fulton, *From Judgment to Passion: Devotion to Christ and the Virgin Mary, 800–1200* (New York: Columbia University Press, 2002), esp. 351–404.

aspirations of the times in ways that other strains of medieval religious life did not.[11] Petit often effectively apologizes for medieval
authors that they were incompletely in conformity with later doctrinal developments they cannot have imagined, as though his
commentary need redress their error, so making their works suitable
for a modern orthodox readership. This tendency is most evident
in his discussion of early Premonstratensian writers' incomplete
embrace of the notion of the Immaculate Conception.[12] For the
most part, since Petit's generation, scholarship has purported to
take the past more or less on its own terms, not embarrassed by its
differences from the beliefs of later times, and with appreciation
of its characteristic perspectives.

All of these traits of Petit's analysis—the unabashed advocacy
of Prémontré's excellence relative to other medieval religious
groups, the way he addresses his readership, his general ease in
reference to biblical, patristic, and medieval sources, even his welcome to his readers into the Premonstratensian community as "we"
(and indeed many of his original readers were members of the
order, as some of this translation will be)—are preserved here.
Finally, Petit's frequent, deeply French reference to human beings
in their spiritual lives as *âmes*, souls, is spared in this English version
from paraphrase that might distance it from his exact sense, that
Norbert of Xanten touched the souls of many Europeans such that
souls then followed him into religious life.[13] Such terms, anomalous
in English, convey Petit's distinctive perspective with an accuracy
a more idiomatic rendering would obscure. While some effort has
nonetheless been made to adjust a rambling French text to English
standards of economy of style, it has seemed best to change Petit's
sense as little as possible so that his voice may emerge the more
transparently.

Toward the same end, because Petit found it essential that his
notes include much more substantial quotations from Latin sources
than modern publishers and readers generally invite, his full textual
footnotes are reproduced here. Many of his citations are from the
Patrologia Latina (PL), which is indeed available to Latin readers in

[11] Petit, 34.
[12] Petit., 255–56.
[13] Petit, for example, 11.

both hard and electronic copy in many libraries worldwide. Petit seems in some instances to have emended PL texts, perhaps in comparison with other editions unmentioned by him, and this translation reflects his readings. Others of his source quotations, however, are from seventeenth- and eighteenth-century Continental publications to which access is difficult even in the United States and Britain. Petit's rich notes are in any case a gateway to all readers, especially those with flexible Latin, to the rich, full repository of the literature of the medieval Premonstratensians. This publication of Petit's study in English, therefore, preserves that path into their religious culture. It invites those whose interest in the order is new to engage with its texts more fully in their entirety, in both the PL and various early modern collections of texts on religious life in the twelfth and thirteenth centuries.

In general, Petit's source references are revised to include the full bibliographical details he sometimes omitted. When he cites the works of major theologians or canon law collections available in multiple editions, indicating no preference, his citations remain here as standard text divisions. Similarly, where he refers to the *Acta Sanctorum* or sermon collections by date or feast day, those designations are preserved. In a few instances, Petit cites small local publications or other obscure works for which bibliographical details are inaccessible even through electronic cataloguing tools; his references in those cases are included as he left them. Throughout, the editor's intent has been, where possible, to ease access to Petit's sources without burdening his text with the recent bibliography to which readers of this foreword will in any case be directed.

Translation of cited passages in the body of this text has privileged Petit's readings in his own French version rather than adjusted their sense to conform more exactly to the Latin of the notes. Meanwhile, it would be impossible to supply all the citations of the scriptural allusions that Petit and his sources would immediately have recognized but most moderns would not; again, therefore, in regard to Vulgate, patristic, and even literary citations, Petit's text is here left much as he intended, with English adjusted to the Douay Bible.

One further aspect of this English representation of Petit's *Spirituality* requires explanation in this context. Since this work's original publication, manuscript and textual analysis have indisputably

revealed that the so-called "Sermon of Saint Norbert," which Petit
included in an appendix and which he clearly hoped was the
founder's own text, is a later work.[14] No word thus survives from
Norbert of Xanten's pen—an uncomfortable circumstance from the
point of view of anyone interested in the history of the Order of
Prémontré, whether from a scholarly or devotional perspective. The
editorial board of this series indeed considered carefully whether
this sermon, reputed for many centuries to be authentic, ought to
be omitted from the present volume. Our conclusion, as supported
by the translator, Victor Szczurek, O. Praem., has been that because
of the long reception of the sermon within the order as Norbert's
own, and because François Petit included it not only for its reflection of the founder's ideas but also to support his discussion of the
influence of this text in the medieval and later order, it should be
reproduced here.[15] Translation of the "Sermon of Saint Norbert" is
therefore included at the end of this volume. Readers are nonetheless reminded that, demonstrably proximate though the sermon's
central notions are to the thought of Norbert's immediate followers,
these are not his precise words.

The present volume thus offers Petit's vision of medieval
Prémontré to a twenty-first-century readership sensitized by recent
scholarship to the centrality of spirituality in medieval culture and
to the important place of this work's subjects, the white canons, in
the great reformation of the twelfth century. This translation draws
the reader's attention to Petit's many documentary, theological,
hagiographical, and liturgical sources as well as to the Latin origi-
nals imbedded in his notes. Those readers who may pursue further
investigation of the medieval order and its several eminent authors
will wish to consider the recent bibliography on aspects of Premonstratensian history and the order's authors assembled in the Classics
of Western Spirituality volume, *Norbert and Early Norbertine Spirituality*, edited by Theodore Antry, O. Praem., and myself. This CWS
collection of Premonstratensian sources envisions a readership

---

[14] Wilfried M. Grauwen, "Die Quellen zur Geschichte Norberts von Xanten," in
Norbert von Xanten: Adliger, Ordensstifter, Kirchenfürst, ed. Kaspar Elm (Coligne:
Wienand, 1984), 15–33, esp. 20–21.

[15] Petit, 273–82.

similar to that of the present volume and so emphasizes works in English.[16] Interested readers may also wish to review the bibliography on the first great Premonstratensian writer, Anselm of Havelberg, in the first number of this series, Premonstratensian Texts and Studies.[17] Petit would have been gratified to know that his own work has found a place alongside the dialogues of Anselm, Norbert's close friend and powerful instantiation, among English-speakers worldwide.

Carol Neel, for the editors of
Premonstratensian Texts and Studies
December 7, 2009
Feast of Saint Ambrose

[16] Antry and Neel, esp. 285–300.

[17] Anselm of Havelberg, *Anticimenon: On the Unity of the Faith and the Controversies with the Greeks*, trans. Ambrose Criste and Carol Neel, Premonstratensian Texts and Studies 1, CS 232 (Collegeville, MN: Cistercian Publications, 2010), esp. 219–25.

Introduction

The history of spirituality is a field of study new to the Church. How have souls sought to encounter God during different periods of history? How have they prayed? With what thoughts have they been nourished? What devotions have inspired them? What penitential practices have they embraced? How have they received the sacraments? Many such important questions bear on the psychology of religion, opening up for us the heart of the Church. In fact, everything ecclesiastical—the Church's hierarchy, its works of mercy, its relations with secular authority, its intellectual life, its canon law, its religious orders—has always had as its final goal to support the spiritual life of Christians. Spirituality is a wisdom shaping all others, and anyone who lives at the heart of the Church is not surprised to see a pope such as Leo XIII attribute more importance to his encyclicals on the Sacred Heart or the rosary than to those that treat of Thomist theology or the situation of the modern working class. Yet before the nineteenth century spirituality seemed not to have had a history; spiritual life appeared to have essentially been the same for all souls at all times, consistent in its shape and expression. None of the great spiritual writers of history were thought to have been innovative, rather to have recovered the essence of Christianity without intending to shed light on different points of view or engaging in novel practices.

Today we wish to know, however, about the historical development of this inner activity of souls. Although the broad lines of this past are now well known, large areas are still to be explored; these areas are not barren, as they might heretofore have seemed, but rather are rich in teaching, examples, and beauty. The spiritual history of the Premonstratensians during the twelfth and thirteenth centuries is one of these little-known regions of the past. Yet even at first glance it is clear that a religious order embracing more than a thousand European houses, serving many rural parishes and exercising influence evident throughout the long medieval period, must have been endowed with a deep spiritual richness. Close investigation here will allow us to see and to judge this as an age of great spiritual transformation distinguishing the Christian devotion of antiquity from modern piety. Authors of great genius—Saint Bernard for example—may mislead modern readers regarding a more general history because their own personal conceptions and sensibility shape rather than reflect their milieu.

Among the medieval Premonstratensians, however, we witness the ascetic and mystical development of the great mass of people guided by their priests. We see the development of an increasingly tender devotion to the humanity of our Lord and the Virgin Mary. We witness the first large-scale attempt to provide the priesthood with not only a stimulus to perfection but also a powerful means of raising itself to spiritual heights. We admire a movement toward the divine life that goes beyond the cloister and draws the laity—both men and women—toward sanctity. The splendor of Cluny and the austerity of Cîteaux are here integrated in an apostolic movement seeking to revive in priests and clerics the intensity of the religious life of the first Christians gathered around the apostles: this is the central character of the first centuries of Prémontré. Men trained, equipped, and steeped in pastoral spirit developed this movement. We do not know everything about them. The most skilled florist in the world, even Glycera herself, can put into a bouquet only what she can find, but the interest in this aspect of medieval spirituality is immediately evident.

The first part of the following work will explore the lives of the founder, of his first followers and of the first writers of the order, as well as their tendencies and notions regarding the spiritual life, in chronological order. The second part will investigate the great syntheses of the spirituality of the order set forth by the two principal Premonstratensian writers of the later twelfth century, Philip of Harvengt and Adam Scot. Finally, the third part, revisiting all this material, will offer a general discussion of Norbertine life during the Middle Ages.

Part 1

Historical Development

Chapter 1
The Canonical Way of Life
before Saint Norbert

The Order of Prémontré, like many other important human institutions, came into being only after a variety of attempts to achieve similar ends. Its eventual development was elicited and enabled by a specific combination of circumstances. Saint Norbert's vision is clarified by its historical context in the earlier development of the canonical way of life—hence the inclusion here of a summary of earlier historians' perspectives on this complex past.

Since the beginning of Christianity a few men and women adhering wholeheartedly to the counsels of the Gospel text have founded their search for God in self-denial. Ascetics, virgins, and widows were obliged in early Christian times to live in the world, first in secular families, later in religious communities as monastic life developed. These individuals' ascent toward a life of perfection was guided by bishops, priests, and deacons—especially by bishops, whose role it is to carry both the whole Church and its individual souls toward perfection. But what was the character of the personal life of these clerics, these spiritual masters? What example did they offer? What elevation of thought, purity of heart, and sanctity of life was appropriate to their lofty rank? Did they embrace the self-imposed renunciation of the ascetics? The personal sanctity of many of these clerics leaves no doubt—and the number of martyrs that they have given to the Church irrefutably attests—that they indeed were ascetic, but did their model leave its mark on clerical institutions? Since the establishment of the Church, the canons of the various councils have required of the clergy not only an exemplary life but also true personal asceticism. Celibacy was gradually imposed. Clerics were required to renounce economic engagement, involvement in secular affairs, frequent travels, cohabitation with women, games of chance, and many other worldly occupations. Further, attempts were made from time to time to encourage priests and clerics to live in community after the manner of monks. The most important of these efforts was Saint Augustine's.

When Monica's son converted, he turned at the same moment to the Catholic Church and to the monastic life he had come to know in reading the life of Saint Anthony. Augustine established a monastery in his home at Tagaste. When he became a priest of Hippo, he transferred his monastery to this town, but after he was made bishop and could no longer live where his brothers did he transformed the bishop's residence into a religious house in order to live there in common with his priests, deacons, and subdeacon. "I wished," he explained to his people, "to have here a monastery of clerics, *monasterium clericorum*."[1] Like many other expressions flowing from Augustine's pen, this phrase was wonderfully apt. Those whom the illustrious bishop gathered around him were not monks but clerics maintaining their duties as priests and deacons at the service of the Church and the Christian people. Yet their house was at the same time a true monastery offering the means of sanctification practiced by monks: chanting the psalms at the canonical hours, reading sacred scripture, manual labor, silence, common meals, frequent fasting, stability in community. These clerics were bound by strict poverty after the example of the Christians of Jerusalem and the apostles. Augustine did not demand such a life for all clergy; if an individual did not want to embrace asceticism the bishop was glad to transfer him into another church. But the clerics of Hippo might not abandon poverty, that is, strict community of possessions, without breaking their vows and falling

---

[1] Augustine of Hippo, *De vita et moribus clericorum*, Patrologiae cursus completus, series Latina (Paris: J.-P. Migne, 1857–66), 39, cols. 1570–71. Migne's great edited collection is hereafter cited as PL.

from their holy profession. Meanwhile, all dressed as did Augustine himself, in an undecorated linen garment taken from the community's vestry. This small community of Hippo—a seedbed of saints, breeding ground of bishops, and the first sustained experience of a clerical religious life—would remain the paradigm for all later regular canons, the Premonstratensians in particular, wishing to establish monasteries of clerics in order to seek priestly perfection through the asceticism of regular religious life. In itself Augustine's community was a magnificent success, but it lasted only a little longer than the incomparable bishop who had devoted himself to it. Nevertheless, it would not be forgotten.

In the eighth century another such attempt was made on a large scale by Saint Chrodegang, bishop of Metz (A.D. 746–66). Up until that time canons—that is, clerics attached to major churches and living according to the laws or canons of the ecclesiastical councils —had lived separately in their respective homes. In order to direct them toward a loftier lifestyle and to increase the fruits of their apostolate, Chrodegang ordained that these canons live in community near the cathedral. To constrain such clerics to the Rule of Saint Benedict then widely in use would have indeed been difficult in practice. Chrodegang instead wisely composed a new rule necessarily retaining a number of Benedictine observances but refashioning them in a novel way.[2] The canons of Metz remained together during the night but in the morning after their chapter—a meeting of the community at which the word of God was preached, daily tasks and obediences distributed, then faults corrected—they went to the cathedral or into the different churches of the town to perform the divine service and to be of use to the faithful. The clerics took their meals in common and they returned to their cloister as often as their duties allowed them. In one regard, however, their lives were less well-ordered than those of the clerics of Hippo: Chrodegang left to these canons the ownership of their respective inheritances, so that they held in common only the revenues of their church. This concession would have disastrous consequences for the canonical way of life for a long time to come.

---

[2] Chrodegang of Metz, *Regula canonicorum secundum editionem Labbei*, PL 89, cols. 1098–1120.

With respect to spirituality, Chrodegang insisted above all on humility because the Carolingian clergy were inclined to pride, imperiousness, and harshness. The canons' principal pious practice was the divine office. Chrodegang, promoting Gregorian chant, had introduced Roman usage in the singing of the psalms in Gaul. His followers celebrated the office with profound reverence, but private prayer also had its place. Reading and meditating on sacred scripture followed the chanting of the nocturns. Novices learned the psalms by heart. Penitential practices were numerous. Manual labor was assigned during the morning chapter by the bishop, archdeacon, or *primicerius*;[3] canons confessed at least twice a year; they maintained fasting and abstinence; superiors reminded the community of their faults and imposed penance upon them; the canons did service to the poor and the sick in the town hospice. They were encouraged to receive the Eucharist frequently, at least on Sundays and feast days. They held zeal in high esteem.

These developments were grounded in the clear-headed, practical spirit that would come to mark the future. Chrodegang's attitude toward inheritance, however, left undefined any separation of regular from secular canons according to whether they accepted complete renunciation of property. Nonetheless, the role he attributed to liturgical prayer and his institution of monastic asceticism and service to the sick and poor would become essential characteristics of the canonical way of life. The rule composed by the bishop of Metz solely for his own cathedral was quickly accepted by a number of churches. Although it was a practical and precise canonical document, however, it lacked the spiritual stature of the Rule of Saint Benedict. When prelates commented on it in their chapters it failed to encourage varied and substantial instruction. Furthermore, it was unsupported by any strong ecclesiastical authority.

In 817 the Council of Aachen therefore produced another rule at the behest of the emperor Louis the Pious.[4] This rule did not contradict the work of Chrodegang, rather amplified it. Amalarius,

---

[3] Translator's note: The *primicerius* was a dignitary of a diocese either in charge of the liturgy or perhaps director of the cathedral school.

[4] *Forma institutionis canonicorum et sanctimonialium*, PL 105, cols. 821–976.

a priest charged with the composition of such a work by the bishops of the council, made a great compilation of writings of the Latin Fathers on the priesthood and the clerical life. He added the canons of the various prior ecclesiastical councils on the same subject. Saints Isidore of Seville, Gregory the Great, Jerome, Julianus Pomerius, and Augustine, whose discourse on the life and morals of the clergy Amalarius cited in its entirety, furnished the essential texts. The complete rule of this Council of Aachen is divided into sixty-five chapters. Its selections from the Fathers embrace little theory; its entire content is practical and pastoral, not to say commonplace. The text's consistent teachings are that priesthood demands sanctity and that nothing is so deplorable for the Church as a cleric unconcerned with his own moral perfection.

The Rule of Aachen would become the subject of pious homilies, yet it lacked canonical clarity. The world for which the Fathers had spoken and the ancient councils had legislated had long since disappeared. Meanwhile Amalarius' compilation added a few practical provisions, reproducing those of Chrodegang in their entirety but without the same precision. It continued to stress the importance of the divine office, of beautiful liturgical chant and of service to the sick and poor. Wise provisions addressed the administration of canonical schools where young men preparing to enter communities of canons were formed. These small schools, seminaries before the term existed, were strictly run. The cantor taught Gregorian chant, other canons taught other subjects according to their respective skills and a general supervisor took charge of the program as a whole. Since the ninth century the cloister of canons has thus necessarily been a house of studies. To observe God's commandments, to live soberly, to embrace fasting, to prefer nothing to Jesus Christ, to obey the bishop, to love and help the poor, to celebrate the divine office with great respect, to maintain claustration, to study, to do useful manual labor, to do everything to maintain peace among the brethren: this is the ideal presented by the Rule of Aachen. From the point of view of poverty, however, this rule remained faithful to the views of Saint Chrodegang in refraining from imposing on the canons any renunciation of familial goods, instead charging them to live in common from the revenues of the Church.

A third rule—this one anonymous—was drawn from the preceding, widely known rules of Chrodegang and of the Council of Aachen. It seems to date from before the eleventh-century Gregorian Reform.[5] Some of its elements are of interest for the history of spirituality. The prayers of the chapter, the martyrology, the prayer for the day's work, the reading of the rule, accusation of faults, the superior's announcements: all these aspects of spiritual practice had by this point taken on the form still represented in the modern breviary. Common recitation of the general confession began around the same time. Correspondingly, this third canonical rule gave instructions on mental prayer, conceived above all as confession both as acknowledgment of faults and praise of God. Sacramental confession became frequent, emerging as an instrument of perfection. Finally, the responsibility to preach regularly in a manner intelligible to ordinary people was imposed on the canons.

All three Carolingian rules remained in use during the tenth century and the first part of the eleventh, but would soon afterward prove to be insufficient. In the feudal context serious abuses appeared among the clergy. The grave heresies of simony and nicolaism were widespread. Bishoprics and abbeys were made into virtual fiefs and purchased like lay benefices: simony. In order to keep such offices in their respective families as seigneurial possessions, clerics attempted to contract marriages: nicolaism. Soon all holy offices and ritual objects such as parishes, canonical prebends, relics, and churches became objects of simony, such that moral depravation pervaded the ecclesiastical hierarchy.

Even in this gloomy period in the history of the Church, its centuries of iron, heroic saints nonetheless emerged to stem disorder. Hildebrand, later the pope-saint Gregory VII, and Saint Peter Damian, cardinal bishop of Ostia, were eminent among these heroes. Their straightforward goal was to bring the clergy back to the life of the apostles. In 1059 at a council in Rome over which Pope Nicholas II presided, Hildebrand, then a cardinal deacon, praised those canons of Rome who had just renounced all property in order to embrace a life in community like that of the early

---

[5] *Regula canonicorum secundum Dacherii recensionem*, PL 89, cols. 1057–98.

Church. This formulation would be key to the entire later movement. Now there would be no question of the clerics' retention of their inherited goods while living off the revenues of a given church. They would be required to embrace a poverty like that of monks and that practiced by the first Christians of Jerusalem who had gathered around the apostles. Their common life would render concubinage and other misconduct impossible, while poverty would protect the Church from simony.

The same Roman council required that priests, deacons, and subdeacons live in community in immediate proximity to the churches to whose service they had been ordained and where they would now also eat and sleep. The council also enjoined them to the common life, that is to the complete renunciation, according to the apostolic model, of such personal goods as had been given them. Peter Damian, with his indomitable energy, supported his letters and accounts about this council by detailing its participants' views. For him the mandate of clerics was framed in two passages from scripture. The first is taken from the Acts of the Apostles: "The multitude of believers had but one heart and one soul. Neither did any one say that aught of the things which he possessed, was his own; but all things were common unto them" (Acts 4:32). The second is found in the Gospels, in Christ's commission to the apostles: "And he commanded them that they should take nothing for the way, but a staff only; no scrip, no bread, nor money in their purse" (Mark 6:8).[6]

Thereafter canons were divided into two groups. Those who desired to keep their familial goods and hold in common only the revenues of the Church were called secular canons. Their property did not prevent them, during the Middle Ages, from living together in a canonical house. Others, the many clergy who embraced complete poverty, were, in contrast, called regular canons. Their existence affirmed that the call of the saints and of the Church had indeed been heard, so great was the need for serious reform. Many cathedral chapters and lesser collegiate churches embraced apostolic poverty in the same places where their clergy had the care of

---

[6] This identification of a twofold scriptural source for apostolic poverty reflects medieval notions of an evangelical spirit and the apostolic spirit.

souls. These regular canons' aim was the better ordering of their clerical life and fulfillment of their duty. Thus Arnulf, patriarch of Jerusalem, formed a college of regular canons from the chapter of the Church of the Holy Sepulcher in order that life in community be pursued by an exemplary clergy in the very place where the apostles had first established it. Regular canons embracing the reform of poverty founded other churches, particularly in the suburbs of large towns beside the tombs of important local saints, to house clergy seeking a perfect life. These included Saint Quentin of Beauvais (1073), Saint Victor of Paris (1110), Saint-Jean-des-Vignes of Soissons (1076), and Mortain (1082). Arrouaise was founded in 1097 by three hermit priests—Heldemar, Conon, and Roger—who had joined together in order to live in community according to the new dispensation; the same Conon appears again in the story of Saint Norbert. Those new houses in which the care of souls was less urgent made more use of monastic practices, as might be expected. Among the latter foundations emphasis lay more on the religious life of clerics than on their apostolate—inevitably so, for their clergy were too numerous for all of them to be occupied with laypersons.

In general, after some discernment, the regular canons of the seventh and eighth centuries adopted the Rule of Saint Augustine, although this text did not appear in exactly the form in which it does today. After a preamble on the love of God and neighbor, the Rule presented a brief set of strictures for the monastery. Saint Augustine's authorship of this work has been denied by some scholars, but Mandonnet and others along with him consider it an authentic spiritual commentary recorded in a letter of Augustine to the religious of Hippo. The entire text forms only a slim booklet, but one of rare spiritual richness.[7] This Rule contains the description of the ancient liturgical office as it existed before the development of the psalmody of the Rule of Saint Benedict.[8] Conforming to Eastern traditions, this older text of the Rule of Saint Augustine notes that the office—that is, the chanting of the psalms as separate

---

[7] See Pierre Mandonnet, O.P., *Saint Dominique, l'idée, l'homme, et l'oeuvre*, Vol. 2 (Bruges: Desclée de Brouwer & Cie, 1938), 107–9.

[8] *Alia regula incerti auctoris*, PL 66, cols. 995–98.

from the readings and at hours set by the Church—is essential to daily monastic practice.

Next in the text of the Rule of Saint Augustine comes a simple statement of the order of activities: among the various hours of the office, manual labor from morning to noon, *lectio* or divine reading from noon to three o'clock, then rest and work again until *lucernarium*, that is, our vespers. After further reading followed by psalms—what would become compline—came retiring for the night until midnight, when the night office was sung. After this the confreres returned to bed until the morning, when the day began with the chanting of what we today call lauds. These observances are very simple and severe, assuming complete poverty. No one possessed anything for himself, neither clothes nor anything else. This was the apostolic life the regular canons sought: *apostolicam enim vitam optamus vivere.*[9] This text alone was enough to make the Augustinian Rule precious. No murmuring; obedience to the superior and his assistant; reading at table; when confreres were required to go out, they went two by two, like the apostles sent by Christ; silence in the house; the expulsion of those who did not keep the rule—all this on one page. A later commentary by Saint Augustine did not have the same administrative precision and would be insufficient for establishing a community life, but this related text was nonetheless rich in spiritual teachings concerning all that was essential to religious life in the West.[10] Above all it insists on the complete renunciation of temporal goods, following the example of the Church in Jerusalem, as on chastity, obedience, and brotherly love.

The Rule of Saint Augustine was accepted with enthusiasm because of the poverty that it imposed. Nevertheless adjustments were necessary because this African rule was impractical in its detail in the north of Europe. Furthermore, the office had evolved in the intervening period, as had monks' daily fast, now extending until the middle of the afternoon, with the three hours of *lectio* in the

---

[9] "We wish to live the apostolic life." Augustine, *Regula secunda*, PL 32, cols. 1449–51. This is a famous phrase of the Middle Ages, and one that we shall find time and time again.

[10] Augustine, *Regula ad servos Dei*, PL 32, cols. 1377–84.

middle of the day and manual labor occupying most of the remaining time. Such monastic practices were unsuitable to the needs of the clerics. Thus on August 11, 1118, Pope Calixtus II wrote to the canons of Springiersbach, who had consulted him in this regard, counseling them to observe with the grace of God all the good practices contained in the rule but to celebrate the office according to the general custom of the Church and to keep fast and perform manual labor according to local conditions and practicalities. This papal advice would enable adaptations to the Rule of Saint Augustine. Although the spirit displayed in the commentary was to be preserved, appropriate statutes might be substituted for some of the Rule's content. After 1150, the attached commentary would disappear from almost all the manuscripts and the Rule itself would take the form in which it has since been known. Saint Augustine could not have foreseen the general success of this small work written for a specific context. His Rule had so striking a rhythm that it was as memorable as a verse of Corneille; it was so rich in content that the abbots and provosts could comment on it to the full extent of their learning and zeal. The Rule especially appealed to the lovers of spiritual beauty who sought in it the instrument of their perfection.

Alongside the desire for the reform of the clergy expressed in the revival of the Rule of Saint Augustine was another important eleventh- to thirteenth-century effort for the renewal of Christianity, characterized by contemporaries as an apostolic movement.[11] The great medieval reform, as yet little researched but nonetheless one of the most important in the history of the Church, saw three phases. It began with the foundation of new religious orders, among them the Order of Prémontré. It continued in a proliferation of heretical groups when the new orders could no longer contain its influence. Finally this apostolic movement was restrained and reshaped by the development of the mendicant orders of the thirteenth century. Its governing notion was a return to the perfection of the early Church. Clerics reformed themselves by embracing the poverty of the apostles, while their public preaching of this ideal led the laity to wish to take part as well. Why, the faithful asked

[11] See Mandonnet, Vol. 2, 163–64.

themselves, should the apostolic life be reserved to the clerics? They are indeed the successors of the apostles, but did not Saint Luke say that at Jerusalem the multitude of believers gathered around the Twelve, having abandoned their individual goods to common use, persevered in prayer and adhered to the teaching of the apostles and the breaking of bread? Desire for religious life took hold of the masses. Men offered themselves to monks or clerics in order to assist them, but even more women were so moved. They gave their humble service daily with the devotion of servants. Among the villages daughters of peasants renounced marriage in order to live under the direction of priests. Even married folk wished to live the religious life. Why did they not become monks in the ancient abbeys? Perhaps there was a lack of space, but more probably they desired a life less contemplative than the Benedictines. They thirsted for work and devotion.

Bernold of Constance assures us that such lay devotion was widespread in Germany.[12] If he had been familiar with the orders of Grandmont, Fontevrault, Arrouaise, Savigny, and Prémontré, he would have realized that it was no less common in France, because in the foundations of all these orders the number of brothers and nuns far surpassed that of the clerics. The Order of Cîteaux itself, faithful though it was to the ancient monastic spirit, was the most important manifestation of the apostolic movement's rapid expansion. The movement grew thus: an apostle, often a saint, began to preach from town to town. In an age when parish priests no longer proclaimed the word of God he was enthusiastically received, often arriving with a companion according to the Gospel model of the apostles' traveling two by two. This preacher was dressed like a hermit, in a habit of wool or of lamb or goat skin. A hooded mantle completed his attire. His life was absolutely selfless; he was poor, without money like the apostles themselves, inflamed with the poverty of Christ and the ideal of the early Church. Stephen of Muret, Robert of Arbrissel, Bernard of Tiron, Vitalis of Savigny, and Norbert of Xanten all conformed to this model. Their eloquence won hearts because they preached not only an ordinary Christian

---

[12] Bernold of Constance, *Bernoldi Chronicon*, PL 148, col. 1407.

life but the perfection of the first Christians. Eventually each of them founded a double monastery in order to gather there both clerics and the men, women, and children who followed them. The founders themselves continued their itinerant preaching with the same ardor after establishing their communities and, in some cases, giving them monastic rules. Grandmont and Fontevrault were among this group. Others, realizing more clearly the importance of the clergy in the new institutions, incorporated their foundations into the movement of regular canons: Prémontré, Arrouaise, Marbach. The monasteries of the new religious movements in general were double. Next to a common church they housed clerics and brothers on one side and women religious on the other. The practice of double communities was, however, short-lived because related difficulties ensued. In 1120, for instance, Saint Vital moved his community's women religious elsewhere. Hugh of Fosses, first abbot of Prémontré, and Walter, third abbot of Arrouaise, soon followed suit, but the tendency toward double monasteries would reappear at each subsequent renewal of the apostolic movement.

Because of this great revival religious life flourished greatly between the eleventh and thirteenth centuries. Between 1050 and 1150 the number of religious houses tripled; the new monasteries, composed especially of peasant men and women, cleared more land and built more churches, farms, and barns in the next hundred years than Europeans had since Roman times. Such then was the spiritual climate in which Saint Norbert began the foundation of the Order of Prémontré. It was an age in which religious communities would expand, diversify, and rejuvenate with fervor, in order to render service to the Catholic Church for the good of souls and the support of the poor. Regular religious life was now a social force adapted to all the needs of the Christian world.[13]

---

[13] Until that time religious life had been completely monastic and consecrated to the individual salvation of those who embraced it.

Chapter 2
The Spiritual Ideas of Saint Norbert

The most influential and well-developed of the canonical communities, the Order of Prémontré, takes its name from the small village in Aisne between Laon and Soissons, where it was founded in 1121 by Saint Norbert. For the Premonstratensians, as for any religious order, the life of the founder and the circumstances behind his work determine its spirituality. Thus far this volume has treated only the circumstances of the origin of the Order of Prémontré, but now we come to the decisive moment at which Divine Providence effected its appearance in history. Norbert of Gennep, the founder of the Premonstratensians and eventual illustrious archbishop of Magdeburg, was a marvelous figure of the early twelfth century. His contemporaries, unaware of the prestige the future would attribute to the writings of Saint Bernard, instead assigned Saint Norbert the higher rank.[1]

The story of Saint Norbert's life is well known from several virtually contemporary sources. Norbert died in 1134. In 1149 Herman, a monk of Laon, wrote a history of the miracles of Our Lady of Laon in which he recounted at length the foundation of

---

[1] Herman of Tournai, *De miraculis Laudunensis de gestis venerabilis Bartholomaie episcopi et S. Norberti libri tres*, PL 156, col. 995: "One might commend Dom Bernard, abbot of Clairvaux, who at that time accomplished so many great works. But be careful here, for he did not found an order. . . . He was not the one who planted the new tree in the Church's field; he simply watered it and helped it grow numerous strong branches. Norbert, on the other hand, planted the fruitful tree of Prémontré; he was truly a founder."

Prémontré.[2] Likewise, around the year 1155, a Premonstratensian began a continuation of the famous chronicle of Sigebert of Gembloux; this author included the principal elements of Saint Norbert's life.[3] At about the same time the Premonstratensians of Cappenberg in Westphalia wrote the history of Saint Godfrey, their founder. This text as well contained much on Saint Norbert.[4] Finally, between 1155 and 1164 an explicitly biographical account appeared. Two versions survive: a work of German origin (*Vita A*) discovered in a manuscript of Saint Peter's, Brandenburg;[5] and another redaction from France (*Vita B*) copied at the behest of the blessed Hugh of Fosses, the successor of Saint Norbert in Prémontré.[6] Despite the similarity of these two lives throughout much of their respective texts, their precise relationship is difficult to establish.

Fewer than thirty years after his death Saint Norbert's memory was thus already secured in the historical record. Documents of other kinds—letters, papers, charters, and books—might enable reconstruction of Saint Norbert's life even if the surviving, precious accounts had disappeared, but Norbert did not leave behind any works from his own hand. From the perspective of the history of spirituality this is a serious lacuna in the sources. We do not know Saint Norbert's ideas on the spiritual life except from secondary records. Our sources are sufficient, however, that other documents can corroborate their historical testimony with only a few small gaps. Regarding the saint's ascetic and mystical life, these extant sources are true to the master's own tradition. Their authors, notably, were not inspired evangelists and each purports to expound precisely this matter of spirituality, yet their writings are useful with the caveat that, while opening up for us the thought of Saint Norbert, they offer as well the views of the entire first generation of Premonstratensians on the founder and his work.

---

[2] Herman, cols. 987–99.

[3] Sigebert of Gembloux, *Chronica*, PL 160, cols. 57–546.

[4] *Analecta Norbertina*, PL 170, cols. 1343–50.

[5] *Vita Norberti archiepiscopi magdeburgensis*, Monumenta Germaniae Historica Scriptorum 12, ed. Roger Wilmans (Hanover, 1956), 663–703. [Editor's note: This series is cited hereafter as MGH, and this version of Norbert's life as *Vita A*.]

[6] *Vita S. Norberti auctore canonico Praemonstrantensi coaevo*, PL 170, cols. 1257–1343. This version of Norbert's life is hereafter cited as *Vita S. Norberti* in notes or, in the text, occasionally as *Vita B* to emphasize its later composition.

To tell the entire history of Norbert is impossible here. Besides, it is accessible to all through many books—and good ones at that. Here, nonetheless, are the stages in the life of Norbert of Gennep:

1085(?)–1115: He spent his youth in the cloister of Xanten, at the court of the archbishop of Cologne, and at the court of Emperor Henry V. This was a joyful period, but also turbulent. Norbert was wasting his life.

1115–21: Norbert saw lightning strike close to him in the country-side. He converted, then received both the diaconate and the priest-hood; soon afterward he went out barefoot to preach the Gospel.

1121–26: During this period he founded the Order of Prémontré.

1126–34: Saint Norbert was named archbishop of Magdeburg. He worked for the reform of his diocese, for the expansion of his order, for its missions in northern Germany and in the struggle against the anti-pope Pierleoni. He died exhausted, worn out from penance.

Norbert founded his canonical order during the shortest of these periods (1121–26). At that time he clearly already had framed his spiritual doctrine in its fullness. That doctrine was so ample that the memory of those fertile years has never ceased to nourish Saint Norbert's spiritual children.

The Psychology of Saint Norbert

Investigation of the genesis of Norbert's ideas on the regular religious life is an important task, and the psychology of the future founder is in turn crucial. Norbert was from the start a person of extraordinary energy and imagination, endowed with irresistible attractiveness. He was handsome of face, slender in stature, rather tall,[7] and of cheery demeanor, never pallid,[8] smiling.[9] He was refined in his courtesy

---

[7] *Forma decorus, statura gracilis ac paululum longus. Vita S. Norberti,* PL 170, col. 1257.

[8] *Non vidit eum quisquam vel ad modicum pallescere. Vita S. Norberti,* PL 170, col. 1335.

[9] *Aspectu hilaris, vultu serenus.* Bartholomew of Laon, *Donationes piae S. Norberto et Praemonstratensibus factae,* PL 170, col. 1359.

and delightful in his manner,[10] so effortlessly able to be all things to all men. Further, his voice was attractive, his speech articulate and moderate, mature without pretension, so that it is no surprise he fascinated others. Men and women alike flocked to him. Important individuals like Godfrey of Cappenberg and the highborn Adele of Montmorency and Ricwer of Clastres asked that he invest them in the religious habit. Popes Gelasius II, Calixtus II, Honorius II, and Innocent II enjoyed his charm. Emperors Henry V and Lothair, bishops Bartholomew of Laon, Josselin of Soissons, and Godfrey of Chartres as well as important monks like Saint Bernard and Guibert of Nogent—all these lavished upon him their esteem and admiration. To see him was to love him.

In regard to his interior life, Norbert had so lively an imagination that in his youth he could not endure long periods of quiet or prayer—yet he would become a great contemplative.[11] His tastes were lofty. From his childhood he loved beautiful horses, fine clothes, and perfect cleanliness. He would later apply these standards to the altar and the splendor of divine worship. Like his contemporaries, he was sensitive to symbols as metaphors for more concrete notions.

Although always self-possessed,[12] Norbert was also sensitive. He was embarrassed at receiving gifts even though he himself gave generously and magnificently.[13] He wanted everything he saw, beginning with pleasure, and he especially craved intellectual enjoyment. Eventually he would wish to gain Christ himself. Such an external comportment, lively imagination, and delicate sensibility bear witness to an exceptional temperament; and Norbert added to this a transparent intelligence. He studied first in the cloister of Xanten where, from the age of eight or nine, he was registered in the chapter as just such a scholar as the Rule of Aachen had envisioned in its establishment of canonical schools. Later, according to the local practice, Norbert may have attended the monastic school of Siegburg. As a young subdeacon he was further trained

---

[10] *Gratus omnibus et habilis universis.* Bartholomew, PL 170, col. 1359.

[11] *Religionis et quietis impatiens.* Bartholomew, PL 170, col. 1359.

[12] *In manu consilii sui positus.* Bartholomew, PL 170, col. 1359.

[13] *In dando profusus, in accipiendo pudibundus.* Bartholomew, PL 170, col. 1359.

in the court of the archbishop of Cologne, then among the chaplains of the emperor,[14] in that form of education provided by lords to their future knights, pages, and horsemen. The life of Saint Norbert demonstrates that this was the general experience of young clerics as well. In ecclesiastical courts during the intellectual renaissance of the twelfth century, pleasure was the general rule.

But Norbert also studied. *Eloquio excultus, homo litteratus:*[15] he was widely known for the cultivation of his speech and his profound literacy. The program of studies he experienced had likely not yet risen to the high standard of the later twelfth century, because learning was still recovering from the prior ages of iron. And yet, if, as is quite probable, the dialogue between a monk and a cleric of Rupert of Deutz concerns Saint Norbert, Philip of Bonne Espérance's remark about that interlocutor holds special interest:[16] "That cleric probably had not read the letters of Saint Jerome, or if he did he did not remember them, but if in respect to knowledge of Porphyry or Aristotle, he would surely have been unrivaled. Indeed he would have far surpassed the monk, for, he was well schooled in secular literature and eloquent in debate. But he had also studied religious works so deeply that, in the debate he had with the monk, the teachers of the school of Laon asked about the matter judged his position to be the better."[17]

Norbert certainly was skilled in the Latin literary craft of his time. He was thoroughly familiar with both sacred scripture and the teaching of the Fathers, and indeed from his model we better understand those prescriptions for education that appear in the canonical rule of 817. Meanwhile at court he saw at close hand the administration of a vast diocese. He learned about the important affairs of the state; for clerics as the only literate persons were necessarily consulted in those regards—a rich education for an intellect as sharp and broad as his. Yet Norbert was not then and never

---

[14] *In curia regis mecum pariter nutritus est. Vita S. Norberti,* PL 170, col. 1274.

[15] "He was gifted with eloquence, a man of letters." *Vita S. Norberti,* PL 170, col. 1257.

[16] Rupert of Deutz, *Altercatio monachi et clerici, quod liceat monacho praedicare,* PL 170, cols. 537–42.

[17] Philip of Harvengt, *De institutione clericorum tractatus sex,* PL 203, col. 807.

would be an intellectual, strictly speaking. He was an acute observer of life and learned at least as much from men and situations as from books. His intellect turned toward the practical in the noblest sense of that word. As for secular politics, he understood them well. He granted the religious habit to Godfrey of Cappenberg but refused it to Theobald of Champagne, whose entry into religion would have thrown the kingdom of France into disarray. Norbert's engagement with various emperors was also consistent, following what has been termed the *politique lorraine*: devotion to the empire on the condition that the Church's liberty would be fully respected.

Norbert distanced himself from Henry V when that emperor treacherously captured Pope Paschal II. He then went to ask the pope's pardon for the part that he had unknowingly played in that incident. After his conversion Norbert sought out Pope Gelasius II although Emperor Henry supported the anti-pope Maurice Burdin; he had previously turned down the bishopric of Cambrai because he would have been required there to uphold lay investiture. He would later give excellent advice to Emperor Lothair on overcoming the schism of Pierleoni. As a result, Lothair unhesitatingly made Norbert his chancellor for Italy, but in the very church of the Lateran he refused this office in the presence of the pope. Innocent II had there been ready to grant the emperor ecclesiastical investitures in recompense for Norbert's appointment.[18] Norbert thus demonstrated himself completely in agreement with the reform of Gregory VII. Thus, although his family's alliance with the emperors and dukes of Lorraine, as well as his relations with the kings of France and their counselors, lent him a keen political sense, he was before all else a man of the Church even before his conversion, in his commitment to honorable fulfillment of the duty of his office. He was that much more a churchman when he came to believe that ecclesiastical life required sanctity. But Norbert understood feudal society thoroughly and committed his time, eloquence, and strength to settling the private wars rending Christendom.[19] He thought on a large scale and held justice paramount, so nothing infuriated him

---

[18] This episode, unknown to some prior historians of the saint, had been recorded in the *Vita Norberti A*.

[19] *Vita S. Norberti*, PL 170, cols. 1278–82.

so much as seeing persons of bad faith refusing to respond to reason. Unhappily he was often so grieved.

Norbert's clarity of thinking was matched by a steadfast will. Protestant critics of our day have accused him of stubbornness and obstinacy. These words are too strong; the even-handedness of this apostle precluded any narrow-minded or egotistical action. Rather his energy was indefatigable.[20] Once he decided something, his enemies—and he did have them—would know that it was impossible to divert his plan. The words of Saint Jeanne de Chantal about Saint Francis de Sales are equally applicable to Norbert: "He never gives up." As his life notes, "To hold fast was his firm desire."[21] Norbert was then a great enthusiast with a clear, fair-minded intellect.

Conversion

Norbert nonetheless took a long time before making complete use of his gifts. Although some who knew him thought that he should be ordained a priest, he remained a subdeacon. He initially avoided the responsibilities of the priesthood because he had a very lofty notion of it, and he had not yet found the courage to live so holy a life. He was too faithful to be a bad priest and too attached to his rich and easy life full of amusements—perhaps too attached to his delightful and absorbing secular studies—to have the resolve to live fully as a priest. This was the dilemma with which he was confronted.

Then in 1115, on his way to the town of Freden, Norbert was surprised by a sudden storm. Lightning threw him from his horse. After a moment of stupor or unconsciousness he heard a voice commanding him from the depths of his heart: *Turn away from evil and do good: seek after peace and pursue it* (Ps 33:15). This word from God pierced him like a sword and he was converted; but he took his time in declaring this conversion. All would eventually know that he wanted to be at once priest and saint. "He preferred to receive the clothing and adornments of his new life at the same time:

---

[20] *Vita S. Norberti*, PL 170, col. 1259.
[21] *Vita S. Norberti*, PL 170, col. 1326.

the religious habit and the dignity of the priesthood."[22] We must, however, take care here not to misinterpret his actions. Norbert still was unsure what form his religious vocation would now take, whether it would be the same religious vocation he already had embraced, as that canonical status was then understood in Church law—whether he would remain a canon under the Rule of Aachen, take on the garb of a pilgrim, hermit, or monk, or become a regular canon. He still did not know. But in any case it would be the habit of a poor man. At the same time that he received the priesthood he would publicly vow to follow the Gospel to the letter. He would both be a priest and aspire to holiness.

Before this profession, however, Norbert would undertake purification. According to the words of Jeremiah, rooting up and tearing down must precede planting and building (Jer 1:10). To change a savage and ravenous hawk into a simple and sweet dove is a daunting task, yet Norbert would undertake this battle with himself quickly and forcefully. "He gathered all his strength, fortified his soul, framed lofty ideals, then transformed his tastes and goals in order to redirect them completely."[23] Norbert imposed upon himself a sort of novitiate, "training strenuously for his future conversion."[24] He disappeared from court, returning to live at his family's home at Xanten or at the Abbey of Siegburg with the saintly abbot Conon. He read the lives of the saints, studying and meditating on sacred scripture. He then contemplated the life he would undertake, the poverty he would embrace, and the sufferings and struggles he would surely encounter. For the brave, to meditate on suffering is to relieve suffering: "He was comforted by untiring meditation."[25] Evidently he struggled, impatient, with his own impetuousness. Norbert reminded himself, however, that Jesus Christ had to wait for his own hour as determined by his Father. The disciple could certainly wait as his Master had done. Besides, the gifts received at his ordination would be the more precious for the wait. In the end

---

[22] *Malens simul novi hominis indumentum et ornamentum suscipere, illud quidem in habitu religionis, istud vero in dignitate sacerdotii.* Vita S. Norberti, PL 170, col. 1262.

[23] *Mutavit funditus atque convertit omnia vitae suae studia ad vias alias et omnino diversas.* Vita S. Norberti, PL 170, col. 1261.

[24] *Tirocinia quaedam futurae conversionis exercens.* Vita S. Norberti, PL 170, col. 1261.

[25] *Infatigabili meditatione levigabat.* Vita S. Norberti, PL 170. col. 1261.

—beat calmly, great hearts of the Middle Ages!—the devil's dismay would be the greater in the glorious triumph of the magnificent King in his servant.[26]

The time finally arrived, likely during the Ember Days before Christmas in 1115. At the feet of his archbishop, Norbert asked to receive diaconate and priesthood at the same time. His preoccupation was consistently this: that priesthood and renunciation of the world go hand in hand as a twofold vocation. The archbishop was astonished. To receive two sacred orders on the same day was contrary to canon law. Norbert explained himself with great feeling. The prelate did not understand Norbert's reasons, but he saw that the candidate was committed to his plan and he understood that this ordinand was acting under the secret inspiration of the Holy Spirit. Finally, the archbishop's affection for Norbert moved him to grant the request and he gave his dispensation.

On the appointed day Norbert presented himself at the cathedral of Cologne. Ever since the incident at Freden he had had a hair shirt under his clothes, but he had continued to wear his rich attire over it. Norbert wore under his cloak an ermine or marten garment lined with silk—the dress of a nobleman, appropriate for an emperor's chaplain. His attire showed nothing of the Church. Such was then the convention, that, except for the regular canons, the clothing of clerics and that of the laity was indistinguishable outside of church. But at the moment the sacristan presented him with the sacred vestments, Norbert turned toward the servant who had accompanied him. He took off his lavish clothes and put on a sheepskin garment, nothing more, to the great surprise of those present. Over this, the humble garb of hermits and itinerant preachers during the twelfth century, the ordinand put on his sacred vestments. At this period, when luxurious fur marked the higher social classes, Norbert's abandonment of his accustomed attire signified before the Church and Christian people that he had renounced all pomp, vanity, and works of the devil and that he would henceforth belong completely to God. The ceremony came to a close. Norbert received his orders and publicly trampled upon the judgment of men. He would now be a priest and would live as a poor man.

---

[26] *Ac per hoc malignus spiritus se gravius in circumstantium conspectu rueret, quo magnificus Rex in Norberto gloriosius triumpharet.* Vita S. Norberti, PL 170, col. 1262.

Norbert spent the next forty days on retreat among his friends, the monks of Siegburg. He needed to become skilled in the priestly practices, especially in the celebration of the Mass. He also learned the particular ways of the religious life.[27] For Norbert there would always be this same conjunction: priesthood and religious life. Nor would this be the last time that Norbert would open himself to the instruction of others; he welcomed their teaching. An educated layman like Saint Francis of Assisi would improvise the form and organization of his order; Saint Norbert and Saint Dominic, on the other hand, submitted themselves to tradition as was appropriate for them as learned and inspired. The orders that they founded were shaped by their model. Norbert would later study in Laon, where he again sought the company and the counsel of holy men.

But let us return to Xanten for the solemn celebration of Norbert's first Mass. The new priest took his place in the embrace of his collegial chapter as was entirely natural. As he assumed, he might live there in holiness and poverty. The Rule of Aachen followed at Saint Victor's was not a rule for religious, but if closely observed it might indeed bring sanctity. Norbert ascended the altar, then, after the Gospel, turned and preached—an extraordinary innovation. The world was dying of spiritual hunger but apart from some eccentrics—fools, heretics, or saints—almost no one preached.[28] And Norbert was not content to live poverty; he was determined also to preach it.

The content of this new convert's preaching is of course of interest. He preached the doctrine that had moved him to change his own ways, that worldly pleasures pass and fall away.[29] They are ephemeral, entirely without meaning for whomever clings to them or loves them. Glory slips away, ambition is blind, riches perish, pleasure passes, rest deceives, and even security is uncertain. Nothing remains but the severity of a vengeful God who does not allow

---

[27] *Et accepti sacerdotii addisceret usum et certa religiose vivendi caperet documenta. Vita S. Norberti*, PL 170, col. 1263.

[28] Pastoral preaching was almost nonexistent at the beginning of the twelfth century, in part because the faithful no longer understood Latin and the modern languages had not yet acquired a sufficient suppleness and literary quality to be used easily from the pulpit. Preaching in Latin remained the practice in cloisters.

[29] *Vita S. Norberti*, PL 170, col. 1263.

those attached to such empty goods to enter into his kingdom. This first sermon of Norbert reveals much, reminding us of the first meditation in the *Spiritual Exercises* of Saint Ignatius, beginning with man's end and going on to advocate complete detachment and lofty perfection. Norbert would preach exactly this throughout the rest of his life. By the power of his own conviction he would bring forth from these basic elements a mighty impulse toward sanctity.

Such preaching, however, has powerful effect. The very next day, at the daily chapter after prime, Norbert spoke again. He had in his hand the Rule of Aachen and he cited the texts of Saint Gregory the Great and Saint Isidore on prelates. Norbert reminded his chapter's dean of his duty to form his confreres in virtue and holiness. The dean and the older brothers said nothing, moved and pensive. The younger confreres murmured; nevertheless, all of them wished him well before they took their leave. His humble attire drew their respect. The next day, however, Norbert preached once more, this time to draw attention to the names of those who committed an infraction against their canonical rule the day before.[30] The others did not at first take Norbert's conversion seriously, but he persevered. Every day he made similar statements in the chapter. One day, the cleric serving as warden lost his temper and spat in Norbert's face.[31] Norbert wiped himself without saying a word but later, alone before God, was unable to hold back his tears.

For the next three years Norbert maintained this manner of living and his poor man's dress. He preached and maintained himself in great continence. He was often at Siegburg among the Benedictines, at Klosterrath among the regular canons, or with the priest-hermit Ludolph. He even visited recluses, sharing with all these holy friends the tribulations of his preaching and learning from them about spiritual life. He drew consolation from them in their conversations about heavenly things.

---

[30] The universal practice in religious houses was that every one, in chapter, announce the names of those whom he had seen commit an infraction against the rule.

[31] According to the biography, this cleric was such a vile character that if Norbert had had him thrown into the mud, everyone would have said, "Well done."

Norbert now saw more and more clearly that he would not be able to remain at Xanten. The Rule of Aachen indeed envisioned that some brothers in a chapter might renounce everything but it did not enforce such complete sacrifice. Then further Norbert had as yet been unable to effect total renunciation even for himself. He indeed lived as if he were poor but he was not utterly poor. He retained basic possessions, including ecclesiastical benefices; he had servants although he acted as if he possessed nothing. In this way Norbert was like the later Saint Jean Baptiste de la Salle, also a canon at Reims, living with his first Christian Brothers and urging them to trust in God and the spirit of poverty. He would have no success until he stripped himself of everything. We do not know why he hesitated. Grace comes when and as it wills. Perhaps the sons of the counts of Gennep were not free to dispose of their goods. Indeed in that period Norbert made a gift to the monastery of Fürstenberg of the property that he is said to have shared with his brother Herbert. In short, our saint wore a habit which he consecrated to God but it was not yet a religious habit in the modern sense of the word.

In 1118, however, the council of Fritzlar met with Conon, cardinal-bishop of Preneste, presiding as papal legate. The cardinal was a regular canon, one of the three founders of the Order of Arrouaise and the second abbot of that house. The canons of Xanten brought before Conon their confrere Norbert and questioned his exceptional behavior. Why, they asked, does he preach when he is neither a bishop, nor a pastor, nor a superior? Why does he conduct himself with such rigor and severity? Why does he dress as a poor man while maintaining his personal goods? One cannot be both a religious and a property-holder at the same time, and custom does not allow the nobility to wear poor garments of sheep or goat skin. The accused tried to justify himself:

> I am being reproached for preaching. Is it not written that whoever saves a sinner from his follies will also save his soul from death and cover a multitude of sins? At my ordination the bishop told me, "Receive the power to preach the word of God." What form of religious life do I profess? A religious life that is pure and untainted, says Saint James, consists in visiting the orphans and

widows in their abandonment while keeping oneself unsullied by the world. Am I decried for my humble clothing? Yet Saint Peter says that God is displeased with lavish clothes? Saint John the Baptist wore a garment of camel hair and Saint Cecilia wore a hair shirt. Then too when God drove Adam from the earthly paradise he clothed him not with a crimson tunic but in animal skin.

To argue was useless. From the point of view of canon law, Norbert's defense was weak.[32] He had not yet officially been appointed to such an apostolate, but his speech bore witness that he was an ardent and generous soul unafraid to break existing boundaries when the common good demanded it. No sentence, apparently, was pronounced against Norbert. He was neither condemned nor affirmed by his judges. Yet Conon, who had left all to lead a very austere life, surely did not believe that a secular canon could profess to strive for sanctity.

Norbert's conversion had not yet produced the effect he wished. His own conversion remained without wider influence. In order to spread it he would have to abandon all his possessions and give himself completely to God. The saint now understood this. Returning to the council he renounced his ecclesiastical benefices before the archbishop of Cologne; he sold his patrimony and distributed his money to the poor. He parted with everything he had inherited, all his property, keeping only one mule, twenty pieces of silver, and a portable altar for the celebration of Mass. Norbert then departed for Belgium with two servants who had remained faithful to him and who wished to follow him in his new way of life. Having arrived at Huy, Norbert still resolved further to follow the naked cross, himself naked. He now gave away his mule and twenty marks. Now he was not simply living as a poor man, he was truly poor.

[32] Norbert did not distinguish the powers of the clerical order he received in his ordination from the power of jurisdiction given by the ecclesiastical superior. This distinction was generally not clearly made in this period, and Rupert of Deutz reasoned just as Norbert did when the former asked for the power to preach for monk-priests. He simply said: *Mitti ordinari est*, "to be ordained is to be sent." Rupert of Deutz, *Super quaedam capitula regulae divi Benedicti abbatis*, PL 170, col. 534.

Norbert was thus an authentic apostle. Even in the heart of winter he walked barefoot, clothed in a simple tunic and cloak, having neither hearth nor home. Christ alone was his guide.[33] Norbert's passionate love for the poor, wandering, suffering, and crucified Christ would make him one of the pioneers of that new piety that, from the eleventh century on, would rouse affection for the humanity of Christ and the Blessed Virgin Mary. This poor pilgrim followed the well-known pilgrimage routes that lead to Rome or Santiago, but he also stopped at the tomb of Saint Gilles in Provence because Pope Gelasius II was there in exile. Saint Norbert was troubled in his delicate conscience for having received two sacred orders on the same day in a fashion contrary to canon law. He asked for absolution, imploring the counsel of Christ's vicar.

Itinerant Preaching

This extraordinary priest was clearly determined to be a religious in the full sense of the word, but it was as yet unclear whether he would be a canon, a monk, a hermit, or a pilgrim. Like any saint, Norbert did not have a coherent plan for his life. The will of God would decide it for him. The pope sent him, for the moment, to preach wherever he wished. Souls were dying of hunger and preachers were needed who would follow the Gospel, going forth like the apostles with only the clothes on their backs and without money or walking sticks. Robert of Arbrissel (d. 1117), Bernard of Tiron (d. 1117), and Vital of Savigny (d. 1123) all did precisely this. They died at their work, wounded in its conduct by the opposition of the bishops and of secular clergy who reproached them for living off of alms and wearing the clothing of the poor, as if these practices were unworthy of priests. All of these apostles founded monasteries, as might be expected of God's own converts. And Norbert followed their common course. Pope Gelasius found Norbert educated, eloquent, ardently devout, and ripened in persecution. The pope granted him all the faculties necessary to preach, to hear confessions, and to baptize. The apostle immediately returned to the north, traveling barefoot through the cold and snow of winter. One

---

[33] *Solo Christo duce.* Vita S. Norberti, PL 170, col. 1272.

by one, others slowly joined him. Several of these were unable to endure this rigorous life and died of exhaustion. The work of Norbert's followers would be founded upon this suffering and sacrifice of lives. And what lives they were! For the next ten years Norbert led the life of a missionary, accompanied by Hugh of Fosses, a chaplain of the bishop of Cambrai who had joined him. Hugh apparently did not preach much himself, rather accompanied Norbert as Barnabas accompanied Paul, because these apostles too went out in pairs as our Lord had commanded their predecessors.

Our two saints would arrive in a small town. Bells would ring, people would gather, and Norbert would sing Mass. Anything brought to the altar during the offertory, as was the practice then, would go to the poor and to lepers; these two men of God had not left behind great riches in order to store up small goods. Then Norbert would preach. As the sermon came to a close a long catechism would follow. Norbert would speak, ask questions, and respond to questions posed to him. He would discuss confession, penance, property, married life, how salvation might be achieved in this world—so making a great attempt to adapt Christian asceticism to the life of the laity. When evening came Norbert would take shelter wherever he could. The townsfolk would quarrel over the honor of taking him in. Norbert would be filled with joy because he had so observed the Gospel, having neither wallet, walking stick, nor shoes. His belongings consisted simply in his portable altar and his psalter.

On another occasion our apostles might find themselves at the door of a monastery or a cloister of canons. They would be introduced to the chapter. Norbert would preach and then immediately pass on to the familiar conversation, the dialogue of questions and answers. Among clerics questions might arise regarding the different orders and their rules for religious life, the habit they might wear, the institutions of the Fathers, the life and morals of superiors, and the obedience of ordinary brothers and sisters. Norbert would speak most of all of heaven, one of his favorite topics. Now his life has come far from what he knew in Xanten. In the north of France and in Belgium hearts were hungry for the truth.

Whenever there was some discord in a town, for feudalism gave rise to many private wars, Norbert would intervene, for he was an apostle of peace.[34] He would courageously address the heads of the warring households, embracing them, pleading with them, even threatening them as necessary. His source of strength was here as throughout his life his long hours of prayer. "Vigils are fatiguing," he would say, "but they bring forth great fruits of salvation." Norbert imitated Christ, his master, who so often passed the night in prayer. So he was constant in his vigils and prayers, ardent in his work, pleasant to hear, gracious in his appearance, kind to simple folk but stern with the enemies of God.[35] Hence it is no surprise that he did such good.

Alone with his companion, Hugh of Fosses, Norbert would then set out to preach again. He would offer counsel on poverty and on pastoral vigilance—on how to convert sinners and improve the just; on the importance of that humility and simplicity leading us to heaven; on that obedience bringing us knowledge of the mysteries of God; on patience, chastity, virginity; and again on his beloved poverty. Such ideas were indeed current in Norbert's time. No book on spirituality fails to treat these subjects. But he spoke of them with such emphasis and conviction of faith that contemporaries exclaimed, "What excels in Norbert is faith, as humility excelled in Milo of Thérouanne and charity in Bernard of Clairvaux!"[36] His faith was not only a virtue but a charism, such a faith as moves mountains and souls as difficult to move as mountains. Saints often preach ordinary things, common and elementary doctrines, but they make them new by the outpouring through them of the Holy Spirit. Soon Norbert's words would be so influential that they would draw into religious life clerics, laity, women, young ladies, the rich, the nobility, and the peasants. He always offered them the same simple message: "Nothing on earth is worth attaching oneself to. Follow Jesus Christ in poverty and obedience." And soon Europe was covered with new monasteries.

---

[34] *Reconcilians male dissentientes et inveterata odia et bella ad pacem reducens."* Vita S. Norberti, PL 170, col. 1270.

[35] *Patiens in vigiliis, sedulus in labore, gratus in verbo, gratiosus in visu, benignus in simplices, severus contra hostes Ecclesiae. Vita S. Norberti,* PL 170, col. 1277.

[36] *In Norberto eminet fides, in Bernardo Claravallensi: charitas, in Milone Tarvanensi: humilitas. Vita S. Norberti,* PL 170, col. 1269. Milo, a disciple of Saint Norbert, the first abbot of Saint-Josse-au-Bois (Dammartin) in Artois, became bishop of Thérouanne in 1131 and died revered as a saint on July 16, 1159.

The New Conception of Religious Life

Norbert might then have gone on, gathering new companions, to found an order of mendicant preachers. His personal ideal seems to have been thus, and he indeed led such a life until he became archbishop.[37] Neither the canon law of the time nor contemporary practice—nor even the notion of the apostolic life—so directed him, as circumstances were.

On February 2, 1119, Pope Calixtus II succeeded Gelasius II. When Norbert asked the Council of Reims to renew his apostolic permission to preach, the pope acceded to his request. Norbert would continue to preach as much as he wished, continuing to lead the evangelical and apostolic life he chose, but he would now forge a canonical link to a particular church. The pope entrusted Norbert to Bartholomew of Jur, bishop of Laon, a great man and great ascetic who himself would later become a Cistercian and be the canonical founder of Prémontré. Significantly, when the first Premonstratensians arrived in Palestine, the patriarch of Jerusalem behaved similarly. He was delighted at the canons' ardent and efficacious apostolate, but he insisted on the canonically correct foundation of a chapter.

Apparently Calixtus II did not share the antipathy of many prelates to itinerant preaching. At the Council of Reims Saint Vital spoke before this pope, who approved of him heartily. "No one," the pope said, "has spoken to me more articulately concerning the duties of my office." But Vital had founded a monastery to which he then was canonically attached, as was not the case for Norbert. "We must not serve God according to our will, but according to his will," as he had himself said a few days earlier.[38] A community of itinerant preachers was not yet possible; Saint Dominic would found one a century later, but in that later society towns were more developed, universities flourished and formed many clerics, and in general the rapid pace of intellectual, artistic, and commercial exchange prepared townsfolk to listen to preachers loosely connected

---

[37] The *Vita S. Norberti* holds for this view so much that, while deploring Norbert's absences, it applies to him in regard to his preaching the words of Psalm 103:23: Man shall go forth to his works. *Vita S. Norberti*, PL 170, col. 1287.

[38] *Vita S. Norberti*, PL 170, col. 1279.

to their humble convents, who were in one place one day and on the following obediently preaching in another part of the world.

In the twelfth century, however, society was still rural, and religious life necessarily remained so as well. Abbeys were the earlier period's independent and self-sufficient centers of activity. Scholastic theology had not yet been established. Clerics and monks were formed slowly and over a long period of time through the maternal pedagogy of ecclesiastical ritual and patient meditation on scripture. Intellectual exchange was as yet undeveloped, and attitudes differed from region to region. In these circumstances eminent preachers might indeed emerge if they were exceptionally gifted, but formation of itinerant preachers was not yet appropriate, as yet unsupported by large and stable communities. Likewise, religious life had not made the transition between the old monasticism and the new mendicant orders. This great change would soon happen through the appearance of the orders of Chartreuse, Cîteaux, Fontevrault, and Prémontré. These new orders' houses were rural and independent, models of Christendom as had been the Benedictine abbeys of the past, but they shared solid ties, focused on the same observances and grew under shared, attentive supervision. They thus prepared the way for more centralized, mobile, and flexible orders, more easily adaptable to apostolate. But in these new monastic communities of the twelfth-century, family life, with its wonderfully sanctifying paternal authority and mutual fraternal education, still prevailed.[39]

The Foundation of Prémontré

Norbert established himself at Prémontré in 1121. He needed only to appear in public to find companions. Now the organization of the new churches of Notre Dame and Saint John the Baptist would proceed. Norbert was now surrounded by forty clerics and even more laity. He urged them to remain faithful to their resolution to give themselves to God and to the voluntary poverty they embraced.

---

[39] While the theology of the Catholic Church in the Middle Ages was the same as that of today, the conception of a particular church remained much as in Christian antiquity—a notion much obscured in our day.

All trusted him, for his words lifted their hearts to heaven. No one asked anything else of him; all they required was to be followers of Norbert, but their founder thought more was necessary. Norbert and his disciples wished to maintain their evangelical mission, *evangelica institutio*, that is, to go out and preach the Gospel in poverty as our Lord had commanded the apostles. Further, they wished to pursue their apostolic mission, *apostolica institutio*, that is to imitate the life of the Church of Jerusalem as it gathered around the apostles.[40] This was a noble ideal, but for it to be realized they must, Norbert said, belong to an order—to observe a religious rule and to preserve the practices of the Fathers. Only in this way might they know the will of God with certainty and keep it to the end, so deserving the commendation of Christian folk. Norbert had wasted his time neither at Xanten nor in the monasteries he had visited. Again, Francis, son of Pietro di Bernardone, would later compose his own rule because he lacked clerical education and had not frequented monasteries on the ancient model. His rapidly developing way of life would therefore obviate the ancient pattern. New wine does not belong in old skins. But Norbert was a cleric of refined taste and education, with a love of tradition. He would change anything he needed in order to adapt it but, so far as he could, he would preserve the practices that had formed so many saints.

Various plans emerged. Religious of every style of dress, as well as bishops and abbots, variously insisted on drawing the new community into their preferred way of life. Would Norbert's followers be hermits, anchorites, Cistercians? Norbert himself waited, reflected, and prayed. His personal vocation was not at issue. He who had preached like Bernard might indeed have been Cistercian, but

---

[40] *Sine quibus non posset observari apostolica et evangelica institutio. Vita S. Norberti,* PL 170, col. 1292. In this text (c. 1160) there is less distinction between these two elements than in the writings of Saint Peter Damian. At the time of Saint Norbert the distinction was even less clear, as the formula of profession bears witness: *secundum evangelium Christi et apostolicam institutionem et regulam B. Augustini* ("according to the Gospel of Christ and the apostolic institution and Rule of Saint Augustine"). Attention to Adam Scot will demonstrate that, thirty years later at Prémontré, these texts were no longer understood. The apostolic movement was more narrowly defined and a religious order strictly speaking had been initiated.

the question now was the future of his religious establishment and soon the future of an entire religious order. Once, while he was among the Premonstratensians of Cappenberg at their daily chapter, Norbert said, "I know a brother of our congregation who searched with care for a rule for us to follow. Not through his own merits, but because of the prayers of his confreres, the blessed Augustine appeared to him, handing him with his right hand his golden rule and identifying it with these luminous words: 'I am Augustine, bishop of Hippo. Behold the rule that I have written. If your brothers are henceforth to be my sons, serving wholeheartedly under the banner of this rule, they may face God's judgment without fear.' "[41] No one doubted that the confrere in the story was Norbert himself.

This testimony is strong, but not only in the indisputable authenticity of the vision it relates. Its persuasiveness bore proof, then as it does now. Norbert was a canon, as were all the clerics who gathered around him, and they wished in no way to do insult to their ancient profession. They wanted to preach and the canonical life allowed them to do so by dedicating them to the ministry of souls.[42] They wished to be in a religious order and they could both be religious and still be canons. All that was required was the foundation of a monastery of regular canons. The institution proved robust. It was supported by the ecclesiastical hierarchy and demonstrated the flexibility to allow both holy religious life and fruitful apostolate. Surprisingly, however, Norbert did not yet know the Augustinian Rule except by hearsay. He needed to procure a copy—an easy matter given that it was already in use at Saint Denis of Reims and Saint-Jean-des-Vignes of Soissons. Nothing then appealed to the founder more than adopting a rule saying, "We desire to live the apostolic life."[43] Norbert found this rule brief, but rich in substance.[44]

---

[41] *Analecta Norbertina*, PL 170, col. 1346.

[42] *Ne professioni canonicae cui . . . attitulati fuerant ab infantia injuriam inferre videretur. . . . Apostolica enim vita quam in praedicatione susceperat jam optabat vivere.* Vita S. Norberti, PL 170, col. 1292.

[43] *Apostolicam enim vitam optamus vivere.* Augustine, *Regula Secunda*, PL 32, cols. 1449–51.

[44] *Vita S. Norberti*, PL 170, col. 1292.

On Christmas Day of 1121 many made religious profession at Prémontré; and the formula they chose signaled the community's future. They gave themselves to God in three ways: *secundum evangelium*, according to the Gospel, that is, to a life of preaching in poverty as prescribed by Christ for the apostles he himself sent forth; *et dicta Apostolorum*, according to the precepts of the apostles, that is, with the organization described in the Acts of the Apostles; *et propositum sancti Augustini*, that is, according to the Rule of Saint Augustine as the detailed application of the first two points to life in community.

From that day forward Norbert would no longer speak about the *instituta patrum*, the customs established by the Fathers, those venerable texts cited by the Rule of Aachen and according to which he had lived until now. All the other Fathers receded in importance relative to Saint Augustine's. The same phenomenon took place in the intellectual life of the period. Except for Saint Gregory, who was still widely read, all the ancient lights of the Church were gradually dimmed during the course of the twelfth century relative to the master of masters, the incomparable Saint Augustine. To adopt his rule, however, was a complex matter. Again, this venerable text comprised two parts: a succinct, practical, and complete rule, then a spiritual commentary rich in doctrine but insufficient for the organization of common life. Some specific strictures could not be applied to Norbert's and his followers' situation, for instance, the celebration of the divine office according to the Roman usage. Further, the austerities of Hippo were unsuitable to life in Northern Europe. Then again, as noted above, three years before the foundation of Prémontré, Gelasius II had effectively ordered Augustinian canons to write up a more precise rule to be placed at the head of their existing text. The elaboration of this specific legislation would now present additional problems.

Some of Norbert's disciples were fearful of this decision, others hesitated, and still others became lax; clearly different communities of canons had adopted very different practices. Norbert was not surprised. Diverse patterns of life need not be in mutual opposition, and no one is obliged to adopt his neighbor's ways. To preserve the bond of charity with fellow religious through wise flexibility—this is paramount. The Rule enjoins that we love God first of all, then our neighbor. Meticulous observance does not establish God's kingdom, rather it is advanced by good conscience and attention to the Ten Commandments. The holy doctor Augustine speaks of charity, work, fasting and abstinence, clothing, silence, obedience, courtesy among the brethren, and the honor rendered to the father of the community. This suffices for salvation in religious life.[45]

One central question regarded clothing.[46] If we become canons, Norbert's followers said to him, we should dress as canons, in the regular canons' traditional garment, a simple surplice of linen. Norbert would come more and more to agree. At the end of his life he allowed the Premonstratensians of Magdeburg and of Gottesgnaden regularly to wear such a surplice with a black cape. He would himself take up the surplice once again, but for the moment he held fast to the woolen tunic which he wore during his apostolic wanderings.[47] He asked whether there were in the Rule, or in the Gospels or Acts of the Apostles, any prescriptions regarding the whiteness, the blackness, the fineness or the roughness of clothing. If there were such, he asked that these texts be discussed.

Two central points were then established: first that the angel witnesses of Christ's resurrection appeared in white attire and second that the law and custom of the Church suggest that penitents be clothed in wool. Like all wise men and spiritual people of his time, Norbert sought to base his decision on the Old Testament. Scripture speaks of the priests of the Old Law as appearing before the people in woolen garments but using linen in the sanctuary. Therefore, Norbert concluded, since among the Fathers and other historical models preachers and canons were understood to repre-

---

[45] *Vita S. Norberti*, PL 170, col. 1293.

[46] *Vita S. Norberti*, PL 170, col. 1293.

[47] *Pater Norbertus lanearum tunicarum in clero inductor, idem ipse suae institutionis postmodum exstitit improbator. Etenim cum esset junior cingebat se et ambulabat ubi volebat, sicque per novitium fervorem et iuvenilis animi robur in illam simulationem adductus est. Cum autem senuisset, jam factus archiepiscopus Ecclesiae, cedens auctoritati simul et antiquae consuetudini, tamquam cinctus ab alio, tunicas ipse lineas recepit, simul et suis qui sibi parentes erant discipulis, ut eis vestirentur praecepit, volens hoc ipsum in toto suae institutionis clero effecisse: sed praeventus est morte et a multis recepta consuetudo subito auferri non potuit.* Arno of Reichensberg, *Liber de ordine canonicorum,* PL 188, col. 1112.

sent the angels of the resurrection, no one might object to his followers' use of white habits. But since they were both penitents and their office obliged them to appear before the people, they should wear woolen garments, but when they entered the sanctuary, they should also don vestments of linen.[48]

Norbert's solution would quickly become the whole Church's, except in a few longstanding religious orders in which earlier customs prevailed: an ecclesiastical habit of wool and a different vestment for the choir, where the surplice is important. The decorousness of the divine service would be enhanced by the wearing of vestments reserved for that purpose. For the Premonstratensians the symbolism of their habit would be very clear: white, because such is the color of clerics, and woolen, because wool is the fabric of penance. Only these reasons for this custom appear in documents of the period. Later Premonstratensians are proud and happy that their vestments are the colors of the host and the immaculate Virgin, but this more recent symbolism should not obscure the real motives behind the founder's choice. Norbert's order is clothed in white wool because they are both priests and penitents.

As for further observances, the divine office could not be performed exactly as it was described by Saint Augustine, but Norbert wanted to maintain everything else his Rule prescribed, including perpetual fasting and manual labor for most of the day. These two elements would nonetheless eventually prove impracticable. The Premonstratensians would have to be content with fasting from September 14 until Easter, and would dedicate more than the three hours provided for by Saint Augustine to divine reading (*lectio*) and study. Already, among the underbrush and marshes around Prémontré, Norbert offered his community religious formation. The new foundation was connected to the regular canons by the Augustinian Rule and by the education that the founder and his first clerical disciples had received; this context in general preserved the traditions of canonical life. The many lay brothers and sisters outnumbering the clerics and likewise dedicating themselves to Norbert's work, however, marked the new foundation as part of

---

[48] *Vita S. Norberti*, PL 170, col. 1293.

the new apostolic movement described above. Norbert and his clerics wished to be true apostles while their lay brothers and nuns were like "the multitude of believers" (Acts 4:32) gathered around the first twelve. For Norbert's contemporaries this represented a true reformation of the Church, returning it to its primitive form. They had no intention of forcing anyone to undertake their way of life. Nonetheless, they wanted to found as many communities of regular religious as they could. Monastic tradition could indeed be brought into the service of this ideal, as did the contemporary orders of Grandmont or Fontevrault, particularly the Cistercians, demonstrated. At Prémontré, however, Norbert wished to enshrine distinctively canonical traditions. The canons themselves, although the minority in the community, were its essential members. Indeed the number of brothers and nuns was to decrease rapidly and Norbertine chapters reduced almost completely to their clergy. Among traditional canonical practices Norbert emphasized three: the worship of God, correction in the chapter, and hospitality. He pledged that communities observing these practices would not suffer more than they could bear.

Divine worship was the fundamental obligation of the canons. On the very night of Norbert's arrival at the blessed site of Prémontré, he had seen a procession of men walking through the valley, dressed in white and bearing in their hands crosses, candles, and censers. The founder insisted on decorousness and precision in worship. The canons were to be clothed in undyed wool for work, but in the sanctuary to wear linen for the celebration of the sacred mysteries and for handling the Blessed Sacrament. This practice was to be consistent, for the sake of purity and for the honor of God. In the same way the altars were meticulously maintained. "It is at the altar that one shows his faith and love for God."[49] The later Premonstratensians would understand their founder's thought: they would therefore adopt many of the Cistercian practices but never the austerity of Cîteaux in divine worship. The use of dalmatics, copes, tapestries, and stained glass would from the very beginning lend splendor to their liturgical functions.

[49] *In altari namque exhibit quisque fidem et dilectionem Dei.* Chrodegang, PL 170, col. 1295.

The daily chapter of faults took place from the beginning of the twelfth century among both monks and canons, and its origin was again canonical. This morning meeting of the community was especially necessary in clerical houses whose members were often away for the rest of the day attending to the salvation of souls. It is also found in the Rule of Saint Chrodegang.[50] Norbert knew full well that excesses and negligence would arise in any human community. If such things were not corrected immediately, everyone would suffer and fervor would diminish. Norbert therefore wished that correction be made first of all in chapter—hence this meeting's existence—but also anytime it proved necessary. He was, we are told, severe in his own correction of other's faults. He had many disciples and the more their numbers grew, the more urgent it became to diminish their individual wills as much as possible in order to replace them with the Holy Spirit. A large community will not endure except through the unity brought about by its common vows and fidelity to customs. "The care one takes in purifying one's conscience," said Norbert, "is proof of the charity that one has for oneself."[51]

Finally, Norbert's third major emphasis was hospitality and care for the poor. This evidently had been the earlier canons' primary charitable work, and Norbert held firmly to this tradition. At Prémontré he built, then generously endowed by his own efforts, a hospital with a guest house for travelers, a hospice for the poor, and an infirmary for the sick. The male religious looked after the men while the female religious looked after the women. The kindly Ricwer of Clastres gave her whole life to this hospital and wished to be buried in the cemetery of her beloved poor. Later the community's hospital would be transferred to Saint-Quentin. At Magdeburg Norbert would choose for his confreres the church of Notre Dame because it had an affiliated hospice.[52] This poor monastery,

---

[50] Saint Chrodegang calls it "our little institution", *institutiunculam nostram. Regula canonicorum secundum editionem Labbei, PL* 89, col. 1102.

[51] . . . *in conscientiae purificatione, curam sui. Vita S. Norberti, PL* 170, col. 1295.

[52] *Cum plurima antecessoris nostri piae memoriae Adalberti munifica largitate quaedam domus hospitalis juxta ecclesiam beatae et gloriosissimae Mariae constructa fuisset, ipsam, quod non sperabamus, pene annihilatam invenimus, ita quod hi qui in ea stipendium quotidianum accepturi erant indecenter et miserabiliter medicarent, quorum necessitate et*

Protestantized in the sixteenth century, exists today ~~as an orphan-age~~—a remembrance of Norbert's charity. At Steinfeld, Vire, Paris, Neuffonts, and many other places this eleemosynary tradition endured for a long time. As the founder said, "We show our love for our neighbor at the hospice."[53]

Religious ritual, discipline, charity: these were the three central precepts of the father to his children. They wrought extraordinary community at Prémontré in the founder's own presence. The spirit of poverty was such that confreres were ashamed to wear new habits. Instead they sewed worn patches onto new garments and disdained no work, even the most vile. Their poverty was voluntary and spontaneous, as descriptions in historical documents repeatedly attest.

Critics have often compared Augustinian, monastic poverty, mandated in the Acts of the Apostles as a life of renunciation completely in common like the life of the poor, to the poverty of the mendicant orders as embraced and preached by Saint Francis of Assisi. The latter represents rather the love of the poor Christ, stripped of every comfort in the course of his preaching and naked on the cross. This second type of poverty was indeed already sought in the eleventh and twelfth centuries. At Grandmont Saint Stephen of Muret wrote: "If the Son of God, in coming to earth, had known a better way to heaven than poverty, he would have chosen and followed it."[54] This very ideal suffuses the entire apostolic movement. Yet at Prémontré the desire to be poor like Christ and to follow the Gospel to the letter still seems novel: "To follow the Sacred Scriptures and have Christ as their leader."[55] The main difference between the Premonstratensians and the mendicant orders

---

miseriae compatiens, consilio et consensus majorum nostrorum, eadem domum hospitalem fratribus nostris in ecclesia beatae et perpetuae Virginis Mariae constitutis cum omnibus eidem hospitali attinentibus regendam et disponendam jure perpetuo tradimus. Bartholonew, PL 170, col. 1359.

[53] *. . . in hospitum et pauperum susceptione, dilectionem proximi. Vita Sancti Norberti,* PL 170, col. 1295.

[54] Edmond Martène, *Sentences de Saint Étienne,* in *De antiquis ecclesiae ritibus,* (Venice, 1763), 318, c. 1.

[55] *Sanctas scripturas sequi et Christum ducem habere. Vita S. Norberti,* PL 170, col. 1293.

appearing a century later, however, was that the Premonstratensians would spend their life working on common land, not begging. The Church did not yet want mendicant clerics because in the twelfth century there was as yet no resolution to the problem of clerical vagabondage. Contrary to the tendencies of a twelfth-century society rediscovering the comfort and riches lost since the fall of the Roman Empire, however, fervent and educated clerics as well as rich and noble lay brothers and high-born women who populated the monasteries rose up as if to defy those norms—not because they could not attain these things but because they had discovered the Gospel and understood that the riches of this world are worthless.

The community at Prémontré added to this practice of poverty their prompt obedience to the commands of superiors. Confreres reportedly would have thrown themselves into fire if commanded under obedience so to do. Obedience is essential in all religious life, but promptness in obedience among Norbert's followers is emphasized in both the *Vita A* and *Vita B*, as in the work of the Premonstratensian who continued the chronicles of Sigebert of Gembloux and in the so-called sermon of Saint Norbert. What was modeled at Prémontré was then soon imitated in the other monasteries founded by Norbert himself or his disciples. Indeed, the urgency of obedience was perhaps too great, for a series of diabolical obsessions and possessions ensued from the state of tension in which the confreres lived. When Norbert was present, however, all was peaceful. His incomparable personal dynamism drew souls to his cloisters. Later, however, when Norbert became archbishop of Magdeburg, he would need to introduce an element of stability by naming abbots for his monasteries. An important vision, nowhere directly attributed to Norbert but nonetheless worthy of mention as shedding light on the thought of the first Premonstratensians, came to one of the first confreres there. He fasted and prayed to know where the community should build the monastery church. This religious saw the crucified Christ surrounded with seven rays of light on the exact spot where the temple of God should be built. In this vision, pilgrims came from four paths leading into the valley; they prostrated themselves before the cross and then returned by the ways on which they had come. The role of Prémontré as head of the order and the model for its collegial life was clearly indicated in this vision.

In 1126 Norbert, founder of Prémontré, was named archbishop of Magdeburg. The role that he played in this great city of the north is not at issue here although it calls for close historical study of his work there. To date, Norbert's archiepiscopal career is the weakest element in published studies of his life.[56] For the present work, however, interest lies rather in the spiritual life of Archbishop Norbert.

As archbishop, Norbert met with bitter criticism. The curious twelfth-century dialogue between a Cluniac and a Cistercian includes these strange remarks: "Some say that the founder of the Premonstratensians, Lord Norbert, apostatized. He who had earlier traveled barefoot or donkey-back later wore shoes and rich attire astride his caparisoned horse. Once a hermit, he later lived at court. Once contemptuous of the world, he became its powerful broker."[57] This criticism presages the words of the archbishop of Reims against Saint Joan of Arc during her imprisonment. Saints cannot escape unfair judgments any more than did their divine master: "Behold a man that is a glutton and wine drinker" (Matt 11:19). In fact, even as archbishop, Norbert remained a soul in love with God just as he had been since the day of his conversion.

Contrary to custom, the archbishop retained the habit of his order, to which he would later add the surplice of the canons regular as was worn by the Premonstratensians of Magdeburg. There, more devotedly than ever, he kept liturgical vigils and consecrated his nights to private prayer. He celebrated Mass every day as he had done since his ordination—something unusual in his period. Indeed he performed most of his miracles during the Holy Sacrifice and he loved to preach as he came down from the altar. He has been criticized for having been too authoritative with others, but only so

---

[56] Emiel Valvekens' recently published biography in Dutch seems to remedy this lacuna: *Norbert van Gennep* (Bruges: De Kinkhoven, 1943).

[57] *Auctor eorum, dominus Norbertus dicitur apostatasse, factus de nudipede ascensor asini bene calceatus et bene vestitus, ascensor phalerati equi, de heremita curialis, de contemptore mundi magnus actor causarum mundi. Dialogus inter Cluniacensem et Cisterciensem*, ed. Edmond Martène, in *Thesuarus novus anecdotorum*, Vol. 1 (Paris: 1717), c. 1614, 19.

could he bring about the requisite moral reform resisted by both the clergy and nobles of his diocese. Norbert never balked in his duty, showing great sensitivity and profound sympathy toward the poorest of men. The chronicle of the archbishops of Magdeburg notes that he was always "a man in whom outcasts were sure to find refuge and unfortunates consolation—a prelate able to exercise both love for men and hatred for sin. He was good to all and full of patience. He had no enemies except those scandalous clergy who did not wish to bear the Lord's yoke. He treated gold and silver, despite the power they can exercise over mortal men, with such indifference that he emptied the treasury of his church without hesitation when necessity required it."[58]

The archbishop of Magdeburg necessarily led a life different from that of a simple missionary, but the soul of Norbert soared above riches and comfort. His whole heart and all his strength belonged to Christ and the Church. He died young, worn down by his efforts. Pope Gregory XIII, in numbering him among the saints, respectfully testified that all of Christendom had been nourished by the merits and virtues of Norbert.[59]

---

[58] *Chronicon Magdeburgense*, cited in *Acta sanctorum quotquot tot orbe coluntur*, ed. Society of Bollandists, vol. 20 (Brussels, 1643–present), 58. [Editor's note: This great series is hereafter cited as AASS.]

[59] This discussion omits reference to the *Monita spiritualia* attributed to Saint Norbert by D. Albrecht: *Manuale canonicorum praemonstratensium* (Strassbourg, 1742). Texts preserved in a seventeenth-century French document at Sainte-Marie in Pont-à-Mousson and translated into Latin there are likely inauthentic.

Chapter 3
The First Disciples of Saint Norbert

Hugh of Fosses and Walter of Saint Maurice

After Saint Norbert founded the Order of Prémontré, he at first continued his preaching and then eventually became archbishop. For him the word of God was clearly more important than the details of community organization. Meanwhile, however, Norbert's preaching—like that of many of the saints—was focused on the recruitment of religious vocations. It therefore addressed sanctity, not ordinary Christian life. Yet Norbert did not abandon Prémontré but watched over it for a long time. The inspiration it expressed was so powerful that new foundations continued to grow from those Norbert had already begun even after his departure from his first foundation. As archbishop of Magdeburg, Norbert then depended on his order to hasten the conversion of northern Germany. Still, as the saint's biographer notes, "when the standard-bearer leaves the army, the troops lose heart for the battle."[1] Norbert's foundations required superiors to form the souls they embraced, to organize their common life and to prepare for their future.

The first abbot of Prémontré and first abbot general of the order was the blessed Hugh of Fosses. His life was parallel to his master Norbert's. As a youth Hugh was educated in the school for clerics

---

[1] *Absente signifero ubi bellum geritur. Vita S. Norberti*, PL 170, col. 1287.

of the chapter of Fosses. In due course he became a canon there under one of the existing canonical rules, then was fostered at the court of Burchard, bishop of Cambrai. There he met Norbert during the period when the saint was clothed as a beggar.[2] Hugh was able to visit Norbert many times when the exhausted apostle lay ill at Valenciennes. At that time Hugh revealed to Norbert that he wished to follow him: "O my Father, you have bound me to you with an unbreakable bond."[3] The two would now be missionaries together. After the Council of Reims, Hugh parted briefly from his master in order to give away all his personal goods. He then returned to Prémontré, where he became first a regular canon and, soon after, prior. In 1128, two years after becoming archbishop of Magdeburg, Norbert appointed Hugh abbot of his order's first house.

Hugh might then have followed Norbert's model closely in all regards, but this was not the case. As Hugh's biographer has noted, the two men were quite different:

> Norbert was the inheritor of a great name, a descendant of great feudal lords, and moved with ease at princely courts. As an apostle, he was a soul seized by a sublime ideal—a man of battle taken up in an intense and difficult apostolate, oratorical duels and a constant pan-European engagement in various endeavors, sowing the good word with eloquence and lively persuasiveness. Hugh, on the other hand, was a contemplative—ascetic, mild and patient, strongly preferring the cloistered life. An enemy of all pomp and restlessness, he was reserved with the important figures of this world, timid before crowds and humble to the point of obstinately refusing appointment to any bishopric. Hugh preferred the solitude of the cloister to public gatherings, distant travels and rousing preaching. Yet he was unequalled in the government and organization of the new congregation whose reins he held firmly and which he directed wisely in its early expansion.[4]

---

[2] *Vita S. Norberti,* PL 170, cols. 1274–78. On Hugh of Fosses see also Hugues Lamy, *Vie du bienheureux Hugues de Fosses* (Charleroi: Éditions de la Terre Wallonne, 1925).

[3] *Vinculo indissolubili colligasti me, Pater. Vita S. Norbert,* PL 170. col. 1275.

[4] Lamy, 6.

He was no less saintly than Norbert, no less esteemed by popes and kings, and no less devoted to the reform of the Church; he was the perfect complement to his master.

Immediately after his abbatial election, Hugh applied himself to the great task at hand. Two abbots had already been created before him for Prémontré's first daughters: Walter of Saint Maurice for the abbey of Saint Martin of Laon and Henry for the abbey of Vivières in the diocese of Soissons. Three more would be added at the same time as Hugh: Richard for Floreffe, Waltman for Saint Michael of Antwerp, and Odo for Bonne-Espérance in Hainaut. The abbot of Prémontré immediately called together these first prelates in a general chapter in order to maintain their common purpose and brotherly love as well as to safeguard their obedience. This general chapter, in imitation of the Cistercians', would build unity within the order.[5] Its members numbered six in 1128, nine in the following year, twelve in the third year, and nineteen in the fourth. Hugh lived to see one hundred and twenty abbots gathered around him. This great expansion was possible only through great attentiveness and exertion. Although Hugh was mild, he was also tenacious. Again and again he asked the supreme pontiff to prevent bishops from blocking the order's annual reunion and to command its abbots to attend. The individual houses would have been reduced to dust without this bond of unity. Hugh was thus in large part responsible for building a religious order lasting for centuries directly because of this cohesion.

The principal work of the chapter was the development of the order's statutes. Because the Rule of Saint Augustine had been preserved with no details of the customs of daily life surrounding its composition, it required completion with details of practice. Soon the charters of the abbeys would state that a given monastery was established under the Rule of Saint Augustine and the institution of the Premonstratensians or, again, under the Rule of Saint Augustine and the institution of the venerable Norbert. These counsels standing in place of the customs of Hippo and developed by the general chapter, were generally composed of dictates beginning with the

[5] *Vita S. Norberti*, PL 170, col. 1330.

words: *Statutum est;* "It has been decided. . . ." Thus they were called "statutes."[6]

From the perspective of a historian of spirituality, the early statutes of the Order of Prémontré are striking in making no provision for active apostolate. The organization they envision is for an entirely contemplative life. Their text is largely copied from the customs of the Cistercians. Canonical traditions, of course, are intact, but everything that might be borrowed from the monks' practice indeed was. The ideal of the regular canons—to arrive at priestly perfection through monastic asceticism—was thus realized in this document. Parochial ministry was not completely pushed aside, but was to be exercised only collegially: "We shall not have parochial churches unless there is also an abbey."[7]

Within the monastery the life of the canons was much like that of monks: they chanted matins at midnight according to the canonical practice, then all rested. Upon awakening, they chanted prime. Then they celebrated Mass individually, while in choir they sang the morning Mass for the Dead for the deceased of the order. The chapter followed. Next the community engaged in manual labor for the relaxation of the spirit and for self-mortification as well as for the physical exercise indispensable for general health. Work was never lacking because most of the land given to these new monasteries during the twelfth century still needed to be cleared. The bulk of the manual labor was done by the lay brothers, but the clerics also lent a hand. Before the solemn Mass the canons undertook an hour or two of sacred reading, *lectio divina*, and they resumed this task during part of the afternoon. On Sundays and holidays all of their time outside of the office was reserved to *lectio*, as was generally the practice in Christian and monastic spirituality of the past. In the last hour of the morning the canons solemnly celebrated terce, solemn Mass, and sext in choir. This was the most

[6] The most ancient text known of the Premonstratensian statutes was edited by Raphael Van Waefelghem: *Les premiers statuts de l'Ordre de Prémontré: le Clm. 17.174 (XIIe siècle)* (Louvain: Smeetes, 1913). However, a text published by Martène in the *De antiquis ritibus*, Part 3, 312–14, is proximate to the customs of Cîteaux in the passages where it depends on that source.

[7] *Non recipere altaria ad quae cura animarum pertinet nisi possit esse abbatia. Les premiers statuts*, 45.

solemn moment of the day—the heart of the canonical life. The afternoon would be spent between similar activities, principally manual labor. Vespers followed, and then again *lectio divina*. Finally came the evening meal, immediately followed by the reading of a chapter of a collation or spiritual conference of Cassian, then the chanting of compline. We know from other texts of the statutes that the Little Office of the Blessed Virgin was regularly added to the canonical office.[8] In this practice the religious orders of the twelfth century spiritually expressed their unity with the crusading movement. Often they also sang the Office of the Dead. Overall, the life of the first Premonstratensians resembled that of Trappists today.

Lay brothers, of whom there were many, were present only at matins, the morning Mass, and compline. The rest of their time was spent in manual labor and agricultural work. Women religious initially lived in a part of the monastery set aside for them. Canonesses or choir sisters were not yet present, but only simple lay sisters. These were present at matins and the morning Mass, then they worked in silence. If they were educated, they were permitted some reading on Sundays.[9] The whole day thus centered on prayer and penance,

---

[8] See Luke of Mont Cornillon [recte], *Moralitates in cantica: Sic sancta Mater Ecclesia dicit in ejus quotidiano servitio: Quasi cedrus exaltata sum in Libano.* ("Thus Holy Mother Church says in her daily service, 'I am exalted like a cedar of Lebanon.'") This passage *Quasi cedrus* is the reading for vespers of the Little Office in the Premonstratensian Rite. Luke, *Moralitates*, PL 203, col. 513; cf. Ezek 31:3.

[9] The statutes are rather brief regarding women religious. Here, however, is a beautiful passage from Herman of Tournai, who allows us to get a glimpse of their fervor: *Feminis . . . mox ut conversae fuerint perpetua deinceps lex manet semper intra domus ambitum clausas retineri, nunquam ulterius progredi, nulli viro non modo extraneo sed nec germano nec propinquo loqui nisi ad fenestram in ecclesia, duobus viris conversis cum viro externis et duabus feminis cum illa internis residentibus et quidquid dicitur audientibus.*

In ipso etiam conversionis initio, mox ut suscipiuntur, ad resecandam omnem superbiam et carnalem voluptatem etiam capilli earum usque ad aures tondentur, utque magis Christo caelesti sponso placeant, pro ejus amore in fragili et illecebrosa carne omnino deturpentur. Nulli deinceps pretiosam vestem nisi ex lana vel ovinis pellibus licet habere, nulli velum sericum more quarumdam sanctimonialium, sed vilissimum panniculum nigrum super caput portare. Et cum in tanta districtione et vilitate cum silentio sciantur esse reclusae, miro tamen modo Christi operante virtute, quotidie videmus feminas non modo rusticas vel pauperes, sed potius nobilissimas et ditissimas, tam viduas iuvenculas quam etiam puellulas, ita conversionis gratia spretis mundi voluptatibus, ad illius institutionis monasteria

with no organization of apostolic work noted in the statutes. This need not mean, however, that no one preached or administered the sacraments, because we know that Waltman and the religious of Saint Michael's of Antwerp, Luke and the canons of Cuissy, Abbot Altman of Floreffe, and Provost Eberwin of Steinfeld, among many others, preached continually even during this period of meditation and reflection. The blessed Garembert likewise maintained his service to the pilgrimage chapel of our Lady of Bony.

Apart from the early statutes' brief comment on the work of the novice master, they do not provide for the organization of schools. Nevertheless, schools did exist, both for the young men of the abbey and for the even younger oblates brought up there.[10] Manual labor was not exclusively agricultural; some members of the community were involved in the copying of manuscripts. We can still admire today the wonderful illuminated books from the Abbey of Cuissy,

---

festinantes, et quasi ad mortificandam teneram carnem currentes, ut plusquam decem millia feminarum in eis hodie credamus contineri. ("As for the women, once as they have entered the community, their governance is thus: they are enclosed within the confines of the house, never going out again. They may speak to no man, not even to a brother or other relative, except at the window in the church, and then only if two lay brothers are with the man on the outside and two women of the community with the woman on the inside. These attendants hear everything that is spoken. As soon as women are received into the community, at the very beginning of their conversion, their hair is cut to their ears in order to diminish all pride and carnal lust. Thus, to please Christ, their heavenly spouse, their fragile and libidinous flesh is disfigured because of their love for him. From that point none may have a rich garment, only one made of wool or sheepskin. None is permitted to wear silk veils over her head as do certain nuns, but only very crude black cloth. Although the sisters are thus enclosed with great strictness and abasement, including silence, nevertheless the power of Christ works in them in an extraordinary way. Daily we see women—not only rustics and the poor, but even the noble and rich, both young widows and even little girls—who in the grace of their conversion shun the pleasures of the world and hasten to monasteries so governed. They rush there to mortify their tender flesh. We believe that today there are more than ten thousand women dwelling in these monasteries.") PL 156, cols. 996–97.

[10] Adam's sermon for the feast of Saint Nicholas is addressed solely to the young oblates. Adam himself lamented the fact that he had not been thus brought up in the monastery of his profession: Adam Scot, *Sermones fratris Adae, Ordinis Praemonstratensis: Twenty-Eight Discourses of Adam Scotus of Whithorn* (Edinburgh: Blackwood, 1901).

and we know that Pope Innocent II thanked Hugh of Fosses for a magnificent codex copied for him at Prémontré.[11]

In short, the statutes are an incomplete record of their audience's life, and indeed to try to imagine their practice from such written legislation invites error. A collection of prescriptions concerning apostolic activity would have been difficult to frame without a precedent, and none indeed existed. The Premonstratensian way of life and its associated customs would eventually be recorded as law. Nevertheless, that the blessed Hugh of Fosses and his colleagues did not craft a more original body of statutes is indeed regrettable. Following as they did the custom of another institution they rightly admired, the Cistercian Order—although it did not share their aim and characteristics—they placed their apostolate outside its documentation. Yet this ministry was essential to the order and always practiced by its confreres. The Premonstratensian life has then always been more widely engaged than its legislative records directly affirm.

Under the impulse of Hugh and the first abbots, however, the whole of the order was rather oriented toward meditation and contemplation, and for clear reasons. First, the apostolic movement had been successful beyond measure. Too great a number of laity, both men and women, had become attached to the priests, just as the first Christians of Jerusalem had been attached to the apostles. Herman of Tournai affirms that more than a thousand religious were at Prémontré and at its dependent houses, with ten thousand in the whole order; during Herman's day more than five hundred confreres belonged to the monastery of Saint Martin of Laon. Evidently then, during the first generation, the canons themselves were overwhelmed by this lay enthusiasm.[12] Although the early statutes set forth that the prior should hear the confessions of all his community's religious, he would certainly have needed help. Nor could he give all the collations for these religious by himself, especially

---

[11] *Chronique de monastère d'Oudenbourg*, ed. Ferdinand van de Putte (Ghent, 1843), 64: "The words of the pope: 'Tell Hugh that we thank him very much for having sent us the volume of Saint Augustine's *De civitate Dei*; it is well written, elegantly and richly adorned.'"

[12] Herman, PL 156, cols. 992, 997.

since the abbey was at some distance from the granges and farms where both the male conversi or lay sisters lived.[13] Preaching rarely occurred outside of the abbey because of the many duties within it: the copying of manuscripts, ministry in the cloister or on its territory, and the instruction of the young clerics likely engaged most of the priests.

Meanwhile monasteries multiplied at a dizzying pace in the first third of the twelfth century. When Bartholomew of Jur was elected bishop of Laon, he found only five abbeys—three of them very poor—in his diocese. When he stepped down from that office in order to become a monk at Foigny, the diocese embraced fifteen abbeys, all prosperous and flourishing: "He dedicated one to Benedict, four to Bernard and five to Norbert."[14] This enumeration omits one Carthusian community and other monasteries of lesser importance. Everywhere the religious movement was similarly prolific. Regular canons multiplied across Europe so that, where there had been almost no apostles, a few years later there were almost too many.

The religious formation of a community, however, requires time. When Norbert and his companions came together in 1121, all of them had already been canons and had received parallel formations. The prestige of the founder was enough at that time to unite

---

[13] James of Vitry, qtd. in Daniel Papebroch, intro. to *Vitam S. Norberti*, PL 170, col. 1250: *Habent autem curias et prioratus non solum hominum sed et feminarum, in quibus tam clerici quam laici, secundum quod a superioribus suis injungitur, commorantur.* ("They have both manors and priories embracing women as well as men; both clerics and laity live in these communities and are directed by superiors there.")
In the priories of the women religious, the same author says, *commorabantur seorsum ejusdem ordinis sacerdotes et clerici, viri probati et religiosi qui eis in divinis officiis servientes, confessiones earum per fenestras audiebant et eas certis temporibus verbis divinarum Scripturarum instruere et informare studebant.* ("Priests and clerics of the order live separately from the women. These are upright and religious men who serve at the divine office; they also hear confessions through a window, instructing and forming the women at various times with appropriate words of sacred scripture.") Papebroch, PL 170, col. 1251.

[14] *Benedicto contulit unum, Bernardo quatuor, Norberto quinque piavit* ("He brought forth one for Benedict, four for Bernard and honored Norbert with five") from an inscription engraved on the tomb of Bartholomew of Laon in the cathedral church. Translator's note: The entire text can be found in *Bulletin monumental ou collection de mémoires et de renseignements pour servir a la confection d'une statistique des monuments de la France, classés chronologiquement*, Vol. 10 (Paris: M. De Caumont, 1844), 668.

their minds and hearts, but his first disciples were now scattered, themselves masters of their own brothers. They now needed to retire before the huge influx of recruits into a labor of asceticism as lengthy as it was necessary. Hugh's personal preference for contemplation and admiration for the Cistercians, as well as the disadvantages he attributed to the frequent absences of Norbert, strengthened this realization in him.

Hugh of Fosses was moreover strongly supported in his personal views by his confrere Walter of Saint Maurice, abbot of Saint Martin of Laon, an individual of great importance although as yet little recognized by historians. Even before the foundation of Prémontré, Bartholomew of Jur, intending to reform the church of Saint Martin outside Laon, had offered it to Norbert. This church was at the time poorly served by a chapter of canons, and Norbert soon was defeated by their ill will. Another prelate, Robert, had no more success. Finally, in 1124, the bishop of Laon renewed his entreaties to Norbert and the latter sent some religious from Prémontré. At their head was Walter. "We believe that, through the prayers of Saint Martin, God immediately granted such a grace that one could repeat what the angel said to Raguel regarding his daughter Sara: 'To him who feareth God is thy daughter due to be his wife: therefore another could not have her' [Tob 7:12]. Although none of the several potential reformers previously granted the administration of this church by the bishop had yet been successful, the charm of Walter and the benefit of divine grace were such that in twelve years he had gathered around him more than five hundred to serve God." [15]

The canons of Saint Martin lived in great poverty and want. During those first years they had only one donkey, named Burdinus after the anti-pope. Each morning they would take Burdinus down to the marshes of the valley of Ardon, where they would load him with dead wood to sell in the village for money to buy bread. Often

---

[15] *Cui Deus, orante sicut credimus beato Martino, tantam confestim gratiam contulit ut de ipso quoque illud videatur posse dici quod de sacra puella Ragueli patri ejus angelus dixit: Propterea nullus potuit habere eam quoniam huic timenti Deum debetur conjunx filia tua. Similiter eam beati Martini ecclesiolam cum plures ad episcopo regendam suscepissent, nullusque eorum ibi proficere potuisset, huic abbati Gualtero tam bona fortuna per divinam gratiam comes adhaesit ut infra duodecim annos plusquam quingentorum fratrum Deo servientium tibi conventus inveniretur.* Herman of Tournai, PL 156, col. 993.

they did not earn enough until late in the afternoon, but Walter consoled his brothers and encouraged them in their divine service. They did manual labor the best they could, so well in fact that, after some years, Saint Martin of Laon became the richest abbey of the diocese, itself establishing a dozen more monastic foundations. From this house and its daughters would eventually spring one hundred fifty foundations of regular canons. Yet Dom Hujben rightly remarked that Walter of Saint Maurice was a resolute supporter of the contemplative life, as attention to the foundation charters of Saint Martin's daughter houses demonstrates.[16]

All the bishops who established these abbeys placed the following text at the head of their charters: "Although we are generally committed to care for all the faithful of our diocese, nevertheless we have a special love for those who are happily shipwrecked and, throwing overboard the cargo of this world, swim to the quiet, peaceful port of contemplation from the turmoil of this world." The language of this formula was borrowed from Saint Gregory the Great, but that is not to say that its words only mimic the model established at the mother abbey. In 1135, when the general chapter decided to divide the double monasteries and sequester their women, so that the sisters of Saint Martin were resettled at Dione in the diocese of Reims, Archbishop Raynaud wrote them, "Although I am constrained to care for everyone, my zeal for charity moves me to special regard for those who, seeking to live for God alone, out of love for him trample the enticing filth of the world, and who, throwing overboard all the cargo of transience and tumult, have in happy shipwreck escaped from the waves of this world to the tranquil harbor of happy contemplation."[17] Raynaud's text is not a copy, yet it conveys the same idea and image in different language. Clearly the charters were both conceived and written at Saint Martin. They allude to phrases of Saint Norbert in the sermon of

---

[16] *La vie spirituelle* (May 1, 1939).

[17] *Etsi omnibus vigilantiam debemus, in eos tamen zelo caritatis impensius intendentes compellimur qui Deo soli vivere quaerentes saeculi blandientis illecebras pro ipsius amore calcarunt, projectaque omni fluxae et caducae substantiae sarcina ad tranquillum jucundae contemplationis portum, de mundi hujus fluctuante pelago felici naufragio evaserunt.*

See these texts in Hugo, *Monasteriologium praemonstratense*, in the different daughter houses of Saint Martin, Vol. 1, p. 513; Vol. 2, 156; supporting texts, Vol. 2, col. 513.

his first Mass, apparently among his favorites.[18] In short, for Walter of Saint Maurice the Premonstratensians were contemplatives.

Because of the lofty stature of Saint Martin's, its abbot was second in the order only to the abbot of Prémontré, with precedence over the other prelates. Walter's personal prestige was further increased by his succession to the episcopal see of Bartholomew in Laon, so of the see in which Prémontré, Saint Martin, and Cuissy— three of the first four houses of the order—were situated. This dignity, along with his own moral valor, the work he accomplished at Saint Martin, the immediate proximity of Prémontré, and the influence he exercised over the monasteries he founded, lent compelling authority to his views, already in harmony with those of the abbot general. Still, the entire Order of Prémontré was not so fully engaged in contemplation that it abandoned its active apostolate. At least two important branches resisted the centralizing tendencies and monastic ends of the mother house.

First of these was the circary of Saxony, proud to preserve the spirit of the founder himself. Saint Norbert, in establishing the monastery of Our Lady of Magdeburg, had proclaimed its dependence directly on him and his successors in the archbishopric. Norbert had permitted the religious there to adopt some of the practices of other regular canons: to wear the rochet and black cape, and to pray the office according to the rite of the cathedral of Magdeburg rather than of the church of Prémontré. The founder granted the same privileges to the monastery of Gottesgnaden. Perhaps seeking to promote active apostolate, he seemed to resist strong centralization. At the time the circary of Saxony was primarily a missionary endeavor, but it would eventually include thirty-two monasteries, among them the cathedral chapters of Havelberg, Brandenburg, and Ratsburg, so establishing a chain of spiritual fortresses from Magdeburg east toward the Wends and north toward the shores of the Baltic. Yet when Norbert was named archbishop, the entire region was still pagan, if not legally at least practically.

---

[18] Translator's note: See the comment in the introduction above on the historicity of this sermon, an important text in the Norbertine tradition although more recent scholars have established that it is not indeed Norbert's words, rather the product of a later hand.

By the middle of the twelfth century the apostolic work of the Premonstratensians would make it a Christian region.[19]

The south of Germany saw the same commitment to the care of souls, but less systematically, in that the circary of Magdeburg alone was able to remain practically independent of Prémontré. The curious dialogue between a Cistercian and a Cluniac, composed in the period between 1150 and 1170 and published by Dom Martène, shows that the Premonstratensians of southern Germany refused to be called either Norbertines or monks, but instead canons, preachers, or curates. In this region the views of Hugh of Fosses clearly had not prevailed.[20] In any case, local differences decreased little by little. The general constitution of communities changed when women were separated and the number of lay brothers rapidly decreased, but parishes entrusted to the abbeys multiplied: seven hundred in France alone. A century later the life of the mendicants demonstrates that, for a clerical order, the ideal pattern for religious life is not imitation of the Cistercians. In spite of some monastic customs, vestiges of the twelfth-century organization, the Order of Prémontré remained faithful on the whole to the traditions of the regular canons. Two immediate disciples of Saint Norbert left behind spiritual writings suggesting the order's early tendencies: Luke, abbot of Mont Cornillon in Liège, and Anselm, bishop of Havelberg and beloved friend of the holy founder. Attention to these two authors is of great interest, since Luke fully represents the contemplative tendency of the West and Anselm the apostolic impulse of the Magdeburg branch.

Luke of Mont Cornillon

The Premonstratensian abbey of Mont Cornillon was immediately outside of Liège. It had been founded in 1124 by the bishop of the city, Albero, to whom an oratory at that place had been given during the prior year along with the income necessary to establish

---

[19] See Franz Winter, *Die Prämonstratenser des zwölften Jahrundert und ihre Bedeutung für das nordöstliche Deutschland* (Berlin, 1865).

[20] Martène, *Thesaurus*, Vol. 5, cols. 1614–15.

clergy there. The bishop immediately considered inviting the Premonstratensian religious of Floreffe, who were already in his diocese, to this church. At his request a small contingent began a new colony, with the blessed Luke as its head. This figure has for a long time been a legend in the order as one of the first to join Saint Norbert after he had cast his net in the school of Laon in 1120. As abbot of Mont Cornillon, Luke was, likely rightly, famous for his devotion to the holy angels, especially his guardian angel. Certainly he was one of the first prelates of the order and a contemporary of its foundation; he left behind a spiritual record whose importance demands consideration here. Only two of his works are known. The first is a continuation of the commentary of Aponius on the Canticle of Canticles. This work was dedicated to the blessed Milo, then abbot of Dammartin and afterward bishop of Thérouanne. The second is titled *Moralitates in cantica canticorum*.[21] Luke undertook to write this work at the insistence of a friend who had heard him preach— no doubt in his monastic chapter, for preaching on the Canticle of Canticles was rare outside of the cloister—and who had begged him not to allow such beautiful thoughts to fall into oblivion.

---

[21] Luke, PL 203, cols. 489–584. This work was first published in 1621 by Nicolas Chamart, abbot of Bonne Espérance, among the works of Philip of Harvengt. [Translator's note: The PL reproduces Chamart's version in Philip of Harvengt, *Opera omnia* (Douai, 1621).] It was unsigned, but it is nonetheless surprising that Chamart did not immediately recognize that the work was not Philip of Harvengt's. The author reveals his name in an acrostic: "The last and least of the servants of God, whose name is contained in the first five letters of the first volume." Philip is a name of nine letters (*Philippus* in Latin), and thus cannot be indicated, but the five letters are still at issue. Chamart read *primi tomi* in error, so positing M P Q S S when he should have read *primorum tomorum*, yielding VCAS. The letter designation [Translator's note: evidently L for LUCAS], of the first volume was missing because, according to the editor, it was struck out, illegible, in the manuscript. This signature is a riddle by a shy author fond of jests, as will later be the more apparent. Moreover, these *Moralitates* were dedicated to two Premonstratensians, Milo, bishop of Thérouanne, and Hugh of Fosses. Many authors named Luke wrote in the twelfth century, but it would be too coincidental for Milo to have had two friends named Luke, both Premonstratensians, exegetes, preachers, and specialists in the study of the Canticle of Canticles. It has been rightly said that the stylistic traits of the two works are not identical, but their rhetorical divergence likely resulted from Luke's attempt to imitate Aponius even in style as he continued the prior author's work, as Cornelius a Lapide noted. Even if the identity of the author of the *Moralitates* were unknown, however, the importance of the work would be evident.

The prelate at first hesitated. He then reflected that, the more he absorbed himself in his work, the less careful he would be to avoid the sicknesses to which his weak health subjected him. Yet he worked without intermission. When he had finished, he was apprehensive, cautious about presenting his work widely. He feared the harshness or ill-will of his critics. Indeed, the beginning of the twelfth century was a time of stridency about purity of doctrine, even of affectation. In such circumstances Luke knew that he must be careful of what he wrote. Critics abounded. As it happened, however, this book was delightful to many contemporary readers, although today a thorough reading seems tiresome. Its rhetorical style is unfamiliar and the author's frame of mind is antithetical to our own. To read this work, however, is nonetheless fruitful for study of the history of spirituality because it demonstrates how the first Premonstratensians—and they barely differ on this point from all their contemporaries—nourished their minds and souls on sacred scripture; it reveals their spiritual practice. Luke's style is similar to all twelfth-century spiritual writers', if perhaps a little clearer because he lacked the literary gifts to veil his meaning in a variety of rhetorical forms.

Contemporaries of Luke founded their reading of sacred scripture on allegory—not as bizarre or exaggerated perspective but, according to the teaching of Saint Gregory the Great, because the soul is more easily raised to mystical contemplation when it meditates on imageries of belief. In this period beginners were normally nourished with the historical, literal level of interpretation of sacred scripture, while more mature souls found in allegories of doctrine their more powerful and nourishing drink.[22] Such interpretation corresponds to spiritual experiences different from our own, but nonetheless real. Luke, well schooled in sacred scripture and the Fathers, especially Saint Ambrose, Saint Jerome, and Saint Augustine,

---

[22] Adam Scot also expounded this notion in the preface to his *Allegoriae in sacram scripturam* and in that of his *De tripartito tabernaculo*. Allegory, therefore, is not for our authors a simple process of rhetoric or an intellectual pursuit. It is rather the means to penetrate the mysteries of the Holy Spirit, of breaking the shell in order to nourish their souls on the kernel. Some authors who have treated the sermons of Saint Bernard are likewise so distant from the profound thought of their subject as to miss this point.

had no difficulty in finding beneath the symbolism of the Canticle of Canticles the substantial marrow of its mysteries. Frequently the meanings he discerns are delightful, but he had little rhetorical skill and his allegories follow too rapidly—as if he were indeed able to find the pure gold in ore, but allows us to admire it too briefly.

Luke's devotion to the Savior was lively but as yet does not embrace such tenderness as might lead to a detailed meditation on Jesus' earthly life. His work shows nothing of this new spirit. When he speaks of our Lady he is more evidently moved. At a time when only the joys of the Virgin drew souls, he paused also to contemplate her sorrows: "You will truly show yourself his mother when you, with the deep love of your heart, suffer with him as he dies on the Cross."[23] Again he writes, "Those who are wounded by the weapons of vice must implore the help and protection of Mary, holy mother of God, and say to her from the depths of their heart: 'We have taken refuge in your protection, where so many of the sick have recovered their strength.'"[24] Saint Bernard would have written further. Luke's eloquence is too brief; we nonetheless sense a deeply filial, affectionate trust.

The other topic dear to Luke was the monastic life: "He who has converted and spends his life well, living in a holy and religious way within the cloister, known for his irreproachable life and for drawing others to conversion to God, he whose dove-like peace and fraternal charity mark him as beloved of his brethren . . . about him we should say: *Thy name is as oil poured out* [Song 1:2]."[25] Further, after an invective against religious who, under pretext of a more austere life, leave their cloister to go to another only to leave that one as well, he exclaims: "O how happy, how blessed the soul

---

[23] *Sicque veram ejus genitricem te esse comprobabis cum ei in cruce morienti intimo cordis affectu compatieris.* Luke, PL 203, col. 572.

[24] *Qui ergo . . . vitiorum telis vulnerati dolent isti sine dubio necesse est ut auxilium et opem sanctae Dei Genitricis Mariae implorent et ex intimo affectu cordis dicant: sub tuam protectionem confugimus ubi infirmi acceperunt virtutem.* Luke, PL 203, col. 520.

[25] *Qui ad conversionem vadit et in claustro bene et sancte et religiose conversatur, et qui bona fama irreprehensibilis vitae animat et attrahit ut ad Dominum convertantur, et insuper qui columbina pace et fraterna dilectione animis fratrum suorum amabilem se reddit . . . huic sine dubio dici debet: Oleum effusum nomen tuum.* Luke. PL 203, col. 533.

that pines with the love of God!"[26] Such exclamations are frequent in Luke's works. Although his soul was on fire it reveals itself only timidly and occasionally, then returns to its allegorical explanations. In short, we are scarcely able to love him or even to keep company with him, but he must have been a delightful guide for his brothers. Given their spiritual state, he worked to kindle in their souls the living flame of the love of God. He surely wanted no other recompense.

Anselm of Havelberg

Reading Luke of Mont Cornillon is instructive, if not always enjoyable. His allegories are powerful and intelligent, but their many symbols grow tedious. Anselm of Havelberg, on the other hand, is an author of high merit. He wrote little, especially on spiritual matters, but his few works are both readable and enjoyable. His intellect is lively and penetrating, while his rhetorical sensibility is well-suited to stir and persuade. Anselm appears in history without father or mother or genealogy. He certainly came from the Rhineland or Lower Lorraine, where the name Anselm, almost unknown in Saxony, was common. As a youth he was likely a pupil of Ralph of Laon, so was one of those students from Lorraine whom Saint Norbert attracted during his first preaching at the renowned cathedral school there. Anselm later appears at Magdeburg in the company of Norbert who, as metropolitan, in 1129 made him bishop of Havelberg, a city still inhabited by pagans. Anselm therefore remained in Magdeburg with his master, at whose side he stood during the violence fomented there by the saint's enemies. Only later would Anselm be able to take possession of his episcopal see, where he then established Premonstratensians in the chapter of his cathedral church. He subsequently lived in community with them, afterward contributing to the foundation of the Norbertine abbey of Jerichow.

Life was harsh and dangerous in the marches of the north, at the far limits of Christendom: "In my manger at Havelberg I dwell, a poor

---

[26] *O quam felix, quam beata anima quae languet amore Dei!* Luke, PL 203, col. 538.

man of Christ among my brothers, also Christ's poor. Some of them
build defenses against the enemy; others keep watch against attacks
by pagans; others again attend to the divine services while daily
awaiting martyrdom; some purify the souls they will soon return to
God by means of fasting and prayer; still others occupy themselves
in divine reading and holy meditation, thus following the example
of the saints. All of us, as the naked and poor of Christ, follow him
in his poverty and nakedness as best we can." [27] As bishop, Anselm
also played a major role in the evangelization of the Wends. Like
Norbert, he was embroiled in the politics of his day, collaborating
with Wibald, abbot of Stavelot, to reconcile pope and emperor. In
1133 Anselm accompanied Emperor Lothair and Saint Norbert to
Italy and won the favor of Innocent II, who asked him to preach in
his presence at the solemn liturgy of September 8. He also was often
in the company of the emperors Conrad and Frederick. Anselm
traveled to Constantinople in 1136 to ask on Frederick's behalf for
the hand of the daughter of the Greek emperor. On this occasion
he conducted interesting conversations with the Greek masters of
theology on the subjects of the procession of the Holy Spirit and
the use of unleavened bread. At the request of Pope Eugenius III
he would later commit these conversations to writing. Afterward,
in 1154, he negotiated the coronation of Frederick I with the am-
bassadors of Eugenius III. Eventually named archbishop of Ravenna,
Anselm received the pallium from the hands of Hadrian IV on the
same day the pope crowned the emperor. He died suddenly
August 12, 1158, during the imperial siege of Milan.

---

[27] *In praesepio meo Havelberg pauper Christi cum fratribus meis pauperibus Christi
maneo, ubi alii turim fortitudinis aedificant a facie inimici, alii sunt in excubiis ad
defendendum contra insultus paganorum, alii divinis obsequiis mancipati quotidie
martyrium expectant, alii animas suas Deo reddendas jejuniis et orationibus purificant;
alii lectionibus vacantes et sanctis meditationibus insistentes et sanctorum vitam et exempla
imitantes seipsos exercitant, at omnes nudi et pauperes nudum ac pauperem Christum
quantum possumus sequimur.* Anselm of Havelberg, *Epistola CCXXV Ad Wibaldum
abbatem*, PL 189, cols. 1319–20.

This beautiful text shows us the fervor of these first missionaries of the north.
Their method of evangelization is unrecorded, but it seems similar to that of the
Benedictine abbeys of England: to establish exemplary Christian communities
around which the new faithful might rally.

Anselm was the spiritual successor of Norbert in northern Germany. Although he had neither the dynamism nor the asceticism of the great archbishop, he nonetheless evinced a skillful political flexibility. Except for a brief exile from court under Conrad, he was always able to support both popes and emperors. His learning made him the greatest theologian of contemporary Germany. Remarkably, he attained a subtle and sympathetic understanding of Orthodox theology. His historical sensibility was the most developed of his century. Anselm's clarity of thought was penetrating. When Conrad, Norbert's successor at Magdeburg, died, Anselm installed Wichman in the metropolitan see; the latter would become a great peacemaker between the ecclesiastical and imperial power. The qualities of Anselm's heart, however, were no less lofty than his political acumen, despite his occasionally satirical tone. His graciousness was such that, in his dialogues at Constantinople, the audience applauded him although he represented an opposing world. Anselm maintained a moving filial piety for the memory of Norbert. He appreciated that his relationship with the saint was the greatest honor of his life. His devotion to the Order of Prémontré was so great that appeals came to him from far and wide that he seek pontifical or imperial privileges for the work of Norbert. Anselm's spirituality demonstrated a particular devotion to the Holy Spirit, refined in his contact with the Easterners. For Anselm, the Catholic Church is living because the Holy Spirit animates it. Its vitality is sapped by those timid folk who cling to the past in fear that all novelty is corruption, attached as they are by habit to old practices and frightened by necessary change. The Holy Spirit is everywhere, *pantepiscopos*, the universal bishop watching over and sanctifying all Christ wills in the unfolding of time. Anselm's love for poverty and for the ideal of apostolic life was according to the exact frame of mind and lived example of Saint Norbert.

In his very boldness the bishop of Havelberg incurred enmity. When he died, some critics attributed his unexpected demise to divine punishment, blaming Anselm for having accepted translation to another episcopal see. Moreover, his manner was insouciant, so alienating the stodgy. One day when he was suffering a painful sore throat, he approached Saint Bernard: "Father, you cure the poor and silly women. Can you not cure me of this sore throat?"

Bernard answered, "If you had the faith of those little weak women, you could cure yourself." Anselm rejoined, "Then I myself lack such faith, cure me by your own." Bernard touched him and the swelling disappeared.[28]

The present work will not treat Anselm's dialogues, *antikeimena*, the record of his conversations with the Greeks. This work merits study in the context of a full biography. It shows how weak awareness of the schism from the East was in the twelfth century and what effort this northern bishop exerted to communicate the Roman point of view to the Greeks. It also clarifies differences between western and eastern theological perspectives. But Anselm can indeed be considered a spiritual author in his apologetic letter on behalf of the regular canons, a work addressed to the abbot of Huysburg, [29] and again in the first book of his dialogues, treating the internal development of the Catholic Church.

Anselm's Apologetic Letter

The bishop of Havelberg sat alone absorbed in *lectio divina*, studying the letters of Saint Jerome, an inexhaustible source of the monastic spirit, when a religious approached holding out a newly written work. Anselm exchanged his old reading for the new material. He took the manuscript, read the first line he saw, then read on. Here he learned nothing new, but found the tract's tired old ideas irksome and boring. He then looked at the title. It was a work of Ekbert, abbot of Huysburg, against the regular canons. It was thus an element in a lively and important polemical literature— lamentable yet providing the opportunity to clarify the Church's theology of asceticism by explaining the relationship between the priesthood and regular religious life.[30] When monks and regular

---

[28] Cited by Fleury, *Histoire de l'Église*. [Editor's note: Petit here likely refers to Claude Fleury, *Histoire ecclésiastique* (Paris: Delaroque, 1856).]

[29] Anselm of Havelberg, *Epistola apologetica pro ordine canonicorum regularium*, PL 188, col. 1120–22.

[30] Monks, although a great many were priests and clerics, were not considered a clerical order in the Middle Ages. The monastic state is complete in itself without requiring the sacrament of orders.

canons reopened this discussion in the seventeenth century it regarded only precedence, their respective places in public processions. In the twelfth century the issue was rather whether the monks, under pretext of greater austerity, had the right to undercut the monasteries of canons by luring away their best converts, as unfortunately then transpired. Lambert of Saint Ruf and Arno of Reischensberg wrote on behalf of the canons; Abelard and Rupert of Deutz for the monks.

Today the authority of the Church has judged in favor of the regular canons in this controversy and the reason is evident.[31] In theory, canons surpass monks in the dignity of the holy orders to which they have been called by virtue of their institution and by the superiority of the mixed life over the purely contemplative life.[32] In practice, however, the superiority of the institution means little in comparison to the superiority of souls. A person leading an active life can be a saint while another giving himself to the contemplative life can remain lukewarm, while yet another embracing a mixed life—inherently the loftiest path—is dissipated. In the twelfth century this observation begged attention and Anselm's response to Egbert fulfilled that need: I do not call someone good because he is a monk but because he is good. I call another good not because he is a cleric but because he is good. I call him such and befriend him because he is. I call a man good or evil not because he is a layman.[33] Reciting such truisms is worthwhile only because ambiguity had afflicted the terminology of ascetic and mystical experience.

Now, when we speak of the contemplative life, we mean a life organized in such a manner that those who lead it easily arrive at contemplation supported by fasting, the singing of psalms, silence, and study. When we speak of the active life, we understand a life

---

[31] *Canonici regulares praecedunt monachis. Codex iuris canonici,* c. 491. § 1.

[32] *Sicut majus est illuminare quam lucere solum ita majus est contemplata tradere quam solum contemplari. . . . Sic ergo summum gradum tenent in religionibus quae ordinantur ad docendum et praedicandum, quae et propinquissimae sunt perfectioni episcoporum. Summa Theologiae,* II.II, q. 188, a. 6.

[33] *Ego monachus non sum, attamen monasticum ordinem tecum defendere paratus sum. . . . Ego nec clericum, quia clericus est bonum, diligo. Ego nec laicum, quia laicus est, aut bonum aut malum judico.* Anselm, *Epistola apologetica,* PL 188, cols. 1120–21.

oriented toward active apostolate and works of mercy, and embracing education and practical studies alongside brief but thoughtful and fruitful devotions, with a certain freedom in the use of time and the organization of work. One can indeed arrive at contemplation in the active life—Saint Francis Borgia, the General of the Society of Jesus, was an outstanding contemplative—while the strictly contemplative life does not ensure access to contemplation. As for the mixed life, its every feature facilitates contemplation but allows the contemplative in the ordinary course of his experience to allow the overflowing abundance of his soul to be engaged in the work of active apostolate, constrained by time and space but fructified in its intimate union with God.

Saint Thomas Aquinas holds this all to be clear, but the Fathers understood the distinction between these two pathways of religious life differently, as Thomas often notes. For them, the active life means the beginning of the spiritual life, a time in which moral virtues are instilled. The contemplative life is then the spiritual life of the perfect, in which the theological virtues are exercised constantly and more and more simply. The mixed life lies outside this distinction, yet of course the greater perfection of monks, contemplatives—except for regrettable but individual lapses—is easier to credit than that of clerics, active persons vowed to apostolate. Because an individual always has the right to abandon a less perfect life in order to achieve one of greater perfection, it seems a great accomplishment to win the best souls from cloisters of canons for the benefit of monastic institutions. Exactly this had happened. Peter, provost of the canons of Hammersleben, had just became a monk and other monks were indignant that his former confreres had reminded him of the vows of "his profession of the common life according to apostolic institution."

In retrospect the debate concerned at once the possibility of new forms of religious life—for the monks reproached the canons as latecomers in the Church—the value of the care of souls, the usefulness of the sacrament of orders for the sanctification of those who received it and finally the superiority of the mixed over the contemplative life. The issue was complicated, however, by the fact that authors among the canons considered monks as such—assuming that monastic profession did not imply priesthood—while monastic authors assumed that most choir monks were indeed raised to priesthood or diaconate. In England, for example, Benedictine monks dedicated to the care of souls in the cathedrals were effectively regular canons. Nonetheless canons are by their very nature priests dedicated to the ministry of souls even unto death, as are bishops; Saint Thomas himself noted that monks are not priests by virtue of their monastic institution, hence not obligated to any ministry.

Anselm insists above all on the superiority of the mixed life, while arguing against the derogation of monasteries by discrediting either way of life. "I am not a monk," he wrote, "but I am ready to defend with you the monastic order if it is attacked." Then, in order to support his thesis, he shows first of all that the greatest saints of the Old Law (Abel, Noah, Abraham, Jacob, Moses, Joshua, David, and the Prophets) were at once contemplatives and actives. Anselm places greatest weight on the example of the Son of God himself, the exemplar of both the contemplatives and actives who made his apostles (Peter, James, and John) both contemplatives and actives. Egbert objects, quoting Christ about the contemplative Mary, "Mary has chosen the best part, which shall not be taken away from her" (Luke 10:42). Anselm invites Ekbert to consider that there are three persons in that Gospel story: Martha, Mary, and also Jesus, the contemplative of the Transfiguration and Gethsemane here actively teaching humble women the word of life. He is himself the paradigm of the mixed life. The term "mixed life" is absent from the works of Anselm but his description clearly suggests it:

> Jesus Christ himself, the Son of God and Man, head of the Catholic Church, model of contemplatives, exemplar of all actives—does he seem to you to have been contemplative or active? . . . Martha, engaged in her ministry, indeed signifies the active life while Mary, who sat at the Lord's feet and attentively listened to his word, appropriately represents the contemplative life of which the Lord said, "Mary has chosen the best part which shall not be taken away from her" [Luke 10:42]. Did he want "the best part" to be understood as a comparison between Mary and Martha, or rather was he speaking about Martha alone? Jesus Christ, as he so sat and taught, played the teacher's role. Christ teaching, Mary listening and Martha ministering are three persons. Which of the three

seems to you to be the most worthy? Of these three roles, which seems to you to be the most worthy? Surely no one doubts that the most worthy office was Christ's own.[34]

Need we add, the author asks, that not all monks have arrived at contemplation? He begins a denigrating characterization of certain cloisters but soon breaks it off, recalling the great sanctity of many monks. Nevertheless, as he points out, the Church could still live if she had no monks. She would be unaffected in the most basic aspects of her life. On the other hand, without an established and holy clergy she would no longer be the Church. Anselm thus presents a magnificent ideal of the canonical life:

> With my poor brothers in Christ, I—the least of God's servants and poor little instrument in the Lord's temple, last of those who serve the tabernacle of the covenant—shall with all my strength carry the ark of the covenant with God's other priests. With his other ministers I shall faithfully assist and humbly rouse the Christian people to hasten toward the promised land, to fight earthly desires and defeat the devil's forces. I will exhort them with the trumpets of sacred scripture until the enemy is conquered and the walls of Jericho come crashing down . . . until we all enter into the heavenly Jerusalem.[35]

[34] *Ipse Dei et hominis Filius Jesus Christus, caput Ecclesiae catholicae, caput contemplativorum, caput omnium activorum . . . utrumne tibi videtur fuisse contemplativus an activus? . . . Martha scilicet dum circa frequens ministerium satagebat, activam vitam non inconvenienter significabat; Maria vero dum secus pedes Domini sedens verbum illius avidissime audiebat, contemplativam vitam non incongrue figurabat; de qua etiam cum Dominus diceret: Maria optimam partem elegit quae non auferetur ab ea, numquid optimam partem intellegi voluit comparatione sui ipsius et Marthae, an potius non sui sed potius solius Marthae? Jesus Christus sedens docebat, doctus doctorum gerebat. . . . Christus docens, Maria audiens, Martha ministrans tres sunt personae: quae harum trium tibi videbatur esse dignior? Tria sunt officia, quid horum trium tibi videtur esse dignius? Profecto officium quoque ejus dignissimum fuisse nemo dubitat.* Anselm, *Epistola apologetica*, PL 188, cols. 1131–32.

These texts must be cited because persons today sometimes deny that the Middle Ages had any concept of the mixed life. I acknowledge that "mixed life" is an equivocal and poorly framed term. The mixed life is not a mixture of contemplation and action but a state beyond contemplation embracing a higher order of action.

[35] *Ego autem cum fratribus meis pauperibus Christi, minimus servorum Dei, qualecumque vasculum in templo Dei, ultimus eorum qui serviunt tabernaculo foederis, pro viribus meis*

The tone of this letter is on the whole profound and measured, as a bishop's should be. But Anselm is sometimes rhetorical and sometimes loses his temper. He is exacting, occasionally revealing more ill-will than he should. Thus, referring to the obese Rupert of Deutz, he cites the Greek proverb: "A fat belly does not give birth to a fine mind."[36] Still, Anselm clearly is loath to violate the bonds of charity even to support his cause. After all, he was a Christian before a canon. "We are all one in Christ." In his mystical body are different ranks and roles, but unity necessarily underlies them all.

The First Book of the Dialogues

Anselm's dialogues or *antikeimena* were written in 1143 and addressed to Pope Eugenius III, the Cistercian and disciple of Saint Bernard to whom the saint dedicated his *De consideratione*. On the whole this work of Anselm's is the redaction of what we would today call the conversations at Constantinople between the Orthodox *didascalos*, or official theologian, Archbishop Nicetas of Nicomedia and our Anselm as the Latins' spokesman. This essentially theological work nonetheless contains spiritual elements. For a Westerner to learn to call the Holy Spirit by the Greeks' "light through himself and life through Himself, dedicator of temples, God-maker, spirit of the filiation of the Son of God and by adoption spirit of our filiation"[37] was not to learn heretofore unknown mysteries, rather to appreciate an accent on perspectives unemphasized in the Latin world. That was certainly beneficial. In composing this work, however, Anselm was able to win as his audience the pope, indeed all of Christendom. This opportunity, he realized, would support his defense of the new religious orders in a prefatory book entitled *On the Unity of the Faith and the Many Ways of Living from Abel the Just to the Last*

---

arcam testamenti cum caeteris sacerdotibus Dei portabo, cum ministrantibus fideliter ministrabo, populum christianum ad terram promissionis properantem, ad expugnandas carnales concupiscentias et ad debellandas spiritualis nequitiae turmas, tubis divinae Scripturae humiliter excitabo donec, victis hostibus, muri Jericho corruant . . . donec omnes in caelestem Jerusalem ascendamus. Anselm, *Epistola apologetica*, PL 188, col. 1138.

[36] *Pinguis venter non gignit tenuem sensum.*

[37] *Per seipsum lumen et per seipsum vita . . . templificativum, deificans, spiritum filiationis.* Anselm of Havelberg, *Dialogi*, PL 188, col. 1182.

of the Elect.[38] Here Anselm would argue on behalf of the Premonstratensians but also the Cistercians, barely older than they, and so
would please Pope Eugenius III.

In a time of religious ferment like the twelfth century both new
forms of life and opposition were inevitable. Great sanctity and
moral wretchedness coexisted with multiple heresies and as many
true reform movements, so disconcerting even the best-intentioned.
"Why so many novelties in the Church of God, so many novel religious orders of clerics and varieties of monks?"[39] Some were recom-
mending specific ways of life as leading to the kingdom of heaven
while others warned against the same practices. What one discarded
as sacrilege, another considered salutary and commendable. Simply,
why did the Premonstratensians not live like the other canons?
Why did the Cistercians not embrace the same liturgical pomp as
the Cluniacs? Why new rules of psalmody, new modes of abstinence? Anselm had already written to the abbot of Huysburg:
"A practice is neither more or less contemptible or acceptable because it is newer or older."[40] Alone, Anselm seems to have proposed
the real distinctiveness in his devotion to the Holy Spirit renewed
in his contact with the Greeks: the reason for the novelties is that
the Church, a living institution, is both singular and multiform as
are all living things. She is the mystical body of Christ and the Holy
Spirit is her soul, yet the Spirit himself is also both one and multiple, subtle, mobile. He shares his graces as he wills.

Anselm's thought here is irreproachable and, it may now seem,
somewhat elementary, but neither the Latins nor Greeks of the
Middle Ages had yet expressed it. But even when he is innovative,
as was frequently the case, Anselm always understands himself as
faithful to venerable antiquity. The Cistercians believed that they

---

[38] *De unitate fidei et multiformitate vivendi ab Abel justo usque ad novissimum electum.*
Anselm, *Dialogi,* PL 188, cols. 1141–62. [Editor's note: Anselm of Havelberg, *Anti-
cimenon: On the Unity of the Faith and the Controversies with the Greeks,* trans. Ambrose
Criste and Carol Neel, CS 232 (Collegeville, MN: Cistercian Publications, 2010).]

[39] *Quare tot novitates in Ecclesia Dei fiunt? Quare tot ordines in ea surgunt? Quis
numerare queat tot ordines clericorum?* Anselm, *Dialogi,* PL 188, col. 1141.

[40] *Non quia novum est, aut novum fuit, aliquid plus minusve est contemptibile, nec quia
vetus est aut vetus erit, aliquid plus minusve est acceptabile.* Anselm, *Epistola apologetica,*
PL 188, col. 1122.

renewed Saint Benedict just as the regular canons believed that they revived the Church of Hippo and the Acts of the Apostles. Anselm demonstrates his thesis through the historical development of religious life in the world: God gently leads his people like a teacher or doctor.[41] Divine revelation extends from the beginning of the world to Christ and the Apostles, then continues to unfold. An age of the martyrs follows the apostolic age, then ensues the struggle against heresies. Finally, regular religious life appears, with its new patterns. Anselm offers magnificent praise for Saint Norbert as for Saint Bernard, attesting that that the Holy Spirit continues to effect the Church's eternal youth through the marvelous actions of providence.[42] Such was the fervor Christendom experienced, roused by these saints after the somnolence of the investiture controversy into a tender and vigorous spiritual efflorescence.

The Saxon circary here deserves special attention. It always appeared to be a degree rebellious and suspicious to Prémontré, but nonetheless glorious for the order, with its saintly bishops Evermode, Isfrid, and Ludolph. It was eminently apostolic, so that Winter wrote in 1865: "No religious order can lay claim to the conversion of a province as can the Premonstratensians of the Middle Ages for the country of the Wends."[43] This circary demonstrated filial loyalty to the memory and frame of mind of Saint Norbert and at the same time wisdom and contemporary engagement in their great and noble Anselm. Saint Norbert seems to have foreseen the discord between Prémontré and Magdeburg when, on the very day of the consecration of the Mother Church, he saw the altar stone fracture: "The order will break," he said. As if to explain, he added: "This church will some day need reconsecration."[44] His first interpretation was the more exact. Still, we must not exaggerate.

---

[41] *Paedagocice et medicinaliter.* Anselm, *Dialogi* PL 188, col. 1147.

[42] *Et fit mira Dei dispensatione quod a generatione in generationem succrescente semper nova religione renovatur ut aquilae juventus Ecclesiae.* Anselm, *Dialogi*, PL 188, col. 1157.

[43] Winter, intro.

[44] Saint Norbert had similarly prophetic intuitions on several other occasions, but he seems to have been uncertain how to interpret them. Thus, having said to Saint Bernard that he was sure that the Antichrist had been born, he then said in response to his interlocutor's query that at least the Church would meet with general persecution. In fact neither occurred, rather Norbert anticipated the schism of Pierleoni.

Saint Norbert and his community at Magdeburg were becoming closer and closer to regular canons, as was Hugh of Fosses to the Cistercians. After the death of the founder confusion and misunderstanding occasionally arose, but no definitive rupture before the Protestant Reformation.

Archeologists note that the cathedrals of Magdeburg, Havelberg, and Brandenburg—the latter two Premonstratensian—closely resemble the cathedral of Laon. This is symbolic. The Premonstratensians of the far-off circary never ceased to look toward the country of Laon and the wilderness of Prémontré, whose name they bear and which Norbert chose to establish the foundations of his canonical work. They cannot forget that, while canonically their monasteries were daughters of Our Lady of Magdeburg, most of their early religious and their great missionaries came from Prémontré, Floreffe, and Cappenberg.

Chapter 4
The Heroes of the Apostolic Movement

Religious orders are founded to produce saints, and so they should. To ask a given order not long after its foundation, "What results have you obtained? What has been the spiritual return on your enterprise?" is then well-justified. Yet at the same time not every one of an order's saints need be buried under an altar, for this would be impossible. Nothing would be more misleading than to judge the holiness of an order according to the number of canonizations honoring its members, especially with respect to orders founded before the thirteenth century. Indeed, in the eleventh century the Order of Cluny had served the Church well. The entire Gregorian Reform was founded on this order, and Cluny would see many of its sons raised to the altar, beginning with its first abbots, Saints Odo, Mayeul, and Hugh. The Cluniacs had devoted themselves to a liturgical splendor, something very good in itself but antithetical to the ideal of poverty embraced at the beginning of the twelfth century. The new orders—the Carthusians, Cistercians, Premonstratensians, and Camaldolese, as well as the orders of Fontevrault and Grandmont—were founded to an extent as a reaction against Cluny. These orders had no wish for canonized saints. The Carthusians have very few even now: Saint Bruno; Saint Hugh, bishop of Lincoln; Saint Roseline. The Cistercians, after having supported the canonization of Saint Bernard, resolved in a general chapter not to request liturgical honors for their saints "lest they be devalued on account of their great number." The Premonstratensians, similarly, participated in no canonization processes because they feared that throngs of pilgrims would ensue, invading their cloisters and disturbing their contemplation. Besides, it seemed to them more perfect to renounce all glory—even posthumous glory—except for the glory of paradise. Therefore, in the Order of Prémontré, Saint Norbert alone has been canonized. Even he was only so honored in the sixteenth century; liturgical honors for the blessed were accorded to only fifteen or so members of the order before the eighteenth century. The Norbertine family has nonetheless piously preserved the memory of certain abbots, canons, lay brothers, sisters, and even hermits who were vested in the white habit of the order and died in the odor of sanctity.[1]

A close examination of each of these saintly figures would be impossible here. There are too many even among the foremost of them, while preliminary research remains incomplete for most. Here, therefore, we will consider only the beginning of the order, studying four representative cases: Garembert, the founder of Mount Saint Martin; the family of Deacon Nicholas of Soissons; Oda, a sister of Bonne-Espérance; the blessed Frederick, founder of Mariengaarde. We thus may participate, even as moderns, in the development of a monastery in the north of France, the conversion of an entire family to the religious life, the sacrifice of the daughter of a noble family and finally the journey of a cleric embracing the apostolic life with complete enthusiasm. All this occurred when the Order of Prémontré was only just beginning to establish itself, when it was less a formal religious order than the fresh expression of that apostolic movement we have mentioned above.

Garembert

Garembert or Walembert—both spellings appear in the charters of the period and the Picard pronunciation explains the variant—was born in 1084 in the village of Wulpen, in Belgium near Furnes.[2]

---

[1] See Georg Lienhardt, *Ephemerides hagiologicae ordinis praemonstratensis* (Augsburg, 1764).

[2] *Histoire du vénérable serviteur de Dieu le bienheureux Garembert* (Cambrai, 1769). [Editor's note: Petit attributes this anonymous work to a Fr. De Villers.] The appendix to this volume includes *Acta vitae beati Garemberti*. The archives of the department

His parents' names were Baldralan and Raghanild. He had a sister of the same name, later spelled Reginalda, whom we shall soon meet again. Garembert probably studied at the collegial school of Saint Walpurga at Furnes but he did not at first enter the clerical life. He did, however, feel the desire early on to give himself to God and, as was the case with other religious founders like Bruno, Norbert, Dominic, and Ignatius, he turned toward France to begin his new life. Whether this change of place was on account of an apparition, a dream, or simple inner movement matters little. Garembert always had the clear intent to serve the Blessed Virgin at a place called Bony. Although he had never seen this spot, he knew its topography by heart. God had reserved for him a site near an imperial highway, where a wooded slope overlooked a wide valley.

One day, when Garembert was about twenty-two—perhaps under the pretext of studying French—he left his parents and went to Cambrai, where he reappeared in the service of a townsman, perhaps in order to earn a living or perhaps because young bourgeois such as he were accustomed to attach themselves to patrons just as the young nobles did to kings and as young clerics to bishops or emperors—so that they might be fostered there. From time to time Garembert inquired about a place called Bony but no one knew of it. After four years he left Cambrai and went to Saint Quentin, where he was employed by two brothers, Baldwin and Oylard, the latter of whom was mayor of the town. Again he was in the service of another but his divine imperative continued to trouble him. The young man could not continue in this way, instead becoming so ill that his patron, alarmed, inquired what the matter was. Garembert responded that he must serve the Blessed Virgin at

---

of Aisne (Ms. 126) house another source on Garembert's life: Fr. Bévièr, *Mémoires historiques relatifs à l'abbaye du Mont Saint-Martin et la vie de Garembert un fondateur* (1664). Lepaige includes a life of Garembert with charters relative to his foundation, but these documents are spurious: *Bibliotheca praemonstratensis ordinis*, ed. Jean Lepaige (Paris, 1633). Lepaige thought he could cobble together reproductions of appropriate documents because the abbey's cartulary had been lost, but it reappeared subsequently in the library of Colbert. See the charters in Hugo, *Monasterioliogium*, Vol. 2, 154ff. See also Ignatius van Spilbeeck, *Vie du B. Garembert*, (Namur, 1890).

Bony but that he did not know where it lay. Oylard, as it happened, knew the place well; it was one of his own territories. He took Garembert there the next day and offered that, if the young man saw fit, he could become a hermit there—a remarkably simple resolution. The strength of the religious movement was evidently such in the twelfth century that laypeople who did not embrace the cloistered life were as enthusiastic in it as those choosing such a life. Garembert now went to Bony and recognized the place even though he had never seen it before. There, with the permission of Burchard, bishop of Cambrai, friend of Saint Norbert and protector of Hugh of Fosses, Garembert settled in a hut in the forest. He invested himself joyfully and completely to contemplation and penance in this place where he found his rest.

The new hermit, however, soon became famous. Others came to converse with him or to be healed of their sicknesses. A companion named Alberic came to live under his direction and Garembert did not have the courage to send him away. Some time later the great number of their visitors made the two hermits' life together impossible and they prepared to move, but the people of the nearby parishes begged them to stay. Garembert yielded to their wishes and agreed to remain. Then Alberic recruited yet another companion, then more came in droves—clerics and laity alike wishing Garembert to form them for religious life. Never had he thought that he would become the father of a community but now his duty was clear. Moreover, since the confreres were still not self-sufficient because the undergrowth was being cleared away and the earth was not productive, the master of these solitaries would go out among the neighboring villages. As he went he drove a small donkey carrying baskets for alms to nourish his children. In the meantime the number of religious continued to grow. Garembert now had to consider replacing the huts with a church and monastery.

Garembert's building project was made possible in 1119, two years before the foundation of Prémontré, by the donation of the land where he lived. The Picards are a cautious people and were unwilling to fund the project before they were certain it would move ahead. The land that Oylard had promised belonged to him, but the mayor shared it with his brother Baldwin and the renowned chapter serving the collegiate church of Saint Quentin. The chapter, "trusting in Christ and in those who love him," was easily persuaded by Garembert's personal appeal. They granted him the land to build a church in honor of our Lady, Saint Cassian, and Saint Nicholas, along with a cloister, living quarters, and a garden. Oylard and Baldwin, "animated by a holy zeal and attentive to the Lord's invitation, *Give and it shall be given to you* [Luke 6:38]," gave away all proprietary rights to this new church. Even in the seventeenth century, after many wars and other disasters, the stone flooring of the church and the small tiles paving the cells were still visible. During the church's construction agriculture also proceeded; the community labored, spreading lime on some fields and manuring others, clearing the brush so effectively that for a long time the area was still called "Garembert's Clearing." On this territory the community soon built a farm at Bellicourt and sent several brothers there. The chapter of Saint Quentin first granted this right and ten years later fully abandoned its claim to the land.

Since this new community of religious included a certain number of clerics, they established a college of canons. Garembert was blessed as their abbot by the bishop of Cambrai sometime between 1130 and 1136. The clerics' canonical profession gave them the right to serve parishes. They would soon care for the church of Mount Brehain. Moreover, they established a monastery of sisters near their abbey with Garembert's sister, Raghanild, as prioress. Bony could then have remained an independent abbey and even become the head of an order, as did Arrouaise or Prémontré, but Garembert was both humble and aware of the dangers of isolation. Well-constructed statutes, regular and thoughtful visitations, the authority of a general chapter—all these elements were important to a monastery's well-being. Therefore, with the permission of Liutard, bishop of Cambrai, Garembert approached Walter of Saint Maurice, abbot of Saint Martin of Laon, asking him to make Bony a daughter house of his community. Walter gave his consent and sent a dozen or so clerics there under the direction of a religious named Oderan.

These confreres from Saint Martin were surprised to see the abbey situated in a location without running water, for the Scheldt lay half a league away in the valley. They decided to transfer the community to the mouth of the river, to a place called Mount Saint Martin because the holy apostle to the Gauls had long ago demolished a pagan idol there. The sisters, however, remained at Bony near the original church; in 1212 they were also transferred, but to the valley of Macquincourt. Garembert naturally resigned as abbot when the canons came from Saint Martin. The former master now became the pupil, entering with his sons into the Order of Prémontré, and in his stead Oderan became the abbot of Mount Saint Martin. The memory of Bony, however, pulled at the heart of Garembert. From the abbey he could see the church of Our Lady on the hill above. He soon asked permission to continue to serve it, then lived there until his death surrounded by the sisters. The sanctuary at Bony quickly became a center of Marian pilgrimage. In the Middle Ages, the wills of the people of Vermandois list as many bequests for Masses at Our Lady of Bony as at Our Lady of Liesse. And in his solitude there Garembert could slake his thirst for prayer. Heaven attracted him so much that he disdained the earth. In the evening he continued his *lectio divina* almost until matins. After the office he recited the rest of the Psalter almost until the dawn. During the day he gave his service to the poor, sick and orphaned.

Nonetheless, Garembert quarreled with his successor over the matter of women religious. Oderan dreaded the responsibility for directing sisters, wishing only to care for Garembert's female relations and then to let the convent die out. Garembert, however, insisted that the sisters be kept. "All these virgins are dear to me," he said. "I have espoused them to Christ. All of them will remain here. If not, I myself shall go with them from door to door as a beggar to supply their needs." Oderan then yielded to Garembert. Not only did he keep the women religious at Bony but he took it upon himself to form them according to the rule of the order. Garembert, for his part, was happy to be present at the consecration of his church at Bony. As he felt death approaching he asked that he be carried into the church to receive the sacraments. He was so full of joy that he raised his arms toward heaven as if, it was said, he had wings. After consoling his brothers, he returned to prayer, immediately reciting the words of the Psalmist, *O Lord, direct my way in thy sight* (Ps 5:9), so rendering his soul to God on December 31, 1141.

Although Garembert has never been recognized with a cult, in his own region his memory has always been especially venerated, even to our own day.[3] The pattern of the foundation of Mount Saint Martin was repeated hundreds of times in our order. Attention to the origins of our monasteries reveals that, because its new houses seemed to be inhabited by saints, the generosity of the faithful allowed these communities to multiply at a previously unimaginable rate.

The Family of the Deacon Nicholas of Soissons

Many entire families converted in the twelfth century, offering themselves up to religion in order to lead the apostolic life. The example of a family of Soissons is interesting for several reasons.[4] Norbert had gone to Laon during the winter of 1120 to visit some relatives who lived there, to speak with Bishop Bartholomew, and to learn French. He had not yet founded Prémontré but his reputation for holiness was widespread in the area, where he was said to be the perfect imitator of the apostles. At the beginning of December, a lady of Soissons named Hedwig came to see him. Although she had been married for several years, she had no children. She found the secular world tiresome and was attracted to religious life, so wished to find out whether she might separate from her husband in order to place herself in God's service. Norbert listened to her, then exclaimed, seized with the spirit of prophecy: "No, this is not what you are to do. God will give you a son. You must raise him not for the world, to someday be your heir; rather he is to be consecrated to God from his infancy. After him you will have other children and offer them all to God. Your whole family will thus enter into religious life." Hedwig trusted in the word of the saint. She had a son and named him Nicholas because Norbert

[3] This veneration is demonstrated in the name of Garembert, given at baptism, and by the images of Garembert on the stained glass windows of Bony and Câtelet. The clock of Bony, before 1914, was named Garembertine. I myself blessed a marble plaque in memory of Blessed Garembert in the church of Bony on July 4, 1932.

[4] The history of Deacon Nicholas is found in *Vita A* of Saint Norbert, c. 11, although other early historians of Norbert did not know of it. Nicholas' life is also recounted by Guibert of Nogent, *De pignorbus sanctorum*, PL 156, col. 616, without mention of Norbert's role.

had made this prediction around the feast of that saintly wonder-worker.

In those days the leaders of the Gregorian Reform depended on the people's support to turn priests away from the heresy of nicolaism. They forbade the laity to attend any Mass celebrated by a married priest or by one who had a concubine. In the same year that Norbert spoke to Hedwig, the council of Soissons promulgated this prohibition in the northeast of France. Meanwhile, however, the erroneous belief spread among the faithful that consecration of the Eucharist by sinful priests was invalid. Years later in Antwerp, the companions of Norbert found hosts consecrated by such priests and kept in boxes, but without honor, in case they might have some usefulness. This heresy was effectively countervailed in regions influenced by Norbert. "If Peter baptizes," Saint Augustine had said, "Christ really does. If Judas baptizes, still Christ really does so." The validity of the sacraments does not depend on the holiness of their ministers.

In 1125, then, Hedwig went with one of her sisters and her little son Nicholas to a church to pray. A married priest was at the altar and she did not receive lest she violate the council's prohibition. Suddenly the child, who until then had barely spoken, said to his mother: "Mama, look up and see the beautiful child, more beautiful than the sun, whom the priest is holding above the altar and whom he adores as God." She answered, "My son, is the beautiful child you see the figure on the cross?"[5] "No mama, he is in the hands of the priest. Now the priest is covering the child with a linen cloth." The priest, of course, was covering the chalice with the corporal. Once again the truth came out of the mouths of babes. But this child who had so seen God always was fragile; heaven was always drawing him closer. He would nonetheless eventually enter religious life, then die after his ordination to the diaconate, but live long enough to see the fulfillment of Norbert's prophecy. His father, mother, brothers, and sisters, and a number of his relatives all gave themselves to God to lead the apostolic life, likely although not certainly at Prémontré.

---

[5] Crucifixes of the twelfth century were sometimes clothed in a long robe, hence the mother's misinterpretation.

Such episodes offer us a precious glimpse into medieval history. Because many souls shared the feelings of the family of Nicholas, such men as Norbert, Bernard, Robert of Arbrissel, and Vital of Savigny had but to speak out and their monasteries multiplied. The reform movement deeply touched hearts and souls. Even the disruptions leading to the Gregorian reaction were small in scale compared to the sanctity that the reform caused to blossom throughout all of Christendom.

Oda of Bonne Espérance

In the life of Blessed Oda we first encounter Philip of Harvengt, abbot of Bonne Espérance in Hainaut, to whom a long chapter is devoted below. Philip composed the biography of this young woman at the request of her companions; he wrote so with all his heart and in a sophisticated style.[6] In Philip's text the moral strength of these daughters of great nobility who renounced all to follow Christ is immediately striking. No one more accurately accounted riches, comfort, honors, and power all as meaningless. These sisters' will was as strong as the swords and lances of their brothers, and their commanding manner lent such authority to their devotion that, unsurprisingly, Robert of Arbrissel entrusted the women of Fontevrault to an abbess rather than a male prelate.

Our Oda was born in 1120 in the chateau of Allouet, near Andelmes. Her parents were named Gilbert and Thescalina. They were noble Christian folk, although the apostolic movement did not affect them personally. Their daughter wished to sustain the honor of their house in her aspiration to sanctity. From infancy she was in love with purity. To better preserve this virtue she yearned for cloistered life—all the more when she considered how many souls are lost in the secular world. Therefore, in early adolescence Oda made a vow of chastity but, realizing that she was too young to be received into a convent, she continued to live with her parents. She kept no ordinary society, however—no friendships with thoughtless young girls, only long conversations with God.

---

[6] Philip of Harvengt, *Vita beatae Odae virginis*, PL 203, cols. 1359–74.

Years passed. Oda knew the moment was approaching when she would become a religious. Her parents, however, were unaware of the vow she had made. They had not planned for their daughter to become a nun, and the young virgin knew that they were strict and stubborn, so she spoke to one of her relations whom she loved very much—one thinks of Saint Joan of Arc when she revealed her vocation to her uncle Durant Laxart—asking him tearfully to keep a secret for her. Oda then spoke about her vocation and asked her trusted relative to inform the blessed Odo, founder and first abbot of Bonne Espérance. Oda believed that the abbot had enough influence over her parents to make them consent, but her confidant betrayed her, revealing the girl's plans to her distraught parents, Gilbert and Thescalina. They quickly gathered their family to take counsel on a marriage for Oda.

In feudal society love was one thing, marriage another. Parents chose spouses for their children according to the common interest of their two families. Oda's parents thus sought a match for the heiress of Allouet. They chose a wealthy and well-regarded young man named Simon, who joyfully agreed to this apparently felicitous union and swore to marry Oda. The day of the marriage was set. Meanwhile the girl herself was at first untroubled, confident that the father abbot would intervene, but she soon learned that her secret had become public. She grieved but, as the daughter of a knight, faced the coming trial willingly. The appointed day drew near and the family castle was decorated with sumptuous tapestries. Oda's father's retinue rejoiced in her good fortune while she herself was woeful and desolate. On the eve of the wedding, Oda's father feared that she would take flight. Sadly, this knight—although he was reputed to be faithful of heart and indeed wished to be—proved blind to his daughter's betrayal: "Do not grieve, my child. Enjoy the flower of your youth. If this wedding saddens you then I will delay it."[7] The father thus deceived his child hideously, but the girl did not suspect such faithlessness from him and so was calmed by his words.

The next day the young groom arrived at the castle with his relations and many rich, noble guests. Her mother and father sent word

[7] Philip, *Vita Odae*, PL 203, col. 1364.

to Oda to put on her wedding dress and come to join them. Not understanding, she nonetheless obeyed. Because the church was far away the wedding was arranged at the castle. The priest asked Simon three times, "Do you consent to marry Oda?" The groom replied that he had come for just this reason; he promised to perform his marital duties. Then the priest addressed the young girl. She did not respond, but blushed and bowed her head. "How arrogant!" some thought. "What a fool!" said others. One woman stood beside Oda and encouraged her to respond fearlessly. Finally the girl spoke: "You want me to say that I am pleased to marry this young man, but you should know that I do not want to marry him or any other. I have been bound from my childhood to another Spouse to whom I have vowed my virginity. Neither love, riches, threats from my parents, even beatings can ever separate me from his embrace."[8] The company was stunned. Simon was embarrassed, feeling mocked, and he declared that he wanted nothing to do with Oda. He then mounted and rode off with his companions. Oda's parents and the other guests were furious, heaping her with their reproaches. Gilbert realized that any delay would make the misunderstanding irreparable, so he set out after Simon with a few of his friends and tried to make the spurned groom believe that he could persuade the girl to consent so that there might still be a happy ending, but the father's attempt failed.

Oda now understood what she must do. She ran to her mother's room and slammed the door, then seized the sword hung at the head of her parents' bed. She tried to cut her own nose off but in her trembling could not sever the cartilage. Furious, she cried "This sword is so dull that it cannot even disfigure my beauty!"[9] She tried again, cutting her nostrils and bleeding profusely. The damage was small but the amount of blood frightening. When Thescalina, banging on the door, at last forced her way in, she found her daughter fainting. The mother herself then fell to the ground, sobbing. Gilbert returned and he too began to weep. Oda, however, regained her calm and—now disfigured—feared marriage no longer.

[8] Philip, *Vita Odae*, PL 203, col. 1365.
[9] Philip, *Vita Odae*, PL 203, col. 1366.

These events were so well-known in the region and so disturbing that their report reached Bonne Espérance. Abbot Odo sent two canons to Allouet to console the valiant young girl. Gilbert and Thescalina now received them warmly. Oda, on her part, spoke to them of her frustrated desire to enter the cloister. In their presence she begged her father once again to allow her so to do. Gilbert, sorrowful, still resisted, but Oda declared that, if her desires were not respected, she would continue to disfigure herself so that neither noble nor peasant would want to marry her. Gilbert, now defeated, at last gave his consent. The two canons returned to their abbot and Abbot Odo, filled with joy, himself returned with a few brothers to bring the maiden to the monastery. The latter said good-bye to her parents and soon received the habit of the Premonstratensian sisters from the venerable abbot. Oda's biographer sums up her profound humility, desire for sanctity, detachment, and obedience: "She aligned her steps to the Gospel teaching." [10] This was indeed the ideal of Norbert's first disciples: "To have Christ as one's guide and to follow the Gospel literally."

Oda was so rigorous in her fasting and self-mortification as to exceed caution. Her heretofore glowing skin paled and troubling patches appeared on her hands. Those around her believed that she had contracted leprosy, saying, "Oda is a leper and must be isolated." They quickly built her a hut in the middle of the garden and chose an old sister to be her infirmarian, but the elderly woman refused, saying she preferred to disobey than to be forced to look at Oda's lesions. The elder was chastised, but younger sisters were generous enough to seek the honor of attending her. Oda meanwhile remained serene. Jesus was struck over all his body in this way, humiliated as if he were a leper, crucified. Believing herself blessed in so resembling her Bridegroom, Oda tenderly kissed the hand where her infirmity had first appeared. The ailment was not leprosy, however, and the spots gradually disappeared. Oda re-entered the monastery and placed herself under obedience again, with more fervor than ever.

Oda was soon named prioress. She was an ideal superior: sweet, maternal, and vigilant. She was both feared and loved. Oda under-

---

[10] Philip, *Vita Odae*, PL 203, col. 1369.

stood the sisters' different characteristics and temperaments, accommodating herself to the distinctiveness of each in order to form Christ in them. To the poor she was generous and giving, sometimes quietly sending to the needy things from the common store. "Pious pilfering," she said, "succors Christ."[11] Oda began to become known outside of the monastery, for saints often have attractive and uplifting charm, but a soul such as hers was not long for this world. She was soon struck with a chest ailment lasting six months: fever, pain, fits of anguished coughing. Unable to sleep, Oda prayed night and day while continuing to direct the sisters. When she could no longer take nourishment, she was given extreme unction. Her sisters said to her, "Remember us in heaven," but she replied, "How could you say to such a sinner the words that were said to the apostles and saints? Only ask pardon for my sins and commend me to our good God's mercy."[12]

After vespers on Easter Sunday, April 18, 1158, in the presence of Philip of Harvengt and their brothers and sisters, Oda rendered up her soul to God. All wept as, according to the liturgy of the order, they recited the Hallel Psalms and repeated the *In exitu* that had just been sung at the Paschal vespers. The following day they brought her body to the abbey of Bonne Espérance. Gregory, the Cistercian abbot of Elne, sang the requiem Mass. The venerable Odo, first abbot of Bonne Espérance—retired but still living—was also present. Philip of Harvengt, his successor and a learned prelate with great interest in Greek etymologies, said during the ceremony: "She bore her name well. She has been a magnificent ode to the glory of God."[13]

The Blessed Frederick Feikone

The biography of the blessed Frederick Feikone, who died in 1175, attests that the apostolic ideal was still alive in the north of Europe at the end of the twelfth century. Our understanding of this figure

---

[11] *Dicebat enim illi pium hoc esse furtum quo infirmo misericorditer subveniret, quo Christum in nudo paupere operiret.* Philip, *Vita Odae,* PL 203, col. 1372.

[12] Philip, *Vita Odae,* PL 203, col. 1373.

[13] Philip, *Vita Odae,* PL 203, col. 1374.

—if not complete, at least very clear—is based on the brief account of one of his successors, Sibrand, abbot of Mariengaarde. This record is precise and full of vivid details.[14]

Frederick was the son of Suitberge, a poor widow from Hallum, in Friesland. His mother sent him into the fields to tend the sheep but, instead of playing like the other children, Frederick would recite the Lord's Prayer and build chapels and altars out of clay, then reenact the ceremonies of the Church. The leading members of his parish noted these hints of an ecclesiastical vocation and urged Suitberge to allow him to study but, lamentably, she was so poor that she hesitated. All were eager to assist him, however, and the curate of Hallum gave Frederick his first lessons in Latin. The child was intelligent, determined, and virtuous—soon the best student in the pastor's class, not only in knowledge, but also in goodness. After he finished his initial studies, he left for Münster in Wesphalia to study the liberal arts, and especially sacred scripture, at its famous school. The program of that time embraced the *trivium* (grammar, rhetoric, and dialectic) and the *quadrivium* (arithmetic, geometry, astronomy, and music). Theological teaching, in which the entire program culminated, emphasized the allegorical explanation of sacred scripture.

Frederick's three central devotions, characteristically, reflected his love for purity: to the Blessed Virgin, Saint John the Evangelist, and Saint Cecilia. He was not content with praying for the preservation of his virtue but wore a hair shirt to keep himself always on guard. "No one," he said, "is exempt from the effects of the original stain." A few years later Saint Cecilia appeared to him in a dream, telling him to think not only of his personal progress but to work also for the salvation of his neighbor. Obedient to her command, Frederick left Münster and returned to Hallum. Since he was not yet a priest he could not preach, so he became a teacher, recruiting students to prepare for the priesthood. When he reached the canonical age, however, he was ordained a priest and at the request of his old curate became the elder's vicar. Frederick's zeal and devotion were admirable. Upon the death of his pastor, he was chosen

---

[14] Compare AASS, March 3.

as his replacement. At first he hesitated because he wished instead for a religious life. He had been in contact with the Premonstratensians many times already and wished to join them, but the will of God was apparent. Frederick would be the curate of Hallum and would compensate for not being a religious with nights of wakeful prayer, fasting every Friday, and celebrating Mass in honor of the Blessed Virgin every Saturday. He would practice poverty by giving away all his surplus food and clothes on Christmas and Easter.

One day he saw a poor, sick woman trying vainly to ford a stream. He took her in his arms and set her on the other side, but caught a cold from going into the river and fell dangerously ill. During this time he dreamed that all mankind was driving chariots full of wood. "Why all the wood?" he asked himself. "In order to heat the furnace of Babylon," replied a voice. Frederick knew, therefore, that he needed to leave the earthly Babylon so filled with danger. Saint Peter then appeared to him, embodying the famous apostolic ideal seizing so many souls during the twelfth century: "We have left all," Peter said, "to follow the Lord Jesus, and he has promised us a hundredfold return." Frederick had already set aside his money in order to found a hospice at Hallum, but the will of God would surpass his own. He now called together companions to form a community with one heart and soul, always the apostolic ideal, and together they would serve the poor. But obstacles arose: discord in the parish, violence in the street, fire in the church, murders—all slowing his effort. In addition, the zealous pastor was still caring for his elderly mother, but she then died and was buried in the church of Hallum. The parishioners showed their curate great sympathy and many came to the funeral. Frederick spoke: "You are accustomed to make offerings to the church for the repose of the souls of the dead. I do not pass judgment against you for this but, as for me, I find that I possess nothing worthy of offering for the soul of my mother. I shall therefore offer myself, making sacrifice to Jesus Christ and the Blessed Virgin in order to serve them both perpetually. I will do so no longer under my own governance but according to the Rule of Saint Augustine."

The next day Frederick went to find the bishop of Utrecht, to ask him for permission to build, in the Augustinian formulation, "a monastery of clerics." He then received the canonical habit and went to the Norbertine abbey of Marienweerd for his novitiate. He returned with a copy of the *Ordinarius*, the ordinal or ceremonial, as well as other necessary books, then set out for the towns and villages to recruit companions. The Cistercians, recently established nearby, gladly received the rich and noble, but Frederick had already spoken many times to recruits of this type. For his part, he would more willingly accept the poor. In 1163 he built a conventual church in honor of Our Lady and Saint John the Baptist; he subsequently built a monastery. The location was so fertile and pleasant that it was called Mary's garden, Mariengaarde. Novices soon came. Among the clerics was Tadocon, who later founded two other abbeys, as well as Alard, Meinold, and Elsard. Among the women religious was Synoeris, the daughter of the wealthy bailiff of Reysum, and Gertrude of Dresum, who was soon named novice mistress. Among the brothers was Godescalc, a wealthy and well-regarded knight who would attract many laity to the religious life. Here we find again, forty years after the foundation of Prémontré, the double monastery of the early days—the primitive expression of the apostolic institution: again the multitude of believers gathered around the priests like the Christians of Jerusalem around the apostles. This form of monastic establishment had, however, been already characterized as problem-ridden by Hugh of Fosses and the general chapter, and the other regular canons shared their views. Frederick therefore accepted their judgment and founded the monastery of Bethlehem for the sisters at some distance from the men's community. He always had a special love for Bethlehem. He took such great care in forming the religious women there that "one might have believed that their house preserved the very beginnings of the early Church." These simple words, written by the sixth abbot of Mariengaarde more than fifty years afterward, demonstrate how deeply the founder had impressed his ideal on his community.

Frederick was thus serving as both abbot of Mariengaarde and superior of Bethlehem while still remaining the curate of Hallum—no easy feat. Meanwhile the abbot of Marienweerd had agreed to form Frederick in the religious life and to admit him to vows; the latter had not formally accepted the position as father abbot of Mariengaarde and his new foundations were not, strictly speaking, attached to the Order of Prémontré. Frederick therefore went to

Steinfeld and sought to have Mariengaarde received among that abbey's daughter houses, already three in number. The abbot of Steinfeld understood Frederick's situation. He immediately offered Herman, his prior, as assistant at Mariengaarde. Frederick did not formally resign from his abbatial duties, as Garembert had done, but Herman in practice governed Mariengaarde while Frederick divided his time between Hallum and the monastery of Bethlehem. He sent two confreres to live near the sisters' monastery to teach them to read and to perform sacred chant, since after the women's separation from the principal monastery they would need to become full choir canonesses. Frederick believed that literate sisters were more easily formed in religious life and contemplation. The aftermath affirmed his hopes. Meanwhile the men's community developed a renowned school for clerics.

A variety of undertakings thus began to flourish under the direction of the blessed Frederick, but he was growing old. He fell ill at Bethlehem. Knowing that death was near, he bade farewell to the sisters and returned to his church in Hallum, where he celebrated a final Mass in honor of the Blessed Virgin, so entrusting his parish to that divine protectress. He then mounted a horse and went to the Mariengaarde to die. On his last day he called together his parishioners to bless them. Then, addressing himself to his religious, he said to them: "My heart yearns for one thing, that you pray for me often because I have not done as much for the poor as I would have liked because our monastery has been so poor." The thought of the hospice he had planned clearly remained with him. Frederick exhorted his confreres to perfect observance of the rule and assured them that he would not abandon them as long as they were faithful to it. He then rendered up his spirit as they recited the prayers for the dying on March 3, 1175. Miracles happened at his tomb so frequently that many pilgrims visited the church of Mariengaarde.

Again, these examples are but a few chosen from among hundreds as edifying and memorable. The principal descriptions are gathered in Lienhardt's *Ephemerides hagiologicae*, a much later work but on the whole founded on solid sources. Clearly, many new monasteries wanted to enter the Order of Prémontré not only because it was a solid organization with clear statutes but because its enthusiastic spirit made it a faithful revival of the early Church, so providing powerful encouragement to the perfection of the saintly life.

Chapter 5
The Spirit of Crusade

The importance of the idea of the crusade to the religious hearts of the Middle Ages cannot be exaggerated. It was as central to them as was the reform of the Church. In 1214 Gervase of Chichester, abbot of Prémontré, wrote to Pope Innocent III: "How happy I am that Divine Providence has raised you to the pinnacle of apostolic dignity! And for these two principal reasons: that you have always aimed both to help the Holy Land and to procure for Holy Church an honorable increase in the sanctity and the number of her children."[1] This was the battle cry of three centuries of Christianity—the eleventh, twelfth, and thirteenth. The same notion survived even in the midst of the struggles and sufferings of the fourteenth and fifteenth centuries.[2] The preoccupation with crusade was deeply rooted among the Premonstratensians. Attention to the origins of this interest will reveal how it shaped the spirituality of the order.

---

[1] *Gavisus sum ex quo divina Providentia vos vocavit ad apicem Apostolicae dignitatis circa duo praecipue: vestra semper intentio versabatur ut subveniret Terrae sanctae et ut Ecclesia Dei tam in moribus quam in personis incrementum semper susciperet honestatis.* Charles Louis Hugo, *Sacrae Antiquitatis monumenta*, vol. 1 (Etival, 1725), 5. Gervase of Chichester, who died as bishop of Sées, was from the start an exceptional abbot general. His letters are not only important historical documents but were copied as stylistic models and its clausulae merit particular attention as exemplary of the rhythmic prose dear to writers of the twelfth and thirteenth centuries.

[2] Saint Joan of Arc never lost hope of resuming Christian action against the Saracens.

Preoccupation with Crusade

The founder of the order, Saint Norbert, spent his life in the atmosphere of the First Crusade. He was still a child when it was organized and blood ties connected him too closely to the crusader leader, Godfrey of Bouillon, for him not to have been elated at the conquest of Jerusalem on July 15, 1099. For Norbert himself, however, clerical reform was the most important concern from the moment of his conversion. He had no time for involvement in the Holy Land, although his disciples here would differ.[3]

In 1141, Blessed Hugh of Fosses, Norbert's successor at Prémontré, made an important decision. Baldwin II, King of Jerusalem, offered Saint Bernard a site called Saint Samuel (*Nebi Semouil*), eight kilometers north of Jerusalem, along with a thousand gold crowns, to establish a monastery there. The place was on a high hill called Mount Joy (*Mons gaudii*) by the crusaders because from there, when they arrived from the north, they first set eyes on the holy city of Jerusalem after many battles, sufferings, and privations. The French wished to make of Palestine another France in respect to religious and feudal organization, but they had a further reason immediately to found contemplative monasteries: the crusaders were at once ill-prepared for the attractions and ease of the Orient and enervated by the extreme heat. The Christian army was thus in tumult and the Cistercian model of austerity might be useful for recalling them to their mission. But the abbot of Clairvaux himself acknowledged that the risk of Saracen raids and unhealthy climate made him hesitate to send his monks. He also was aware that the Cistercians could not, without changing their pattern of life, exercise an effective apostolate among the crusaders. He therefore decided to offer this ministry to the Blessed Hugh of Fosses, who accepted it. In the meantime Baldwin II died and was succeeded by Fulk, count of Anjou. A contingent left Prémontré for Palestine, warmly recommended by Saint Bernard to Queen Melisende: "You will find them honorable men, firm-hearted, willing to face suffering, powerful in

---

[3] Nevertheless, a letter of Saint Bernard says that it was rumored that Norbert desired to go to the Holy Land. Bernard of Clairvaux, *Epistolae* 355, PL 182, cols. 557–58.

word and deed. They are clothed with the armor of God, girded with the sword of the Spirit, that is God's own word. . . . Welcome them as peaceful warriors, gentle to men and fearsome to demons."[4] The newcomers would indeed fulfill the hopes Bernard placed in them. Their conventual church—where the reputed tomb of the prophet Samuel had been venerated by Muslims, Jews and Christians alike—remained until recently the final vestige of the Premonstratensian monastery, but it was destroyed by Ottoman artillery in 1917.

Shortly before the foundation of Saint Samuel, in 1136, the renowned Premonstratensian monastery of Floreffe also reached out into Crusader territory. Almaric, prelate of Floreffe and former prior of Gottesgnaden, was so well-known for his preaching of penance that Pope Innocent II sent him to the Holy Land. Almaric, armed with a pontifical license, set out from Floreffe with a small contingent of confreres. Fulk, king of Jerusalem, and the venerable patriarch William, himself a regular canon and former prior of the Church of the Holy Sepulcher, received them joyfully. The abbot of Floreffe and his companions had come to preach, and indeed they immediately began a series of missions throughout Palestine and Syria. God blessed their preaching in both churches and encampments as they urged the crusaders to good behavior and converted numerous schismatics, and even some Muslims. Islam is not, indeed, impervious to conversion. Despite their success, however, conditions were hostile to such a group of itinerant preachers. They were already canonically attached to a church but the patriarch William further insisted on giving them a house in Jerusalem. They preferred, however, the solitude of the monasteries of Saint Habakkuk and Saint Joseph of Arimathea in Ramla. They also frequently went out to preach at the request of various bishops. In 1152 Amalric became bishop of Sidon. Several others of his religious followed him to the episcopate.[5] After the reconquest of Jerusalem by Saladin in 1187,

---

[4] *Invenientur, nisi fallor, viri consilii, spiritu ferventes, in tribulatione patientes, potentes in opere et sermone. Induerunt se armatura Dei et gladio Spiritus, quod est verbum Dei. . . . Suscipite illos tamquam bellatores pacificos, mansuetos ad homines, violentos ad daemones.* Bernard, *Epistolae* 355, PL 182, cols. 557–58.

[5] See especially Hugo, *Monasteriologium*, "Saint Habacuc" and "Probationes." Lepaige, *Bibliotheca*, on the these sites.

the Saracens killed the religious of Saint Samuel and some of those from Saint Habakkuk. Others sought refuge at Saint John in Acre, the only town left under Christian control. When, a century later in 1291, Saint John also succumbed, remnants of the two communities nonetheless remained, for twenty-six Premonstratensians were then burned or butchered by the infidel. Abbot Giles of Marle was dismembered before his confreres to persuade them to apostatize, but neither he nor any of his confreres shrank from martyrdom.

The defeat of 1187 was terrible for Christendom. The pope died of a broken heart. His successor, Albert of Mora, who took the name Gregory VIII, was probably a Premonstratensian.[6] He was pope only

---

[6] Despite the assertion of the later author Guy of Clairvaux, who identifies this pope as a Cistercian and others who claim him as a Benedictine of Monte Cassino, the following texts offer ample proof of Gregory VIII's Norbertine profession at Saint Martin of Laon. First, an anonymous chronicle written at Laon in 1219 by a religious of English origin well-informed of events in Picardy and Champagne, related: *Urbano Papae successit Gregorius. Gregorius iste fuit hujus nominis octavus. Hic fuit Albertus de Benevento, cancellarius, vir magnae sanctitatis et laudabilis parsimoniae: in omnibus actibus suis religiosus fuit: ecclesiam beati Martini in qua habitum religionis sumpsit semper cordi habuit, quae etiam ei annuatim vestes secundum regulam procuravit.* ("Gregory, the eighth to bear this name, succeeded Pope Urban. He was Albert of Benevento, chancellor and a man of great holiness and praiseworthy frugality, religious in all his ways. Dear to his heart was the church of Blessed Martin, in which he received the religious habit and which provided his clothes each year according to its rule.") Second is the necrology of Saint Martin of Laon, cited by Dom Luc d'Achery in his edition of the works of Guibert of Nogent, in the entry for the eighteenth day before the Kalends of January: *Bona recordatio domni Gregorii Papae, hujus ecclesiae canonici.* ("The happy memory of Lord Gregory, Pope, a canon of this church.") Guibert, *De vita sua*, PL 156, col. 1186. Third, the chronicle of Ninova (1291) records for the year 1187: *Iste Gregorius VIII qui prius dictus est Albertus Cancellarius canonicus fuit Laudunensis.* (Gregory VIII who, earlier known as Albert the Chancellor, had been a canon of Laon.") Hugo, *Sacrae antiquitatis monumenta*, vol. 2 (Nancy: 1736), 171.

Here are added the following considerations: (A) Albert as chancellor twice defended the rights of Saint Martin of Laon. In particular, on May 10, 1171, he reproved the canons of Prémontré for having elected an abbot general in the absence of the abbot of Saint Martin. (B) The sanctity of Gregory is energetically confirmed among Premonstratensians. See the preface to the letters of Gervase of Chichester and especially the chronicle of Saint Marian of Auxerre, where he is proclaimed *vir litteratura facundiaque clarus, sed puritate vitae et animi intergritate praeclarior suique corporis vehemens castigator* ("a lettered man known for his eloquence, but more famous for his purity of life and integrity of spirit, and a zealous chastiser of his

for fifty-seven days, but he had enough time to express the sorrow and hope of the Church in the beautiful metrical style of which, as chancellor, he had instructed the Roman Curia: "Saladin came with a multitude of armed men. The king, the bishops, the Templars and Hospitalers, and the barons and knights all went forth to battle with the native people and the cross of the Lord. They were sure that the holy cross, with the memory and faith of the passion of Christ who hung upon it and so redeemed the human race, would be their sure defense against the attacks of the pagans. The battle began. Some of our men were overcome, the cross taken, bishops massacred, and the king captured. Almost all were either killed by the sword or fell into the hands of the enemies, and only a few escaped in flight."[7] The pope then asked for prayers and alms and ordered five years of fasting on Fridays and abstinence on Wednesdays and Saturdays, but, lamentably, the Holy Land had been definitively lost. The Christians did not give up, however, and for about the next hundred years preachers of crusade traveled across Europe, recruiting soldiers and receiving offerings toward their supply.

Letters of the abbot of Prémontré, Gervase of Chichester, show that he was constantly occupied with asking for information and negotiating dispensations for those who had taken the cross improvidently, expediting departures, and—in case the crusaders were successful—reclaiming the rights of his order over the monasteries of Saint Habakkuk and Saint Samuel. He also frequently assured the king of Jerusalem of the prayers of his religious and affirmed

---

own body"). (C) From December 29, 1181, to March 19, 1184, the registers of the Roman Curia list at least thirteen privileges for the Order of Prémontré, all from the hand of Albert. (D) In the same registers, matters regarding Laon and Champagne come always to Cardinal Albert as informed in the affairs of these cities.

[7] *Accessit Saladinus cum multitudine armatorum ad partes illas et occurrentibus eis rege et episcopis et Templariis et Hospitalariis, baronibus, et militibus cum populo terrae et cruce Dominica (per quam ex memoria et fide passionis Christi qui pependit et genus humanum redemit, certum solebat esse tutamen et contra paganorum incursus desiderata defensio) facta congressione inter eos et superata parte nostrorum capta est Crux Dominica, trucidati episcopi, captus est rex et universi fere aut occisi gladio aut hostilibus manibus deprehensi ita ut paucissimi per fugam dicantur elaps.* Bull of Gregory VIII. [Translator's note: Petit cites P. Labbe, *Histoire des conciles,* for A.D. 1187, perhaps indicating Philippe Labbe, *Sacrosancta concila ad regiam editionem exacta,* Vol. 10 (Paris, 1671–72).]

his trust in him. Gervase wrote many letters to the pope, to legates, to the patriarch of Jerusalem, and to the royal court of Palestine. The bishop of Saint John of Acre, the famous James of Vitry, asked that Hillin, the abbot of Floreffe, accompany him in his preaching. Gervase then warmly recommended Hillin, the worthy successor of Almaric, to the patriarch of Jerusalem, Albert of Château Vautier, himself a regular canon of Mortara. During the same period Emo, provost of Wittewierum in Friesland, worked to fund a ship for the crusaders. Documents in the history of the order attest hundreds of like incidents.

When the time had come finally to abandon the Holy Land, the Premonstratensians would remain as close as possible to that beloved region. They founded the abbeys of Kalabrita near Patras and on Cyprus, Episcopia (Laïs), where Prince Hayto, son of the king of Armenia, would receive the white habit. These abbeys would remain until the definitive victory of the Turks in 1571. The summary of Crusade events presented here, however, awaits detail in future research. Little is known, in particular, about Premonstratensian preaching of crusade.

The Influence of Crusade on Spirituality

The crusade movement necessarily influenced the spirituality of Prémontré just as it shaped almost all the other religious orders of the period. First, crusade effected religious vocations, forming an entire group of saints for whose entry into religious life the apostolic movement does not alone account. For these individuals the religious life was another way of taking up the cross. Such a figure was Saint Gilbert.[8] During the reign of Louis VII, the encouragement of a Premonstratensian named Ornifiers, first abbot of Dillô in Burgundy, inspired Gilbert to join the Second Crusade. Originally from Auvergne, this Gilbert was a knight of the higher nobility. After the defeat of the expedition promoted by Saint Bernard, this crusader resolved with his spouse Petronilla and his daughter Pontia to consecrate himself to God in religious life. He gave a part

---

[8] See Gilbert's life in AASS (June 6) and in Lepaige, *Bibliotheca*.

of his goods to the poor and built a monastery for Norbertine sisters, where Petronilla and Pontia entered. Then, after himself taking the white habit at Dillô, he built a Premonstratensian abbey at Neuffontaines. Gilbert became abbot of that monastery, adding a hospice quickly famous for its saintly prelate's miracles, especially involving sick children. Gilbert died in the odor of sanctity on June 6, 1152. Out of his love for the sick, he wished to be buried in the cemetery of the poor who had died in the hospice.

Gerlac, also a knight, was Gilbert's later contemporary.[9] Grieved at the death of his dear friend, he went to Rome barefoot. Pope Eugenius III granted him the indulgence of a third of his sins and sent him on to Jerusalem, where he lived for seven years, working at the hospice as a humble swineherd. Gerlac then returned to Rome and, with the permission of Pope Hadrian IV, became a hermit at Valckenburg, between Utrecht and Aachen. Some hermits wear a simple robe of linen and a hood while others adopt the habit of a religious order, wearing for example the garb of the Cistercians or Premonstratensians and adhering to their respective institutions in somewhat the fashion of tertiaries in modern times. Gerlac thus wished to wear the white habit of the sons of Saint Norbert. His diet was a continual fast, his dwelling the hollow trunk of a huge oak. He attained such eminent sanctity that the holy Hildegard sent him the crown given her by the bishop of Mainz on the day of her profession. The Premonstratensian monastery built at Valckenburg preserved Gerlac's relics.

Blessed Hroznata, founder of the abbey of Teplá, was also a crusader.[10] He had been married and had had a son, but mother and child both died prematurely. Hroznata then resolved to dedicate his goods to the Lord, founding the monastery of Teplá in the diocese of Prague. Afterward, though, he took up the cross and vowed to go to the Holy Land. He first went to Italy but his expedition was halted there, so he went to Rome to ask Pope Celestine II for dispensation. The pope granted it on the condition that he build another monastery. This second foundation was Chotesov, a convent for Norbertine sisters. When this task was completed, Hroznata

[9] AASS (January 6).
[10] AASS (July 14).

returned to Rome, where the pope gave him the Premonstratensian habit. He then returned to Tepla, where the superiors of the community put him in charge of its temporal administration. Hroznata was so devoted to the task, however, that he made enemies. One day he was ambushed while visiting Tepla's granges and farms. Hroznata was then spirited away to Germany, where he was held captive and cruelly maltreated. He died in prison on July 14, 1237, and was honored as a martyr.

More remarkable still was the life of Blessed Gertrude, daughter of Louis of Hesse and Saint Elizabeth of Hungary.[11] At a very young age she became an oblate of the Norbertine monastery in Altenberg. She later took the veil, then became prioress at age twenty-four. When Pope Urban IV called the Christian world to the crusade once again, Gertrude was a zealous supporter of the movement in Hungary. She herself took up the cross with her sisters and a large group of noblewomen; as the letters of Gervase of Chichester demonstrate, clerics or married women often took up the cross in this way, of their own volition, like knights. For them the crusaders' vow consisted not in going overseas, for they were strongly discouraged from so doing. Instead, in order to be dispensed from their vow, they made a material offering that would support a crusader knight in their stead. All of Christendom thus was involved in the crusade. Many alms, prayers, fasts, and penances were offered for that cause that, although unsuccessful, nonetheless gave Europe a boost of religious fervor the like of which has not been seen again.

Still more significantly, not only individual religious but an entire province brought the crusader movement to the Order of Prémontré. Henry Sdyck, bishop of Olmütz, witnessed the work of regular canons while on pilgrimage to Jerusalem in 1136—first the canons of the Holy Sepulcher, then the Premonstratensians who, under the direction of Almaric, were preaching penance to the crusader forces.[12] Until then Sdyck had never known any religious other than the Benedictines, who had ten abbeys in Bohemia and three in Moravia. But the new Order of Prémontré, founded on the life of the apostles in Jerusalem in the aftermath of the Ascension,

---

[11] AASS (August 13).

[12] Zak, *Henricus Sdyck in Analecta Praemonsratensia*, first ser.

attracted him. "I remembered," he wrote, "the words of Saint Jerome: 'It is not having been in Jerusalem, but having lived there well, that is worthy of praise.' By the inspiration of God from whom all good things come, I resolved to put off the old man with all his deeds and to put on the new man recreated in justice and holiness, so that I might serve God under the Rule of Saint Augustine and in the religious habit. I revealed my desire to the Lord Patriarch and all the brothers in the same religious habit who serve God at the sepulcher of our Redeemer."[13] The Patriarch of Jerusalem in fact acted as abbot for the regular canons of the Holy Sepulcher, so receiving their professions according to this formula: "I, Brother N., offer up myself to God's mercy in order to serve the Church of the Holy Sepulcher of Our Lord Jesus Christ, to live under the canonical Rule of Saint Augustine without personal property and in chastity. I promise obedience to the Lord Patriarch and to his successors, whom the wiser part [*pars sanior*] of the religious congregation elect by God's will."[14] This was not a purely honorary profession, for Gerlac, Premonstratensian abbot of Milovǎ in Bohemia, wrote in 1184: "Henry Ždyck received our habit, which he had seen in Jerusalem at the sepulcher of life, with a great outpouring of tears. He renounced the use of meat and every comfort of life in order to bring to Bohemia a new man and a new order."

When Henry Ždyck then wished to establish this new order in his own country, he adopted as his site Strahov, near Prague. He gathered together there every soul of good will who wished to take part in this work, giving them as their superior a man named Blaise. To affiliate this house with the church of the Holy Sepulcher, where he made his profession, was impossible because there were then only thirty canons of that community and their daughter houses were only a few parish churches. Further, they were isolated, barely surviving without traditions or governance. Henry Ždyck therefore earnestly wished to come to know the Premonstratensians, so he went to Steinfeld and asked for some religious from Eberwin, provost of that monastery, whose community was a model of observance. Meanwhile the bishop gave Ždyck's new foundation the name

---

[13] Zak.

[14] Ordinal of Holy Sepulcher, published in *Analecta Carmelitana.*

Mont Zion in memory of the Holy Land, where his heart lay.[15] The introduction of the Premonstratensians into Bohemia thus grafted onto the order a vigorous branch able to survive many storms. The body of Saint Norbert still rests in the church of Strahov.

The crusades brought not only new recruits to the religious orders but a new direction as well. Historians generally acknowledge that in the eleventh and twelfth centuries pious souls approached the mystery of Jesus' sacred humanity with an affection unknown to prior times. Modern scholars initially wanted to credit Saint Bernard for this change, but the movement has earlier origins, evident for instance already in Saint Anselm. Nevertheless, this attachment to the humanity of Christ developed widely after Europeans began to undertake frequent pilgrimages to Calvary, Nazareth, and especially Bethlehem. As Pope Gregory VIII said, "It is marvelous beyond words that the God who willed to be incarnate, by whom all things had been made, in his ineffable wisdom and incomprehensible mercy willed to work our salvation in the Holy Land through the weakness of his flesh, his hunger, thirst, cross, death, and resurrection, as is written: *He hath wrought salvation in the midst of the earth* [Ps 73:12]."[16] Nevertheless, such tender piety did not itself inaugurate the devotion proper to the crusader movement. When Godfrey of Bouillon had gained control of the sepulcher of the Lord, his first concern was to place canons there to celebrate the divine liturgy; these clerics then became regular canons in 1111. Other canonical communities were soon established at the Temple, Mont Zion, and the sepulcher of the Blessed Virgin.

The devotion of these communities was founded on the traditional liturgical sources. It took its vitality from rediscovery, through direct contact with their origins, of clearer and more moving meaning in scriptural passages recited or chanted in the rest of Christendom. Naturally, all of Christendom fixed its eyes on the Holy Sepulcher

[15] The church of Mont Zion in Jerusalem recalls the memory of the institution of the Holy Eucharist and the Dormition of the Blessed Virgin. It was, therefore, a eucharistic and Marian title.

[16] *Imo, quod maximum et ineffabile est, Deus qui voluit incarnari, per quem facta sunt universa, per ineffabilem sapientiam et incomprehensibilem misericordiam suam, per infirmitatem carnis, esuriem, sitim, crucem et mortem et resurrectionem salutem notram ibi voluit operari, juxta quod dicitur: Qui operatus est in medio terrae.* Labbé, Vol. 10, 1749.

just as it did on Rome during other periods. The Order of Prémontré followed the model of the church of the Holy Sepulcher very closely. The first ordinal of the Premonstratensians and the ordinal of the Holy Sepulcher are strikingly similar, much closer to each other than to the rites of Laon, Cîteaux, Cluny, and others. Whether the ordinal of the Holy Sepulcher, written in 1111, served as the direct model for the Premonstratensians'—or whether the latter imitated the customs of the same French church as the community in Jerusalem followed—matters little. The Premonstratensians' offices for Holy Week, save for some minute details borrowed later from the Roman Rite, are today carried out as they were at the Holy Sepulcher at the time of the crusades.[17] This liturgy is indeed a triumphal celebration; the torments and humiliations of the Lord barely appear except in the ancient chants taken from the Gregorian antiphonary —not a word about Gethsemane, the *via dolorosa*, or Pilate's praetorium. The processions and stations are at the temple, the cenacle, the sepulcher of Mary, and the Ascension. Emotional emphasis lies on the cross and the Holy Sepulcher. Indeed, the holy cross had been heretofore venerated for a long time; the feasts of the discovery and the exaltation of the holy cross were already celebrated throughout Christendom, and since the time of Alcuin the Mass of the Holy Cross had been properly said on Fridays. Attention to the cross now, however, took on a new depth and enthusiasm. Rather than moving hearts to pity, Christ's victory was sung: "Sing, my tongue, of the victory of the glorious contest."[18]

Today our office for Good Friday, on account of the dark tone of later accretions, is mournful, but such gloom is not reflected in its antiphons and hymns. When it is celebrated in a great church with vibrantly red dalmatics and copes, it still assumes an aspect of praise and rejoicing. This manner of devotion to the holy cross was very much emphasized in the Order of Prémontré, revealing itself particularly in the practice of private prayer added to the prior form of the Mass in the twelfth century: preparatory prayers at the

---

[17] Nevertheless, not all of these rites were adopted at the beginning. The Rite of Jerusalem for the blessing of palms followed upon a more ancient Premonstratensian practice. See Placidius Lefèvre, *L'ordinaire de Prémontré* (Louvain, 1941), 55 n.

[18] *Pange, ligua, gloriosi / Lauream certaminis.*

foot of the altar, offertory prayers, preparation for Communion after the *Agnus Dei.* Ascending the altar of Prémontré, the priest kissed both the altar and the cross on the Missal, reciting the antiphon: "We adore thy Cross, Lord, and we honor thy glorious Passion. Have pity on us, you who suffered for us." [19] After Communion, at least in certain churches like Averbode, the priest recited the following verses: "Christian medicine, save us; heal the sick. What the human heart cannot do, let it be done in thy name. O thou, the Consecrator of the Cross, hear us who assist at its praises. And after this life, bear us, the servants of thy Cross, to the palace of true light." [20] In the twelfth century the Mass of the Holy Cross served as the Friday conventual Mass. Adam Scot wrote a beautiful sermon on the glories of the cross, in which he sums up its praise: "It makes all impurity and strengthens all weakness." [21] Although the cross was itself unclean, it sanctifies and glorifies those who carry it; although it bespoke weakness, it becomes a firm protection for those who lean upon it. Devotion to the Holy Sepulcher meanwhile occupied a place our imagination today can scarcely conceive. We naturally experience a particular affection for the buried Christ, as the epistles of Saint Paul suggest, but that is a later notion. In the twelfth century, however, devotion to the Holy Sepulcher itself reflected devotion to the Savior's Resurrection. The chapter of that renowned basilica was even called the Chapter for the Veneration of the Resurrection.[22] Today, the seal of the Order of the Knights of Malta is still of white wax and represents the resurrected Christ.

The Church has always had a particular veneration for the paschal mystery. In the Roman Missal as in the Roman ordinal, the feast of Easter is as much the feast of baptism as it is the feast of

---

[19] *Tuam Crucem adoramus, Domine, tuam gloriosam recolimus Passionem. Miserere nostri qui passus es pro nobis.*

[20] *Medicina Christiana / Salva nos; aegros sana / Quod non valet vis humana / Fiat in tuo nomine / Assistentes Crucis laudi / Consecrator Crucis audi / Atque servos tuae Crucis / Post hanc vitam verae lucis / Transfer ad palatia.* Adam of Saint Victor ["*Inventio crucis*"; Digby S. Wrangham, trans., *The Liturgical Poetry of Adam of St. Victor: From the Text of Gautier,* Vol. 2 (London: Kegan, Paul, Trench and Co., 1881), 52 (Ed.)].

[21] *Sacrat immunda et munit infirma.* Adam Scot, *Sermones fratris Adae,* ed. Grey Birch, May 3.

[22] *Capitulum venerandae Resurrectionis.*

the Resurrection, for the two mysteries are closely connected according to the Pauline doctrine. Beginning in the eleventh century, perhaps under the influence of Lanfranc, the Resurrection nonetheless began to have more prominence in its celebration. Saint Norbert in fact gave his companions the white habit, the paschal color—the canons of the Holy Sepulcher wore a black cape at this time—because the angels announcing the Resurrection of the Lord wore white vestments. When Norbert's disciples Philip of Bonne Espérance and Adam Scot explained the white vestments of their order, they again adverted to precisely this motive.

The Premonstratensian ordinal itself attests the place the paschal triumph of the Lord held in the minds of Saint Norbert's sons, as in those of the clerics of all French and Belgian churches. During Paschaltide, we still employ the Sunday Mass "in honor of the holy Resurrection" throughout the entire week except for Saturday;[23] thus we preserve the memorial of the Resurrection at all conventual Masses. Even on the feasts of saints one of the two Alleluias is for the Resurrection. Each Sunday the procession refers to Easter, even when a feast precludes the use of the Sunday office and the conventual Mass is then the Mass *Resurrexi* of Easter Day. Clearly this practice is less focused on the Resurrection than is the rite of the Church of the Holy Sepulcher, in which Paschaltide extends to Advent. But it is more extensive than in the Roman Rite.

In one of his sermons Adam Scot seeks the place where Christ's body lay. He finds four: the womb of the Virgin, the crèche, the cross, and the Holy Sepulcher. For him, the womb of Mary represents those who are filled with the word of God. The crèche signifies those who abandon themselves to the Blessed Virgin. The cross represents those who in their suffering are supported by the passion of Christ. "O to be so filled! O to be so strengthened! O to be so supported! But the Sepulcher represents those who have entered into the contemplation of God. "O to feel that joy!"[24] As Adam says, "I mention this refuge last because it surpasses the first three in its beauty, its value, its repose, its security, its tenderness, its

---

[23] *Propter honorem sanctae resurrectionis.*

[24] *O impleri! O institui! O inniti! O frui!* Adam Scot, *De ordine et habitu canonicorum Praemonstratensium,* PL 198, col. 474.

delight and sweetness. Here I mean that Sepulcher where the holy women saw the angel robed in white."[25]

Alongside the medieval devotion to the Holy Sepulcher, Bethlehem also attracted many of the faithful. The Epiphany, more theological, took second place to Christmas, easier to understand, more popular, and more emotionally moving. Here—more than in contemplation of the passion, barely evident until its thirteenth-century development by the Franciscans—began what we would call the flowering of religious feeling. Such feeling appears clearly in Saint Bernard, but just as much in our Premonstratensian authors. Adam Scot, for instance, contemplated the Divine Infant in the crèche: "O Majesty so lowly! O sublimity so humble! O immense, eternal, and ancient of days! O earthly and infant Lord!"[26] Moreover, Philip, abbot of Bonne Espérance, delighted in representing the Blessed Virgin as embracing her Infant so tenderly and so sweetly that all her sorrows and torments vanish. Bethlehem thus led to Marian devotion. The Little Office of the Blessed Virgin, added each day to the canonical office, was also a crusader practice. Although it was instituted by Saint Peter Damian among the Camaldolese, the Council of Clermont, at which Urban II proclaimed the holy war, first prescribed that all clerics recite the Little Office for the success of Christian armies. Repeated each day in the choir, this prayer placed the Premonstratensians in communication with the defenders of the Holy Land.

The love of the holy places, finally, was so great among the Premonstratensians that the very names of their monasteries suggest another Holy Land: they included several Holy Crosses as well as Palmarum, Bethlehem, Sepulcher of Mary, Siloam, Jericho, Mount Olivet, Mount Zion, and Temple of the Lord. Such devotion would gradually lead to emotion-laden meditation on the mysteries of Christ and the Blessed Virgin, imbuing the order's spirituality with a humanity, tenderness, and compassion less familiar in the earlier Christian past.

[25] Adam, *De ordine*, col. 474.

[26] *O Majestas! o vilitas! / O Sublimitas! o humilitas! / O immensus! aeternus et antiquus dierum! / O parvus, temporalis et infans!* Adam Scot, *Sermones*, PL 198, col. 244.

Chapter 6
The Writers of the Order

T he Order of Prémontré has had few spiritual writers, fewer still whose works have been published. This situation has resulted not from any lack of richness in the intellectual life in Premonstratensian cloisters, but because the most skilled and able confreres always worked in the care of souls. All abbeys had a number of incorporated parishes. The order's statutes, like common sense and the good of the Church, directed that the most gifted religious be assigned to these "benefices." Many towns, even villages, thus often had as their curates doctors of the Sorbonne. Had they not been religious, such men would never have been in such positions. The Order of Prémontré was nonetheless honored to have reserved for this rural ministry—a ministry with no glamour but of the greatest importance—its intellectual elite. Despite their busy ministry, however, some religious would nonetheless find the means to produce a few distinctive works useful in revealing the spiritual life of Norbertine monasteries.

Emo

Emo, the first abbot of Wittewierum in Friesland, is an engaging and interesting figure, yet only a few have ever read his work.[1] Just as some authors today employ the novel or essay form to communicate

---

[1] On Emo, see Hugo, *Sacrae antiquitates monumenta*, Vol. 1, *Chronicon Horti Floridi*, hereafter cited as Emo.

103

their life stories, he chose to tell his through the literary genre of the chronicle. He divides his narration, as did prior monastic annalists, into yearly entries. From time to time, in order to preserve the traditions of the genre, he mentions the election of a pope or the sessions of an ecclesiastical council, but principally he offers us a record of his personal experiences. Like Lécuy, the last abbot of Prémontré, many years later, Emo titles his work *Historiae vitae meae*, the histories of my life. This account is as filled with feeling as an adventure novel; it is enlivened with thousands of delightful details for which the modern historian would search in vain anywhere else, even in such an interesting biography as the blessed Frederick's. Nevertheless, we mention Emo's work here not because of his personal adventures—for his foundation had many vicissitudes, as he recounts—but rather for the spiritual insights to which he devotes much of his text. These observations reflect the author's distinctive frame of mind, the result of his often sorrowful experiences.

Notably, Emo was not ignorant of knowledge derived from reading. He was certainly intelligent—not only a theologian but also a canonist, grammarian, musician, and teacher endowed with such gifts as might make his canons and sisters into an elite of distinguished minds. He loved books so much that he was always involved in copying, illuminating them, and supplying the neumes for plainchant.[2] Emo had little interest, however, in the material affairs of his religious house. Although meteorology fascinated him, he apparently knew about farming only from the Georgics. His first two disciples, in contrast, had broad practical knowledge. The first, Sifrid, helped Emo as his prior in the abbey's organization of discipline and administration in its school. The second, Thitard, was an excellent treasurer, extremely pious and assiduous in choir. Thus Emo was able to attend to prayer, study, and the spiritual and intellectual formation of his brothers and sisters.

The foundation of Wittewierum was a difficult process. A cousin of Emo, also named Emo, had decided to give his lands at a place called Verum for the building of a monastery. He proposed this

[2] The history of the blessed Frederick demonstrates that Friesland had an intense intellectual life at the beginning of the thirteenth century.

plan first to Benedictine monks but quickly came into conflict with them. While waiting for a new possibility to emerge, the former Emo was living on his property as a solitary when a priest who was his cousin came to join him with another friend. These three began together to live the canonical life and in 1208 turned to the Order of Prémontré with the hope of being allowed to enter. The second Emo, the figure of primary interest here, took charge as provost of the governance of the small community. With the arrival of Sifrid and Thitard the community then numbered five. Emo as prelate wanted to develop a community of clerics who would celebrate the divine office and invest themselves in *lectio divina* and scriptural meditation. One night he heard a voice singing to him from Psalm 2:8: *Ask of me, and I will give thee the Gentiles for thy inheritance, and the utmost parts of the earth for thy possession.* He awoke joyful. The next morning a cleric arrived, bringing with him his young niece, who wished to become a religious. The cleric did not persevere but the girl was among the first members of a monastery of nuns called Rozenkamp, or Field of Roses. As his communities thus grew, Emo visited Prémontré in order to learn how to live the life of the order more fully. His joy was now complete, for there he saw a "truly apostolic church." At Prémontré he copied liturgical books: the ordinal, the missal, gradual, antiphonary, and book of collects. He carefully wrote down the common tones and the musical program, then returned to Wittewierum with his precious booty. At home he experienced difficulties in administering his religious house in the context of the wishes of the founder (the other Emo), in respect to the jealousy of some of the confreres, because of his own weak skill in the management of temporal goods, and finally from numerous natural disasters—floods, droughts, great storms, and incursions of seawater. These circumstances were all difficult travails, but they did not keep the two monasteries from growing.

Interest here lies instead in Emo's spiritual life. His delicate sensibility led him into trials of conscience that he then describes with candor and insight. A host of temptations assaulted his chastity despite his calm, temperate personality; such struggles can befall anyone because they are part of human nature. This trouble helped Emo understand, however, how temptation can be useful when courageously resisted. Just as the flesh corrupts without gall, so the soul grows weak without temptation.[3] In 1217, however, Emo's trials became so violent for a time that love, fear, and shame—that trinity, his threefold trial—made him flee like a fish from a broken net. But Emo had recourse to powerful remedies: the Eucharist, *lectio divina*, and prayer. The Eucharist was especially effective for him in combating the fires of the flesh. He realized that he must subdue carnal vice in order to become its worthy minister.[4] Emo then gradually came to understand the distinction between a passing thought which is not a sin, that lack of vigilance which is a purely venial fault (*"culpa non tamen crimen"*), and finally such acquiescence to ill-doing as is truly sinful. If consent becomes habitual and obstinate, then the state of the soul worsens, but resistance to such temptation strengthens virtue. Finally, Emo was able to appreciate the necessity of grace.[5] All these stages in spiritual understanding are obvious to us, for they are clearly set forth by Saint Francis de Sales in his *Introduction to the Devout Life*. The problem of temptation and acquiescence, however, still preoccupies many. Adam Scot treated it in detail in one of his sermons and Abelard argued with his judges on the subject of the role of intentionality in sin.

Emo struggled as well with another problem of conscience: at the beginning of his conversion, devotion came easily to him but, as his community increased in number, his distractions grew as well. He experienced real conflict between his commitment to prayer and the care he owed his confreres. The provost tearfully begged God to safeguard both his devotion and his official duties. Emo then began to manage this difficulty little by little. Later in his writings, he returned to memories of his prior life, recalling his youth as not yet very pious and recognizing that God had nonetheless preserved him thus from grave sins. After he became a priest and curate, he schooled himself to be humble, for he was so loved and honored that he was continually asked to come speak with visitors, but then he fell in love with poverty, finding great consola-

---

[3] *Sicut caro sine felle sic anima sine tentatione corrumpitur.* Emo, 452.

[4] *Eucharistia contra carnis incentive. . . . Sic enim vitia carnis edomanda sunt ut ad usum Eucharistiae semper minister sit.* Emo, 452.

[5] *Omne optimum ex dono est.* Emo, 454.

tion in easing the suffering of the poor even before he had set aside all that he owned. Emo recalled that, in his bed during the winter, he often wept at the thought of the poor and homeless. For all this he was deeply thankful.

In 1220, after a terrible calamity, Emo deeply grieved the faults of his native region. Despite the Church's desire for reform and the efforts of so many saints, the northern lands in which he lived were filled with error: legal trial by hot iron was still practiced, churches resistant to episcopal authority sold sacred chrism, ordinations took place without proper authorization, priests frequented taverns, ecclesiastical celibacy was violated, tithing was scorned, and simony was widespread. Emo's conscience was again troubled, now about whether requiring novices to bring money with them when they entered religious life might likewise be simony, that is, the sale of spiritual goods for temporal goods. He reassured himself, however, that his monasteries were so poor that not to ask for this money would effectively be refusing all novices. But he was also troubled when offerings were brought to him, worrying that they might be the fruit of usury. It seemed to him that this money was in fact impossible to restore to its owners, that it should be given to the poor and that, as a poor man himself, he might properly accept it.[6] On one occasion, he offered money to an adversary who laid claim to one of the monastery's parish churches in order to avoid a legal action, and he worried that this too might be the purchase of spiritual goods with money. Fortunately Saint Augustine long ago decided this matter: "Money may indeed be spent to purchase peace."

In 1223 an unfortunate series of events loosed a storm in Emo's heart. He had not succeeded in so extinguishing his desire for worldly prosperity that he could love God in a completely detached way, without fear of the misfortunes already assaulting his foundations. Nonetheless he placed his confidence in God's grace, saying that the pursuit of glory in tribulation and charity before all else were paramount. Charity is the sign of the Holy Spirit's presence in the soul, enabling patience with a penitential spirit even in adversity; such patience in turn inures the soul to misfortune. Emo realized

---

[6] Emo, 466.

that he needed to change his nature through moral practice so that he might say: *I live, now not I; but Christ liveth in me* (Gal 2:20).

The abbot of Wittewierum focused intently on the organization of life in parish rectories, in the granges of the lay religious and among the sisters' chaplains. Where he was able to place two priests, he exhorted them to love each other, to share preaching responsibilities, and to take turns in chanting the office and in receiving confessions. The first curate took care of the parishioners while the second remained at home, but both were in church before and after the people and made visitations in the parish. When such clerics serving parishes returned to the abbey, they again participated in the community's observances, refraining from borrowing too many books. Many other of Emo's provisions supported them to persevere despite the solitude in which they lived and the distance their responsibilities necessitated from their ideal of sanctity.[7] Regarding the discretion Emo permitted in his directives to canons engaged in active ministry, one of his successors applied the words of Scripture: *the faithful and wise steward* (Luke 12:42). For the Order of Prémontré to maintain religious fervor despite the large number of its small houses was a major difficulty because its conventual life was designed for well-peopled abbeys. Much care was needed in discerning what elements were both possible and necessary so that religious life be maintained even when numbers were small.

Emo's chronicle ends with a long reflection in which he considers the human soul with its passions and its faculties, as well as the theological virtues and our lot after death. He noted that fear at the moment of death is often a sufficient expiation for small faults, enabling direct access straight to heaven. His style is not as elegant as Adam Scot's but his work clearly represents the lucid speculations of a fine mind. His last words are written as a director of souls: "If the soul is not cautious in the discernment of spirits, it loses itself among all manner of vanities."[8]

Emo died in 1237 at Rozenkamp following a mild, humid, fever-bearing winter during which he hardly rested. When the first chills of his own illness passed, he rose to care for and console the

---

[7] Emo, 515.

[8] *Si mens cauta non fuerit per discretionem spirituum multis vanitatibus se immergit.*

others who were sick. On the feast of Saint Lucy, to whom he had always had great devotion, he asked her if he might join her in eternal rest. The brothers and sisters surrounded his deathbed, but he rather than they offered comfort and strength. After he breathed his last, they clothed him in sacred vestments and took him to Wittewierum, where he was buried in the chapter room. He had loved that place, where he confessed, received, presided over conventual meetings, read, and meditated. Numerous miracles occurred at his tomb. Emo's successor, Menko, summed up his life: "Day and night he thought only of advancing the worship of God."[9]

Biographies

Medieval lives of individuals representative of the spirituality of the order are less numerous than we would like, nor are they all skillfully recorded, but a survey is nonetheless useful here. The life of Saint Godfrey of Cappenberg, in its surviving form, is an anonymous work published by the Bollandists among the saints celebrated on January 13 and by the Monumenta Germaniae Historica in the twelfth volume of its great series of medieval texts, Scriptores.

Anyone familiar with the story of Saint Norbert knows this Godfrey. Along with his wife Jutta and brother Otto, he placed himself under the direction of the founder and offered as a gift to the Order of Prémontré his castle at Cappenberg, transforming it into a monastery; he also gave the order Niederkloster, Varlar, and Ilbenstadt. Godfrey received minor orders at Prémontré and died young, on January 13, 1126, in his monastery at Ilbenstadt. He is one of the most likeable and radiant figures of the order's first years. Norbert could utterly depend on him: "When I am forced to pause, exhausted, in my preaching, I urge on my son Godfrey, the two of us like stags with hunters on their trail."[10] Godfrey's life might thus have generated an especially engaging biography, but his hagiographer lacked literary talent. The author nonetheless preserved for

---

[9] *Cum diu noctuque de ampliando Dei cultu sollicitus cogitaret.* Menko, in continuation of Emo, 516.

[10] *Vita Godefridi comitis capenbergensis* [sic], ed. Philp Jaffé, MGH 12, 513–30. See c. 5.

us some extremely valuable traditions about Saint Norbert as he was remembered by the community of Cappenberg but, not having known his hero personally, he was not able to offer a lively portrayal of Godfrey, instead replacing detail with pertinent spiritual reflections. The authentic enthusiasm of the apostolic movement is unreflected in his text.

Another anonymous work published by the Bollandists for October 25 tells us of the life of Ludwig, count of Arnstein, who transformed his castle into a splendid abbey. This Ludwig belonged to a family whose origin, like Norbert's, was of the Salian Franks. His father—also a Count Ludwig from Arnstein, a marvelously picturesque site in the Rhine Valley—was a very powerful and astute baron who, after having honorably married off his seven sisters, himself married and fathered our hero. He and his wife both died soon after. The vassals of Arnstein were brigands, like many nobles of the time waylaying merchants and travelers along the roads. The younger Ludwig never participated in these attacks himself, but he later had great remorse for not having stopped them. Once he had reflected on his life, however, his conversion was complete. The abbey of Gottesgnaden ("Grace of God") in Saxony sent him twelve Premonstratensian canons and twelve lay brothers at whose head was Maurice, the former schoolmaster of the Magdeburg canons, who then became the provost of the new monastery. Ludwig himself made his profession as a lay brother in 1139. His chaplain and notary Marquard, his seneschal Swiker, and five of his knights all entered the Order of Prémontré as well. Guda, Ludwig's wife, became a recluse, following the offices of the conventual church from a window in her small adjoining lodge. The new abbey was dedicated to Our Lady and Saint Nicholas; it was richly endowed by Ludwig, who also made donations to the foundations at Münster-Dreissen, Bethlenrode, Enkenbach, Gammersheim, and Beselich.

Ludwig did manual labor and administered his foundation's goods with untiring fervor under three provosts: Maurice, Godfrey, and Eustace. He died on October 25, 1180, in Gammersheim. His biography is written in a sophisticated style with complex metrical embellishments and numerous pedantic scriptural and patristic citations. The engaging details that would have delighted us as modern readers, however, are completely lacking. Still, this biography, like the life of Godfrey, allows us to see the degree to which the authors of the lives of Saint Norbert and Saint Herman-Joseph surpassed their contemporaries in their literary craft and descriptive content.

On the other hand, the small work of the Jew Judah of Cologne, who became a Premonstratensian and later abbot of Scheda under the name Herman, is free of the defects of the accounts of Godfrey and Ludwig. Here the author recounts for us his conversion to Christianity with ample life and warmth. His gratitude for God's illumination movingly animates his confessions.[11] Judah was of a Jewish family of Cologne. His father's name was David, his mother's Sephora. His whole lineage was deeply attached to Judaism, but his parents imprudently sent him to the court of the bishop of Münster to collect outstanding debts. This prelate, unwilling or unable to repay the Jews, immediately took Judah into his household for almost five months and had many conversations with him. Herman listened eagerly to the sermons of the bishop and rejoined with his own comments on scriptural issues. The Christians, respecting the young man's moral strength, were intent on his conversion to Christianity. Even Rupert of Deutz debated with Judah, later composing an apologetic work based on that experience.[12] Judah then visited the abbey of Cappenberg, so coming to know the Premonstratensians, with whom he was deeply impressed. On his return to his parents' home, the elders of the Jewish community accused him of excessive proximity to Christians, correcting him harshly. Meanwhile, Judah had not yet reached the point of conversion. Instead he fasted for three days in order to obtain a revelation from God. He then began again to meet with clerics and hold discussions with them.

In order to bind him to the religion of his fathers, Judah's family then married him to a Jewish girl whom he loved deeply, but his conscience still troubled him. Christian friends, notably Bertha and Glitmuch, two nuns of Saint Maurice of Cologne, prayed fervently for him. Judah then travelled to Worms, where he audaciously preached Christ in the synagogue. From there he fled to Mainz,

---

[11] Hermannus Judaeus, *Opusculum de sua conversione*, PL 170, cols. 803–36.
[12] Rupert of Deutz, *Dialogus inter christianum et judaeum*, PL 170, cols. 559–61.

where his younger brother converted along with him. On the Wednesday before his baptism Judah dreamed of Christ carrying a cross on his right shoulder as a triumphal symbol and recalled the words of Isaiah: *the government is upon his shoulders* (Isa 9:6). The Christ of Judah's dream thus carries on his shoulder the sign of his authority. Such a soul as this dreamer's could clearly not be content with an ordinary Christian life. Using the Pauline privilege, he exited his marriage and entered the abbey of Cappenberg where, after five years of Latin studies, he received holy orders. He later became provost of Scheda. His Latin, nourished by sacred scripture, was thus a late acquisition, but is nonetheless clear, animated, and vibrant. His work is moreover well-crafted, as touching in its sincerity as it is lofty in spirit.

Theological Treatises

A few theological and exegetical works of the period shed some light on the spiritual life of their authors, so enriching the impression made by the early Premonstratensian hagiographies. Vivian, a canon of Prémontré and one of Saint Norbert's first disciples, wrote one such work, a treatise on free will and grace composed around 1130 and titled *Harmonia*.[13] The author uses this musical term in the modern sense of simultaneity of several notes, suggesting that free will and grace act not successively and respectively but together, holistically, in our good works. Vivian's little work was inspired especially by Saint Bernard but also by others, foremost of course by Saint Augustine. The author dedicated it to Gerard, dean of the chapter of Saint Quentin. Vivian distinguishes within free will, or the deep-seated faculty of spontaneous action, both freedom with respect to sin and freedom with respect to misery. His doctrine accords with what has been widely taught in the Church but he is distinctive among theologians in noting that mystics, in their contemplation, in some degree enjoy such heavenly freedom as do the blessed. Vivian also carefully describes the role of Christ in the restoration of our freedom. Like all adherents to

---

[13] Vivian of Prémontré, *Harmonia*, PL 166, cols. 1319–36.

Saint Augustine's thought, however, he acknowledges little difference between the natural and supernatural orders, accounting creation as among the blessings of grace in the sense that it has no end in itself, rather is made for Christ and for heaven.

While remaining a speculative theologian, Vivian does not neglect to discuss the asceticism by which we recover a part of our free will: fasting, vigils, continence, and works of mercy. All such actions earn merit, so constituting the seeds of hope, the flames of charity, the signs of a secret predestination, and the foreshadowing of eternal happiness—in sum, the pathway of the heavenly kingdom rather than the source of the earthly order. Vivian seems to have had important influence on the theology of Adam Scot, but certainly many others among his own brothers must have drawn immense spiritual and intellectual profit from his teaching. His style is dense and unembellished, but balanced and elegant. This "least of Prémontré's poor men"[14] may have produced only this work because the extreme precision he loved and the careful research it required made such writing too difficult for him—or perhaps because premature death cut short the life of this splendid master in his prime—because Vivian remains otherwise unknown. None of the early authors of the order spoke of him, although his work was published by Dom Martène, who discovered it in a manuscript of the Royal College of Navarre.

Zachary of Besançon (Chrysopolitanus), on the other hand, was already characterized as eminent by his first publisher in 1535. This Zachary, the schoolmaster of the cathedral of Saint John in 1130, became a canon regular of Saint Martin of Laon in 1157. Although several authors describe him as a bishop, he probably never left his monastery, distinguishing himself among his confreres only by his diligence in study. He wrote two works: a *Commentary on the Harmony of the Gospels* and a collection of sermons preserved in manuscript form at the abbey of Aulne-sur-Sambre. Unfortunately the latter work remains unpublished, so that Zachary is known only for the scriptural commentary.[15] This work is on the

---

[14] *Vivianus pauperum Praemonstratae ecclesiae minimus.* Vivian, PL 166, col. 1319.

[15] Zachary of Besançon, *De concordia evangelistarum libri quatuor*, PL 186, col. 11–621.

whole simply a chain, *catena*, that is a collection of citations from the Fathers, explaining each Gospel passage. The texts are taken principally from Saint Augustine, but also from Saint Bede the Venerable, Saint Ambrose, and Rabanus Maurus, sometimes from Origen, Saint John Chrysostom, Saint Hilary, and Saint Remy; in the ensemble this commentary is nonetheless a work of rich significance.

Like the *Harmonia* of Vivian, Zachary's text attests the scope and solidity of the theological work in the first Norbertine abbeys. It not only reflects immense reading and research but also testifies clear and vigorous intellect focused on essentials of the faith. It reveals no useless curiosities or dogmatic allegories. Instead, Zachary sought clarification of the Gospel text and its moral implication. Just as Adam Scot's collection of *Allegories on Sacred Scripture* preceded his later sermons, so Zachary prepared himself for his preaching by an extensive exegesis, at the same time writing a text to serve his confreres. In a period in which devotion to Christ's humanity renewed all spirituality, Zachary chose the unfolding of the entire text of the Gospels as his object of study. The concordance of Ammonius, upon whose text he commented, is of little interest for today's historians, for it attributes to Saint Matthew a historiographical rigor we do not recognize and at the same time is untroubled in reordering the dramatic sequence of the Gospel of John, but Ammonius' commentary on each episode in Jesus' life nonetheless is useful.[16] Zachary adds little fresh material, although he here reveals that his thought is fully compatible with that of his order.

In Zachary's short glosses he further reveals the importance he attributes to preaching: "The Lord teaches us to neglect lesser in favor of greater goods. It is a greater good to preach than to bury one's father. He who buries his father hides a body in the earth,

---

[16] Zachary is uncertain that his concordance is Ammonius'. He might have preferred Tatian's concordance but it was unavailable: Zachary, PL 186, col. 36. Perhaps his wish was fulfilled. Ammonius' concordance is found in PL 68, cols. 251–358 (*In evangelicas harmonias Ammonii*), under the name of Victor of Capua, who, according to Dom Frénaud, took it from the *Codex Fuldensis*, where it was derived from Tatian's *Diatessaron* of Tatian. Frénaud refers the reader to Lagrange and Lyonnet, *Introduction à l'étude du N. T.*, Part 2, II, 272–73.

while a preacher raises the dead to life."[17] Later he writes: "Jesus did not deny his mother as if he had been born from a ghost. It is as if he had said, 'My mother is he who gives birth to me in believers by preaching.'"[18] Zachary expounds the symbolism of his order's white habit: "The Angels of the Resurrection proclaim the glory of the triumphant Christ not only by their words but also by their splendid garments."[19] He offers explanations of liturgical symbolism, always in relation to that mystery of Easter that was, as we have seen, the object of special devotion in the Middle Ages: "Note that the holy women do not prostrate themselves, only bow. So the custom was established in the Church that, whether in memory of the Lord's Resurrection or in the hope of our own, on all Sundays and during all of the season of Easter we pray without kneeling, but only by bowing our heads."[20]

Meanwhile Eberwin, renowned preacher and first provost of Steinfeld, sought simply to fight against the heresies of his time rather than to write a spiritual work; he nevertheless deserves to be mentioned here. In a letter to Saint Bernard, Eberwin explains the errors against which he must fight. The majority concern spiritual life, for they were effectively deviations from the apostolic movement: " 'You others,' say the heretics to Catholics, 'add house to house and field to field. If even the most perfect among you, the monks and the regular canons, have no individual property, they still hold ample wealth in common. But we are the true poor men of Jesus Christ. We wander without rest and without home from town to town, like sheep in the midst of wolves. We suffer persecution as did the apostles and martyrs.' Others say: 'the ordination of

---

[17] *Docet nos Dominus minora bona praetermittenda pro utilitate majorum. Majus enim bonum est praedicare quam patrem sepelire. Nam qui patrem sepelit, carnem in terra abscondit; qui vero praedicat, mortuos ad vitam suscitat.* Zachary, *De concordia evangelistarum libri quatuor,* PL 186, col. 177.

[18] *Non negavit matrem quasi de phantasmate natus . . . ac si diceret: Mater mea est qui per praedicationem me generat in credentibus.* Zachary, PL 186, col. 192.

[19] *Angeli non solum verbo sed etiam fulgenti habitu, annuntiant gloriam triumphantis.* Zachary, PL 186, col. 591.

[20] *Nota quod sanctae mulieres non in terram cecidisse, sed vultum dicuntur inclinasse. Unde mos obtinuit ecclesiasticus, ut vel in memoriam resurrectionis, vel in spem nostrae, omnibus Dominicis diebus et toto quinquagesimae tempore non flexis genibus sed declinatis in terram vultibus oramus.* Zachary, PL 186, 592.

priests is invalid because apostolic authority has been corrupted by priests' engagement in secular affairs.' " Eberwin asked Bernard to intervene in this dispute, to refute the counterfeiters of the legitimate apostolic spirit of their times.[21]

Bernard, abbot of Fontcaude, took on a similar task in his treatise *Against the Waldensians*.[22] This work reports on discussions between Catholics and Waldensians moderated by the renowned Raymond of Daventry. As Bossuet said of this Bernard, "His writing is distinguished by its clarity and good sense." The Waldensians, in their imitation of the poverty of the apostles, believed that both their men and women might preach the Gospel. Meanwhile, because they asserted that their disobedience to priestly authority proceeded from the unworthiness of pastors, Catholic apologists rejoined that even wicked priests have the right to preach, for grace is independent of the vehicle by which it reaches the faithful. So Catholics demonstrated their adherence to orthodoxy, condemning slander against pastors and demonstrating that ungoverned and ill-directed preaching in fact undercuts the weak and ignorant. Most of all, such proponents of orthodoxy took a stand against preaching by women, whose role in the Church does not, as they pointed out, embrace this responsibility. Finally, orthodox Catholics showed the Waldensian heretics that they were wrong to reject prayer for the dead and to absent themselves from churches in their desire for solitude.

Richard the Englishman, still another Premonstratensian author, wrote a mystical treatment of the canon of the Mass preserved at the end of a copy of the works of Hugh of Saint Victor. This treatise, whose author was until recently unknown, is titled in one manuscript "Sermon of a Canon of Prémontré to the General Chapter of the Order of Cîteaux." Another manuscript preserved in Lisbon notes the name of this Premonstratensian, whose work is among the most valuable sources for the state of eucharistic devotion in the early years.[23] Other Premonstratensian authors have certainly

---

[21] See Eberwin's letter after Saint Bernard's Sermon 64 on the Canticle.

[22] Bernard of Fontcaude, *Adversus Waldensium sectam*, PL 204, cols. 793–840.

[23] Richard the Englishman, *Libellus de canone mystici libaminis, ejusque ordinibus*, PL 177, cols. 455–69. See Barthélemy Hauréau, *Notices et extraits de quelques manuscrits de la Bibliothèque Nationale*, Vol. 24, pt. 2, 145ff.

gone unidentified, yet those discussed here suffice to represent the teaching of spirituality during the first two centuries of the Premonstratensian Order.

Chapter 7
The Flowering of Tenderness

M any of the Premonstratensian saints of the thirteenth century differed markedly from the heroes of the apostolic life mentioned above. In this period the order was more and more clearly distinguished from the apostolic movement in which its origins lay, now on the one hand thrown off course by heretics and on the other reframed in the new mendicant orders. The spiritual models for the new century were not brilliant Augustinians bent on learning and, in particular, on scriptural study. The cross, the crèche, the tabernacle, and the Virgin Mary as loving mother: these images occupied the new generation. Devotion to the crusade, the affectivity of Saint Bernard, the preaching of Saint Dominic, and the tears of love of Saint Francis of Assisi gradually renewed Christian culture—hence this chapter's title, "The Flowering of Tenderness."

The Blessed Herman Joseph

A clear picture of the blessed Herman—surnamed Joseph from his devotion to the Blessed Virgin—emerges from a biography written by the prior of Steinfeld shortly after the saint's death. Various small devotional works composed by the saint or written in his time and under his inspiration reveal him further. Numerous additional texts might have allowed us to enter still more deeply into this figure's inner life, but these have disappeared. Small devotional works thus often serve their purpose, are enjoyed, profit their readers, and then are lost. Their copies are worn out and no one thinks to preserve them for posterity. Fortunately, at least some sources on Herman Joseph survive.

The Biography

The biography of the blessed Herman Joseph is a dense text detailing the spiritual life of a Rhenish abbey at the end of the twelfth and beginning of the thirteenth century; it treats as well the notion of sanctity prevailing in that strongly mystical environment.[1] The author, who represents himself as the superior of his hero and who names both the prelate and the subprior of Steinfeld, must then have been its prior. Some months after the passing of his saintly friend, this biographer wrote an account of Herman Joseph's death and the miracles worked around his tomb. Then, in response to strong interest in Herman, he returned to compose a more detailed work on the saint's life and virtues. Close study of these two texts suggests the literary stature of their deeply cultured author. None of the order's early writers present a more tasteful Latin style—serious, gracefully metrical, clearly expressed without miscues or repetition, and sufficiently flexible and vivid that its narrative episodes seem like small bouquets. Herman's biographer was a theologian well aware that God needs only truth for praise.[2] His precise, delicate judgment was skeptical of miracles unsupported by holiness of life yet confident that such holy life is indeed accompanied by miraculous signs. In real experience, holiness attests the miraculous, although the relationship between holy action and miraculous signs seems in mere verbal expression to be tautological.[3]

---

[1] *Lilium inter spinas: Vita beati Ioseph prebyteri et canonici Steiveldensis ordinis Prae-monstratensis*, ed. Jean Chrysostome Van der Sterre (Antwerp, 1627). Pagination here refers to the Van der Sterre edition, but the text was reprinted in AASS for April 7, and in Lepaige, *Bibliotheca*, Vol. 1, 534–76. Lepaige, however, omitted the important preface.

[2] *Ficta laude non indiges, mendacium exsecraris. Lilium*, 2.

[3] *Ut vita mirabilis commendetur per miracula et per vitam mirabilem miraculorum veritas commendetur. Lilium*, 4.

The author of the life of Herman Joseph was aware of the problems posed by mystical theology regarding apparitions, prophecies, and other extraordinary signs; he made no pretense of settling these issues, rather distinguished clearly between sanctity's signs and its content. Further, the biographer understood charity as heading of the hierarchy of the virtues, and shrewdly assessed their manifestations. His critical spirit prevented him, unlike many hagiographers, from writing of anything but his direct experience of Herman or the reminiscences of those closest to the saint. He omits anything unfounded in a proximate source, even though such meticulousness meant the sacrifice of wonderful or moving elements. Finally, this author seems a man of good judgment, seeing in Herman a humble soul whom he judged to be also very holy. The writer did not always understand his friend; certain of the saint's patterns of behavior were beyond the biographer's understanding, so that he asked himself whether they were rooted in humility or dullness of wit. The author, however, decided that these traits were indeed humble because he recognized in them an effect of the Holy Spirit sometimes surpassing human judgment. He also distinguished carefully between what in Herman's life should be imitated and what should simply be admired. For all that, the biographer stressed first and foremost the daily office. Time had not yet turned history into legend and the composition of his own two works on Herman obviated the possibility that he write more fancifully.

To critique such a biography by eliminating as implausible anything extraordinary it might recount is indeed possible. Renan addressed the Gospels in such a fashion, but here no such approach would be scholarly because Herman's biographer stands in authentic witness to a series of religious experiences. His work resonates powerfully with the lives of other Rhenish saints of the twelfth and thirteenth centuries, but comparison with the experience of saints of other times and places emphasizes its distance from their experiences. We are then obliged to interpret the life of Herman Joseph in its own terms, without judging it according to our own times' and places' standards. Our goal need not be to assert the truth of all the visions the text mentions in the same fashion as we believe in the apparition of Our Lady to Bernadette of Lourdes, for such credulity would be naïve. We have no such obligation, especially since such graces of the imagination, poetic and consoling though they might be, are from a theological perspective less mystical and marvelous than the smallest act of faith. Regarding the miracles reported for Herman Joseph, we should then note that the Congregation of Rites does accept as evidence toward canonization of a saint such occurrences as the healing of toothaches, nervousness, or paralysis. Therefore this discussion will treat the text for what it represents without assessing the truth of the miracles it recounts.

The mystical marriage of the blessed Herman Joseph with the Virgin Mary is sometimes seen as problematic, yet the incident is not unique. Saint Edmund of Canterbury experienced the same devotion and later, in the seventeenth century, Saint John Eudes entered into a similar mystical marriage. In the twelfth century the heresiarch Tanchelm parodied such a union sacrilegiously. In these figures' period, the Canticle of Canticles was an effective manual of Marian devotion, as is shown by the commentaries mentioned above as well as many anthems in the Premonstratensian Order's liturgies for the feasts of the Blessed Virgin. The contemporary record of Herman Joseph then should be understood in this context with one caveat: that it is not an autobiography and that the prior was necessarily unable to render the experiences of Herman as precisely as they might have been described by the saint himself. In fact, while the biographer represents the apparitions to Herman Joseph with a fresh and lively imagination, he reports the saint's properly mystical experiences in exactly the theological terms of sacred books, so communicating little distinctive about them. His account is thus far less precise than what we know of Saint Teresa or even Adam Scot. The author acknowledges that he was unable to find out as much specific description as he wished. The blessed Herman Joseph lived a very long life (1150–1241), but his biographer knew him only in his last years, when the elderly saint may have elaborated rhetorically on the events of his youth without even realizing it as he generously shared them with his young friends. The major events of Herman's life then frame his prior's description.

Born in Cologne in 1150 to a family of comfortable means that shortly thereafter fell into poverty, Herman Joseph entered the Norbertine ~~abbey~~ priory of Steinfeld as a young man. After receiving the habit, he was sent to Friesland to study.[4] When he returned to Steinfeld, now ordained a priest, he first worked in the refectory and later became sacristan, a post that he occupied for the greater part of his life. When he was old and sick he was finally relieved of this duty. He was also for a time chaplain to a monastery of Cistercian nuns. Herman maintained many relationships with families friendly to the abbey. He died away from his monastery, among women religious, on April 4, 1241.

Herman Joseph had a sensitive, artistic temperament. He was handsome, especially in his youth, with bright, expressive eyes. He was self-possessed, reserved with strangers but merry with those he knew well. In his earlier years he was extraordinarily, untiringly strong. A great traveler, he read, wrote, and built clocks. The Louvre's magnificent reliquary of Saint Potentin, built for Steinfeld in the second half of the twelfth century, demonstrates that its sacristan must have wonderfully fulfilled his responsibility to administer the gifts given to the Church, as that he had exquisite taste. Later, however, Herman became very sick with profound fatigue. Only an absorbing task, like writing a book or building a clock, could make him forget his sufferings. He remained shy, sometimes awkward. Some of his confreres disliked him, while others, among them the more educated and intelligent, considered him a saint. The majority of the community forgot about him, unaware of his greatness until they witnessed the miracles at his tomb. Herman nonetheless possessed great richness of spirit and was endowed with mystical gifts from early in his life: apparitions of the crucified Lord, visions of our Lady, and conversations with Saint Ursula and her companions, for whom he had a great devotion, as well as perceptions of sweet fragrances when he entered the church or pronounced the name of the blessed Virgin Mary.

Two apparitions stand out among the rest. The first is Herman's mystical marriage with the Blessed Virgin.[5] Some confreres gave him the nickname Joseph, so mocking him for his Marian devotion. He was annoyed by this, promising to report these brothers to the chapter the next day, but in the evening he was praying in the choir

---

[4] Here again the lofty intellectual stature of the abbeys of Friesland is evident.
[5] *Lilium*, 128.

of the ~~abbey~~ church, as was his custom between compline and matins, when suddenly the building was filled with light. The Blessed Virgin appeared, seated on a throne on the bottom step of the sanctuary. She was radiant, accompanied by two dazzling angels. One of the angels spoke, asking: "Who shall be the spouse of this Virgin?" "Who merits that role more than this brother here?" responded the other. The angels then signaled for Herman to approach. The saint at first hesitated, but then obeyed. One of the two angels said to him: "This illustrious Virgin will be your spouse." Herman regained his speech only to plead his unworthiness, but the angel took his hand and placed it in our Lady's, saying: "I give you this Virgin for your spouse. Henceforth you shall be called Joseph."

The second apparition took place during major military disturbance of the region when Herman took the night watch against potential robbers on the ~~abbey~~ grounds, especially around the sacristy.[6] Weary, he failed to say the long poetic garland in honor of the joys of Mary that was his usual practice. As he walked along the cloister, he passed by an old woman, completely hunched and shriveled. Angered to see someone violate the monastic enclosure, he asked her what she was doing there. The apparition responded, "I am the guardian of this monastery. I have been for a long time." Herman then recognized his heavenly Protectress. Calling her by the name he was accustomed to use, without adding any preface— so terrified was he—he asked: "Is that you, Rose?" "It is I," the Virgin responded. "But why have you taken on this aged, shriveled appearance?" "I appear to your eyes as you see me in your heart. I have become old for you. Where now is the recollection of my joys? Where is the happy memory of the angelic salutation? Where is that fervor of your devotion, the youthfulness of your soul, the spiritual exercises you have been wont to offer me? These things made me young to your eyes and you young to mine. I do not want you to fail to serve me so that you may guard the monastery. I shall guard it myself, better than you." This stern lesson bore fruit, for Herman no longer failed in his daily homage of long prayers in honor of the Blessed Virgin Mary.

[6] *Lilium*, 134.

Other similar incidents marked Herman's life. Many times the Virgin Mary took him aside into a gallery of the church in order to listen to his concerns and calm his easily troubled conscience. Indeed, such apparitions were not always purely joyful for Herman. They were intimately tied to his spiritual progress, becoming less and less frequent, while his ecstasies, especially at the altar, came more and more often.

Alongside these spiritual favors, however, the saint experienced painful trials, as his biographer emphasizes. Such bitter experiences are integral to the experience of saints, inevitable in spiritual life because they prepare the soul for God's action in it, creating a void that the Holy Spirit may then fill. For Herman Joseph, many of these trials were external. If he suffered through nights like those of Saint John of the Cross, he said nothing of these internal sufferings, except perhaps in his reference to troubles of conscience, or perhaps to his prior. Sickness played a major role in the life of the blessed Herman, however, and he felt responsible for his own sickness, for despite his delicate nerves he had a strong constitution. During his youth others as well as he believed that he never tired. He fulfilled his duty as sacristan. In a church with many priests and daily solemn liturgy, this task was hardly easy and Herman Joseph got too little rest. Moreover, after compline he knelt in the choir until about half an hour before midnight in order to finish his self-prescribed spiritual exercises. He then sounded the first bell for matins and, while the confreres were getting ready, lay down until the third bell. At midnight he returned to the choir and finally retired only after the office, even then sleeping on a wooden plank with a rock for a pillow. He saw any ease for his body as superfluous. After some years, predictably, he began to suffer from an intestinal sickness with intermittent fever, just as did Saint John Chrysostom, and for the same reason. He could no longer eat anything but the lightest food: soups, warm beer, cooked pears. He fainted frequently as well. This physical distress lasted perhaps a half a century. Such minor illnesses were manageable, but whenever a feast day approached, Herman experienced other strange maladies lasting until the beginning of the feast. As he said gracefully: "Feasts are no feasts for me." And for these sufferings there were no successful treatments. Further, God afflicted Herman with numerous privations: the obligation to travel on foot, abstinence from certain foods, refusal even when traveling of comfortable beds. The saint's scruples, especially regarding the Holy Eucharist, were also difficult. Purifying the sacred vessels at Mass tormented him because he was never sure whether some particles of the Host had escaped his notice. This distress was a cruel martyrdom.

Still further, Herman was misunderstood. His persecutors were not many, but his meticulousness in celebrating the Mass, his prolonged ecstasies at the altar, his frequent forgetfulness of the hours for meals, as well as his clumsiness and timidity gave them occasion. He was nonetheless unable to change these things and so suffered frequent mockery and reprimand, the worse for him given his sensitive and delicate heart. He probably experienced other, still more hidden suffering. He prostrated himself before Christ with tears in his eyes, refusing to rise until he obtained mercy for a given individual or community. We thus perceive that his solicitude for all churches and souls was thus for him a source of great dismay. Nevertheless all these troubles did not sadden Herman Joseph's joyful personality. He loved nature and, like all true followers of Saint Augustine, understood it as a jumping-off point from which to rise up to the contemplation of God. He also enjoyed every heavenly consolation almost every morning, especially at the altar. This reward compensated for his many hardships.

Herman Joseph's virtues were radiant. First among them was a wonderful humility, that master virtue his biographer characterizes as "the virtue of Joseph." He was always quick to accuse himself and excuse others, while he was loath to give any reprimand. He willingly praised his confreres, but if they tried to return that praise he quickly changed the topic of conversation with a joyful pleasantry. He called himself a nothing, the zero of an algorithm, *cifra algorithmi*—an act of humility bespeaking a learned mentality, because the zero had only lately been invented by Arab mathematicians. Meanwhile, Herman Joseph's clothes were always poor. He mended his cloak himself, claiming that the new tunics were too heavy for his weak frame. The prior defined his humility as spurning the world, spurning no one, spurning himself, spurning even being spurned.

The author of the *Imitation of Christ*, Thomas à Kempis, had analogous views and formulas. Humility, however, is but weakness of spirit unless it is driven by love, while Herman was inflamed with the love of God. With deep sighs he spoke of his desire to enter into God's presence. As for his neighbor, he listened to souls who came seeking his advice and support with profound compassion. He was able always to be patient with others since he was himself never without his own sufferings, about which he never complained. His obedience not only placed him completely in the hands of his superiors but moved him even to respond generously to the personalities and habits of those whom he knew. Thus he spoke of perfection with the perfect and at the same time played happily with children, who saw him as one of them. To enter into their world, God knows, requires great grace, simplicity, and skill. Such traits are inborn; they mark a saintly soul even more than do miracles and visions.

Nothing can replace this first biography of Herman for the reader who wishes to discover him. It conveys numerous vivid, precise details, while the author's surprisingly modern reflections show that the spirituality lived at Steinfeld was distant from the theories of authors directly in the tradition of Saint Augustine. Adam Scot seems not, to the modern reader, a contemporary of Saint Francis of Assisi, but Herman Joseph is distinctly so.

The Works of the Blessed Herman Joseph

Herman wrote extensively. His literary craft, indeed his prolixity, makes his writing wearisome to read, as we know from the apparent abridgement of one of Herman's works made by his prior, a man of impeccable taste. Little survives, however, of the saint's written oeuvre. Herman Joseph wrote a lost life of Elizabeth, a Cistercian nun of Hoven. He also composed a commentary on the Canticle of Canticles developing a Marian exegesis, but this again has disappeared. Two books of revelations dealing with Saint Ursula, attributed to Herman Joseph by the Bollandists among the texts for October 21 are, moreover, now considered spurious. Thus, only a few prayers remain from his written work for our attention. These will be helpful in shedding light on private devotion in the last years of the twelfth century and the dawn of the thirteenth century. Five of these prayers are extant.

The first, a short poem, was well-known all throughout Christendom. It is a brief eulogy of the five joys of the Blessed Virgin Mary.[7]

> Rejoice, o gracious virgin,
> By a word you conceived the Word:
>> Hail Mary.
>
> Rejoice, o fertile ground
> Who brought forth the Fruit of life:
>> Hail Mary.
>
> Rejoice, beautiful Rose,
> Growing anew in Christ's Resurrection:
>> Hail Mary.
>
> Rejoice, glorious Mother,
> At Jesus' Ascension:
>> Hail Mary.
>
> Rejoice in the delights of heaven,
> You rose, joined to a lily,

[7] *Gaude, Virgo gratiosa*
Verbum verbo concepisti,
   Ave Maria.

Gaude, Tellus fructuosa,
Fructum vitae protulist,,
   Ave Maria.

Gaude Rosa speciosa,
Christo vernans Resurgente,
   Ave Maria.

Gaude, Mater gloriosa,
Jesu caelos ascendente,
   Ave Maria

Gaude, fruens deliciis
Nunc Rosa juncta lilio
Emunda nos a vitiis
Et nos junge Filio.
   Ave Maria.

Herman Joseph's verse was published by Van der Sterre at the end of the saint's biography. See also Herman Joseph, *Opuscula*, ed. Ignatius van Spilbeeck (Namur, 1899).

Cleanse us of our faults
And unite us to your Son:
   Hail Mary.

Such devotion to the joys of Mary would eventually lead to the development of the rosary, when the need to recite the angel's salutation added sweetness to the memorial of this Christian mystery. Herman's biographer says of this prayer: "Here the angel hails the Mother of God, mirroring her joys with his own as he repeats the verses of his salutation." The biographer implies here not that this listing of the Virgin's joys was original with the saint but that these verses' reference to the Virgin as a rose and the inclusion of the poem-prayer in a Steinfeld manuscript representing the poetry of Herman, as well as its phrases in his style such as "Growing anew in Christ's Resurrection" or "You rose, joined to a lily," connect these lines to his other poems. Dom Wilmart found the same verses in a thirteenth-century manuscript at Clairvaux and again in a psalter of Lyra from the end of the same century. This provenance is unsurprising given that Herman's ministry was largely among Cistercian nuns.

The second extant prayer of Herman Joseph's is a long poem addressed to Saint Ursula and her companions, to whom he, like any good Christian of Cologne, was tenderly devoted. It begins, "O springtime roses of Christ."[8] Herman's authorship is affirmed by the appearance of the word *columbellae*, little doves, which his biographer notes was a habitual usage of the saint:

O virgins, little lambs,
Little darling doves of Christ,
Free of cunning, free of guile.[9]

The authenticity of the poem is again demonstrated in this stanza in the saint's characteristic voice:

---

[8] *O vernantes Christi Rosae.*
[9] *O puella, o agnellae*
   Christi carae columbellae
   Sine dolo, sine felle.

O great throng, before you
Goes that blooming Rose,
The one outstanding Rose,
Nor is there any such
Who can equal her,
That noblest of mothers
Who bore heaven's Lord.[10]

Next among Herman's verses is a prayer addressed to the Lord and taken primarily from the Canticle of Canticles. It begins thus:

O Jesus, sweet and lovely,
Wonderfully fragrant Rose,
My loving Spouse,
My beloved, beautiful.[11]

Herman's distinctive figure of the Virgin as Rose returns here:

May our lily-filled home
Be ornamented with the Rose
For he is our well-beloved.[12]

This poem comprises twenty-six paired stanzas. Each has five lines, of which the first four are a rhymed couplet and the fifth rhymes with the fifth verse of the other stanza in the pair. This was the saint's preferred verse form. For him, as for the monastic Middle Ages in general, the Canticle of Canticles was the manual of love.

[10] *Te o turba generosa*
Praeit illa florens Rosa
Sola Rosa principalis
Nec est ibi Rosa talis
Quae sit sibi coaequalis
Mater tota curialis
Quae tulit coeli Dominum.

[11] *Jesu dulcis ut decore,*
Rosa fragrans miro more,
Sponse meus amorose:
Dilecte mi pulcherrime.

[12] *Domus nostra liliosa*
Delicata sit cum Rosa
Nam et noster est dilectus.

The fourth poem is Herman Joseph's longest, with no fewer than the eighty stanzas he promised to recite each night in honor of our Lady. It begins:

> Rejoice, applaud, dear Rose.[13]

Its most beautiful stanza represents Herman Joseph's craft as poet well:

> Rejoice, my beauty,
> To thee I call: Rose, Rose,
> Beyond all beauty, comely,
> More lovesome than all others
> You alone unequalled. . . .

> Rejoice, feast of my heart,
> O solemn spouse of God,
> Whatever passes from my heart,
> Grant that it enter thine,
> Incline thy ear to me. . . .

> Rejoice, pure maiden,
> Damsel of the Lord.
> Secure under thy mantle,
> The wretched need not fear
> And the fearful find refuge.[14]

---

[13] *Gaude, plaude, chara Rosa.*

[14] *Gaude, mea speciosa,*
Tibi clamo: Rosa, rosa,
Pulchra nimis et formosa,
Super omnes amorosa,
Tu sola sine compare . . .

Gaude, festum cordis mei,
O solemnis sponsa Dei;
Quod de corde meo meat
In cor tuum fac ut eat
Huc aurem tuam porrige. . . .

Gaude, pura tu puella;
Domnatoris domicella
Cujus tuto sub mantello

Herman's fifth extant verse work is strictly liturgical, the sequence *Virginalis turma sexus*, "tower of the maiden sex," heretofore used in the churches of Germany in honor of Saint Ursula. It represents musical dictation to the saint, in which the choir chanted a melody as he carefully recorded it. He asked them to repeat the difficult parts several times until he was able to write it exactly.

A final prayer is in prose, comprising twelve short expressions of thanksgiving for the mysteries of Christ's life, for example about the coming of the Magi: "Thanks to thee, Lord Jesus Christ, that a star led kings to thee, the King of Glory. So may thou, through thyself, lead us also to thee."[15] In nearby Cologne the Magi were never forgotten. As a child Herman saw their precious relics deposited in the cathedral during the episcopate of Rainald of Dassel. This and the other prayers of Herman Joseph, as they have come down to us, thus suggest his spirituality. Notably, except for the sequence "Virgin, tower of the maiden sex," they are private prayers. In much of the long Christian past, chanting of the psalms had seemed to suffice. Hymns and common prayers were added as the liturgy opened up to such private prayer as contemporaries experienced. New elements of worship thus entered the liturgical framework, which so became flexible and varied. Although it was not geographically varied, liturgy was open to the development of devotional practice, so was filled with life as it again would be in seventeenth-century France.

Beginning with the eleventh and twelfth centuries, however, a more uniform Latin liturgy tended to become fixed, no longer changing except by the Church's canonical authority. It seemed enough for the liturgy to express the sentiments of the Christian community, as indeed is its proper goal. More and more, though, pious souls could not find in the established liturgy such formulas of prayer as might best express their feelings, so they composed

---

Nullus timor est misello:
Sed timidis latibulum.

Translator's note: No replication of Herman's rhyming or metrical patterns is attempted here.

[15] *Gratias tibi, Domine Jesu Christe, quod ad te Regem gloriae stella reges duxit. Et tu, per te, perducas nos ad te. Amen.*

new formulas, meditations, verses, and expressions of desire. Little by little, outside of the divine office, private prayer exceeded its prior role as allegorical meditation on Scripture or as pilgrimage to various altars of the Church. It now took on the form of spiritual exercises and pious practices as well-established like formal rites, such as the rosary or the stations of the cross. These individual practices were later added to the liturgy in response to the tendencies and needs of those incompletely satisfied by in the Church's solemn prayer. Christian antiquity had had no such devotions because the official liturgy was in itself adequate to such expression in those times, but now, in the Middle Ages, the blessed Herman Joseph spent his silent nights of prayer on just such private spiritual exercises. Private prayer like his therefore indicated the new tendency of medieval devotion, privileging meditation on the mysteries of Christ's life and tender feeling for his sacred humanity as for the Virgin Mary and the saints and angels. This religious practice was less formal, perhaps, than the prior age's, but it sprang more from the heart, with more feeling, both joy and compassion. Heaven now came down to earth as pilgrims from beyond the sea wept for joy at Bethlehem and for sorrow at Gethsemane and the Holy Sepulcher. Great-hearted Saint Bernard supported this trend with his lofty religious and mystical authority.

In this context, then, Herman Joseph composed his twelve acts of thanksgiving. Three bear on the mysteries of the Epiphany: the Magi, our Lord's baptism, and the wedding feast of Cana. These scriptural events were elements of special local devotion in the region of Cologne. Herman also mentioned and venerated in his prayers of thanksgivings, however, the institution of the Holy Eucharist and the specific details of the passion. No longer, like the authors of the past, did he seek Christ in allegorical imagery, rather directly in the scenes of the Gospel, presented to worshipers' imagination so that they might harvest its fruit, as later happened in the recitation of the rosary. A similar process is reflected in Herman's prayers on the five joys of our Lady. His two long garlands of prayers composed in honor of Christ and our Lady represent outpourings of affection tirelessly interwoven—albeit tiresomely, from our modern perspective—in his belief that love in its boundlessness is never repetitive. No liturgical prayer can proclaim such sentiments.

Even the Psalms, moving and feeling-laden as they sometimes are, do not address the humanity of Christ. Moreover, except for some sweet passages like the *How lovely are thy tabernacles* (Ps 83:2), they offer only weak expression of the intimate union between God and the soul in the prayer of contemplation. In contrast, our poet calls out, intoxicated with love:

> Already my heart is joyful,
> Already delighting in thee,
> Knowing thy presence
> In foretaste of sweet grace.[16]

Again Herman yearns for the presence of our Lady and expresses his joy in it:

> I wish, I desire to know thee.
> Grant that I may know thy presence,
> Incline thine ear to me,
> For thou art the heaven's gentle Queen,
> And to thee I offer my entire self.

On the whole, the prayer of Herman is similarly completely joyful, and he eagerly recalls the Virgin's joys, for him five in number as had been traditional since the eleventh century. Later the Virgin's joys were numbered seven, corresponding to the seven sorrows we still memorialize today, and finally fifteen, the number established by the blessed Alan de la Roche for the mysteries of the rosary. In reminding our Lady of her joys, Herman's intention was to console her for her sorrows. He recalls to her that her five joys correspond to the five wounds of Christ. Again in "Rejoice, applaud, dear Rose," he writes:

> Rejoice for the sad fear
> Which thou had in his death.

---

[16] *Iam cor meum dilatatur,*
Et jam in te delectatur
Sentit vere te praesentem,
Praegustat suavem gratiam.

That cruel torture
And the fastening of the nails
That thou bore in thy love.[17]

Such recollection of the Virgin's sorrows, commonplace in the affective piety of the fifteenth century, appeared only rarely in Herman's time. On the whole his period's devotion was joyful. In the twelfth century such a canticle of contemplative souls seemed a prelude to the delights of heaven. A distinctive nuance of Herman's Marian devotion, however, was his imputation to her of a role as teacher, in the loftiest sense of that word—guiding, enlightening, and supporting those on the way leading to God. "O teacher of well-ordered life," he addresses her.[18] Indeed the Blessed Virgin fulfills this role for Herman with diligence, patiently enlightening him in his conscientious introspection.

In their formal style Herman's naïve compositions lack the grandeur of the pontifical or even the French prayers of the seventeenth century. They pertain to a popular genre honoring nimble, quick, graceful, and pretty language, yet Herman lacked a sense of when to stop. To know when to keep silent, "when to cease, even concerning the most beautiful subjects," is a worthwhile skill, valued since classical times. But Herman had little taste for antiquity, which he found too pagan. Evidently his trembling soul propelled his pen and he could scarcely control it.

Herman Joseph is sometimes identified as the first poet of the Sacred Heart. In fact, he speaks of the Sacred Heart in "Jesus, sweet and comely":[19] "From the chalice of Thy Heart / Grant me the choice wine."[20] The image evoked here by the chalice is the great legend of Holy Grail epic, the "choice wine," the blood of Christ in the upper room sought by the Knights of the Round Table despite every

---

[17] *Vellem, vellem te sentire;*
Quod sis praesens fac me scire
Aurem tuam huc inclina
Caeli mitis es Regina,
Me totum tibi offero.
[18] *O magistra disciplinae.*
[19] *Jesu dulcis et decore.*
[20] *Cordis tui de cantini*
Principali da de vino.

obstacle. The mysterious drink from the chalice is divine love to the point of rapture, yet it points toward still more. The works of Saint Bernard had included a salutation to Christ's heart. A series of hymns in the same meter in honor of the feet, hands, knees, and breast of Christ, is then attributed to the Cistercian Arnulf of Louvain, who died as abbot of Villers in 1250. Yet the salutation to the Sacred Heart is this series seems not to be Arnulf's because it repeats its salutation to the breast of Jesus. Moreover, this poem's style differs from that of the other metrical compositions with which it is associated such that in 1908, the learned Fr. Blume, S.J., in the scholarly journal *Stimmen aus Maria Laach* (Voices from Maria Laach) attributed it to Saint Herman Joseph. Internal criteria support Blume's argument. Similar verbal usages and stylistic presentation of material mark Herman's other works, including his characteristically wearisome prolixity. The Cistercian nuns whom Herman served for a long time may have asked him for this composition in order to complete the salutations of Arnulf to their liking, for devotion to the Sacred Heart was well-developed in the Order of Cîteaux, especially after the sermons of the blessed Guerric, abbot of Igny. This well-known poem may thus be Herman's:

> Hail, heart of the highest King:
> With joyful heart I salute thee.
> To embrace thee delights me
> And this my heart desires,
> Grant that I might speak to thee!
>
> Spread and open wide
> Like a sweet-smelling rose
> Join Thyself to my heart,
> Anoint it, pierce it:
> What does he who loves Thee suffer? [21]

---

[21] *Summi Regis Cora aveto:*
   Te saluto corde laeto
   Te complecti me delectate
   Et cor meum hoc affectat:
   Ut ad te loquar toleres. . . .

   Dilatare, aperire
   Tanquam Rosa fragrans mire

Obviously attribution by a handwritten medieval superscription would be more secure than such stylistic argument. The Order of Prémontré would rejoice for the first poem written in honor of the Sacred Heart to have been the composition of a canon of Steinfeld. In any case, Herman Joseph had almost arrived at what the canons of Windesheim in the fourteenth century called the "modern devotion": he carefully prescribed spiritual exercises, accessible to ordinary Christians and already prepared to extend the limits of the cloister in order to involve the laity in the pursuit of Christian perfection.[22]

The Blessed Bronislava

Bronislava, a Polish saint, sheds light on the Premonstratensian spirituality of the first half of the thirteenth century.[23] She was born in 1203 and died in 1259. She reveals the influence of Saint Dominic on the Order of Prémontré; Dominic, patriarch of the preachers, correspondingly borrowed some elements from the Premonstratensian Order.[24]

Bronislava was born in the small village of Kamien, in Silesia, of which her father was the lord. She belonged to a family of saints; Saint Ceslaus and Saint Hyacinth were her cousins. Bronislava's paternal uncle, Ivo, was bishop of Cracow. Her father, Stanislaus, married Anna Jaxa, the granddaughter of crusaders. This legacy left its mark, for this visit to the holy places yielded a devotion to the passion of Christ throughout the family. Anna Jaxa poured out her prayers before a crucifix in order to receive the blessing of maternity. The child to whom she gave birth was a girl baptized immediately

---

> *Cordi meo te conjunge*
> *Unge illud et compunge*
> *Qui amat te quid patitur?*

[22] In the story of Herman Joseph's life, the phrase *exercitia spiritualia* is placed on the lips of the Blessed Virgin: *Lilium*, 75.

[23] The sources of Bronislava's life are her canonization process and a manuscript life preserved in Zwierzyniec and used by Van Spilbeeck in his life of Bl. Bronislava (Namur, 1886).

[24] Dominic is often said to have borrowed from Prémontré a bit of splendor, a bit of austerity and a bit of discretion: *Aliquid splendoris, aliquid rigoris, aliquid discretionis.*

after her birth as Bronislava, meaning "she who defends reputation." Anna Jaxa wished to nurse the child herself, violating convention for her social class. She taught little Bronislava to say the names of Jesus and Mary as soon as she began to babble. The child was deeply engaged in nature and often prostrated herself before a little altar, for only the things of God interested her. Bronislava lived with her family until she was sixteen, as was conventional for young nobles of her time. She was charitable, not even waiting until a feast began to distribute the best cakes to the poor: "Our guests always have enough. We cannot give them everything." She traveled by carriage but brought it to a stop when she saw a poor person. She visited the sick with her mother and did labor alongside orphans, even letting them into her room. The young woman did not wish to remain indefinitely at her father's castle, however; she wished to be a religious.

Bronislava's cousins Ceslaus and Hyacinth traveled to Rome to receive the habit from Saint Dominic, who entrusted them with the mission of establishing his new order in Poland. With the assent of their uncle, Ivo, bishop of Krakow, they founded the Preachers' convent in that city. One day, when Hyacinth came to the castle at Kamien, young Bronislava took him aside and shared with him her plan to become a religious. The saintly friar approved and spoke to her father about his daughter's wish, but Stanislaus initially reserved his consent. The young girl, at first dissuaded from her intent by her father's affectionate reproaches, renewed her commitment when the crucified Jesus himself appeared to her saying, "Bronislava, you must be my spouse." Her father, moved at this event, then relented. Bronislava set out for the monastery of Norbertine nuns in Zwierzyniec, a suburb of Krakow. This house had been founded by her grandfather, Jaxa of Mxizeck, the crusader. She was received joyfully into the women's community and received the white habit from her uncle, the bishop. From that moment she began to apply herself to interior recollection, silence, and humility. The founder's granddaughter, however, was accorded no special treatment. "Trample me under your feet," she asked her sisters, "for I am but a bag of dust filled with miseries, unworthy to lie down before you."

A pious hermit from the area was troubled about his vocation. He heard a voice say to him, "Go to the convent of Zwierzyniec, where a holy novice will teach you what you ought to do." He arrived there asking for the nun. Bronislava appeared with her habit still damp from washing dishes, and told him, "Obedience is better than sacrifice. To become a saint requires obedience." The hermit left to commit himself to a hospice where he served the poor.

Bronislava made her profession in 1223, once again at the hands of her uncle, Bishop Ivo Odrowąs. She mortified herself more than ever, disciplining herself with ropes, thorny branches, and nettles. She continuously wore a hair shirt, slept very little, and then only on the floor, and forced sharp objects under her fingernails. Nothing seemed excessive to her in her desire to imitate her crucified Savior. Then Jesus appeared to her again one day, saying: "Bronislava, my Cross is your cross, but my glory shall be your glory." The names of three of her sisters and closest friends are known. The first was Judith, a young woman from Cracow, whose own extraordinary gifts and prophetic insights were so great that she was consulted by many, even the kings of Poland. The two others were Fabislava and Margaret. With these three companions Bronislava shared the inner workings of her soul. Later she was herself named novice mistress, a position she held until 1241.

By God's grace the bishop gave Saint Hyacinth as the confessor to the nuns of Zwierzyniec. Bronislava was therefore able to make good use of the advice and exhortations of this Dominican whom she called her brother, according to the national custom. One early biography tells us that Hyacinth introduced Bronislava to the rosary. Since the personal role of Saint Dominic in the development of the rosary remains obscure, the nature of this devotion during Brinoslava's lifetime is likewise unclear. Certainly, however, Saint Hyacinth was very much attached to the Blessed Virgin and could not but inspire his sister to love that divine Mother still more.

On the feast of the Assumption in 1257, at nine o'clock in the morning, Hyacinth, overcome with fatigue, trials, and mortifications, rendered his soul to God. At that moment Bronislava was meditating on the glories of the Blessed Virgin when she saw a great light over the Dominican church. Within it appeared a multitude of angels, and in their midst was a young virgin surrounded by other virgins, who was holding the left hand of a Dominican, shining gloriously. Bronislava asked, "Madam, I ask you, who are you and who is the brother whose hand you are holding?" The young woman responded, "Do not be surprised, my daughter, to see me appearing here among mortals, but I am the Mother of Mercy, leading the solemn procession into glory of this brother Hyacinth, who showed me so much devotion." At these words the Mother of God intoned the antiphon *I will go to the mountain of myrrh* (Song 4:6), taken from the Canticle of Canticles, chanted each Sunday in procession in the Premonstratensian liturgy of her period. The entire heavenly court then joined in. Coming to her senses, Bronislava told Fabislava and Margaret what she had just seen and all three then went to the Dominican house to console the brothers by relating this vision.

Bronislava and her three sisters' visit to the Dominican house may seem surprising, but for the prior sixteen years there had been no cloister at Zwierzyniec. The abbey had been completely destroyed in the following fashion. On the Friday of Quinquagesima in the year 1241, Bronislava and Judith were praying with their arms outstretched in the form of a cross before the tabernacle. Bronislava heard a voice saying, "The convent will be destroyed." Some days later the Tartars, who had crossed the Vistula, arrived at Sandomir, then Krakow. Bronislava picked up a cross and said to her sisters, "Do not be afraid; the cross will save us." She then led the sisters into the monastery crypt, where they remained while the Tartars pillaged and burned the monastery. With cross in hand Bronislava struck the wall of her and her sisters' hiding place three times and a hallway opened to lead them into the middle of a forest on the mountain of Shornich. The sisters then hid themselves among the crags. Upon their return, however, the sisters saw their convent left in ruins. They were forced to take refuge separately. Some fled to another monastery far away while others, among them Bronislava, built themselves huts in the abbey's garden. The abbey itself was not to be rebuilt until 1595. The saintly nun loved thereafter to return to Shornich to lose herself in contemplation and self-abnegation.

Judith died shortly afterward in the odor of sanctity and was buried in the church of the Holy Savior. Because the cloister could not be reestablished, however, Bronislava found herself after 1241 in direct contact with the poor, as she had been in her youth. Whenever there was an epidemic she stayed by the bedsides of the sick and dying. When she sensed her own impending death, Bronislava made a general confession, visited her beloved sick one last time, and made a final pilgrimage to Shornich in the company of a peasant for whom she had cared when he was sick. Following the sister's orders, he brought along a spade. When they arrived at the mountain's summit, Bronislava said to the man, "I am about to die. I am a great sinner, unworthy of burial honors. So dig a ditch and when I die, cover me with dirt and leave me here." She then fell into ecstasy and died on August 29, 1259, forty years after she had entered religious life. Her remains did not rest on the mountain along however, but were brought to the church of Saint Augustine. Later, however, a chapel built on Shornich was the site of many miracles. The annals of the order include no more tender and focused devotion to the Lord's passion.

Christine of Christ

A child born in the diocese of Mainz in 1269 adds distinction to the end of the period under consideration here both in the sanctity of her life and the favors granted her from heaven. The story of this individual is engaging even seen from afar, in shadowy form. Given her place of origin, she herself of course spoke High German. Her confessor wrote her history and revelations in Latin, but this text has been lost and only a Flemish translation by Fr. Van Craywinckel in 1665 survives.[25] We do not know the central figure's baptismal name, nor how her new name was given in its stead, only that our Lord rechristened her "Christine." This figure appears first in the historical record when she was six years old, as a young boarder at the Norbertine monastery of Rhetirs, a house founded in 1140 near Coninlestein by Count Gerard of Waringeon. This establishment

[25] On Christine of Christ: see Johannes van Craywinckel, *Legende der Levens van de voornaemste Heylige . . . in de Witte Orde van den H. Nobertus* (Mechelen, 1665). See also Georg Lienhardt, *Spiritus litterarius norbertinus* (Augsburg, 1771), appendix; Ignatius van Spilbeeck, *Une fleur cachée: La bienheureuse Christine du Christ, de l'Ordre de Prémontré* (Namur: 1885).

was dependent on the abbey of Romersdorff but had never been a double monastery. From its beginning the sisters were not lay sisters, as at the beginning of the order, but canonesses, *sorores cantantes*. Unable to participate in the office at the abbatial church, these women celebrated the canonical hours in their own oratory by themselves, as did the Benedictine and Cistercian nuns as well as the Dominican and Claretian sisters.

As with the canons, the liturgical life formed the very center of the canonesses' life, day and night. At the church's school holy young girls were nurtured. Unable to aspire to priesthood, they approached the dignity of that role by celebrating the same office and practicing the same manner of life as did the canons. The reasons for which Christine was at this monastery and why her parents had parted from her so early remains unclear. She may herself have asked as soon as she was able to consecrate herself to God, for already when she was ten she requested the habit of the order and began the serious pursuit of religious life. Our Lord himself directed her in that year to turn away from children's pleasures and to apply herself to contemplation when he appeared to her one day, himself as a child, in dazzling light as she chanted the office. One long ray of that light extended to her and she tried to follow it to embrace him, but the vision then disappeared. Christ *hath set his tabernacle in the sun* (Ps 18:6). Only a soul as pure as the sun might merit his divine embrace, but Christine was not yet so pure. Her faults were only the little errors of a child, but nonetheless prevented the divine contact she desired. The little girl therefore wept bitterly over her errors. She then learned that the prelate of Romersdorff, the major superior, would soon be coming to make his canonical visitation to the monastery. Christine prepared a general confession for him. Although her heart was broken with sorrow, she had barely received absolution when the child Jesus appeared again. This time he came all the way into her heart.

Christine made her profession in 1281 after two years in the novitiate. On Christmas she was granted another heavenly vision. Before matins she was hiding in the choir reciting twelve rosaries—clearly not the modern rosary, since that form had not yet been established, but rather a prayer invoking the five or seven joys of Mary with each stanza followed by a *Pater* or an *Ave* much as in the

blessed Herman-Joseph's similar spiritual exercise. Christine genu-
flected at each *Ave* according to the custom of her order. After these
seventy or eighty genuflections, the tired child fell asleep. Jesus then
appeared to her with roses in his arms. "My well-beloved," he said,
"prepare yourself similar roses like these, that is strong virtues. My
tabernacle must be not only as pure as the sun but decorated with
flowers." At the first bell for matins Christine arose and joined in
the singing. At the fifth response, "O great mystery," she saw the
divine infant lying in a crèche on the altar surrounded by twelve
roses—a reference to the twelve rosaries she had just recited. Jesus
then approached Christine and as he came closer he took on more
and more the form of a youth. He sang the office alongside the
young nun, who now understood that she must devote herself not
only to the mysteries of Christ's infancy but especially to his sorrowful passion.

Christine's experience marks a distinct development in medieval
spiritual practice. Thirty years earlier Herman Joseph still addressed
Christ's public life when he spoke of his mysteries; he spoke of
Jesus' baptism, the marriage feast of Cana and the institution of
the Eucharist. Now, however, emphasis had shifted from religious
instruction to religious feeling. Shortly afterward, the modern rosary
would draw the imagination from Christ's infancy directly to the
mysteries of his suffering in a progression such as Christine had
already realized. Meanwhile, however, the young canoness, notably,
was as yet unformed by thorough ascetical teaching, so—although
she was filled with love—thus far her affection was only personal
and voluntary. She never passed the large crucifix in her dormitory
without genuflecting and praying with her arms outstretched in a
cross, a practice praiseworthy in itself but so time-consuming as to
interfere with her other obligations. Christine was therefore disciplined for her tardiness when the issue was raised in chapter, but
she responded by returning to the crucifix with joy and pride that
she, like the apostles, had been beaten on account of Jesus' name.
The divine Master, however, did not see it thus: "My daughter," he
said, "rejoice in God, but force yourself to obey your superior.
Obedience is more pleasing and precious to me than sacrifice."

Christine thus learned from Jesus but she also read the great
book of nature as it was understood by the contemplatives of the
Middle Ages. Hugh of Saint Victor wrote that the entire sensory

world is like a book written by the finger of God. For Christine, however, the natural world was not to be appreciated as signs alone, rather to be enjoyed for its beauty at the same time that it represented God's reflection. The fountain in her cloister overflowed: "So," she said, "God's grace and mercy abound." Flowers are clothed in marvelous colors: "So God adorns my soul with his grace." Trees climb so high in the sky that a child must tilt his head in order to see their tops: "Trees in climbing toward heaven call us too to rise up toward our Creator." The spirit of Saint Francis of Assisi, as Christine's story is evidence, had spread even to the cloisters of the north.

Christine's childhood joys would, unhappily, soon come to an end. In 1282 both war and poverty obliged the nuns of her community to return briefly to their families. By this time Christine was no longer a child but a sensitive young girl, loving and generous toward God but with a sensibility so clear and precise that she always seemed to want to impose her own views. At the same time she seemed drawn to worldliness. At age six she had thought nothing of leaving the world. At twelve or thirteen such abandonment of earthly things was more difficult, perhaps made harder by her having been somewhat spoiled by her sisters before 1282. When she returned to the monastery her circumstances therefore seemed harsh and unjust, as well they might have for one at this awkward age. Now Christine's arduous, even fierce, struggle against evil began afresh. Jesus appeared to her as severe, causing her to undertake bloody self-flagellations. She suffered these not only for herself but for all hearts suffering temptation, for the souls in purgatory. Christine battled first against her memories of the secular world; the Lord showed her his sacred wounds as a place of refuge where she might find consolation and strength. Thereafter she was afflicted with that *acedia* well-known to the early monks; that weariness in the service of God lay in wait for her as well. Christine fought against this *acedia* by lying down in the snow and depriving herself of the sisters' warming-room after matins, instead striking her feet with sticks to drive away the chill. Through these austerities she rediscovered her taste for prayer.

Then Christine was tempted by anger. She was mocked, intermittently reproved, and reproached with offensive words by her sisters. On one occasion her reaction was so violent that in order to contain it she bit her tongue so hard that she bled heavily. Pride also spurred her. In order to humble herself, she therefore asked to be appointed assistant to the infirmarian, a role she then fulfilled with charity and self-abnegation. Laypeople asked to speak with her in the parlor—understandably given her spiritual stature—but she was reluctant to present herself in her work clothes. When she began to arrange her hair, a glance at Jesus crowned with thorns gave her pause and she quickly took up her veil again before visiting with her friends.

Christine might have found some consolation in her struggles through the such little sweets as her community's frugal refectory provided, but under pretext of keeping watch with the sick, she would leave the table before the end of the meal and ask permission to share some of her food with the poor. Thus she showed herself so amiable toward those sisters who had treated her badly or whose traits irritated her that the community framed the maxim: "If you want Christine to love you, mistreat her." These struggles lasted some three years. By age sixteen the young sister had passed through the temptations of adolescence but she had destroyed her health, inviting an early death. It seems, however, that Christine was so united to the divine mysteries that her remaining life became a metaphor for the liturgical year, vibrant and full of sweetness.

Christine's life throughout 1283 is recorded. In the spring she was sick, exhausted, forced to cease her work and her spiritual exercises, even attendance at Mass. She was carried from time to time into the conventual church of Saint Nicholas, where she meditated on the agony of Jesus. One day, as she held her head in her left hand, a vessel in her right eye burst and bled heavily. She remained in bed for seven weeks, favored with heavenly lights and the gift of prophecy. On Easter Sunday Christine meditated on the joy of the just in limbo at the coming of the Savior, as the response of the Easter procession suggests, wishing to know if the souls in purgatory receive deliverance on this feast of feasts as do the just in limbo. Jesus then appeared to her as he is represented in his resurrection, carrying a red banner. He led her to the chapter room, where a benefactor of the convent had been recently buried. He then struck the tomb with the staff of the banner and Christine saw the soul of the dead man rising up with many others into heavenly glory.

God then showed her the sins committed throughout the world, as he had shown Saint John, as well as the errors committed in her own monastery, so causing her deep sorrow. She soon after made numerous predictions while in ecstasy. On the feast of the Assumption she meditated on the relationship of the Blessed Virgin with the three persons of the Holy Trinity. The Virgin appeared to Christine in order to give her advice about approaching God, adopting a role like that which she demonstrated toward Herman Joseph, as mistress of spiritual discipline. She recommended contempt for the things of this world, renewed aspirations, diligence in contemplation, frequent reception of the Holy Eucharist, care for one's neighbor, pursuit of whatever pleases God, and meticulous religious observance without regard to fear or complacency—none of which required revelation. But the Blessed Virgin clearly indicated to Christine that true Marian devotion leads to the divine union and manifests itself by a thirst to do God's will.

Christine then experienced another apparition, this time of Saint Ursula, probably in October. The entire Order of Prémontré practiced great devotion to this saint and her companions. Her feast was celebrated with a double rite for an octave, in the most solemn observance of the period. Then, at Christmas of the same year, the Blessed Virgin appeared to Christine and placed the baby Jesus in her arms, saying: "My daughter, hold your dear Spouse and console yourself with his loving company. Take all your enjoyment here, tenderly embracing him. You are his bride and he loves you very much." This spiritual marriage shows us that the young Christine had reached the high point of her mystical life, but her bodily vitality would now decline rapidly. Her apparitions came less frequently, one at Candlemas in 1289, another on All Saints of 1291, then no more.

This biographical story as a whole communicates the character of Christine's devotion. Naturally, she gave her love and devotion foremost to Jesus Christ, centering her devotion on the two great mysteries of his infancy and passion. More than Saint Herman Joseph, Christine focused on the sufferings of Christ, so showing less joy but a more lively compassion; the stigmata of Saint Francis of Assisi had in the intervening period ignited the world. After Jesus, Christine loved the Blessed Virgin Mary, whom she did not hesitate to call her mother. Christine rested against Mary's maternal heart.

Finally, the young saint was also devoted to the souls in purgatory, according to the model of much prior practice. The Order of Cluny had established the feast of November 2. Cîteaux and Prémontré alike had instituted a morning Mass each day for their deceased confreres; both frequently said the offices of the dead. Then in the thirteenth century the mendicants, both the Franciscans and Dominicans, began to offer many suffrages for the souls of those who had died. Christine joined in these practices. On November 1, 1291, our Lord asked her what she desired and she responded with a plea for the soul of a fervent religious, recently dead, and for the deliverance of three thousand others of the dead. The Savior granted Christine her request under the condition that she assume these souls' punishments. Christine generously accepted.

Some elements of Christine's devotion suggest that she had a particular focus on divine wisdom. Henry Suso, who inspired new interest in this devotion, was not born until thirty years later, and Christine is unlikely to have received much instruction on this subject, which instead was opened up to her by her meditation on the mysteries of Christ and her intense liturgical life. Meanwhile some further spiritual details about her have come down to us in the form of maxims included in sermons or spiritual conferences on the ten rules of divine wisdom, four rules of the discernment of spirits and seven joys of the Virgin in heaven.

The year 1292 was very difficult for Christine. During that year she paid the debt she had assumed for souls in purgatory with a violent nervous ailment, a shaking rattling her whole bedroom, and frequent fainting spells. Christine bore this cruel sickness with complete resignation, awaiting the hour of deliverance, which arrived on November 23, 1292. She was a little more than twenty-two years old. More details of this humble, short life would indeed be welcome. Christine's illuminations touched each one of her sisters, whose hearts she saw open like roses at the reception of Holy Communion and whose entrance into heaven she affirmed almost immediately after their deaths, so proving that the spiritual life in this monastery—and no doubt in many others as well—was fervent at the end of the thirteenth century.

Part 2

The Great Syntheses

Two important medieval writers, Philip of Bonne Espérance and Adam Scot, framed respectively powerful syntheses of Norbertine spirituality. Neither of the two has yet received the close study the expanse and influence of his work merits. Both of these authors were well-educated clerics, thus were deeply grounded in historical models of spirituality.

Saint Lutgard reputedly received the charism of healing the sick, who then came to her in such great numbers that she was unable to pray. She complained to our Lord, who then asked her: "What grace would you like instead?" She responded, "I would like to understand my psalter so as to increase my devotion." She then came to understand better but was still unsatisfied. "Poor woman that I am, ignorant and unlettered woman, what good does it do me to penetrate the hidden depths of the Scriptures?" Our Lord then asked, "What then do you want?" She replied, "I want your Heart."

The whole spiritual history of the Middle Ages can be summed up in the story of Lutgard. The search for God began in meditation on scriptural allegories as the spiritual exercises of Saint Gregory the Great led contemplatives into this pursuit. Gradually, however, direct and affective meditation on the mysteries of Christ—especially on his infancy and passion—grew in importance so that the psalter began to take second place to the Gospels and *lectio divina* to both the rosary and devotion to the Sacred Heart in a process more of enrichment than of suppression or substitution. The spirituality of the new orders of the twelfth century was, however, still deeply monastic. Philip of Bonne Espérance and Adam Scot reveal the influence of the new orientation, but they are not its champions. They investigate the Scriptures at length, with patience and profundity. The metrical flourishes of a figure such as Herman Joseph do not blossom in their hands. Moreover, they are mutually distinctive; Philip was deeply attached to the tradition of Saint Norbert, seeing the Premonstratensians as clerics committed by their vocation to active apostolate, while Adam recurs more strongly to the ideas of the blessed Hugh of Fosses in his special attachment to the contemplative life. The two authors thus demonstrate beautifully complementary tendencies rather than in any way contradicting each other's perspectives.

Chapter 1
Philip of Bonne Espérance

Philip of Harvengt, later called Philip of Bonne Espérance after the name of his abbey, is one of many twelfth-century clerics born into humble families but attaining great influence through hard work and intelligence. He was also one of the period's most distinguished masters of the spiritual life on account of his virtue and religious experience. Philip was a cleric in every aspect of that term. According to him, the identity of the clergy was threefold: a cleric must be a man of the Church, the master of vast knowledge, and he must as well bring that learning to the service of secular souls. When this author addresses his Premonstratensian confreres, he always refers to them as clerics, not as canons. In this way he suggests the notions characteristic of the religious foundations of the following century.

Despite the poverty of his family Philip undertook advanced studies at a major cathedral school, probably at Laon, applying himself with such fervor that he damaged his health. He left behind a vivid description of student life; study, Philip tells us, leads to such great temporal riches, fame, and honor that parents eagerly steer their children toward literary studies and hire expensive teachers for them. When they are still quite small the students learn to read. As they grow older they become greatly concerned with each other's performance, never wishing to be surpassed by their fellows. They had heretofore feared the rod but now they fear dishonor. In all this they strive to write verse and to compose rhythmic prose, gaining command of the different meters. They lose sleep and go hungry

149

in their prideful pursuit of learning, but they are delighted, after studying Priscian, master of grammar, to enter the bright gardens of rhetoric. Then come the subtleties of dialectic. The better students then take on arithmetic, music, geometry, and astronomy. Finally comes sacred scripture, but happy are the few who seek less to know it by heart than to enjoy its fruits.[1] Such study as Philip here describes required much money, for teachers loved rewards and gifts. Students often heard Plautus' famous verse: "If you've brought nothing, Homer, go wait outside."[2] But Philip himself succeeded in all the challenges he met in his studious youth, becoming a master of both classical studies and the holy doctrine of scriptures. Throughout, even when he was quite young, however, one idea recurred to him: that the clerical life requires holiness. He would demand such holinesss at his eventual abbey of Bonne Espérance, then recently founded by Odo, one of Saint Norbert's first disciples. In the meanwhile, endowed with knowledge, Philip was quickly ordained to the priesthood and soon became the abbey's prior, but great trials ensued for him there.

A canon of Bonne Espérance wished to enter the Cistercian life, fleeing to Clairvaux, where Saint Bernard himself accepted the fugitive. The long-lived question arose whether monks, under pretext of greater holiness, may gather to themselves the best among the

---

[1] *Ut possint vel divitiis temporalibus cumulari vel fama et honore pompatico cum caeteris vel forte prae caeteris gloriari. Hac de causa parentes filios suos litterali assignant studio, eorumque magistros non parvo redimunt pretio, ut parvuli aetate adhuc tenera litteris imbuantur. . . . Cum processu aetatis grandescunt . . . quia jam videri inferiores caeteris pertimescunt, studium et diligentiam disciplinae scholaris inardescunt. Et qui, cum essent parvuli didicerunt timore flagellandi, grandiusculi student amore gloriandi. . . . Student igitur et laborant bene versificari, in prosa et rythmo faciendo commendabiles judicari: ad diversa metrorum genera prompti et agiles inveniri. Hujus vero amore studii multa plerumque difficilia patiuntur, inediam, vigilias, contemptum proprium amplectuntur. . . . Lecto Prisciano in quo totius, ut aiunt, versatur plenitudo grammaticae, ut composite sciant loqui, flores et colores aggredientur rhetoricae. . . . Dant operam ut ope dialecticae possint caeteros verborum maculis irretire. . . . Docti igitur grammaticam, rhetoricam, dialecticam quas mundi sapientes appellare trivium voluerunt, doceri appetunt arithmeticam, musicam, geometriam, astronomiam quas appellandas quadrivium censuerunt. Quidam vero ad legendum etiam divinae legis libros accenduntur et utriusque Testamenti paginis instruuntur.* Philip, *De institutione clericorum*, PL 203, cols. 709–10.

[2] [Editor's note: Petit here seems to misattribute this quotation, in fact from Ovid: *Si nihil attuleris, ibis, Homere, foras. Ars Amatoria*, 2.280.]

canons. Bernard maintained that the fugitive had come with the double authorization of the abbot general and his own prelate, but Hugh of Fosses himself, Walter of Saint Maurice, and the prelates of Braine and Steinfeld all denied the white monk's assertion. Pope Eugenius III, who had intervened in order to grant the required permission, failed to procure it from Odo, abbot of Bonne Espérance; nor did the pontiff himself demand it.[3] Yet the errant religious did not return to Bonne Espérance. At that point Philip wrote Bernard two long, harsh letters: "I am grieved that, although religious orders are growing in our times, fraternal charity is in decline."[4] The saintly abbot of Clairvaux never responded, but his prestige was so great that none could attack him with impunity even when convinced of his own right. Jealous confreres began to criticize the prior of Bonne Espérance, accusing him in the absence of his prelate Odo before both the abbot of Prémontré and the bishop of Tournai. The rumor spread that the prior of Bonne Espérance behaved ill. He was a simoniac, some said, and had bought his office. He was ambitious and sowed discord. The general chapter decided against Philip and the bishop of Tournai accepted their ruling. After ten years in office, the prior Philip was thus forced into exile with six other religious, but soon the accusers' prideful behavior discredited their claims against him. Two years later the general chapter reversed its decision, but bitter feelings lingered and Philip had to wait to return. Little by little peace was restored. Philip eventually returned as prior and later, when Odo stepped down, was elected abbot.

Philip was an excellent prelate, for he possessed both spiritual doctrine and the wisdom of a leader. Fifteen parishes were entrusted to him by bishops or patrons of churches so that his religious might serve them. The wealthy families of Hainault showered Bonne Espérance with donations. Following the example of Saint Norbert, Philip wished to endow his abbatial church with precious relics. He obtained ten bodies of martyrs from the archbishop of Cologne. Finally, on Christmas Day, 1182, Philip of Harvengt stepped down

---

[3] Philip, *Epistolae*, PL 203, cols. 77–88.

[4] *Movet me quod nostris temporibus et religionem videmus dilatari et dilectionem fraternam plurimum coarctari.* Philip, *Epistolae*, PL 203, col. 87.

from his office in order to prepare for death, which he met in faith on the following April 27.

Philip's works fill the entire Volume 203 of Migne's *Patrologia Latina*. They include a collection of letters, or rather epistles, for these messages go far beyond the length of ordinary letters and some are effectively small treatises. These letters are the source of the biographical material surveyed here. Philip also wrote an extensive Marian commentary on the Canticle of Canticles. This work's content is of interest here because it is important to the history of Marian devotion. Further, Philip left behind three small theological treatises: on the dream of Nabuchodonosor, on the salvation of the first man, and on the damnation of Solomon. Next, he wrote a massive theological and ascetic work *On the Education of Clerics.*[5] The latter work is one of the Middle Ages' largest-scale efforts to define clerical spirituality as distinct from monastic spirituality; again, a detailed treatment of Philip's text is required here. Several biographies complete Philip's oeuvre: of Saint Augustine, Saint Amand, Saint Cyr and Saint Julitta, Saint Salvus, Saint Follian, as well as the blessed Giselin, Landelin, and that Oda discussed above in the present work, and finally of Saint Waltrud. A number of poems published at the end of the PL volume have been reattributed to Hildebert of Mans by critical scholarship.

In all Philip's works the author sets forth positive theology rather than speculative reflection on scripture. His erudition was vast, both in secular history and in sacred scripture. Even in a generation of intellectuals, Philip was remarkable for the extent and variety of his knowledge. He was a man of letters, even a stylist. Like all great writers he understood that the literary value of a work resides especially in its metrical form and he invented his own. His sentences are constructed in two-, four-, and six-line clauses, with couplets ending in Latin rhymes and each rhyme forming, with the word preceding it, a metrically regular conclusion to each of the sentences' internal verses. This prose meter is complicated, requiring a sometimes wearisome level of craft but often charming, given the author's delicate sensibility. The following description of springtime is an example:

---

[5] Philip, *De institutione*, PL 203, cols. 665–1206.

When the streams again enjoy the freedom of their courses,
when the thawing surface of the earth brings forth fresh grass,
when plants sprout forth and fields smile,
when buds bloom, banks of brooks grown leafy,
when the sun shines brightly and air is fresh,
when all earthly creation is marked with welcome newness.[6]

With respect to the moral life, Philip exhibits a refined taste. He loved his friends with a rare tenderness but he suffered more than others from their derogation, forgiving his accusers but retaining the stinging memory of their insults along with lively gratitude to Our Lady of Bonne Espérance as his liberator and to friends such as Bartholomew of Jur, bishop of Laon, for their support. This sensitivity impelled Philip's tender devotion to Christ himself and the Blessed Virgin in particular. For Philip divine mysteries seemed close at hand. His description of the Visitation is an example:

> You see two women sitting in the same room. They speak to each other in the spirit of prophecy, not in feminine banter. They sing praises and weave prophecies. From time to time Zachary, unbelieving, is displeased at their inattention to him. For three months the Virgin and the married woman live together, supporting each other not only with affection but also in conversation, delighted to be together not to roll fabric the more quickly from their looms but the more easily to unfurl the praise of God with their joyful voices.[7]

This delightful reconstruction of the scriptural scene as prolonged and repeated during Mary's three-month visitation with Elizabeth

---

[6] *Cum reddito cursu aquis libertate solita jam fruuntur, / cum laxata superficie terrae nova gramina producuntur / cum herbae pullulant, prata irridescunt, / gemmae turgent, rivuli jam frondescunt, / cum sol lucidior, aer purior invenitur / cum grata novitiate inferior haec universitas insignitur.* Philip, *De institutione*, PL 203, col. 1135. [Editor's note: Here and elsewhere Philip's metrical inventivness is entirely obscured in translation.]

[7] *Videtis feminas uno in cubiculo residentes, non levitate feminea sed prophetico Spiritu colloquentes: laudes concinere, texere prophetias a quibus se interdum feriari gravatur incredulus Zacharias. Trium enim mensium spatio eodem conclavi virgo et mulier detinentur, in quo non solum affectu sed etiam sermone mutuo confoventur, amantes simul esse non ut textrino operi manus sedulas instantius applicarent, sed ut divinas laudes jucundo eloquio gratius explicarent.* Philip, *De institutione*, PL 203, col. 1130.

imagines their conversations, offering the picturesque representation of the good Zachary as, like all deaf people, finding himself neglected. Here imagination supports intellect and will so that the incident comes to life and the heart is moved.

Clearly not all of Philip's theology is similarly straightforward; it has not attained the degree of development of a series of meditations such as Bonaventure's. On the whole Philip's theological work shows close dependence on the speculations of the Western Fathers. Yet from time to time, even often, a new light appears on the horizon. Philip's devotion remains deeply Augustinian but here and there bloom the little flowers of Saint Francis. Not all the works of Philip, however, are of equal importance for the history of spirituality. His great work on the formation of clerics, *De institutione clericorum*, divided into several tracts, and his Marian commentary on the Canticle of Canticles demand central attention here.

Philip's Treatise on the Formation of Clerics

The Dignity of Clerics

Because all of Christendom was then absorbed with the problem of ascetic life, Philip was constrained to share his thoughts on the relative dignity of clerics and monks. He balked before the difficulty of the task.

> This problem is like the passage between Scylla and Charybdis, a transit rife with danger, from which escape is something of a miracle. Yet if that captain who saved Peter as he began to sink, who commanded the winds and the sea threatening the apostles and calming their tumult—if he guided my vessel, then I would sail forward and arrive at my destination directly despite my boat's fragility. A feat impossible with my own strength is nonetheless easy for him to whom the ways on the sea and the paths of its waters belong.[8]

---

[8] *Inter Scyllam enim et Charybdam eundum est, inter quas navigare res est plena periculi, inde autem evadere digna miraculi. Caeterum si phaselum mea ille velit nauclerus regere, qui Petrum incipientem mergi data manu fecit emergere, qui apostolis periclitantibus ventis imperavit et mari, et eorum fecit tumultus quiescere, ducar et perducar ad optatum*

Each of the two paths of religious life, the author declares, leads to sanctity if it observes its own rule, yet the problem of which holds the greater dignity remains.

> Because one of the two has pridefully misunderstood what it was, the other has no less pridefully wished to seem what it was not. Fair balance fails both, so that for the most part they are unaware of the degree of each other's dignity. Conversation about respective limitations is mean-spirited and laborious as the discussants declare each other motivated by animosity or self-interest. If I unjustly depreciate the clerics, among whose number I happily count myself, then I seem to hate what I am and to love what I am not . . . but if I do not commend the monks, as I ought, I am slapped with the Gospel text: *Whatsoever you would that men should do to you, do you also to them* [Matt 7:12] and struck with the apostolic verse: *Let each esteem others better than themselves* [Phil 2:3].[9]

Thus, in order to avoid comparing the monastic and clerical life, Philip speaks almost entirely of the clerical order.

Unsurprisingly, the author supports the dignity of clerics with allegorical reading of the Old Testament. In general, he discusses Aaron, Eleazar, Ithamar, and the tabernacle according to the typological sense important to his times, but—distinctively in the twelfth-century context—he notes that the dignity of a Christian priest inheres in the Holy Eucharist as consecrated and offered by him; that Eucharist is represented by the ark of the covenant, the center of the tabernacle even as the Blessed Sacrament is the center

---

cursu peragili, quamvis ligno portatus fragili. Quod enim mihi vires meas metienti videtur impossibile, ei cujus in mari viae sunt et semitae ejus in aquis multis omnino est perfacile. Philip, *De institutione*, PL 203, col. 667.

[9] *Quia enim alter eorum superbe contempsit quod erat, alter vero non minori superbia videri appetit quod non erat, utrobique declinavit statera aequitatis, et ideo plerique jam nesciunt utriusque mensuram dignitatis. Hujus autem metas discutere invidiae plenum est et laboris cum hujusmodi plerumque discussores arguantur odii vel amoris. Si enim clericos plus justo depressero, in quorum numero gaudeo esse videbor id odisse quod sum et amare quod non sum. . . . Si autem monachos, prout justum est, non commendavero, incutiet mihi colaphum illud evangelicum: 'Quod vultis ut faciant vobis homines, et vos faciant illis' et illud Apostolicum: Superiores sibi invicem arbitrantes.* Philip, *De institutione*, PL 203, col. 667.

of the Church: "The Ark, made in the desert with the incorruptible wood of Sethim, represents the Body of Christ." [10] Clerics' role is not, however, limited to that dignity, but requires abundant sanctity in addition. God willed that clerics be filled with such moral holiness that by the merit of their lives they might imitate him rather than the created world. For those attaining such lofty dignity not to be completely suffused with the light of sanctity would be inappropriate, for such rank is more a burden than an honor if it does not rest on the foundation of sanctity. Private persons may indeed act perversely and their ill-doing go unknown, at least outside a small circle, but he whose dignity supersedes others' cannot hide his actions because that very rank sheds light on any shame he commits. Thus Boethius says that rank bestowed on the wicked not only does not make them unworthy of it but also reveals their unworthiness. [11]

So lofty a rank as priesthood is then not attained by ambition or conniving; rather Aaron and his sons, Melchizedek, the apostles, and Saint Paul were all chosen by God. The apostles in turn chose those bishops, priests, and deacons who became their helpers and successors. Still, to be chosen is not sufficient in itself, for Judas also was chosen. Such divine choice requires human responsiveness. Many priests have nonethelss solicited holy orders through ambition or avarice:

> All utterly detest Judas Iscariot and all execrate his avarice, but if we attend more closely we note that he valued the Body of Christ highly, for he demanded no less than thirty silver pieces to sacrifice it. Our priests, however, often sacrifice Christ for a single piece of silver or even a copper, as if unaware that Christ did not wish to be accounted at such a price nor that the mystery of his passion to be celebrated in such a perspective. His own words prove this if we read them closely. When Christ suffered at the beginning of his passion, he left the secure pledge of his own self to his beloved disciples, entrusting them with the celebration of the mystery of his Body and Blood. He told them clearly how he

---

[10] *Arca facta in eremo de lignis Sethim, quae nimirum imputribilia sunt, corpus significant Christi.* Philip, *De institutione,* PL 203, col. 668.

[11] *Collata improbis dignitas non modo non efficit dignos, sed prodit potius et ostendit indignos.* Philip, *De institutione,* PL 203, col. 670.

wished this celebration carried out, saying: *As often as you do this, you do it in memory of me.* What then does he mean by "in memory of me"? He means not in memory of a piece of silver nor of any worldly object or advantage, but in memory of me, that is to please me, love me, and offer fitting recompense for my passion so that, just as I offered myself to the Father out of love for you, so each one of you might offer himself for me. Therefore he who does these things but not in his memory does them contrary to Christ's own commandment. Certainly such sacrifices have no efficacy without obedience since, as the Lord said through Samuel, obedience is of greater worth than sacrifices. *As often as you do this,* he says, *you shall do it in memory of me.* Rightly, then, when at each Mass this sentence recurs in the canon, the priest publicly recalls Christ's commandment with his own lips lest anyone excuse himself or cover up his fault with the blanket of ignorance or forgetfulness. This verse offers the just an incentive of love and the unjust an increase of punishment and sorrow. The former, pronouncing these words, are the more fervently spurred to imitate Christ while the latter, abusing the same things, are the more harshly judged. Indeed, the multitude of those who abuse those words is so great that they fill not only the churches but the public places.[12]

---

[12] *Omnes quidem Judam Iscariot mirabiliter detestantur, omnes avaritiam ejus exsecrantur; sed si paulo diligentius velimus attendere, corpus Christi multo ille pretiosius aestimavit qui pro illo immolando non minus quam triginta argenteos postulavit. Nostri autem presbyteri plerumque pro nummo, plerumque pro obolo Christum immolant in altari, non sane attendentes quia tali pretio non se Christus voluit comparari nec hujus intuitu passionis suae mysterium celebrari. Quod ex verbis ejus poterit comprobare qui ea voluerit diligentius retractare. Cum enim Christus sub ipsius passionis articulo agonizaret et certissimum sui pignus dilectis discipulis relinquens, corporis et sanguinis sui celebrandum eis mysterium commendaret quo intuitu vellet agi signanter expressit et ait: Haec quotiescumque facietis in mei memoriam facietis. Quid est in memoriam mei? Hoc est non in memoriam nummi, non in memoriam saeculi, non in memoriam terreni alicujus commodi, sed in memoriam mei, hoc est ut mihi placeatis, ut me diligatis, ut passioni meae vicem congruam rependatis, ut sicut ego pro vobis charitate exigente Patri obtuli memetipsum, sic et pro me charitate reciproca unusquisque offerat semetipsum. Qui igitur haec facit et in hanc memoriam non facit contra mandatum Christi facit. Certum est autem quia contra obedientiam non prosunt victimae cum sicut per Samuelem Dominus dicit, melior sit obedientia quam victimae. Haec, inquit quotiescumque feceritis, in mei memoriam facietis, et pulchre cum missa celebratur idem versiculus in canone replicatur, ut sacerdos ore suo mandatum Christi reducat ad medium ne valeat excusari, ne scilicet per ignorantiae vel oblivionis oppansionem culpa ejus possit aliquatenus obumbrari. Hic quippe versiculus et justis dat incentivum amoris et injustis augmentum paenarum et doloris, dum illi nunc*

Others still violate their holy orders:

> Because their patrimony suffices for them such that they have
> means enough for the present life, they completely scorn ordina-
> tion. They do not want to be honored or made rich, but then too
> they do not want to be restrained by holy orders from the license
> to sin. Indeed they are afraid, because if they were indeed
> burdened by the responsibility of orders, they might then be
> compelled to live better lives. They do not wish to lose the desire
> to sin, so neither do they wish to put away that freedom. There-
> fore, when their bishop or dean or any other prelate desires to
> raise them to holy orders because the Church may have need of
> their ministry, they obstinately refuse. They do not deign to obey
> the command of their superiors, saying that they fear to be in-
> vested with holy orders when they are not leading saintly lives.
> Thus they wish to be supported by the Church's temporal goods
> but do not themselves wish to support that same Church in spiri-
> tual matters. They wish to live by the altar not to serve the altar.
> Hence we see many churches full of canons, yet so lacking in
> priests and deacons that there is hardly anyone to perform the
> sacred functions unless paid vicars are brought in. If, however,
> these men who scorn holy orders see ecclesiastical honors smiling
> upon them—honors they cannot obtain without orders—their
> purported fear is left behind and they hurry to receive the orders
> they once avoided. Now suddenly their youth does not impede
> them, nor their illiteracy, nor their lives invested in vice. Instead,
> oblivious of these conditions, they submit to that yoke of holy
> orders they will be unable successfully to bear. Thus in our times
> many churches are weakened because, by some hidden judgment
> of God, they are led by such priests, brought to their high office
> by their their own presumption rather than the love of Christ.
> These men seek in their rank not the interests of Jesus Christ but
> their own. They devote all their energy to earthly things, like
> children who cling to present goods with no regard for the
> future.[13]

---

replicantes ad imitandum ferventius excitantur et isti contemnentes amplius judicantur.
Horum autem contemnentium tanta est multitudo ut jam eis non tam ecclesiae quam fora
repleantur. Philip, *De institutione*, PL 203, cols. 682–83.

[13] *Quia enim forte eis sua patrimonia suppetunt, et quae ad praesentem vitam satis*
praesto sunt, contemnunt penitus ordinari, non quia nolunt honorari vel ditari, sed quia

The way of life in which Saint Norbert spent his youth was thus unfortunately the norm rather than the exception. Regular canons were also engaged in deplorable practices, for the devil always seeks to weaken the sanctity of their institution. He finds clerics who, if they are not called to orders at an appropriate time, murmur against their prelates that they are unappreciated and scorned. These men do not understand their own vocation, for those who seek holiness in the habit and under the discipline of their rule in fact declare war against vanity with all their zeal. True religious receive holy orders fearfully and under obedience, knowing that refusal is wicked. Then again many others are only too happy to receive orders even if they have not sought them. They accept such orders first in God's honor but also because the dignity pleases them, as they then prove by their great sadness if they are not so recognized. Their own will is still present, a tribute to the devil.

> Every religious should desire the capacity to choose, to the extent that this is granted him, that which divine scripture commands him to love. Our Master made this clear to us in the Gospel text when he instructed us to embrace it zealously, teaching us what we ought and ought not to choose if we wish truly to follow

---

nolunt per ordines a peccandi licentia revocari: Timent profecto, quia si pondere ordinum gravarentur, melius deinceps vivere cogerentur, et cum peccandi nolint deponere voluntatem, amittere nolunt etiam libertatem. Eapropter cum vel episcopus vel decanus vel quilibet eorum praelatus eos voluerit ad ordines promovere, quia forte Ecclesia eorum ministero videtur indigere, contumaciter recusant nec dignantur majorum obedire mandatis, timentes, ut aiunt, sacris ordinibus insigniri, cum vitam non habeant sanctitatis. Volunt quidem temporalibus Ecclesiae beneficiis sustentari, sed eidem Ecclesiae nolunt in spiritualibus suffragari. Volunt de altario vivere sed nolunt altario deservire. Inde est quod nonnullas ecclesias videmus canonicis plenas esse et tamen eisdem diaconos et presbyteros sic deesse, ut vix possint inveniri qui hujusmodi officiis perfungantur, nisi forte vicarii tamquam mercenarii conducantur. Si autem isti contemptores ordinum honores ecclesiasticos sibi viderint arridere, quod sine ordinibus non possunt obtinere, relegato timore quem antea praetendebant, currunt ad ordines quod antea fugiebant. Jam profecto non aetas eos junior revocat, non stoliditas illitterata, non vita vitiis irretita, sed horum omnium consideratione supponunt sub eis procul dubio ruituram. Unde nostris temporibus plures ecclesiae non mediocriter infirmantur quia videlicet eis hujusmodi praepositi occulto judicio principantur, quos cum ad gradum digniorem evexerit praesumptio propria, non dilectio Christi, in ipsa dignitate quae sua sunt quaerunt, non quae Jesu Christi. Totum quippe animum suum rebus applicant perituris, et more puerorum praesentibus inhaerentes nihil cogitant de futuris. Philip, *De institutione*, PL 203, col. 684.

his model. *When thou art invited to a wedding*, he said, *sit down in the lowest place* [Luke 14:10]. . . . But if evident, exterior self-humiliation is denied an individual, he may still preserve the desire for it in his heart, so that he performs true self-humiliation in his heart even if his circumstances accord him the honor appropriate to his rank. Our same Master clearly taught us this as well when he said elsewhere: *Learn of me, because I am meek, and humble of heart* [Matt 11:29], as if to say that one who holds a higher place in rank or honor should nevertheless embrace a lower place in humility of heart. Then at once his rank may receive its due and his humilty remain intact.[14]

Once chosen by God, then, the cleric ought to receive ordination just as Aaron was consecrated by Moses. On that occasion the high priest carried two robes, one of white linen, the other blue. The first represents the splendor of knowledge, the second the justice or sanctity rendering all the cleric's actions heavenly. So clothed with knowledge and sanctity, the cleric can give of his fullness without suffering detriminent to himself, according to the wonderful verse of Ovid: "Who objects that light be taken from the light next to it?"[15] Such knowledge and sanctity are the topics of Philip's two subsequent treatises.

The Knowledge of Clerics

The object of the cleric's knowledge is sacred scripture: "The scriptures themselves state that knowledge of their texts is the special

---

[14] *Est enim quaedam electio, quam unusquisque religiosus veraciter debet appetere, qua seipsum, quantum conceditur, debet eligere, quam, divinarum testimonio Scripturarum jubetur diligere. Ipsa est quam noster ille omnium magister in lectione evangelica designavit, cum ad eamdem amplectendam studiose nos informavit, docens quid eligere, quid non eligere debeamus, si ejus imitatores veraciter fieri peroptamus. 'Cum invitatus, inquit fueris ad nuptias, recumbe in novissimo loco'. . . . Quod si personae cuilibet humiliandi quantum ad exteriora non conceditur effectus, in corde tamen servari debet affectus, ut vera interius humilitas teneatur, quamvis personae pro suo cuique modo exterius deferatur. Hoc etiam idem Magister alibi signanter expressit, dicens: 'Discite a me, quia mitis sum et humilis corde.' Tamquam diceret: Etsi pro alicujus honoris dignitate locum tenetis superiorem, tamen exemplo mei ex cordis humilitate amplectimini inferiorem, ut sic dignitati quod suum est, tribuatur, ne humilitati injuria inferatur.* Philip, *De institutione*, PL 203, cols. 686–87.

[15] *Quis vetet apposito lumen de lumine sumi?* Philip, *De institutione*, PL 203, col. 692.

obligation of clerics."[16] Such a statement is surprising to a modern age accustomed to the study of theology as distinct from biblical exegesis, but during Philip's time university education was still in its infancy. Although tradition was understood to be a source of theology, sacred doctrine was nonetheless sought immediately in scripture. Priests under the Old Law were already able to judge between blood and blood, between leper and leper, so that much more the priests of Philip's time, as he pointed out, should be able to judge between species of sin. Our Lord reproached the Sadducees for ignoring the underlying meaning of scripture, saying to the scribes that they should search the scriptures to find testimony about him.[17] Saint Paul frequently urged Timothy and Titus to study the Bible. But unfortunately children study out of fear of punishment and, later, ambitious students are content to see honors accrue to them despite their ignorance. Still others excuse themselves, asserting that their poverty deprives them of books and schools, but actually they have no desire to make the sacrifices necessary to acquire knowledge.[18]

Even among the regular canons the pursuit of knowledge is flawed. Although they have left all in order to be free to devote their time in a cloistered life to spiritual things, a certain number still refuse to commit themselves to study. Some even accuse the studious of wasting time on books. These restless folk see it as a burden to sit still, to read, and to meditate, so they instead search for all manner of occupations, even asking for permission to busy themselves with work. They are so busy that they neglect their reading, which in turn becomes more and more tiresome for them. Some confreres set it aside because reading actually becomes painful for them. They do not know how to find the allegory beneath the literal meaning of the text and this inability drives them away. In this case the reluctant student must force himself to meditate and to speak

---

[16] *Si quis diligentius velit scire quam certum sit scientiam Scripturarum proprie clericis convenire, revolutis iisdem Scripturis facile poterit invenire.* Philip, *De institutione,* PL 203, col. 693.

[17] [Editor's note: See John 5:39.]

[18] *Malunt apud suos indocti remanere quam discendi gratia apud exteros indigere.* Philip, *De institutione,* PL 203, col. 701.

with Christ in prayer, for such reading is finally about him. Reading brings that better knowledge of Christ necessary to greater love of him and in turn to closer relationship with him. And it teaches that when prayer fails, tears may suffice.[19] Obligation to the care of souls might stand in the way of study, as might manual labor, but all such work ought to be done at its proper time and in charity, not out of curiosity, impatience, or aversion to study.[20] Philip ends his treatise with these valuable thoughts.

The Justice of Clerics

After treating knowledge, Philip considers the justice, that is, the saintliness, of clerics. Their justice consists in two religious virtues: poverty and continence. Poverty is the central subject of the treatise at issue here. Philip, like the first Premonstratensians, always adds the word *voluntaria* to poverty as he represents it. This willed or spontaneous poverty begins in the real and total abandonment of all those things that were formerly possessions. Poverty is in its essence a clerical virtue. Philip does not go so far as to say that one cannot be both a cleric and a proprietor, so setting aside the possibility of the existence of secular clergy. He instead suggests that thorough reading of sacred scripture points to this position:

> The justice of the clerics—rather the fulfillment of their justice and their love—consists in voluntary poverty and continence, among the other virtues. These two attributes, however, are so clearly assigned to clerics by the divine testimony of the scriptures that I do not know whether, without them, that designation is appropriate. This statement is strict but deeply truthful. He who is not rich in the treasury of poverty, whose loins are not girded with the belt of chastity, is not truly a cleric.[21]

[19] Philip, *De institutione*, cols. 703–6.

[20] *Labori . . . manuum vel curis ecclesiasticis non serviat curiosae impulsu levitatis sed purae et sincerae obedientia charitatis.* Philip, *De institutione*, PL 203, col. 708.

[21] *Est ergo justitia clericorum vel potius operatio justitiae et dilectionis eorum, ut de multis duo eligam: Paupertas voluntaria et continentia, quae duo ita divinarum testimonio Scripturarum clericis specialiter indicuntur, ut nesciam utrum sine his possint veraciter existere quod dicuntur. Durus sermo, sed plenus veritatis, non satis vere est clericus, quem non ditat thesaurus paupertatis, cujus lumbos non astringit cinctorium castitatis.* Philip, *De institutione*, PL 203, col. 718.

To be a cleric, in its etymology, is both to be God's legacy and to inherit God himself. Under the Old Law priests and Levites indeed possessed temporal goods, yet they held no lands of their own in Israel, rather themselves represented the legacy of the Eternal. But in the Gospel Jesus goes a step further, instructing the apostles not to carry even a purse.

> Jesus speaks here as if to say, "Your mission is to preach to others the words of life and to invite them with the greatest zeal to a love of heavenly things. I do not want you to convert a ministry of such great dignity into the pursuit of worldy goods. Nor indeed may you who invite others to the riches of the heavenly kingdom appropriately bring along a sack to store up earthly wealth, lest you be found to urge one thing by your words and show another in your example." May that not happen! No listener heeds a preacher's sermon unless that preacher's life is in accordance with his words. So that their preaching might be accepted and he might successfully exhort others to shun transient things, Christ willed that his preachers possess nothing, rather that they offer others the model of poverty.[22]

Christ makes poverty the foundation of the apostlic life in the first beatitude.[23] He promises to make the poor apostles the judges of the twelve tribes of Israel, so making the renunciation of temporal goods the foundation of perfection.

---

[22] *Ac si diceret: Vos qui mittimini verba vitae aliis praedicare eosque summo studio ad amorem caelestium invitare: nolo ut tantae ministerium dignitatis in aucupium terreni commodi convertatis. Neque enim decet ut qui alios ad caelestis regni divitias invitatis, ad recondendum temporalem pecuniam sacculum deferatis, ne inveniamini verbo aliud commendare et aliud, quod absit! exemplo demonstrare. Denique nescit auditor sermonem praedicantium acceptare, nisi vitam sermoni videat concordare. Eapropter, ut eorum sermo commendabilis habeatur et ad contemptum temporalium alios efficaciter hortaretur: eosdem praedicatores nihil Christus voluit possidere, sed formam paupertatis caeteris exhibere.* Philip, *De institutione*, PL 203, col. 719.

[23] *Si ergo clerici sciunt se habere apostolicam in Ecclesia dignitatem, cum eorum vice ligandi atque solvendi teneant potestatem, sciant sibi quoque sicut et aliis voluntariam paupertatem injungi, quam nisi tenuerint judicantium numero non poterunt jungi.* Philip, *De institutione*, PL 203, col. 720. (If clerics know that they have the apostolic dignity in the Church, since by their office they hold the apostles' power of binding and loosing, let them also know that as voluntary poverty was required of the apostles, so it is required of them as well, and that they will not be added to the number of judges unless they hold fast to the judges' poverty.)

> However generous, chaste, just, and holy a man may be, he is not
> perfect as long as he has riches. . . . If you wish to crown all the
> common virtues with the grace of perfection, you must give the
> poor all that you have so that, having laid aside the burden of
> property—a load which does not obstruct all holiness but none-
> theless stands in the way of perfection—your sanctity may win
> you that judgment seat reserved for the perfect. . . . This rule of
> perfection, a formula of generosity, was preached first by Christ
> in the Gospel, then preserved by the apostles and many of their
> successors.[24]

Even the great saints of the Old Testament had not heard such
language. They received riches in proportion to their piety toward
God. "The perfection of the Gospel was first offered to you, clerics,
who follow in the footsteps of the apostles. The privilege of such
sanctity was reserved for you, so that the poorer you are in other
things, the richer you may be in the merit of perfection."[25] So Peter
said to the lame man at the Beautiful Gate: *Silver and gold I have
none; but what I have, I give thee. In the name of Jesus Christ of Nazareth,
arise and walk* (Acts 3:6). Not even a Croesus, despite his wealth,
would have been able to give this gift. Nothing is lacking to those
who have nothing.[26] Poverty is the inheritance of clerics; it is their
profession and their treasure they share as Christ's heirs.[27]

Notably, Philip here does not cite the description of apostolic
life in Acts except in one brief allusion. He thus evokes the evangelical institution rather than the apostolic institution because the

---

[24] *Quantumvis quippe largus, castus, justus, sanctus quilibet habeatur; perfectus tamen
nequaquam judicatur, quamdiu proprias divitias habere comprobatur. . . . Si desideras
virtutum generalium aggerem perfectionis gratia cumulare, oportet te omnia quae habes
pauperibus erogare ut, deposita proprietatis sarcina quae, etsi non sanctitati, tamen
perfectioni non mediocriter adversatur, judiciariam perfectorum sedem tua sanctitas
mereatur. . . . Haec nimirum perfectionis regula, haec formula largitatis Christo in
evangelio praedicante primitus est audita et ab apostolis nonnullisque eorum successoribus
in posterum custodita.* Philip, *De institutione,* PL 203, col. 721.

[25] *Perfectio quidem evangelica vobis, clerici, qui apostolica sectamini vestigia, debebatur,
vobis tantae sanctitatis privilegium servabatur, ut scilicet quanto caeteris estis pauperiores,
tanto essetis perfectionis merito ditiores.* Philip, *De institutione,* PL 203, col. 722.

[26] *Nihil habentibus nihil deest.* Philip, *De institutione,* col. 724.

[27] *Christi pauperiem commendantis facti sunt cohaeredes.* Philip, *De institutione,* PL
203, col. 725.

former addresses the entire apostolic community, including the laity. Although Philip is concerned in this work with clerics only, he nonetheless thus demonstrates the enthusiasm for the apostoloic movement in both Saint Norbert and Anselm of Havelberg. Occasionally his text shows the lyricism that would make Lady Poverty the mystical spouse of Saint Francis of Assisi.

> A clergy able to own property does not contribute to the spiritual progress of its people. Loving money, it is unconcerned with the salvation of souls. Occupied with earthly things, it does not strive for heavenly riches. When the laity see it, they fling insults at their clergy rather than address them with compassion and mercy. . . . Poverty then is the special attribute of clerics, for the Gospel makes it the mother of virtues. Since they have nothing of their own, they may more easily and completely obtain the other virtues. Just as riches breed vice, so poverty increases virtue. Without it the virtues' list is incomplete. The perfection of the other virtues therefore is fostered in the lap of poverty. Christ does not want his clerics, as teachers and leaders of his religion, to have anything in common with the clerics and priests of Pharaoh.[28]

The Continence of Clerics

As noted above, the titles of Philip's works are misleading; the texts in fact address more than their titles suggest. Especially rich, beyond its title's implication, is his great treatise on the continence of clerics, extending to eighty pages in the 1621 edition.[29] The work is divided into three parts, of which only the first corresponds to

---

[28] *Ipsi etiam populo talis clerus profectum non impendit, qui verbo et exemplo docere subditos non intendit, qui amore captus pecuniae animarum salutem non intendit, qui terrenis occupatus apprehendere caelestia non contendit. Talem quippe clerum dum multitudo popularis perpendit, non tam miserando compatitur quam insultando reprehendit. . . . Ideo congrue paupertas clericis specialiter assignatur, quae mater est virtutum, sicut in Evangelio designatur, ut cum inventi fuerint proprium nil habere, facilius et perfectius virtutes possint reliquas obtinere. Sicut enim divitiae non mediocre vitiis dant fomentum, sic nimirum paupertas virtutibus incrementum, ut sine illa istarum catalogus non possit adimpleri, quarum perfectio in illius gremio dicitur confoveri. Denique suos Christus clericos, doctores et principes suae religionis, non vult commune quid habere cum clericis et sacerdotibus Pharaonis.* Philip, *De institutione*, PL 203, cols. 726–27.

[29] *De institutione*, PL 203, cols. 727–840.

the title. The second resumes the topic of the dignity or rank of clerics and compares their canonical profession to the monastic life. The third part represents his rejoinder to Rupert of Deutz, to whom Anselm of Havelberg had already responded. Because Rupert had attacked Saint Norbert, he met with as much opposition by the Premonstratensians of the west as by those of Magdeburg.

Such conflict over the roles of monks and regular canons is puzzling from a modern perspective, yet this controversy was a burning, essential question for the first Premonstratensians as well as for all other clerics who professed the Augustinian Rule. Their place in the Church, even their very existence, depended on the resolution of this controversy. The first part of Philip's work on clerical continence, treating the chastity of clerics and occupying one fourth of the treatise, requires little commentary here. Its content develops a well-known theme: the necessity of sexual continence for clerics as shown in the typology of the Old Law, in our Lord's own words, and by the examples of the apostles and their successors.

> Christ himself wished to represent the chastity of which we speak with such integrity as to mar it with no stain or even suspicion of stain, keeping it as an ornament so perfect as to suffer no blemish of any kind. The Virgin of whom he was born showed the same splendor of perfect continence, remaining chaste after his birth just as she had earlier been. Her chastity was undamaged in her fruitfulness while her fruitfulness in no way damaged her chastity. Indeed, when Christ was embodied in her virgin womb he joined with the Church as his own bride in this nuptial chamber, in no way diminishing his mother's integrity when he was then born of her. Nor did his union with the Church diminish that Church's chastity. The pure union signified his wish that those whom he willed to rule and instruct that same Church in his name, whom he thus ordained to bring forth his spiritual children, might follow his own model in their way of life. They might aspire to such holy office by entirely refraining from carnal embraces and occupying themselves with only the growth of the Church. . . . When he chose his disciples, Christ likewise willed that none of that apostolic rank remain married, bound by carnal union. Just as he did not allow those who had not yet taken a

wife to be married afterward, so he willed that those who had
already married be released from those bonds.[30]

Although this argument seems self-evident now, it did not seem
obvious in Philip's time. Nicolaism had not entirely disappeared,
although it soon would. Although the theoretical position of the
Church regarding clerical celibacy was no longer under attack, to
state it with a precision emphasizing the nobility and the clarity of
its justifications remained useful.

Philip's treatise, having addressed the continence of clerics, then
returns to its central subject, their dignity. Faith, hope, charity, and
the other moral virtues are required of the laity, but further virtues
—vocation (*electio*), knowledge, poverty, and chastity—are required
of clerics. The level of sanctity expected of them is more difficult
because their dignity is more lofty.[31] Philip distinguishes precisely
between dignity as a social rank and sanctity as moral stature. While
some among the monks may be holier than many clerics, that difference has no bearing on the dignity of either order. Although the
dignity of clerics requires greater sanctity than monks', clerics' potential failure to achieve it nonetheless does not damage the dignity
of their role as mediators between God and human beings, resting
in what in modern times is identified as their ministry and Philip

---

[30] *Hanc igitur de qua loquimur continentiam tanta in se integritate Christus voluit
consignare, ut nulla eam vel macula vel suspicione maculae sineret violari: tam integrum
hujusce castitatis servavit ornamentum ut nullum ei ex parte inferret detrimentum. Denique
et in ea de qua natus est Virgine eadem continentia resplendivit quae sicut continens ante
partum sic mansit et post partum: nec illi data castitas fecunditati nec fecunditas
praejudicium intulit castitati. Carnem quippe humanam Christus cum in utero sumeret
virginali sponsam sibi copulavit Ecclesiam in thalamo nuptiali, et nec matri abstulit
integritatem dum de ea nasceretur; nec Sponsae minuit castitatem cum ei jungeretur. Ex
quo satis innuitur quia eos quos ad regendum et instruendum eamdem Ecclesiam vice sua
voluit sublimari et ad generandum spiritales filios ordinari, sibi quoque vivendo voluit
conformari ut ex quo ad tam sanctum officium aspirarent, carnales a se complexus omnino
relegarent, et solius Ecclesiae fecundandis profectibus incubarent. . . . Proinde cum
discipulos eligeret, nullum in gradu apostolico manere voluit uxoratum, nullum carnalis
copulae vinculis occupatum; sed sicut eos qui nondum uxores acceperant non permisit
postmodum nuptiis alligari, sic eos qui acceperant ab eisdem voluit vinculis relaxari.* Philip,
De institutione, PL 203, col. 742.

[31] Philip, *De institutione*, PL 203, col. 738.

called their wonderful power. His and his contemporaries' discussion thus has little resonance with the disputes among religious orders in the eighteenth century. The regular canons of the Middle Ages did not consider themselves a religious order comparable to that of the monks, rather as Catholic clergy maintaining their priestly rank in the ordinary hierarchy but striving under the Church's impulse toward a perfect life. Poverty had not yet been imposed on the entire clergy, as celibacy had lately been.

For Philip, then, their priestly role sets clerics above princes. Princes wield the material sword but clerics wield the word of God, more trenchant than a two-edged weapon. "Wonderful dignity! Wonderful power! Demoniacal forces and sicknesses of the soul are subjugated to the cleric's command. Whatever he wishes bound or loosed on earth is bound or loosed in heaven."[32] Personal sanctity is a completely different matter: John the Baptist was holier than the apostles, yet the apostles among themselves shared a dignity greater than his.[33] Nevertheless, priestly rank requires the priest to strive toward commensurate sanctity. Indeed the apostles attained such lofty sanctity that clerics, although taking them as models, can never equal them. The apostles were the living rule for the early Church that the apostolic movement emulated. They represented, strictly speaking, the Christian ideal as realized by the faithful of Jerusalem who imitated them.

> Indeed the sanctity of the apostles was so great no cleric could equal them however closely he imitated them. Athough we inherit their dignity, their sanctity is reserved to them as properly their own. When the Holy Spirit came upon them they spoke about the things of heaven in many languages. All venerated them on account of this miracle. Then such a new level of sanctity invested them as to strike fear into the eight thousand gathered outside. Those others then promised to live under the apostles' direction, voluntarily submitting to the sweet yoke of Christ. The apostles

---

[32] *Mira dignitas! mira potestas! cujus imperio virtutes daemoniacae et languores animae subjugantur, ad cujus arbitrium quaecumque in terries in caelo quoque solvuntur et ligantur.* Philip, *De institutione*, PL 203, col. 761.

[33] *Apostolus in Joanne majorem aspicit sanctitatem et Joannes veneratur majorem in Apostolo dignitatem.* Philip, *De institutione*, PL 203, col. 763.

then established a new rule of life for their followers, presenting themselves as the exemplars of this rule. They led their community to a perfection uinknown in prior ages. Thus it is written in the Acts of the Apostles: *The multitude of believers had but one heart and one soul: neither did any one say that aught of the things which he possessed, was his own; but all things were common unto them. . . . For neither was there any one needy among them. For as many as were owners of lands or houses, sold them, and brought the price of the things they sold. And laid it down before the feet of the apostles. And distribution was made to every one, according as he had need* [Acts 4:32, 34]. O what novelty! Who, either before the Law or under the Law, had heard of so many thousands coming together in such a unity of spirit, embracing voluntary poverty with such fervor, living together with such harmony, and obeying the laws of a new and perfect sanctity with such unanimity? They were, as the Acts say, all together at the portico of Solomon. That portico was rich, not so much with silver and gold or any other metal of old Solomon, as in the treasury of virtues and the splendor of the new religion.[34]

The ideal of the apostles could not be maintained, however. After their dispersion, the clerics of the newly established churches were

---

[34] *Tanta quippe apostolorum sanctitas fuit ut etsi eos utcumque potest quivis clericus imitari, non tamen eis possit aliquatenus coaequari; et cum ad nos usque eorum dignitas derivetur eorum tamen sanctitas sibi quasi singularis et propria retinetur. Cum de caelis misso Paraclito linguis omnibus loquerentur et vulgato tali miraculo cunctis venerabiles haberentur, tanta in eis effloruit novitas sanctitatis ut timorem incuteret octo millibus congregatis; et ad eorum arbitrium illi promitterent deinceps se victuros et suave Christi jugum cervice voluntaria subituros. Unde Apostoli novam illis vivendi regulam disponentes et seipsos ejusdem formulam regulae proponentes ad tantam illos perfectionem provexerunt quantam nulla retro saecula cognoverunt. Sicut enim in Actibus Apostolorum scriptum est: 'Omnes qui credebant erant pariter et multitudinis credentium erat cor unum et anima una; nec quisquam eorum quae possidebat aliquid suum esse dicebat, sed erant eis omnia communia; et quotquot possessores domorum vel agrorum erant vendentes afferebant pretia eorum et ponebant ante pedes Apostolorum et dividebatur singulis prout cuique opus erat.' O Nova res! Quis vel ante legem vel sub lege tot millia hominum audivit ad tantam pervenisse spiritus unitatem, tam prompto animo amplecti voluntariam paupertatem: in tantum pariter vivendi consensum devenire, tam novae et perfectae sanctitatis legibus unanimiter obedire? Erant, inquit, omnes unanimiter in porticu Salomonis. Dives ille porticus non tam auro vel argento vel metallis quibuslibet illius antiqui Salomonis quam thesauro virtutum et splendore novae religionis.* Philip, *De institutione*, PL 203, col. 766.

too few in number to be able to preserve common life and poverty. They contented themselves with coming to the help of those saints in Jerusalem who adhered to the original ideal but, sadly, even this commitment failed when the holy city was destroyed. Soon, however, this regrettable state would be repaired by the foundation of monastic life, which Philip traces back to Saint Mark and the restorative efforts of Philo.[35]

Our author now dicusses the monks. Like all of his contemporaries, Philip loves etymologies. *Monachus* comes from *monos*, alone, for *monoculus* means one who has only one eye. The monastic profession thus presupposes a certain solitude not as an end in itself, rather as a way of attaining freedom for devotion to God alone. Its door to such freedom is open to all, men and women, the educated and the unlettered. Manual labor, humility, obedience to superiors: these are the distinctive traits of monastic discipline. Chanting of the psalms is widespread among the monks, but the time and solemnity invested in it vary according to the different rules.

Whether priesthood should be a constitutive element of the monastic life remained a major issue. Philip argued that it need not because the first monks were not priests. Nevertheless, he added, necessity soon moved early bishops to ordain some monks, but only for the service of the monastic oratory; those few who, out of love for Christ, separated themselves from the social world and chose to live in solitude could not be forced to lead this life without the sacrament of Christ or to end it in peril, without that same help.[36] In short, the examples of the first solitaries notwithstanding, the Eucharist and the priesthood are necessary for Christian monasteries. Thus, little by little, monk-priests became more numerous. During the twelfth century, among the black monks, Benedictines, only a few religious were not ordained. Clerics, as Philip says, have no reason to complain in this, for no insult has

---

[35] *Haec infirmitas, hic defectus, haec dissolutio clericorum fons quidam et origo, quantum mihi videtur, extitit monachorum.* Philip, *De institutione*, PL 203, col. 769. ("This weakening, this defect, this dissolution of the clerics was, it seems to me, the source and origin of the monks.")

[36] *Ne qui propter Christum a turba remoti elegerant in solitudinibus habitare illic sine Christi sacramento vel praesentem vitam ducere cogerentur vel eamdem periculosius terminare.* Philip, *De institutione*, PL 203, cols. 774–75.

here been done to them. Certainly, nevertheless, ministry outside the monastic community is neither the tradition nor the vocation of monks. If it increased, it would soon damage monastic life because monks' role is not to baptize, to bless marriages, or to commit priests to the celebration of the sacred mysteries in churches.[37] Philip permitted exceptions; his view was close to the modern point of view. A cleric dismayed by life in the secular world and fearful of his own inability to attain sanctity in it might well become a monk. He might not be then appropriately accused of desertion in so doing well. Conversely, for an observant, scholarly monk to supply the need for clerical functions while wearing the monastic habit presents no contradiction. The two orders are proximate, so should avoid all such jealousy as might stand in the way of contemplation of God.[38]

The third part of Philip's treatise on the education of clerics responds directly to Rupert of Deutz.[39] This author had composed a work entitled *Altercation between a Monk and Cleric* on the very subject of interest here.[40] The interlocutors in this debate are generally understood to be Rupert as the monk and Saint Norbert as the cleric, although the text is not the transcript of an actual discussion, rather a work of careful literary craft. The portrayal of the cleric in particular is stylized. Such a discussion did, however, take place and Norbert himself was very possibly Rupert's opponent. Indeed, other evidence suggests that the abbot of Deutz was hostile to the founder of the Premonstratensians. Certainly these two antagonists manifested different characteristics. Rupert was the more learned in patristic studies. His clerical interlocutor, Philip points out, was on the other hand more knowledgeable in philosophy. His views on scripture were, according to the judgment of the masters of the school of Laon, more correct. On the whole Rupert reasoned thus: you are clerics, but so are we. Further, we are monks and you are not. Therefore, we are greater than you.

---

[37] Philip, *De institutione*, PL 203, col. 795.

[38] Philip, *De institutione*, PL 203, cols. 834–35.

[39] Philip, *De institutione*, PL 203, cols. 807–40.

[40] Rupert, *Altercatio*, PL 170, cols. 537–41.

Philip, taking up in his own work the part of the cleric whom Rupert represented, responds: you monks have received sacred orders. Good. We are ourselves the first to rejoice. But while you perform clerical functions, you do not profess the clerical life. A man who occasionally rides a horse is not a knight. The true cleric is he whose life is devoted to the care of souls. By special dispensation you have received holy orders so that you may serve your confreres, not the Christian people generally, for monks' proper role is fasting, vigils, work, compunction, and silence—not to serve their neighbors or have contact with the world. Philip supports this argument by reexamining the texts cited by Rupert in his dialogue. The work of the abbot of Bonne Espérance then ends with the conciliatory declaration that, by a divine grace unusual in the history of the Church, the fervor of both monks and clerics is lively in his own time, in the later twelfth century. Just as at winter's end trees bloom again in spring's warmth, now a fresh dew causes the religious life of monasteries, most prominently Cîteaux, to flower. The monastic order, heretofore moribund, now rises, shaking off the the dust of the past and giving itself wholeheartedly to work, poverty, tears, and silence. It seeks not to draw its support from tithes but to earn its bread by manual labor. In a reaction against the luxurious black cowls previously in use, Cîteaux has adopted another color, the undyed hue of sheep's wool. Although this choice has elicited sarcasm from secular people and from other monks, such criticism is of no importance because Cîteaux thus follows the Rule of Saint Benedict to the letter. Meanwhile Clairvaux (*clara vallis*) is preeminent among the Cistercian monasteries. The humility practiced there makes it a true valley (*vallis*), while the sanctity with which it shines renders it bright (*clara*).[41]

But clerics also have been so graced by Christ, as Prémontré, the exemplary gathering of clerics, demonstrates. It has assembled fervent men whose fervor inspires others far and wide to such religious life as they should have.[42]

---

[41] Philip, *De institutione*, PL 203, cols. 836–37.

[42] *Quosdam fervente spiritu congregavit, per quos ad religionem debitam longe lateque caeteros excitavit.* Philip, *De institutione*, PL 203, col. 838.

The sanctity of the clerics there is so fervent and their fortitude against worldly enticements so great that the apostolic life seems renewed in them. . . . There, the sack of coins is cast aside and the deadly poison of self-will is detested. Ecclesiastical offices previously attained or sought are left behind, while transient honors are disregarded. Meanwhile, work, silence, and poverty are undertaken with such holy diligence as to replicate both the weary suffering of the monks and the saintly, unwavering devotion of the clerics. God expressly willed this to take place in a valley so that the form of its site might fit this salvific work, clearly demonstrating to clerics for whom lofty dignity and freedom of rank had been the occasions for moral ruin that instead voluntary self-abasement and humble penance bring spiritual preferment. This valley is rightly called *Prémontré*, "shown beforehand," to make clear that the humility of the clerics was not thus instituted thoughtlessly or haphazardly, but that divine mercy showed it beforehand as an example for others; the very land bore witness that humility was the path to return to God.

Thus divine providence formed and shaped this valley for its present work and that valley shaped its present work so that the appearance of the place warns of the difficulty and harshness to which its clerics' humility must then respond. The valley is shaped in the form of a four-armed cross, its floor bounded by four corners so that its length extends from east to west and its width from north to south. This very topography, cruciform not through human effort but in its nature, thus shows that those who come there ought no longer to care to live in the world. They ought instead to conform themselves to this landform, rather to Christ himself, in a comparable crucifixion. Further, the entry to the valley is along one of the four arms. In the middle lies a crossroad so that those newly arriving from all directions come together there, whence also the lofty repute of the community flows back into all four directions. . . . *And the vales*, says David, *shall abound with corn* [Ps 64:14]. This grain may be understood to be Christ himself. Falling to the earth, he sprouts forth the more fruitfully; ground in the mill of his passion, he feeds his humble flock with the bread of life, offering his humble clergy the food of salutary refreshment and, as they mature, the ornament of glorious beauty. Christ therefore saw fit in the Canticle of Canticles to call himself *the lily of the valleys* [Song 2:1], revealing that he will swiftly crown with honor and glory those who consider it no burden to bear

the hardships of abasement for his sake. . . . Indeed, the whiteness of the lily signifies the solemnity of that joy with which
Christ will reward the sorrowful humility of his clergy when he
reveals himself to them, face to face.[43]

Philip then offers a final chapter on the symbolism of the Premonstratensian habit. Its white wool, according to Isaiah, signifies
the remission of sins. This whiteness also represents the transfigured
Christ and the angels of the Resurrection. Norbert's symbolism is
thus honored: the habit is white because it is clerical and woolen
because it is penitential. Christ is the supreme whiteness, the
"whiteness of the eternal light." The Premonstratensians are the

---

[43] *Illic quippe tanta clericorum efferbuit sanctitudo, tanta adversus temporales illecebras
fortitudo ut vere in eis vita reformari apostolica videatur. . . . Illic, inquam abjecto sacculo
pecuniariae facultatis, exsecrantes mortifera lenocinia propriae voluntatis, relinquentes eas
quas vel habebant vel ambiebant Ecclesiae praefecturas, ducentes pro nihilo dignitates
velocius transituras tantum studium labori, silentio, paupertati, tantam denique impenderunt
diligentiam sanctitati ut apud eos inveniri posset et laboriosa afflictio monachorum et sancta
ac devota devotio clericorum. Quod profecto signanter Deus in valle voluit actitari ut ipsa
loci forma concors esset negotio salutari: et potenter ostenderet quia clericis quibus ruinae
occasio erat excelsa dignitas et libertas praesidendi, oportuna esset voluntaria depressio et
humilitas clericorum non temere, non fortuitis est adinventionibus inchoata, sed eam divina
misericordia in exemplum caeteris praemonstravit, quibus per hanc revertendi ad se aditum
demonstravit. Nec vacat quod hanc vallem divina providentia sic formavit, sic eam praesenti
negotio vel ei praesens negotium conformavit ut ipsa loci facies videatur quiddam grave et
asperum praemonere, eique praemonenti humilitas clericorum respondere. Ad modum enim
crucis eadem vallis in quatuor cornua dilatatur ejusque planities in quatuor angulis
terminatur, a quo Orientali in Occidentalem tenditur longitudo, ab Aquilonari vero in
Australem ejusdem latitudo. Quae loci facies cui tanta crucis similitudo est infixa, quae
vallis non humano molimine sed naturali opere quodammodo crucifixa, quia monet et
praemonet nisi ut ad eam confluentes mundo vivere jam non curent, sed se illi, imo Christo
crucifixione congrua configurent? Praeterea in eam vallem per quatuor illa cornua devenitur
et in eis medium quodam quadrivio, id est via quadrupla convenitur, ut ei scilicet a quatuor
mundi partibus convenarum grata multiplicitas infundatur et inde in quatuor mundi partes
religionis opinio diffundatur. . . . Valles, inquit (David), abundabunt frumento. Hoc
autem frumentum forte idem ipse Christus est qui cadens in terram feracius pullulavit, qui
passionis mola tritus pane vitae humiles pavit, qui clericis humilibus largitur refectionis
salutaris nutrimentum et eisdem jam adultis confert gloriosi decoris ornamentum. Propter
quod in Canticis lilium se convallium voluit nominare, ostendens quia eos qui propter ipsum
non gravantur abjectionis molestias tolerare, ipse honore et gloria festinate coronare . . .
candor quippe lilii signat solemnitatem gaudii quo humilem clericorum tristitiam munerabit
cum se illis facie ad faciem demonstravit.* Philip, *De institutione*, PL 203, cols. 837–38.

reflection of his whiteness, so "conformed to the brilliance of Christ."[44] The whole of Philip's final chapter on the continence of clerics thus depends directly on the biography of Saint Norbert, yet surprisingly the abbot of Bonne Espérance nowhere mentions the name of the founder. Nor will Adam Scot. Philip makes reference to none of the visions underlying these various symbols although he indeed remarks their signification. Because of Prémontré, then, the monks might no longer say to the clerics that they lack the sanctity required by monastic status. Here dignity adorns sanctity while sanctity brings its strength to dignity.[45]

The Obedience of Clerics

Philip's discussion of the obedience of clerics is less engaging than the preceding treatises constituting his great work on the education of clerics. To read these sixty pages requires great effort relative to its few fruits.[46] Philip's contemporaries, however, may not have been so disappointed. The latter treatise's heavy use of skillfully expounded allegories must have delighted his early readership. Perhaps this exegetical method will some day return to fashion and later readers be surprised that twentieth-century philistines were unable to enjoy its riches, so that we in turn may be humbled. That said, Philip's analogy between the six ages of the world and the six stages of the human life, again explaining six aspects of obedience, presents little interest to us, as do his long figurative explanations of the lives of Abraham and Saint John the Baptist. Reading this material very slowly and in small sections during the long hours dedicated to *lectio divina* might, on the other hand, be more tolerable than analytical reading of scripture concerned with understanding the work as a whole.

Philip here focuses on a philosophical study of the social nature of man as the natural foundation for religious obedience:

---

[44] *Candor est lucis aeternae. . . . Christo candido conformantur.* Philip, *De institutione,* PL 203, col. 840.

[45] *Dignitas adornat sanctitatem et dignitate sanctitas suffragatur.* Philip, *De institutione,* PL 203, col. 840.

[46] Philip, *De institutione,* PL 203, cols. 839–944.

How should we value obedience, my brothers, and must we be
obedient in all things or is it permissible perhaps to avoid obedient submission in some cirucmstances? Obedience is indeed a
perfect virtue, so commended in the scriptures from the very
beginning that no other is perfect unless fortified by it. Even if
charity, greatest of the virtues, attempts to love something contrary to obedience, not only is it rightly condemned but adjudged
not truly charitable because it resists God in loving him outside
the bounds of obedience. Therefore, every rational creature is
constrained to obedience just as all creatures are commanded by
the Creator of all. No creature is so great or of such lofty dignity
that he must not obey a greater power. . . . God thus wills both
that all creatures obediently serve him and that each obey another
so that there is no order, profession, city, or country that may
abuse its own will. Instead each is subject to the power of another.
Even kings, although they are not compelled to submit to other
kings, nevertheless must obey God. They must also listen to
the pontiffs of the Church who act as God's vicars, so that as
monarchs they may order their lives according to the admonitions
of those same popes. Kings must defend Mother Church from
those who attack her, fighting the enemies of the faith with their
obedient arms. Consuls, centurions, tribunes, and other military
officers then offer their obedience to kings. These officers in turn
command others according to well-established rules. Those who
pridefully scorn such authority incur the guilt of disobedience
not only in men's eyes but also in God's. Knights thus owe military service to their lords and lords to their kings, so that when
they must do battle—whether for peace, for their homeland or
for the Church—the lesser immediately respond to the behests
of the greater, aware that they so fight God's rather than men's
battles. Meanwhile, if anger at those higher up provokes disturbance of the peace, the country, or the Church, lesser men should
not support it, for they know that we all must obey God rather
than human beings.[47]

---

[47] *Quaeritur, fratres, quae virtus debeat aestimari et si ei in omnibus obsequi debeamus
vel forte in aliquo liceat refragari. Obedientia quidem virtus est consummata, et in Scripturis
a principio commendata, ut nulla virtus alia perfecti esse meriti videatur si non ejus praesidio
muniatur. Ipsa etiam charitas quae major esse caeteris affirmatur si contra hanc quidquam
diligere moliatur, non solum prudenti judicio reprobatur, sed nec vera esse charitas judicatur,
quia Deo adversari veraciter invenitur, si vel eum diligit aliter quam per obedientiam
definitur. Omnis igitur rationalis creatura obedientiae vinculis alligatur et a Creatore*

Without obedience society knows no peace. Differences among people and the divergences of their opinions bring about disruptions, disputes, and hatreds. A human being is neither a wild ass nor an owl alone on a rook. The salutary constraint of obedience binds even secular people.[48] But that visible obedience sufficing for social peace does not supply virtue and sanctity because it fails to settle charity in human hearts. True virtue requires the desire to obey for God's sake, completing obedience to him. Not all religious professions require the same obedience, but monks and regular canons—indeed all those who wish to reach perfection—must obey their superiors. This obedience is the object of a vow in the rules of Saint Benedict and Saint Augustine, whose goal is fraternal charity. Thus religious superiors are granted the power to apply the rule with prudent discretion and for the good of charity. The prelate himself is bound by the rule to command obedience in charity and for the good of the community, not according to his own whim.[49] His subjects must then obey, but without flattering their superiors; Philip, who suffered such flattery, recommends its studious avoidance. Because the reproaches of one in charge are to be feared, prelates ought not to direct criticism against those whom they fail to love; nor should they try to lavish praise on those who are likable or proximate, for this is to obey men rather than God.[50]

---

omnium creaturis omnibus imperatur nec est ulla tam praecelsae, tam praecellentis dignitatis quae non suscipiat majoris obedientiam potestatis. . . . Vult ergo Deus omnes sibi creaturas obedienter deservire et earum alteri invicem obedire, ut nullus vel ordo, vel professio, vel civitas vel natio abutatur propria voluntate, sed omnes redigantur sub alterius potestate. Reges quidem etsi non aliis compelluntur regibus subjacere, Deo tamen debent obedientiam exhibere, et vice Dei aurem debent Ecclesiam pontificibus inclinare et eorum monitis mores proprios ordinare, matrem Ecclesiam ab incursantibus defensare, hostes fidei armis obedientibus expugnare. Ipsis autem regibus consules, centuriones, tribuni, quinquagenarii subjugantur et eorum aliis alii jure ordinatissimo dominantur, ita ut qui cervice tumida dominantem sibi contempserit principatum, non solum apud homines, sed apud Deum etiam inobedientiae currunt in reatum. Debent itaque milites principibus, principes regibus obsequium militandi, ut cum pro pace, pro patria, pro Ecclesia necessitas ingruerit praeliandi, ad nutum majorum minores non differant praeparari, scientes se Dei praelia magis quam hominum praeliari. Philip, De institutione, PL 203, col. 841.

[48] *Obedientia nectura salutaris.*

[49] *Non suae lubrico voluntatis sed devotae impulsu charitatis.* Philip, *De institutione*, PL 203, col. 928.

[50] Philip, *De institutione*, PL 203, col. 930.

The truly obedient religious knows he belongs to Christ, who redeemed him by a great price. Such an individual has not left the servitude of sin only to make himself a slave of a man. He is instead the servant of Jesus Christ. In obeying his superiors, he obeys God. Thus he should never accede to commands contrary to God's law. Sadly, however, some religious care only about their own advantage or do not dare to reveal the truth to their superiors, the latter being the more common failing. To find another Peter who can willingly accept the observations of a Paul is always difficult, but to find another Paul who dares to chastise Peter is also hard.[51] Certainly if a prelate commands something beyond the limits of the rule, obedience is not required but heroic virtue will nonetheless make this leap even across a great gap, propelled by charity to respond to all it is asked. So spiritual masters should act with sweetness, seriousness, and justice. The Augustinian Rule thus requires that the superior make himself more loved than feared, so maintaining peace in his community. Before all else the prelate and his subjects must carefully preserve the bond of charity. Philip's teaching is summed up in these words: command by love and for love. The brief analysis of his text here, however, lends only an imperfect sense of the luxuriance of his images or the forest of symbols and allegories filling his treatise.

The Silence of Clerics

Philip's treatise *On the Silence of Clerics* is so titled only because the larger work of which it is a part treats the clerical life. In fact, this section might simply have been called On Silence, but in the broadest sense of the term.

> The question arises, brothers, to what extent silence is to be kept—with whom, when, and why, and when on the other hand it should be set aside, since in the scriptures silence is both commended many times and on many other occasions reproved. As

---

[51] *Quoniam vix alter Petrus invenitur qui Paulum arguentem sufferat patienter, vix est Paulo quisquam similis qui Petrum arguat confidenter.* Philip, *De institutione*, PL 203, cols. 931–32.

I see it, there is no easy response to this question, nor can anyone impart to his listeners a precise understanding of silence without first having made the choice himself to dwell in silence within the cloister, so attaining intimate and practical knowledge of it as through his own experience. Indeed, the best instructor is he who knows the truth of what he teaches not so much through intellectual understanding but through direct experience. Such a man does not babble about speculative knowledge alone, like a stream swollen by winter rains, but speaks from the heart, as if drawing the truth of his teaching from a living fountain. Just such a teacher, a wise man, inspires others to imitate him: To me God has given to speak from the heart.[52]

Having lamented the lack of such experience, the author continues:

Silence is highly recommended for regular religious and diligently maintained in monastic communities. No cloister in our times would be regarded as worthy of praise if it did not diligently keep regular silence. As Isaiah says, silence represents the cultivation of justice, because he who strives to maintain justice cannot find grace sufficient so to do if he is so rash as to speak whatever comes to his lips. In fact, when many men come together for a just and well-governed life, abiding in the same space, *the doors being closed for fear of the Jews* [John 20:19], they will have difficulty restraining their verbal contention if the law of silence does not limit their freedom to speak at will. *For, whereas there is among you envying and contention,* says the Apostle, *are you not carnal and walk according to man?* [1 Cor 3:3]. Therefore, in order to live a regular life, the members of a community must be bound by the rein of

---

[52] *Quaeritur, fratres, quod, quibus, quando, quare silentium sit tenendum et e regione commendabiliter seponendum cum plerumque in Scripturis inveniatur silentium approbari, plerumque vero in eisdem nihilominus reprobari. Huic autem quaestioni (ut videre videar) non potest facile respondere suosque auditores dignam satis ad intelligentiam promovere qui non prius elegerit sese intra claustra silentii cohibere et in eis conversatione congrua familiarem illius notitiam obtinere. Ille enim praecipue doctor congruus invenitur qui non tam sciendo quam sentiendo verum esse quod praedicat experitur, qui non velut torrens actus hiemalibus pluviis sola ex scientia verbosatur sed magis ex sententia velut ex fonte vivido veritatem proferre comprobatur. Qualem se esse doctorem ille sapiens attendebat et ut ad imitationem sui provocaret caeteros aiebat: Mihi autem dedit Deus dicere ex sententia.* Philip, *De institutione,* PL 203, cols. 943–45.

silence, so that by the grace of religious life men may converse intimately with God in the silent depths of their hearts rather than chatter with other men. In such spiritual conversation they may so deserve to become like gods rather than men. But the silence of the mouth alone does not merit this grace. The tongue may be silent without the inner man's finding rest. Indeed, exterior quiet often belies great rage within.[53]

Sometimes, indeed, breaking silence drains an infection, so the silence of the lips is not always the best path. Thus the scriptures and lived experience both suggest another, more profound silence.

Philip thus presents the two central justifications for monastic silence: fraternal charity and recollection leading to prayer. Next, he identifies several aspects of silence, each of which he treats at length: silence with respect to both words and signals, silence that promotes good acts, and silence that obstructs wicked acts.[54] Philip's title *On the Silence of Clerics* thus embraces, in addressing such general principles, a treatise on the spiritual life broadly speaking. He defines silence with respect to words by recounting its origins and both its advantages and dangers. Sometimes silence is injurious to the interests of a neighbor, so that the wise man must be able to discern when it is better to be silent and when to speak. The prophets spoke, the Word of God came to earth to speak and the

---

[53] *Silentium quidem a religiosis viris non mediocriter commendatur, in claustris religiosis diligentius conservatur, nullumque claustrum dignum satis laude nostris jam temporalibus perhibetur, in quo diligenti custodia regulare silentium non tenetur. Est enim, ut Isaias dicit, justitiae cultus silentium quia qui justitiae exhibere curat obsequium non potest apud eam sufficientem gratiam invenire, si quidquid in os venerit praesumit effutire. Et revera cum plurimi ad vivendum juste et regulariter congregantur et in eodem conclavi propter metum Judaeorum clausis foribus demorantur non facile cohibent linguas mobiles ne rixentur, si non a vaga licentia loquendi indicta lege silentii cohibentur. Cum enim sit inter vos zelus et contentio, ait Apostolus, nonne carnales estis et secundum hominem ambulatis? Necessario igitur ad vivendum regulariter congregati loro silentii colligantur, ut cum religionis gratia homines non hominibus fabulantur, in secreto cordis sui Deo familiaribus colloquantur, ejusque spiritali colloquio non homines sed dii effici mereantur. Veruntamen ad promerendum hujus muneris gratiam non satis oris silentium invalescit, nec quoties tacet lingua totiesque interior animus conquiescit, imo plerumque quo tenacius illa exterius obmutescit, eo iracundius ille interius inardescit.* Philip, *De institutione*, PL 203, col. 945.

[54] *Est silentium a locutione. Est silentium a bonis. Est silentium a malis.* Philip, *De intitutione*, PL 203, col. 946.

apostles received from the Holy Spirit the gift of tongues in order to proclaim the Gospel. The apostles then went out barefoot to preach, so signifying that their teaching was not obscured by any fear or weakness. Following their example, preachers should raise their voices like the clarion of battle. Even if what must be said is learned from silence, that silence must be united to speech in order to bear fruit. Philip recounts at length the fable of the marriage of Mercury and Philology, noting that Philology is pure verbiage without Mercury, while Mercury without Philology cannot share knowledge, but the marriage of the two brings joy to the Muses and enables all intellectual life.[55]

After the silence of the words then comes the silence of the signs. These have great importance, for Philip goes on to explain at length God's breath calling the flies of Africa against Israel, the gentle wind carrying off Elijah to Mount Horeb, and the trumpet that brought down the walls of Jericho. He then addresses his own times, telling about clocks giving rhythm to the Christian life. Finally he speaks about the written word, the sign purely speaking. Philip searches for the origin of script among the ancients, tracing it back to Enoch. Again, he notes, whether writing or abstaining from writing is better requires judgment. So his long discussion of speech recurs to the theme of silence.[56]

Next Philip takes up that variety of silence he identifies as silence from retribution, that is the failure to punish wrongdoing or the event of postponing the execution of justice. God sometimes does not punish evil immediately either in order to correct it the more sternly later or to allow the sinner time to repent. Such is Christ's silence during his passion and such also is the silence of religious persons persecuted by the world or misunderstood by their superiors in the monastery. Prudence can also require good to be returned for evil. Augustus was prudent in this fashion in regard to Cinna; Philip intriguingly transposes Tacitus' style into metrical prose as Corneille later would into Alexandrian verse: "Take a seat,

---

[55] As Philip notes, this fable is told by Martianus Capella in *De nuptiis Philologiae et Mercurii*. Philip, *De institutione*, PL 203, cols. 978–80.

[56] Philip, *De institutione*, PL 203, cols. 1012–27.

Cinna, sit, and most importantly/ Observe exactly the law I impose upon thee." Philip writes:

> The emperor ordered that a chair be placed nearby and offered
>   it to Cinna.
> The latter, unwitting of Augustus' plan, followed his command.
> The others retired and Augustus spoke: "Cinna, keep quiet a
>   while,
> And listen to whatever I may say in silence."[57]

Unfortunately some men, even some prelates, return evil for good, blindly doing their own will and depriving their flocks of both just treatment and regular discipline. Christ himself was treated thus by the high priests when, unable to accuse him of true crimes, they heaped him with calumnies. Philip here betrays a bitterness revealing that he speaks from experience.

The author then goes on to explore several more varieties of silence. He speaks of silence reserving good deeds.[58] Philip notes that a silence abstaining from positive action can be a matter of discretion, as for instance when pearls should not be cast before swine or when Jesus did not respond to Herod. Such abstention can become culpable weakness, however, as in the silence of Eli when he did not reprove his sons, or when prelates and pastors do not dare to preach an offensive truth. Silence can also take on the form of a chastisement for evil inclinations, as when Christ imposed silence on the Herodians, Pharisees, and Sadducees in the temple or when the angel Gabriel closed the mouth of the priest Zachary.

Finally, Philip discusses the silence that abstains from evil.[59] He distinguishes two types of evil: sin and affliction. Regarding sin, he offers a lengthy discourse on error, on its conception in the soul, and on its exterior effect, by means of an allegory on Job. Then Philip discusses affliction, noting that God sometimes seems to keep silence, leaving the soul in sadness in order to test it. But this

---

[57] *Cui cum praesentato poni juxta se cathedram praecepisset.*
Et ille ad ejus imperium adhuc consilii nescius se dedisset.
Remotis omnibus: Volo, inquit, Cinna, paululum te tacere.
Et quidquid dixero cum silentio sustinere. Philip, *De institutione*, PL 203, col. 1067.
[58] Philip, *De institutione*, PL 203, col. 1089.
[59] Philip, *De institutione*, PL 203, col. 1149.

silence is short-lived. The more bitter it seems, the sweeter its remission. Philip's treatment of these topics is indeed lengthy, but for those fond of the mystical level of interpretation and of reading history long past, it is delightful. The abbot's work thus reminds the reader that, for him, the life of a cleric was one of reading and writing, not only of liturgical duties. These two activities were both pleasurable to him and brought many spiritual and literary joys to his brothers in religious life.

Philip's multipart treatise *De institutione clericorum* is certainly the first major scholarly effort to establish a spirituality grounded in clerical and priestly status. The Rule of Aachen had been only a collection of texts without any logical interconnection, but Philip's treatise forms an organic whole replete with ideas and images. The author pauses on every topic that interests him, but his work is nonetheless solid and coherent as a whole. Philip's expression of canonical spirituality could not shape Christian people generally, as did the models of Saint Francis of Assisi, Saint Dominic, or Saint Ignatius of Loyola, because it was too priestly, but eventually it would be rediscovered as a leaven of renewal for Catholic clergy. Tronson's *Forma cleri*, on the formation of the clergy, one of the outstanding monuments of Sulpician spirituality, enshrines Philip of Bonne Espérance's original ideas.

Commentary on the Canticle of Canticles

The abbot of Bonne Espérance composed another great work. This latter text is dedicated to the Blessed Virgin and titled *Mystical Commentary on the Canticle of Canticles*.[60] Here the wedding song of the Canticle of Canticles is interpreted allegorically, first as the covenant between God and his people Israel and then as the union between Christ and his Church, according to the sacred figure of Christian marriage. Philip also understands the canticle as representing the union between Christ and individual Christian souls as microcosms of the Church to which they pertain. Finally, he interprets this text as the moral union between Jesus and Mary. Many exegetes have understood the Canticle in this last sense after the model of the

---

[60] Philip, *Commentaria in cantica canticorum*, PL 203, cols. 181–490.

liturgy in its frequent use of passages from the Canticle for feasts of the Blessed Virgin: so Rupert of Deutz; William Petit, abbot of Bec; Alexander Neckam, abbot of the Augustinian canons of Ciren-cester; Honorius of Autun; Cardinal Nicholas Hailgrin; Alain of Lille; Placidius; Nigidius; the Carthusian Jean Pic. Like them Philip applied to the Blessed Virgin everything said of the bride in the Canticle:

> The virgin whom Solomon sees, whom the Son of God will thus love and choose for this ministry, is noble of race and eminent in her life—beautiful among the daughters of men, knowledgable in letters, humble in spirit, glorious in merits. I name her: her name is Mary.[61]

This spiritual epithalamium between Christ and the Virgin is of great interest. Its readers are invited to this divine wedding as friends and relations, so we are filled with joy.

Philip's commentary on the Canticle is what we would today call a book of meditations. He examines each word of the text, somewhat in the manner in which Saint Ignatius conceives the third way of prayer in his *Exercises*. For Philip, the Canticle of Canticles is a poem of intimacy between Jesus and Mary. Here the Blessed Virgin manifests herself as the great teacher of prayer and true guide to the contemplative life. The author explains his Marian doctrine fully, at great length. To reorder and synthesize his notions will nonetheless be useful here and is best achieved by presenting in succession Philip's views on the privileges of Mary, then on her roles as Christ's bride and mother at once of the apostles, of Chris-tians, and of sinners.

The Privileges of Mary

Philip's teaching on the privileges of Mary may disappoint the modern reader. His views on the Immaculate Conception and the sanctification of the Blessed Virgin correspond only incompletely

---

[61] *Virgo autem quam videt Salomon sic a Filio Dei diligendam, et ad hoc ministerium . . . eligendam, illa est genere nobilis, insignis moribus, prae filiabus hominum speciosa, litteris sapiens, humilis spiritu, meritis gloriosa, illa, ut tandem eam nominem, Maria est.* Philip, *Commentaria*, PL 203, col. 188.

to the Church's authentic tradition. Although Philip opposed Saint Bernard on other matters, he unfortunately imitates him closely here. His specific statements are entirely clear: "The Blessed Virgin, like all others, was by nature a child capable of anger . . . because according to human nature she was conceived in sin."[62] Meanwhile, Philip repeats constantly that Christ alone was born free of original sin; like a number of other Augustinians, the abbot-author confuses original sin with the presence of concupiscence in the act of conception. Only the Virgin Mary was, in her virgnal conception, unbound by the law of concupiscence. Christ was not therefore alone in his freedom from original sin. For Philip, Mary is honored because she overcame the original stain by actively conceiving Christ with no blemish to herself and with no experience of sensuality. For that reason she is fearsome to the devil, who uncomprehendingly then flees her.[63] Although Philip then did not attribute to Mary the privilege of the Immaculate Conception, he indeed recognized that she was free of actual sins: "Who is she," he says that the angels ask, "who, still living in a mortal body subject to corporeal needs, completed her life unstained, exposed though she was along the way to vices?"[64] In concert with the opinion of several twelfth-century theologians, Saint Anselm among others, Philip attributes the Virgin's complete sanctificiation and confirmation in grace to the mystery of the Annunciation, at the moment of the Incarnation of the Word. For him, the Holy Spirit purifies her in his shadow:

> When the angel hailed her, he delivered to her the message entrusted to him. The Holy Spirit at that moment granted her its power, by which the wicked law no longer prevailed in her and no stain of sin, new or ancient, remained in her.[65]

---

[62] *Virgo autem ut caeteri naturaliter filia fuit irae. . . . Quae quoniam in peccatis naturaliter est concepta.* Philip, *Commentaria*, PL 203, col. 459.

[63] Philip, *Commentaria*, PL 203, col. 441.

[64] *Quae est ista. . . . Quae vivens in corpore mortis necessitatibus obvoluto vitam vitiis obnoxiam cursu peragit impolluto?* Philip, *Commentaria*, PL 203, col. 355.

[65] *Ex quo injunctum sibi verbum Angelus Virgini nuntiat et salutem, sanctusque supervenit et obumbrans ei Spiritus dat virtutem in ea non obtinet suum privilegium lex iniqua, non peccati permanet recens attaminatio vel antiqua.* Philip, *Commentaria*, PL 203, col. 379.

Regarding the other privileges of Mary, Philip's teaching is completely traditional. Not only will the Mother of God always remain a virgin but she was the first person to have made a vow of chastity. She so wished to serve God that she vowed to remain a virgin even though she found this precept neither in sacred scriptures nor in any precedent. Thus the honor of virginity takes it beginning from her. Before Mary no one gloried in virginity and it enjoyed no particular renown. Philip then says that the Virgin's bodily Assumption is plausible. The Mother is with the Son not only in spirit—about which there is no doubt—but that she is with him also in body is in no way unbelievable. The abbot of Bonne Espérance here cites the authority of a text he believed to be Augustine's.[66]

Philip then assigns the Virgin Mary a place immediately beneath Christ, superior even to the angels: "The Virgin knows that all she has of light, all the grace and honor she has received, is from Christ, whose excellence is still greater. He alone surpasses her, while she herself excels beyond the rank of the other saints."[67] "Who then is she who appears to have no need of our support, who is greater than even the angels not by nature, but by grace?"[68] Philip constantly returns to the impossibility of adequately praising Mary. Even the angels cannot achieve this. Still, in this author's characteristic view, the gifts of grace are unquestionably supported in Mary by the gifts of her excellently disposed nature.

> Beauty, nobility and knowledge blossomed in the Virgin with an excellence befitting her rank but beyond what was necessary for her salvation. . . .[69] Therefore, fittingly, the most beautiful among the children of men had a bride whose beauty came of a singular grace, her appearance unmarred by any unsightliness

---

[66] Philip, *Commentaria*, PL 203, col. 488.

[67] *Virgo quidquid lucis obtinet, quidquid gratiae vel honoris a Christo novit esse qui est excellentiae potioris, quo solo minor ipsa sanctis caeteris principatur.* Philip, *Commentaria*, PL 203, col. 453.

[68] *Quae est ista . . . ut nostro etiam videatur jam patrocinio non egere imo ut . . . angelis non natura sed gratia praeeminere?* Philip, *Commentaria*, PL 203, col. 355.

[69] *Forma, genus, scientia quae in Virgine quadam excellentia floruerunt honestati convenientia, saluti vero necessaria non fuerunt.* Philip, *Commentaria*, PL 203, col. 306.

incompatible with her nobility, rather shaped as beloved by that
Love who loves her.[70]

That Love shaped the Virgin is the strongest argument for the
Immaculate Conception but Philip did not appreciate its consequences. All of this text's discussion conforms to the views of other
twelfth-century theologians. In his edition of Philip's works,
Nicholas Chamart, abbot of Bonne-Espérance, cited the authorities
with whom Philip supported his unfortunate assertions. Those
authorities were many, so might indeed have misled elements in
the Catholic tradition.

The Role of the Virgin

Philip's characterization of the intimacy between Jesus and Mary—
the Blessed Virgin's role as bride, from which he drew his notion
of her spritual motherhood—is then important to his spirituality.
The abbot of Bonne Espérance's meditation on the Canticle is built
centrally on his view that Mary is here the bride of Jesus. Her womb
is the marriage bed on which the Word is wedded to human nature.
In marrying Mary, Christ befriends all her brothers; this divine
wedding becomes a great feast. "How solemn she appeared before
her Bridegroom, how festive!"[71] Mary's love for her Savior is like
the turtledove's; she mates only once even if widowed.[72] The Blessed
Virgin is thus joyful only in the presence of the Lord. In his absence
she remains faithful to him unto death. John was given to her as a
son, not a spouse. The Virgin's love surpasses that of the angels,
who recognize that the Virgin loves the Bridegroom more than they
but nonetheless experience no jealousy.[73]

---

[70] *Decet . . . ut speciosus forma prae filiis hominum habeat sibi talem quae singulari gratia pulchritudinem praeferat specialem, cujus faciem turpitudo indigna et degenerans non obscuret, sed dilectam dilectio ei a quo diligitur configuret.* Philip, *Commentaria*, PL 203, col. 274.

[71] *Quam solemnis! . . . Quam festiva.* Philip, *Commentaria*, PL 203, col. 393.

[72] Philip, *Commentaria*, PL 203, col. 257.

[73] *Vident angeli nec invident Sponsum nunc a Virgine plus amari.* Philip, *Commentaria*, PL 203, col. 346.

Mary's love for Jesus presupposes her profound knowledge of him. "He could not have been loved if he had not been known and he could not have been known if he were not loved."[74] Mary's knowledge of Jesus exceeds even that of the evangelist:

> In the bosom of the Bridegroom are contained treasures of wisdom and knowledge entirely hidden even from the prudent and wise men of this world. The Bridegroom, who hides these secrets from so many men who consider themseves great—and for such a long time—rises from the nuptial bed and with his accustomed generosity now reveals them to his little ones. During ancient times these incomparable treasures lay hidden in him, but when he took on the flesh of the Virgin his own breasts swelled wonderfully on his bosom, giving forth not dryness but streams and rivers pouring abundantly into those worthy to approach them. Thus the Virgin does not bid farewell to her Bridegroom or part from him, rather reclines on his bosom in order to effect her own preferment. She suckles from him with a capacity as great as the desire of her pure and fervent soul. She drinks, satisfying her thirst in the sweet abundance of his breasts and milk. There she finds that knowledge and wisdom hidden from the many by God's secret plan. Her profound desire thirsts for it and she perceives that all is clearly revealed to her. Now she need consult neither the angel nor the prophets who have gone before, but she alone reclines on Christ alone, drawing to herself the depths of that wisdom once hidden, as Job wrote.[75]
>
> I am greatly deceived if the beloved disciple of the Bridegroom did not know that wisdom and knowledge flowed from Christ's bosom when, at the Last Supper, that apostle took pleasure less in wine and material nourishment than in resting on the bosom of Jesus, between his breasts, in sweet release. There the disciple saw the Word remaining deep within the bosom of the Father; at the same time he saw the Word made flesh in the virginal marriage bed of the bride-mother; he saw the treasures of wisdom and knowledge illuminated with striking clarity for him but veiled and obscured for the prudent and wise of this world. . . . None

[74] *Nec . . . potest diligi si non fuerit intellectus nec videtur intelligi si non fuerit et dilectus.* Philip, *Commentaria,* PL 203, col. 444.

[75] Compare Job 28.

before, however, and none more perfect has come close to the Bridegroom than she who was found worthy to prepare for him a marriage bed in her womb and who, reclining on his bosom, drew forth and tasted that sweet knowledge and wisdom better than the thought, teaching, or error of the philosophers.[76]

The Virgin Mary's knowledge and love of Christ was for her a source of great sorrows, according to Philip. Ahead of his time, when only devotion to the joys of Mary was fully developed, he thus evinced a lively appreciation of her sorrows. He emphasizes this perspective when he comes to the Canticle's image of pomegranates and when he explains the words: "Arise, O north wind, and come O south wind." "Whatever hardship he suffered at his Father's behest was reflected in commensurate suffering in his Mother's heart. . . ."[77]

---

[76] *In pectore Sponsi thesauri sapientiae et scientiae reconduntur, qui prudentibus et sapientibus hujus saeculi penitus absconduntur; et qui secreta eorum tam multis grandiusculis tempore tanto celat procedens Sponsus a thalamo, bonitate quae sua est parvulis jam revelat. Siquidem auctis retro saeculis in ipso thesauri incomparabiles latuerunt, sed assumpta carne virginis, velut de pectore papillae turgentes mirabiliter eruperunt quae non arentes guttas sed rivos et flumina profuderunt et sese pleno cornu quibuscumque digne accedentibus infuderunt. Quapropter et virgo tamquam valefaciens non declinat sed in ejus pectore proficiendi gratia se reclinat et adhibens eo capacius, quo avidius hauritorium purae mentis, potatur, satiatur ubertate grata uberum et fluentis. Ibi scientiam, ibi sapientiam profundo consilio pluribus occultatam alto desiderio sitit et sentit sibi manifestius revelatam; et jam, sicut angelo sic prioribus prophetis inconsultis, incumbens sola soli, trahit juxta Job et attrahit sibi sapientiam de occultis. Fallor si non et ille Sponsi discipulus quem dilexit de ipsius pectore manare sapientiam et scientiam intellexit cum in Coena positus non tam vino et epulis materialibus acquievit quam supra pectus Jesu inter ipsa ubera grato accubitu requievit. Ibi Verbum carnem factum in virginali thalamo Sponsae matris; vidit thesauros sapientiae et scientiae claritate sibi conspicua luminosos, mundi prudentibus et sapientibus superfusos quodam velamine tenebrosos. . . . Ad quem nemo prius, nemo perfectius inventus est properare, quam illa quae meruit venienti suum uteri thalamum praeparare, quae recumbens, in ejus pectore hausit et sensit ejus scientiam et sapientiam gratiorem sensu, sententia, errore philosophico meliorem.* Philip, *Commentaria*, PL 203, cols. 200–201.

[77] *Quidquid ille mali patitur jussu Patris naturalis fundae circuitu redundat miserabiliter in cor Matris.* Philip, *Commentaria*, PL 203, col. 225. Thus appropriately, Philip—here also very modern—speaks of the heart of the Virgin Mary. Compare Philip, *Commentaria*, col. 273: *Lectulus Virginis est secretum cordis ejus.* The Virgin's marriage bed is the secret of her heart. Col. 356: *Omnibus salutari congruentibus medicinae congestis et attritis in corde Virginis tamquam in mortariolo disciplinae.* ("All these things are ground together as a salutary medicine in the heart of the Virgin, as in a mortar

Let not your consideration of my troubles confuse you as if you were children, as if it were not fitting that my experience be filled with bitter trials."[78]

Notably, then, Philip comes to the idea of the Blessed Virgin's spiritual motherhood from Jesus' and Mary's union of mind and heart—indeed miraculously, had not this teaching already been embraced by Christians long before, as was indeed the case, for the notion of Mary's spiritual motherhood is built on long tradition. Origen clearly presented it, but in the twelfth century this notion had fallen into obscurity. Saint Bernard's writings offer no evidence for Mary's identification as mother of men or mother of Christians. Nor does Adam Scot present this notion. Saints have livelier intuitions than the doctors, however, and among the poems of the blessed Herman Joseph we find these two verses: "Rejoice, thee who call to thine own, / Those whom thou lovest as their devoted mother."[79] Herman Joseph's parallel usage is exceptional but not fortuitous because for Augustinians—and all the twelfth-century theologians are Augustinians—the mother of our souls is that grace of whom the Church sings at the blessing of fonts: "As a mother, may grace bear all men towards one infancy."[80] Thus Adam Scot, in one of his most beautiful sermons, presents the Blessed Virgin as the allegory of divine grace. Conforming with this trend, then, Philip does not title her the mother of men, as would not conform to Augustinian terminology, but this is clearly his notion:[81] "[Christ]

---

of discipline.") Col. 369: *Labia Virginis clausa scientiam legis servant et quae servanda noverant in cordis secretorio coacervant.* ("The sealed lips of the Virgin preserve her knowledge of the law, holding in the hidden depths of her heart what they know must be preserved.")

[78] *Ne ad meas molestias vestra consideratio pueriliter obstupescat, tamquam non sit conveniens ut mea conversatio tribulationibus amarescat.* Philip, *Commentaria,* PL 203, col. 230.

[79] *Gaude quae ad tuos clamas / Quos ut pia Mater amas.*

[80] *Omnes in unuam pariat gratia mater infantiam.*

[81] Philip himself reserves the title, "mother of our souls," for grace. In explaining the text, *Una est matri suae,* he writes: *Una est [Maria] igitur matri suae, quia mater gratia nec primam visa est habere similem nec secundam et quae se pari forma virginem exhiberet et fecundam.* ("[Mary] therefore is the only child of her mother, because mothering grace seems not to have another like her who might similarly show herself a fruitful virgin.") Philip then explains that grace, like the Virgin Mary, is at

becomes the Bridegroom by joining the Virgin to himself in a marriage bond . . . begetting sons in her and through her by his spiritual power, so both he and she may rejoice in the fruit and offspring of their sons."[82]

Nevertheless, the role of the Blessed Virgin is not entirely passive. The prelate of Bonne Espérance carefully explains that everything leading the world to its salvation depended on the Virgin Mary: the flesh of Christ, his sorrowful passion, the wood of the cross, the washing away of our sins, the victory over darkness, our constancy in virtue, and our confidence in future rewards.[83] To this role, however, so fully acknowledged, corresponds a properly motherly activity ceaselessly exercised by the Blessed Virgin from her place in heaven.

> When in another childbearing I lead you out of the darkness of ignorance and by my care and labor bring you forth to the light of truth and knowledge, and when with my affectionate care I shape you with perfect rules for living, do I not as a mother conform you to my heart, rather to my life? And the Bridegroom even says to one of you: Behold your mother.[84]

Mary fulfills this maternal role especially toward the apostles, as Philip understandably stresses, because in an apostolic order like the Premonstratensians the influence of the Virgin on the apostles

---

once mother and virgin, adding: *[Gratia] virginem cognitione provida praelegit, ipsa eam affectu materno suscepit misericorditer et collegit.* ("In foreknowledge grace chose the Virgin, and she mercifully took it up and gathered it in maternal affection.") Philip, *Commentaria*, PL 203, cols. 452–53.

[82] *Sponsus fiat Virginem sibi jungens foedere conjugali . . . in ea vel per eam generans spirituales filios efficacia spiritali ut tam ille quam illa gaudeat fructu et sobole filiali.* Philip, *Commentaria*, PL 203, col. 192.

[83] *Dependet autem in ea Christi caro, carnis passio, lignum crucis, culparum abolitio, noctis fuga . . . virtutum constantia, fiducia praemiorum.* Philip, *Commentaria*, PL 203, col. 468.

[84] *Quae cum pariendi more de tenebris ignorantiae vos educo, cum studio et labore ad lumen veritatis et scientiae vos perduco, cum perfectioribus vivendi regulis affectuosa sollicitudine vos informo, quid nisi matris vice meis visceribus vel magis moribus vos conformo. Et quidem uni ex vobis Sponsus dicit: Ecce mater tua.* Philip, *Commentaria*, PL 203, col. 230.

is the object of meditation and devotion, especially because Mary lived on after the Lord's Ascension for the apostles' sake.

> Her example and her teaching stood before them, for through her the order of their life flourished in their moral discipline. . . .[85] When the care of John was entrusted to the Virgin Mother, her concern for the others was undiminished; rather mysteriously the care shown to one was necessary to all. Nor did John alone care for and venerate Mary, nor the Virgin embrace him alone in the affection of her own devoted attention. Instead, loving all the apostles, she strove to make herself useful to all, giving them such excellent teaching as all could use. . . .[86] None attended to that same Virgin more closely or received through her mediation a more complete knowledge of her Bridegroom than did the apostles, who lived with her both before and after Christ's passion, often hearing from her about the mystery of the Incarnation of the Word.[87]

This affectionate care on the Virgin's part extends to the apostles' successors as well. "By the example and merit of the Blessed Virgin, as the apostles and their successors believe, they have found grace."[88] Mary's loving care extends even further, to all Christians, because of her special place in the mystical body of Christ as its neck, below its Head and above its limbs:

> The Virgin is below Christ, the Head, but she is also surely above the rest of the body, so holding a place halfway between body

[85] *Exemplum Virginis profuit et doctrina nam per eam inter illos ordo vitae morum viguit disciplina.* Philip, *Commentaria,* PL 203, col. 296.

[86] *Cum . . . Joannis cura matri Virgini commendatur, aliorum sollicitudo ab ea non relegatur, sed quod certi causa mysterii uni specialius assignatur, omnibus generaliter esse necessarium designatur. Nec enim solus Joannes Mariam suscipit, susceptam veneratur, nec solum Joannem Virgo affectu devotae sollicitudinis amplexatur; sed omnes diligens studet utilem se praebere, doctrinam praecipuam, imitabilem omnibus exhibere.* Philip, *Commentaria,* PL 203, col. 253.

[87] *Nulli quippe eamdem Virginem familiarius sunt secuti vel ea mediante Sponsi notitiam plenius assecuti quam Apostoli qui ante et post Christi passionem cum ea diutius conversati ab ipsa frequentius audierunt Verbi mysterium incarnati.* Philip, *Commentaria,* PL 203, cols. 213–14.

[88] *Exemplo quidem et merito Virginis. . . . Apostoli et eorum successores credunt se gratiam accepisse.* Philip, *Commentaria,* PL 203, col. 215. Here evidently the successors of the apostles are not bishops but those clerics who lead the apostolic life.

and Head, because the sons of the Bridegroom cannot belong to him without the mediation of the mother. If the Bride is present to us, we may be united with him, but if she is absent, the limbs cannot be united to him as Head. Since we are far below, the Son of God reaches down to us through her; nor can our weakness ascend to him except through her. She is first in rank, most blessed, the recipient of that outstanding role in which the many and diverse have been made one; through her two walls are united in one faith and one baptism so that they come together before Christ and are united in his person. Finally, as intermediary she commends us to her Spouse and Son; she invites us to pray to him and admonishes him to listen to us. At once the mother and handmaid of her Spouse, ruler of us all she brings together those who have gone astray; as a powerful and effective mediatrix she keeps together those who are already united. She sees that we are thirsty but that there is no more wine at the wedding banquet. She knows that a banquet without wine is not pleasing and that, wretched as we are, we will die of thirst, so she hastens with solicitude to prevent this, to bring before her Son this matter of the lack of wine. Jesus' mother, the Gospel relates, thus says to him, "They have no wine."[89] Well knowing that the humble intervention of her pious prayer cannot be in vain, rather for our profit as for all the wedding guests', she says to the servants: "Whatsoever he shall say to you, then do." They hear and, obeying the command of the Virgin, fill the jars with water and and pure wine replaces it. Miraculously our insipidity is turned to savor, our sluggishness to fire, our negligence to love. The Virgin is a good neck, a good intervention, a good mediatrix, connecting to the Head those whom Eve in her wickedness separated. She invites her Son to generosity and us to obedience, so we may offer him our homage and he may confer on us his blessing.[90]

---

[89] Compare John 2:3-5.

[90] *Ipsa est quae invenitur Christo capiti sic subesse ut non sit dubium reliquo eam corpori superesse; et ipsa inter caput et corpus videtur locum medium obtinere, nec ad Sponsum filii Sponsi possunt nisi Matre media pertinere. Praesente ipsa nobis Sponsa, bonum est adhaerere, absente vero non possunt membra capiti cohaerere; nobis longe infra positis per ipsam Dei Filius condescendit, ad quem nisi per ipsam nostra infirmitas non ascendit. Ipsa prior, ipsa felicior accipit grande munus per quod multi et diversi facti sunt unus; per quod duo parietes una fide, uno baptismate sunt uniti et ad Christum concurrentes ei personaliter couniti. Ipsa denique Sponso et filio, interventu medio, nos commendat, invitat nos ad precandum, illum submonet ut attendat. Sponsi mater et ancilla, nostra omnium imperatrix, disjunctos jungit, junctos retinet potens et efficax mediatrix. Videns quippe nos aridos vinum*

In the exercise of this mediation Mary has her preferences: first those defeated in their struggle with sin, for whom she intercedes in order to reconcile them to her Son; then those who are tempted and, lacking precaution or strength, are ready to give up, to whom she extends a triumphal banner; finally the wretched, whose distress Philip knew directly:

> I have experienced that of which I write here. Faced with divine judgment, the sons of my mother have fought against me. While others spared me, my own flesh and blood wounded me. My sadness over this would have caused me to perish had not the Virgin seen fit to reach out her hand to help me. She truly brought me help.[91]

A mother is the first teacher of her child. Philip of Bonne Espérance constantly returns to this observation. Thus the Virgin Mary is our teacher in prayer and contemplation.

Mary herself had been a contemplative for her entire life. Her vision was not obscured by original ignorance. Even before the angel came to her, the Lord was with her. Moreover, the angel did not find her in some public place or in the streets, among feasting or dancing. Still more, according to our author, the angel did not find her occupied with spindle or needle, carding wool or linen— the handiwork of a slave—nor in weaving. Rather she was devoted

---

in nuptiis non habere, et sciens sine vino non digne satis nuptias complacere, siti miseros perituros festinat sollicita praevenire et pro defectu vini fiducialiter Filium convenire. Dicit, inquit, Mater Jesu ad eum: Vinum non habent. Et attendens non cassari piae precis humilem interventum, sed venire nobis, imo cunctis discumbentibus ad proventum, dicit ministris: Quodcumque dixerit vobis facite. Illis autem juxta verbum Virginis aurem inclinantibus ad mandatum implentur hydriae et vinum redditur defaecatum: re digna miraculi nostra insipientia vertitur in saporem, in ignem frigus torpidum, contemptus negligentior in amorem. Collum bonum, bona interventio, bona denique mediatrix quae jungit quos disjunxerat Eva noxia separatrix; quae Filium ad largitatem, ad obedientiam nos invitat, agitque ut et nos deferre obsequium et ille conferre beneficium non omittat. Philip, *Commentaria*, PL 203, col. 260.

[91] *Expertus sum quod aio. Cum divino perurgente judicio filii matris meae contra me pugnaverunt, cum caeteris parcentibus ii quos mea credebam viscera me laeserunt . . . mea ipsius maestitia cogeret deperire, si non Virgo dignaretur extenta manu citius subvenire. Astitit illa mihi.* Philip, *Commentaria*, PL 203, col. 461.

completely to leisure, or strictly speaking to spiritual work, for she was occupied with the scriptures in order to understand them. Mary thus remained embodied but removed from the things of the body. Forgetful of the cares of the world, her serene intellect was absorbed in contemplation, carried into a peaceful rapture in which she possessed a joy oblivious of temporal things but offering her rest in that which she desired before all else.[92] Yet, lofty as her contemplation was, she did not see the divine essence while on earth. Sin did not hold her back, rather only the barrier of embodiment.[93] The Blessed Virgin then does not guard her contemplation jealously, rather allows her children to taste it so that their hearts may rejoice as if steeped in wine, for she realizes that those who have received this gift cannot be without joy.[94]

The prelate of Bonne Espérance often concludes his instructions by recalling the fruits of devotion to the Blessed Virgin.

> Who among you, whenever you hear her name, does not rejoice greatly, applauding in devoted homage and hoping to find her Son pleased and gracious that he has been able to embrace the mother in appropriate reverence?[95] How many monasteries today all throughout the world rejoice in having been strengthened by her patronage, their churches protected by her gentle care?[96]

---

[92] Philip, *Commentaria*, PL 203, col. 191.

[93] *Volebat quidem volens videre facie ad faciem quem amabat, sed a suo eam desiderio lex illa scripta stylo ferreo retardabat. Non videbit me homo . . . et vivet.* ("She greatly desired to see face to face him whom she loved, but the written law held her back from her desire with an iron pen. No one shall see me . . . and live.") Philip, *Commentaria*, PL 203, col. 311.

[94] *Cui gustum suum non invida Virgo notificat, cor illius tamquam vino potum laetificat.* Philip, *Commentaria*, PL 203, col. 468. To these sweet nothings is added a doctrinal illumination: *Nescientibus Virginem Scripturae facies est obscura.* ("For those who do not know the Virgin the surface of Scripture is obscure.") Philip, *Commentaria*, PL 203, col. 375.

[95] *Quis vestrum cum ejus etiam nomen audit devotione non aggaudet, devoto obsequio non applaudit, sperans ejus Filium placabilem et propitium invenire si matrem potuerit digna reverentia praevenire?* Philip, *Commentaria*, PL 203, col. 235.

[96] *Quanti hodie per universum orbem conventus gaudent hujus Virginis patrocinio muniri et eorum ecclesias grata ejus sollicitudine custodiri.* Philip, *Commentaria*, PL 203, col. 235.

Addressing his own confreres at Our Lady of Bonne Espérance, Philip writes: "Leaving aside all the others, my brothers, is this community of yours not gathered in this Virgin's honor, and this place and this church dedicated in her name?"[97]

Philip's Marian doctrine is finally incomplete, even erroneous in regard to the holy Virgin's sanctification, because it partakes in the views of his own time, when even pious and learned persons knew incompletely of the doctrines of redemption and original sin. Yet the few passages in his text we cannot now accept as orthodox need not lead us to set aside his work as a whole. Philip's thought on the Virgin Mary is lofty and sweet. His views are, further, surprisingly modern in their concern with the Blessed Virgin's role in the salvation of souls. They are, most importantly, representative of the Marian devotion of our Fathers, because the devotion of still earlier times had focused principally on Virgin as august queen of heaven and earth, on her as "All Holy," as she is called in the East, or as the woman at prayer, her arms raised to the skies, who ceaselessly intercedes for the world. Henceforth Mary would still be considered a queen but also loved as a sister, a mother, and as "Mother of Mercy," according to the words of the *Salve Regina*. The work of Philip thus wonderfully foreshadows the evolution of Christian devotion.

This long discussion of his works then demonstrates the importance of Philip of Bonne Espérance. His prolixity makes attention to him a large task, however, and his fascination with shades of meaning and metrical ornament requires taxing attention. Still, the depth of his reading, the solidity of his conclusions, and the expressive richness of his imagery compensate these efforts sweetly. Distant though he may appear and despite general modern neglect of his contribution, Philip deserves to be read today.

---

[97] *Ut . . . de aliis taceam, fratres, numquid non iste conventus vester in honore hujus Virginis congregatur, et in ejus nomine locus iste et ecclesia dedicatur.* Philip, *Commentaria*, PL 203, col. 235.

Chapter 2
Adam Scot

The same difference in emphasis as separated Hugh of Fosses and Anselm of Havelberg likewise distinguished Philip of Bonne Espérance, the author we just addressed, and Adam Scot, the abbot of Dryburgh who later became a Carthusian of Witham. Philip emphasized clerical and apostolic life while Adam laid more stress on contemplation, although both nevertheless agreed that contemplative experience was the foundation of the apostlic life. Adam Scot is the most important of Premonstratensian spiritual writers and also the most engaging. For a long time he was forgotten, but the more his venerable figure has emerged from the shadows, the more resonance he has gained with his readers.[1] His work is indeed life-giving.

---

[1] Adam Scot, whose works were edited by Aimé de Fontaine in 1518 and by Ghiselbrecht in 1659, occupies the first part of PL 198. Recent years have seen more works on Adam. In 1901, Walter of Gray Birch edited more of his discourses. Then in 1930, Dom Wilmart discovered a note written on Adam by a Carthusian. In 1932, Margaret Thomson edited a biography written immediately after Adam's death; and Dom Wilmart presented a scholarly edition of that work the following year in *Analecta Praemonstratensia*. Dom Germain Morin wrote a scholarly, *"Gloriosus Magister Adam,"* for *Benedictine Review* 44 (1932): 179. Finally, still more recently I contributed an edition of Adam's fourteen sermons to fellow religious, along with a long introduction: Adam Scot, *Ad viros religiosis: Quatorze sermons d'Adam Scot*, ed. François Petit (Tongerloo: Librairie Saint Norbert, 1934). Work remains to be done but the figure of Master Adam is beginning to appear more clearly. [Editor's note: see now David Jones, *An Early Witness to the Nature of the Canonical Order in the Twelfth Century: A Study in the Life and Writings of Adam Scot with Particular Reference to his Understanding of the Rule of Saint Augustine*, Analecta Cartusiana 151 (1999); Francisco Palleschi, *La dernière écrite d'Adam Scot: Analyse linguistique et stylistique du "De quadripertito exercitio cellae,"* Analecta Cartusiana 168 (2004); Adam of Dryburgh, *Six Christmas Sermons*, trans. and intro. M. J. Hamilton, Analecta Cartusiana 16 (1974).]

The Life of Adam Scot

Adam was born in 1150 in Berwickshire, on the border of Scotland and England. His family was of modest means, but his evident intelligence, eloquence, grace of demeanor, and contagious gaity gained him eminence. His Carthusian biographer would later term him "the illustrious child of ordinary parents."[2] In his schooling, Adam gave himself wholeheartedly to the study of letters. He then was converted to an intense spiritual life and so drawn to the Premonstratensian abbey of Dryburgh, known for its religious life as established by the prelate Robert. This abbey was the daughter house of Alnwick; it had been founded in 1152 on the banks of the Tweed in the diocese of Saint Andrew's. According to the testimony of his namesake, Adam the Benedictine, our Adam, who had been "predisposed from the flowering of his youth to a love of the contemplative life, burned with a happy desire to lead it" in that place.[3] He found freedom of spirit and quietude of the heart at Dryburgh. Adam was extremely obedient and very friendly to all. The practice of the divine office came easily to him and he devoted himself with extraordinary fervor to *lectio* and to meditation on sacred scripture. The occasion of his profession impressed him deeply, as he often recalled: "A good religious rarely or never loses sight of the promises by which he is bound; he does not leave them under the veil of oblivion."[4] Adam was ordained a priest at the age of twenty-four.

Master Adam, as he was always known, was both an intellectual and a contemplative. He read a great deal, not only the Bible—which he knew by heart as did Saint Bernard and which he continually cited effortlessly—but also the Fathers of the Church: Saint Augustine, Saint Gregory the Great, Bede the Venerable, Cassian, Saint Bernard, the Victorines. The Greek Fathers, however, may have influenced him most, especially Origen and Gregory of Nazianzen. Adam's style imitates that of the Greek Second Sophistic school; its metrical

---

[2] "An illustrious son of mediocre parents." Ed. Wilmart, *Analecta Praemonstratensia* 9, 215.

[3] *Amore praeventus vitae contemplativae cujus a primaevo juventutis flore felici desiderio aestuaverat.*

[4] *Vel nunquam vel certe raro quibus se aliquando obligavere promissa, interveniente oblivionis tegmine, a cordis aspectibus abscondat.* Adam, *De ordine*, PL 198, col. 443.

form is built on the balance of the words and the sonorousness of the vowels. In the Middle Ages such metrical prose was called *styles isidorianus* as opposed to the *cursus leoninus*, where meter was based on regularly accented clauses. Adam's works embrace many stylistic devices; he frequently employs pleonasm, paranomasm, repetition, mirrored phrases, anaphora, and antitheses. He also uses frequent assonance, but without pressing it to the point of rhyme, as does Philip of Bonne Espérance. Among his frequently used formulas are: "*tria haec*," "*sed esto*," "*vos autem sic*," "*absit semel et iterum*." Adam's style is thus immediately recognizable. Although his literary craft was skilled, however, Adam's writing was sometimes affected. Even his especially mannered passages are nonetheless made valuable by their content. Their stylistic elaboration supports the author's vigorous and animated thought, while remaining unimpeachably precise.

In the great debate of the end of the twelfth century between traditional Augustinianism and newer scholastic methods, Master Adam clearly sided with the long-standing Augustinian pattern of learning. Scholastic discussion was directed toward the intellect alone; it was purely dialectical, even when it explained and clarified teaching that might later inspire the whole of life. Augustinianism, on the other hand, was concerned with the entire man; it was more literary, more prayerful, and closer to human experience. Although all sacred learning at that time required scholarly organization and precision, Adam's preference for the older pattern is therefore easily understandable.

Adam began to write and preach while he was still a young priest. Around 1180 his abbot, Gerald, fell sick with no hope of recovery and Adam was unanimously elected to replace him. He refused the abbatial blessing from his dearly beloved prelate while the latter still lived, but Adam nonetheless willingly took charge of the community's administrative matters.[5] When the abbot of Prémontré learned of Master Adam's preferment at the general chapter of 1181, he asked the canon of Dryburgh to come to Prémontré, where he was treated with the greatest dignity. Although the archmonastery

---

[5] Adam perhaps refused this honor because Saint Augustine regretted having received the episcopal blessing from the living Valerius, his predecessor.

lacked wine, its well-known guest house served it. While he stayed in the guest house, where the wine from which the archmonastery abstained was indeed served, Adam had frequent occasion to preach at Prémontré and in the environs. The Master of Dryburgh later recalled the reverence with which he was treated with joy, even amazement.

> How much joyful wonder and wonderful joy I have in recalling your affection toward me! I grind it in the pestle of my memory in the mortar of my heart, and the sweetness of the perfume it releases warms my belly. . . . What indeed am I? Who was I then, or what rank or importance? . . . What was my father's house?[6] I beseech you on my knees, prostrate at your feet, to remember me in your evening sacrifices with compassion for my many weaknesses, to present me to the loving eyes of my just advocate, the meek and humble Jesus, so that I might be healed. . . . To these my prayers I add this, if it is not presumptuous or rash: may you cause my name to be written in the necrology of your holy monastery, after I die, along with those of your community who have already departed, because I also belong to you . . . for the church of Prémontré is a wellspring and the other churches of the order flow from it like streams from a fountain. Therefore let that source guard itself against dryness, especially when those streams flow so copiously, lest it run out of the water from which the latter so abundantly flow! . . . The noble ornament of spiritual persons is the sanctity of their full conversion to religious life.[7]

---

[6] *O quanta nobis, in hac recordatione affectus vestri erga nos et cum admiratione exsultatio et cum exsultatione admiratio! Qui et terimus cum ejusdem recordationis pistillo in mortariolo pectoris nostri, ac suavitate fragrantiae quam emittit ex se, refovemus pectora nostra. . . . Quid enim nos? Aut qui nos, vel quales nos, sive quanti nos, ut nos perduceretis hucusque? . . . Et quae domus patris nostri?* Adam Scot, *De tripartito tabernaculo*, PL 198, col. 610.

[7] *Obnixe itaque vos flexis genibus mentis obsecramus, tamquam pedibus vestris prostrati, ut nostri memores sitis in vespertinis sacrificiis vestris, compatientes multimodis fragilitatibus nostris, offerentes nos sanandos piis conspectibus advocati nostri justi, mitis et mansueti Jesu. . . . Sed et hoc petitionibus nostris adderemus, nisi forte temerariae praesumptioni imputandum: scilicet ut nomen nostrum in albo sanetae congregationis vestrae una cum vestrorum qui jam discessere nominibus post mortem juberetis abscribi quia et nos vestri sumus. . . . Nonne velut quidam fons est Ecclesia Praemonstratensis, caeterae vero ejusdem ordinis ecclesiae sic ab ea dimanant ut a fonte rivuli? Caveat itaque sibi a siccitate fons, tunc quam maxime quando copiose fluunt rivuli, ne illo careat liquore quo isti abundant!*

In short, for Adam, the church of Prémontré was truly a terrestrial paradise watered by the four rivers. As prelate Adam developed his exhortation to an ever more fervent and more recollected life of contemplation according to this topographical theme.

In 1184 Dryburgh's old prelate, Gerald, finally died. The subsequent activity of Adam as abbot of Dryburgh must have been minimal with respect to the abbey's temporal goods; not one charter from his administration is found in the abbey's cartulary. He found material matters repugnant and considered the Carthusians, who do not have to busy themselves with churches, parishes, and tithes, truly blessed.[8] Consequently, after the general chapter of either 1188 or 1189, Adam passed through the Carthusian house of Val Saint-Pierre, near Vervins (Aisne), in the company of the abbot of Prémontré.[9] He preached there and was so edified by his visit that he resolved to become a Carthusian. Upon his return to England Adam went to see Saint Hugh, bishop of Lincoln, himself a Carthusian and former prior of Witham. Adam would later enter this very house and for twenty-four years experience the contemplative life he so loved, of which he was indeed an apostle both among the Premonstratensians and Carthusians. Then on Palm Sunday, 1213 or 1214, Adam took his leave of his prior, Dom Robert of Keyford, and all his confreres, encouraging them in charity and fraternal unity. On Tuesday of Holy Week, clothed in a hair shirt and lying on blessed ashes, he died peacefully. Adam is said to have been of average stature and distinctive features, bald at an early age and with a joyful mien. In his old age he became a bit stout but without losing his expansive air and ability to inspire respect.[10]

. . . *Sola nobilitas spiritualis generis sanctitas est religiosae conversationis.* Adam, *De tripartito tabernaculo,* PL 198, cols. 612–13.

[8] *Hanc quidem a saeculo segregationem vos abundanter habetis (o cartusii) qui de redditibus ecclesiarum, parochiarum et decinarum non intromittitis.* ("You have this great separation from the world, you [Carthusians] who do not have to get involved in the dealings of churches, parishes and tithes.") Adam, *Liber de quatuor exercitiis cellae,* PL 153, col. 821.

[9] The text of the Carthusian note bears the words *in dioecesi lugdunensi,* recte *laudunensi.*

[10] *Eum fuisse statura mediocrem, juxta mediocritatem staturae satis corpulentum, facie hilarem, capite calvum et tam pro venustate quam prae aetate et canitie valde reverendum.* Ms. from the Carthusians of Shene, British Library, Cotton Vespasian D IX, fol. 167.

The Work of Adam Scot

Not all the works of Adam Scot have survived. His first known literary effort was *Allegories on Sacred Scripture*, published among the works of Rabanus Maurus.[11] This text's attribution to Rabanus has been contested and now indeed seems incorrect.[12] An important preface precedes the work. Following Saint Gregory the Great, Adam explains in his introductory remarks that there are four senses of scripture, "four daughters of wisdom." Notably, he attributes each of these four senses to a stage in the spiritual life: the milk of the historical sense for still-delicate souls; the bread of allegory for those making progress; the savory nourishment of the moral sense for souls actively striving to accrue virtue; and for those separated from the baseness of this world by the rejection of earthly things, so advanced in their desire for heaven, "the sober drunkenness of theoretical contemplation in the wine of the anagogical sense."[13] This teaching on the four senses of scripture is important for the history of spirituality and was, according to P. Vaccari, a rarity at the time of Adam Scot, so deserving of special notice here.

Adam's *Allegories on Sacred Scripture* are a species of dictionary alphabetically ordering the various allegorical meanings, positive or negative, attributed to the most important elements of the biblical vocabulary. The importance of this work is greater than the casual reader might realize. The authors of the early Middle Ages willingly adopted the allegorical interpretations proposed by the Fathers of the Church, but from the eleventh century on Christian

---

[11] Adam, *Allegoriae in sacram Scripturam*, PL 112, cols. 849–1088.

[12] I proposed this attribution in the preface to Adam's sermons *Ad Viros Religiosos*. Fr. Alès, in *Recherches dans sciences religieuse* 25 (1935): 95, contradicted this position. In *Biblica* 18: 456, Fr. Vaccari, S. J., revisited the problem, concluding that the prologue to the *Allegoriae* is without a doubt from the hand of Adam, and that since this prologue is the appropriate, indeed requisite, introduction to the work, Adam's authorship of the *Allegoriae* cannot be denied.

[13] *Mater Sapientia per hos adoptionis filios pascit: teneris potum in lacte historiae, in fide autem proficientibus cibum in pane allegoriae, bonis et strenue operantibus et operibus bonis insudantibus satietatem in sapida refectione tropologiae; illis denique qui et ab illis per contemptum terrenorum suspensi et ad summa per caeleste desiderium sunt provecti, sobriam theoricae contemplationis ebrietatem in vino anagogiae.* Adam, *Allegoriae*, PL 112, col. 849.

thought was transformed. Dialecticians applied the powerful faculties of logical analysis and synthesis to the text, while mystics
assigned more weight to the illumination of the Holy Spirit; various
readers thus flew on their own wings, working to discover the exact
signification of the words and well knowing that the inner sense
and the superficial meaning differed. The satisfying meat of the
text's nut could only be reached by cracking its shell. The teaching
this process reveals must be Catholic, in conformity with the clear
meaning of Scripture and the teaching of the Church, as Adam was
quick to remind his reader. He nonetheless refused to believe that
the Holy Spirit had ceased to play a role in the Church and that
Scripture had opened all its secrets in the patristic age.

Adam's small subsequent work, his treatise *On the Sweetness of
God*, has been lost. It treated the reasons for praising God in eternity:
our existence, our restoration, our vocation, our justification, our
glorification.[14] Next, however, comes a precious collection of fourteen sermons *On the Order, the Habit and the Religious Profession of
the Regular Canons of Prémontré*.[15] These sermons together represent
the most important early attempt to define the spirituality of the
order. Adam was not completely successful because he was too
distant from the apostolic movement that had animated Saint
Norbert. The Premonstratensians were now already becoming a
formal religious order rather than a spontaneous movement, in
England and certainly at Prémontré as well. In his profound analysis
of the canonical way of life, the Premonstratensian formula of
profession and the Augustinian Rule, however, our author established a body of spiritual doctrine both serious and solid in its
exposition. Although this teaching did not tend toward activity
based in religious enthusuasm, it clearly upheld the primacy of the
contemplative life. Yet these sermons on the Order of Prémontré
were never preached. The sermon form was here a pure literary
device, meant instead for reading in the refectory.

Adam first treats the dignity of canons, aggrandizing it for the
sake of perfecting it rather than for the sake of pride:

---

[14] We know of the existence of this work from Adam himself. Adam, *De tripartito
tabernaculo*, PL 198, col. 757.

[15] Adam, *De ordine*, PL 198, cols. 439–610.

We are held to a lofty standard, my brothers, by our great debt; much is expected of us who have received much. . . .[16] Attend to your vocation, I beg you, and walk worthily in it. You have been called to the canonical order and have professed it before many witnesses. This order is indeed sublime; among all the orders by which the holy Church is exalted, adorned, sanctified, and ruled, ours shines with special dignity. The apostles consecrated this order with their own lives and thus invested it with powerful, distinctive authority. The clerics of the Church have been raised high in their order. They are superior, in the authority of their preeminent power, to the multitude who are monks. . . . Therefore as the meaning of the word instructs us, those clerics who show themselves to be righteous in their lives are called *canons*, for the Greek word canon, as you know, means "rule" and "rule" in turn signifies rectitude.[17]

Rectitude of thought, rectitude of life, and rectitude of intention: Adam insists on this righteousness at length. To avoid every soul-staining fault and every action harming one's neighbor is the straightforward expression of religious life, yet it does not suffice simply to avoid evil:

A sublime name requires a sublime way of life, for often a name is the mirror of life. . . .[18] Those who call certain clerics "secular canons" do not fully understand this. . . . He who wishes to be a friend of this world must be considered an enemy of God, since

[16] *Nos . . . Fratres . . . constricti sumus debito magno: uptpote qui multum accepimus ac per hoc et multum a nobis reddendum scire certissime debemus.* Adam, *De ordine*, PL 198, col. 444.

[17] *Videte, quaeso, vocationem vestram, et ambulate digne in ea. Ad ordinem canonicum vocati estis, ipsumque coram multis testibus professi. Ordo certe sublimis valde, et inter universos quibus sancta exaltatur et decoratur, sanctificatur et regitur Ecclesia ordines, magna quadam dignitate praefulgens. Hunc sua apostoli conversatione consecrarunt et ad sublime singularis cujusdam auctoritatis fastigium evexerunt. Clerici sunt qui ad hunc in Ecclesia ordinem promoti sunt. Qui ipsis quoque in nonnullis sublimiores sunt monachis, quantum ad auctoritatem qua praeeminent potestatis. . . . Usitato vero vocabulo, canonici appellantur ut esse se in vitae rectitudine se demonstrent. Nam canon ut scitis, graece, latine regulam sonat. Regula vero recta ducit.* Adam, *De ordine*, PL 198, col. 445–46.

[18] *Sublime . . . nomen sublimem conversationem requirit. Speculum namque vitae in ipso plerumque nomine consistit.* Adam, *De ordine*, PL 198, col. 461.

his religion is not holy and immaculate, rather he is sullied by the secular world. . . . Black swans—that is what I take secular canons to be. . . .[19] But let us speak now of our own habit, the vestments of us whom the people call regular canons in order to distinguish us from those other men. . . . We must have no luxurious clothing. Our Lord makes this clear when he says that those who are clothed in soft vestments dwell in the palaces of kings, for we fight our heavenly King rather than any earthly monarch. Therefore, as you know, we use linen only for undergarments, considering it praiseworthy not to wear linen on our limbs except in special instances. . . . Yet far be it from us to think it shameful for other religious men to wear such things, for thus we would set ourselves over them as if we were holier than they. I am not explaining our practices to my readers to declare them superior to others'; the sons of holy Church are supported by the foundation of one universal faith, but they do not all follow the same external customs in their pursuit of holiness. . . . Far be it from us, my brothers, far be it from us once and again, always and everywhere, detestably and evilly to presume to disparage in any way the well-ordered customs of any religious house. Rather let us devoutly embrace and heartily approve whatever is in any way useful for souls—whatever discretion, mother of virtues, maintains or assigns to them with pious intent. Still more, let us also regard all others vested in religious habits as better and holier than ourselves, even if we do not see in them the same rigor as we practice in our dress or other external observance. All other good things flow from one chief good as from an ample and unfailing source, so immense as to admit no increase and eternally undiminished.[20]

---

[19] *Illi nomen hoc sublime nequaquam satis acute intellegunt qui quosdam clericos canonicos saeculares appellant. . . . Cum igitur Dei sit constituendus inimicus quicumque hujus saeculi voluerit esse amicus, cum illius munda et immaculata religio non sit qui se immaculatum ab hoc saeculo non custodit. . . . Ut cycnos nigros, sic audio dici canonicas saeculares.* Adam, *De ordine*, PL 198, col. 462.

[20] *Loquamur de habitu nostro, quos ut ab eis discernat vulgus canonicos quoque regulares appellat. . . . Quod autem inter nos luxus vestium reperiri non debeat, ipse quoque Dominus manifestat in eo quod mollibus vestitos dicat eos esse qui in domibus regum sunt. Non enim terreno alicui sed caelesti Regi militamus. Idcirco nostra, sicut scitis consuetudo est non lineis nisi solis femoralibus uti. Sed nec stamineis ad carnem apud nos quemquam indui laudabile est nisi . . . interveniente causa speciali. . . . Absit tamen ut reprehendendos putemus viros religiosos qui talibus vestibus induuntur! aut ut nos super*

In the same manner, for Adam, for other canons to eat meat is entirely acceptable. Nor is it inappropriate for them always to wear the surplice:

> The linen dress of others of the clerical order is entirely appropriate, yet we do not think that we do any wrong in reserving a certain special honor and purity for the divine service by wearing it only then. We regularly minister at the altar only when we also wear a surplice or alb; none dares ascend the altar unless he is so vested. In offering communion or extreme unction, our priests or ministers all wear the surplice. Thus, among us, the surplice is reserved for divine worship. When the ritual is concluded, we take off the linen garment and, after it is laid aside, put it on once again with all the more joy and love.[21]

Adam subsequently addresses the symbolism of the white Premonstratensian habit, drawing from it magnificent teachings about the spiritual life. First, a white garment is the clothing of the angels at the Resurrection and the Ascension. Further, there are four places

---

illos tumide efferamus, quasi eis in hoc sanctiores simus. Neque enim sic ad utilitatem legentium nostra exponimus ut aliena eis supponamus. Nam cum unius fidei fundamento universi sanctae Ecclesiae filii innitantur, non easdem tamen in sanctitate exterioris conversationis consuetudines omnes sequuntur. . . . Absit, fratres, a nobis, absit semel et iterum, et semper et ubique longe sit a nobis hoc detestabile malum ut aliquas ordinatas cujuscumque religiosae domus consuetudines in aliquo vituperare praesumamus. Quidquid animabus utile uno vel alio modo mater virtutum discretio cum intentione pia vel cum rigore tenet, vel cum dispensatione relaxat, devote amplectamur et humiliter approbemus. Non solum autem, sed et omnes qui habitu sunt religionis induti nobis meliores et sanctiores deputemus, etiamsi ad illum quem nos vel in habitu vel in victu, seu certe in aliqua exteriori conversatione tenemus rigorem eos pertingere non videmus. Unum quippe summum bonum est a quo cuncta alia bona emanant utpote fons sufficiens et indeficiens qui nec augeri potest quia immensus; nec minui quoniam est aeternus. Adam, *De ordine,* PL 198, cols. 464–65.

[21] *Multum decet ordinem clericalem lineum hoc indumentum. Nec malefacere nos arbitramur qui specialem quamdam honestatem et munditiam divinis ea induendo obsequiis reservamus. Unde generaliter apud nos statutum est ut omnes qui altari ministrant nunquam ibi sine superpelliciis vel albis appareant nec aliquis, praesente conventu, nisi superpellicio vel alba indutus superiores gradus altaris praesumat ascendere. Ad communicandum quoque vel infirmum ungendum sacerdotes et ministri superpelliciis induuntur. Divino itaque cultui superpellicia deputamus. Cujus peracto obsequio ea exuimus: quia jucundius nonnumquam et gratius poterit repeti quod ad tempus contingit intermitti.* Adam, *De ordine,* PL 198, col. 465.

where the body of Jesus rested: the womb of the Virgin, the crèche, the cross, and the tomb. These four sites represent four degrees of religious perfection: those who bear in their heart the desire for conversion correspond to Mary's womb; those formed in religious life in a monastic community are represented by the crèche; those tried so as to raise their souls above all creation are figured in the cross; finally, the contemplative life of the perfect is signified by the tomb. Contemplation is indeed repose: the sleep sent to Adam when he sensed in himself both contemplation, the virile spirit of command, and action, the feminine principle of obedience; Noah's Ark, enclosed by God against the external world, where the dove brought back the olive branch; the dream of Jacob, when he saw the ladder of angels; the coffin in which Joseph's bones were placed before they were carried to the Land of Canaan; the desert where Moses led his flock and encountered God in the burning bush; the solitude where Elijah fled when pursued by Jezabel. Above all, though, it is the tomb of Jesus. This final site of Jesus' rest—beautiful, precious, restful, stable, calm, delightful, sweet beyond all other places. And the angels at the tomb were clothed in white, like Christ on the day of his transfiguration—clothed in sanctity, clothed in joy, clothed in glory. Adam invites his listeners simply: "Clothe yourselves in white vestments so that you may merit to be clothed in white through eternity."[22] His pages on this topic are magnificent in their oratorical inspiration, their loftiness of thought and the lyricism of their imagery and feeling.

Starting with his fifth sermon Adam begins an explanation of the Premonstratensian formula of profession: "I, brother N. . . , offer and give myself to the Church of Our Lady and Saint N. . . . I promise the conversion of my ways and stability in this place, according to the Gospel of Christ, the apostolic institution and the canonical Rule of Saint Augustine. I promise in Christ our Lord my obedience until death to N. . . , father of this church, and to his successors whom the wiser part of the community elects."[23] Adam's

---

[22] *Induimini candidis cogitationum morum et operum vestimentis . . . ut digni quoque habeamini albis operiri aeternae felicitatis.* Adam, *De ordine,* PL 198, col. 479.

[23] *Ego, frater N. offerens trado meipsum Ecclesiae sanctae Dei Genetricis Mariae sanctique illius; et promitto conversionem morum meorum et stabilitatem in loco, secundum*

material is rich, leading him to speak about conversion and stability in religion and especially to comment in detail on the Rule of Saint Augustine, to which he dedicated his last seven sermons. Here he presented his ascetical teaching in a lucid and complete manner, with less lyricism and fewer scriptural allegories; much good sense, experience of the common life, sometimes even mordant wit are evident in the portraits he sketches. Adam's description of an abbot jealous of his prior is among the more amusing passages:

> What do my prior and I have in common? Who is he? What greatness does he have? In my presence he is not greater than anyone else. He is the same as the least in the monastery. . . . Let him retract his horns and not extol himself on account of his title! He received his title from me and he will hold it only as long as it pleases me. I loaned it; I did not give it. It comes from my abundance; not his inheritance. I exalted him and it is in my power to humble him. This I shall do—and soon.[24]

Adam's final sermons treat the vow of obedience and the devotions of the community. This author, who later as a Carthusian wrote the celebrated *On the Four Exercises of the Cell* on reading, meditation, prayer, and action, indentified only three at this time because in his analysis of *lectio divina* he did not yet distinguish meditation from reading and from prayer. Adam owes his lofty reputation for knowledge and eloquence, acknowledged throughout the order by around 1180, to this work.

Adam wrote *On the Tabernacle* during the same period at the invitation of John, abbot of the famous Benedictine monastery of

---

Evangelium Christi et secundum apostolicam institutionem et secundum canonicam regulam beati Augustini. Promitto etiam obedientiam usque ad mortem in Christo Domino N praefatae ecclesiae Patri et successoribus ejus quos pars sanior congegationis elegerit. Adam, De ordine, PL 198, col. 479.

[24] *Quid mihi et priori meo? Quis ille aut quantus ille? Nullo in praesentia mea major est: par ei est qui omnibus in conventu minor est. . . . Contrahat cornua sua, non se extollat pro nomine suo. Ex me est nomen hoc: durabit quamdiu placuerit mihi. Accommodavi illud, non donavi. Sufficientia mea est, non hereditas sua, non peculium, sed mutuum meum. Exaltavi, meum erit et humiliare. Faciam hoc, et in brevi.* Adam, De ordine, PL 198, col. 567.

Kelso.[25] This work treats of the tabernacle of Moses in three books according to literal, allegorical, and moral exegesis. Here, in addition to the Bible and the Jewish history of Josephus, Adam takes as models the Venerable Bede's work on the tabernacle, Andrew of Saint Victor's commentaries on the Pentateuch, the scholastic history of Peter Comestor, and the royal genealogies of Aelred of Rievaulx. The first book of Adam's work is a literal and historical commentary; it is the most tedious of all his extant texts, although to ground allegorical exegesis on solid investigation of the literal sense was indeed an excellent method.[26] The second book treats the Church, for which the tabernacle was the literary image; in his allegorical explanation of everything found in the tabernacle, Adam reveals many of his theological ideas. In the third book the author speaks of the soul, writing "on the tabernacle of the soul, which is its inner thought"; this book is effectively a treatise on the spiritual life, "a work requiring of me much difficult, nearly impossible work, since discussion of moral life requires the taste of experience more than the smell of knowledge."[27] Here Adam's humility is manifest. Unsurprisingly, every image in the text occasions a discussion of spirituality: the deserts surrounding the tabernacle, the metals found in its construction and its walls, columns, and furniture. This material is interesting but the aims of the work preclude the inclusion of extended, eloquent passages representing the shape of Adam's spirituality.

Adam's *Threefold Nature of Contemplation*[28] must have been composed around the time he received abbatial blessing; it was begun shortly before and finished shortly after. This work is Adam's masterpiece from both theological and literary points of view. He has here revised his style such that he offers neither sermons nor a treatise, but confessions. In this work the author attains fully metrical prose and lyrical movement, occasionally recalling the beautiful

---

[25] Adam, *De tripartito tabernaculo*, PL 198, cols. 609–796.

[26] A colored diagram included in the manuscript but omitted in the published version indeed made the work easier to understand.

[27] *Laboriosum opus et mihi, fateor, non solum difficile, sed pene impossibile, cum mores discutere magis ad experientiae pertineat gustum quam ad scientiae olfactum.* Adam, *De tripartito tabernaculo*, PL 198, col. 743.

[28] Adam, *De triplici genere contemplationis*, PL 198, cols. 795–842.

prefaces of the Roman pontifical. The work presents three parts: God is incomprehensible in himself, terrible in his reprobation of the damned and ineffably sweet in his predestination of the elect.

The first part of the work lifts the soul through the successive stages defined by Saint Augustine in book 10 of his *Confessions*. The same great medieval method seeking God would eventually yield Bonaventure's masterpiece, *The Mind's Road to God*. But here Adam writes:

> Never-fading beauty in my life, never-false sweetness, Lord God, have mercy on my soul, weighed down with sins, muffled by vices, snared by wantonness, captive in its exile, imprisoned in this body. My soul is mired, trapped in the mud, fastened in its embodiment, pierced with care, filled with trouble. It is con-strained by fear, afflicted with sorrow, lost in confusion, ridden with anxiety, restless with suspicion.[29]

In short, the wounded soul asks that the beneficent oil of mercy flow down upon it, then passes on despite its unworthiness to the contemplation of created things. It speaks to the rocks: "Who are you?" They respond, "We are not your God."[30] The soul then turns to the stars and receives the same response. Innumerable creatures make known to its immeasurably creative wisdom. Their greatness lends a notion of the grandeur of God. Their beauty proclaims his beauty; the sounds they produce teach the euphony of the Word of God. The sweetness of their smells suggests the sweetness of God's Spirit and savors move us to taste God. But all lesser creatures do not suffice as a path to God, so we must pass on to contempla-tion of the human soul, casting off the vagaries of our thoughts, for these do not exist in God. Just as the sun makes wax melt and clay harden with one and the same ray, so the same divine will punishes the impious and rewards the just. What a difference be-tween man's will and God's! But let us rise to that loftier region:

---

[29] *Decor vitae meae non marcescens, et dulcedo non fallax, Domine Deus, miserere animae meae quae est peccatis onerata, vitiis irretita, illecebris capta, exsilio captiva, corpore incarcerata: quae est haerens luto, infixa limo, affixa membris, confixa curis, distenta negotiis, quae est timoribus contracta, doloribus afflicta, erroribus vaga, sollicitudinibus anxia, suspicionibus inquieta.* Adam, *De triplici genere*, PL 198, col. 798.

[30] Adam, *De triplici genere*, PL 198, col. 799.

My spirit calls me, Lord God, saying loudly, "Behold, you have studiously and diligently observed in me the six-fold gift: to live, to give life, to feel, to elicit feeling, to think, to will. But climb higher and enter into me. Ascend higher to me, to my loftiness. Enter more deeply into my inner being and see that I am wise, discerning. Although I am indivisible, I am commonly called by different names on account of my different functions: soul because I give life to the parts of the body, sensibility because I relate to material obects, thinking because I perceive, memory because I remember; intelligence because I understand, mind because I am wise, spirit because I contemplate, reason because I discern. . . . Therefore I have wisdom and a rational faculty, as brute animals do not. In this way I am similar to God himself. Therefore I am wisdom and he is Wisdom itself; I am light, and he is Light itself. But the distance between me and him is still great. I am wisdom, but created wisdom; he is wisdom and creative. I am light, but illumined; he is illumining Light."[31]

Adam then discusses man as the image of the Trinity:

You are and you are aware of your existence; you exist and you know it; you know it even as you exist. You are, I say, and you both know that you are and you know also that you know this. Indeed, if you consider this clearly, examining it with subtlety, you will realize that your being and your knowledge give rise to yet a third thing, that is love, for when you see that your being is so worthy and lofty, you love it. And when you see your lucid, profound, subtle wisdom—lucid in perception, profound in

---

[31] *Vocat me, Domine Deus, spiritus meus et dicit ad me magna voce: Ecce studiose et diligenter senariam meam in me scrutatus es: qua scilicet vivo, vivifico, sentio, sensifico, cogito, volo. Sed adhuc ascende et intra ad me. Ascende, inquam, superius ad me superiorem, intra interius ad me interiorem et vide quia sapio, quia discerno. Ego si quidem, cum una indivisibilis sim, ob diversas tamen efficientias meas diversas etiam soleo vocabula sortiri. Unde enim membra vegeto corporea anima sum; unde sensibilitas adhaereo sensualitas sum; unde sentio, sensus sum; unde recordor, memoria sum; unde intellego, mens sum; unde sapio, animus sum; unde contemplor, spiritus sum; unde discerno, ratio sum. . . . Habeo itaque sapientiam et intellectum rationalem quam in se brutorum animantium spiritus non habet. Et in hac re Deo in aliquo similis sum. Sum ego itaque sapientia, est et ipse Sapientia; sum ego lumen, est et ipse. Ego namque sapienta sum, sed creata, ipse vero Sapientia et creans. Ego lumen, sed illuminatum, ipse quidem Lumen et illuminans.* Adam, *De triplici genere*, PL 198, cols. 809–10.

investigation, subtle in comprehension—you immediately love it, approve it, embrace it and take satisfaction in it. Thus a sort of trinity arises in you even as your unity remains.[32]

Clearly this passage is only a distant reflection on a great mystery. Adam, unaware of the subtleties and usages of the scholastics, here attributes being to the Father, wisdom to the Son, and love to the Holy Spirit. This attribution of being to the Father troubled his seventeenth-century editor so much that he adds in a note: "Read here cautiously." Yet these words may easily be interpreted in a completely orthodox way. The first part of Adam's *De triplici genere contemplationis* ends with a lengthy consideration of the Holy Trinity.

Adam then discusses hell—how terrible God is to the damned. His is far from Dante's imaginative description, but Adam nonetheless makes use of the full array of biblical images and figures in order to describe the sufferings of the damned.

Woe to the rational creature, angel or man, who turns away from you, whom his dignity then prevents from returning to complete non-being and whose depravity denies his blessedness![33] Woe then to you, throng of lost souls! Woe to you, flimsy and dry stubble ready for the flames! Woe to you, sterile and dry wood, fit for burning, food only for fire. Woe to you, son of perdition, Cain, standing before your brother bewailing your exile—that is to say standing before the Church of the elect. You envy him and by the pernicious counsel of your bad examples you encourage him to leave its protection so that you may kill him! Woe to you,

---

[32] *Es itaque, et scis; es sciens, et scis existens. Es, inquam, et scis te esse, et scis etiam, te scire te esse. Et ecce, si clare consideras, et si subtiliter intueris, vides profecto quia in te ex his duobus, ex esse scilicet et scire tuo, surgit quoddam tertium, id est amor. Nam cum vides essentiam tuam tam dignam, tamque excelsam, amas nimirum eam. Et cum vides sapientiam tuam tam claram, tam profundam, tam subtilem, tam claram ad intelligendum, tam profundam ad investigandum, tam subtilem ad comprehendendum, statim eam amas et approbas et amplecteris eam, et places tibi in ea. Et surgit in te trinitas quaedam, et unitas manet.* Adam, *De triplici genere*, PL 198, col. 810.

[33] *Vae rationali creaturae, angelo scilicet et homini, avertenti se a te! quae nec propter dignitatem suam ad omnino non esse, nec propter pravitatem suam valet pertingere ad beate esse.* Adam, *De triplici genere*, PL 198, col. 812.

who flee the face of the Lord to living as an exile and fugitive, a wanderer in your disordered covetousness and an exile in your sinful conscience. Your greed sears your flesh while your awareness of your guilt continually gnaws at your mind. Woe to you, I say, who after the the birth of Enoch, your firstborn, built a city on earth, for your investment in present goods has fixed your heart on earthliness. And woe to you, sons of the secular world, who raise their thick necks to charge against God. You abandon the bright and luminous East. Finding there a plain so wide that you cannot see its edge, you take this wide path to perdition. Many are you who take it![34]

The builders of the Tower of Babel, Esau, the wife of Putiphar, Core, Dathan and Abiron, Balaam, Dalilah, the sons of Eli, Saul, Amnon, and Absalom—all these are types of one or another species of sin, therefore objects of similar derogation. And Adam poses the unavoidable problem of predestination:

How terrible thou art toward them, Lord God! Over each of the damned, both angels and men, the secret chastisement of thy just judgment keeps watch, casting them from thy presence and excluding them from among thine elect as vessels of wrath fit only for ruin. Thou neither wash away their evils nor approve their good works; thou hast hardened their hearts that they might not turn to thee and be made blessed.[35]

---

[34] *Vae igitur tibi, massa perditorum. Vae tibi stipula levis et sicca, aeternis incendiis praeparata! Vae tibi lignum infructuosum et aridum, natum in combustionem et cibum ignis. Vae tibi, fili perditionis, Caïn, fratri tuo praesens lugenti exilium, Ecclesiae scilicet electorum invidens, dolosis pravorum exemplorum monitis ad exteriora eum egredi hortaris, ut egressum interficias! Vae tibi quia a facie Domini egrediens, vagus super terram habitas et profugus: vagus per inordinatam concupiscentiam, profugus per peccatricem conscientiam; quia tuam in te et illa carnem urit et haec mentem jugiter rodit. Vae inquam tibi, qui Enoch in primordio generans, in terra civitatem aedificas, quia te bonis praesentibus dedicans, cordis intentionem figis in terrenis. Vae vobis, hujus saeculi filii, qui pingui cervice armati, currentes adversus Deum erecto collo, de lucente et luminoso Oriente receditis; et invenientes campum latissimum, per viam ejus latam ambulatis, quae ducit ad perditionem et multi estis qui ingredimini per eam.* Adam, *De triplici genere*, PL 198, col. 813.

[35] *Et o quam terribilis es, Domine Deus, in illis! Vigilat namque super reprobos singulos, angelos videlicet et homines, secreta animadversio justi judicii tui, projiciens eas a facie tua et a sorte eos electorum tuorum excludens, utpote vasa irae apta in interitum. Eorum etenim*

Here emerges Augustinian doctrine in all its rigor. Based on biblical texts whose Semitic tendency is to see God as the cause of everything that he permits, it terrifies the soul. Nevertheless, divine action in itself does not destroy human freedom; rather, God allows the soul to fall into evil not by so directing it but by allowing it, forbearing to restrain it:. "He is not the author of the fault, yet he ordains the path."[36] At a given moment no one knows whether he is himself worthy of love or hate, whether he is or is not predestined, and this uncertainty holds the soul in fear. Adam's final words here sum up the entire second part of his work on contemplation: God acts in mystery and justice.[37] Few meditations on hell lacking, as Adam's does, imaginative description or invented inclusions can match the eloquence of these pages.

The third part begins joyfully, in contrast. Here Adam considers how sweet and lovable God is toward his elect:

> How happy are thy elect, Lord God, Father Almighty! How happy, I say, are they whose names have been written for all eternity in the book of life. By their Redeemer, thy son Jesus, they have access through faith to that grace in which they stand. They find glory in thy sons' hope of glory. In their hearts the love of God spreads through the Holy Spirit whom thou hast given to them. To their own spirits thy Spirit bears witness that they are thy sons, and as such your heirs and coheirs of Christ. O blessed sons of a blessed predestination! O pure vessels of eternal election! O beloved saints cherished by thee in the odor of sweetness and pleasing unto thee. . . . How gentle, Lord, how wonderful and how sweet is the love by which thou art attached to them. That love calls, gathers, and unites them to thee in an indissoluble embrace of eternal love, so that none can steal them from thy hand! In a

---

non diluis mala nec approbas bona; insuper eorum corda induras, ne ad te convertantur et in te beatificentur. Adam, *De triplici genere,* PL 198, col. 816.

[36] *Non auctor ruendi, sed ordinator incedendi.*

[37] *Et cum praecipiti eidem pravae voluntati qua vult tu, Deus, viam aperies, quodammodo eam inclinas; non tamen impellendo, sed permittendo et non retinendo; nec es ei auctor ruendi, sed ordinator incedendi. . . . Sed haec interna dispositio tua tam occulta est ut ipsas etiam malas voluntates in quibus est lateat; quae ideo suo se putant arbitrio dirigi, quia se sentiunt praeter coactionem proprio appetitu moveri. . . . Juste quidem sed occulte.* Adam, *De triplici genere,* PL 198, col. 817.

wonderful manner thou bringest it about that not only their good deeds, but even their evil ones, work for their good. . . . O pact of serenity! O covenant of peace established by thee with them. Thou smilest upon them with a cheerful face, undeceiving; thou lookest upon them with a kind and peaceful gaze; thou kissest them with the kiss of thy mouth, so purifying them, changing them and perfecting them—purifying them through forgiveness of their sins, changing them through the grace of their merits, and perfecting them in the glory of their rewards. Thus they may be eternally in themselves what they are in thee for all eternity![38]

This text, despite its length, is essential here. Then, after a lyrical passage inspired by Saint Paul, Adam addresses in turn various saints of the Old Testament. He continues with a discussion of predestination elicited by Saint Paul's conversion. Finally he describes the ascent toward God in stages, in an important passage directly describing divine contemplation. Adam writes that the soul rises up, according to the Augustinian method, beyond the things of this world into its very self. It then goes beyond itself to reach its own most profound depths. In contemplating itself the soul there sees three things: being, knowledge, and love. To pass from that point to contemplation of the Trinity we must worship requires divine illumination. There language fails:

[38] *Ceterum quam felices tui sunt electi, Domine Deus, Pater omnipotens! Quam felices, inquam, sunt quorum nomina ab aeterno in libro vitae sunt scripta; et per Redemptorem suum, Filium tuum Jesum accessum habent per fidem in gratiam istam, in qua stant et gloriantur in spe gloriae filiorum tuorum, in quorum cordibus diffusa est charitas Dei per Spiritum sanctum quem donas eis. Quorum etiam spiritui testimonium reddit Spiritus tuus quod sint filii tui. Si filii, et haeredes, haeredes quidem tui, cohaeredes autem Christi. O beati beatae praedestinationis filii! O munda aeternae electionis vasa! O sancti et dilecti quos diligis in odorem suavitatis, complacens tibi in illis! . . . Quam dulci, Domine, quam miro, quamque suavi eis amore conglutinaris; vocans et colligens et uniens eos tibi compage aeternae dilectionis insolubili: ita, ut nemo eos rapere possit de manu tua! Miro modo facis eis non solum bona sed etiam ipsa mala sua eis cooperari in bonum. . . . O serenitatis pactum! O foedus pacis quod cum eis percutis: facie eis hilari et non fallaci arridens, propitio ac sereno vultu super eos respiciens, oris etiam tui osculo deosculans, mundans eos coaptans et consummans! Mundans inquam per veniam peccatorum, coaptans per gratiam meritorum, consummans per gloriam praemiorum: ut tales denique in aeternum sint in se quales ab aeterno sunt in te!* Adam, *De triplici genere*, PL 198, col. 819.

> Now I see in myself thy image, according to which thou hast
> made me; I see thee too to a certain extent in this image. I do not
> yet see thee completely in reality, rather this is a mirror through
> which I see thee as in a riddle, not yet face to face. The mirror
> through which I see thee is my heart if only it is so cleansed,
> enlightened, and purified by thee that thy countenance can be
> clearly seen in it. Thus, as long as thou art behind me and above
> by head, I see thee in this mirror according as thou allowest me,
> but not yet in thyself. Thou art behind me and above my head,
> because I am turned away from thee and different from thee.
> Indeed, thou art just and I am unjust, and thus we are turned
> away from each other; thou art blessed and I am truly wretched.
> So are we different.[39]

Evidently the divine remains transcendent, although the height of
human intellect strains to search the abyss of divinity, especially to
comprehend the problem of predestination. Yet what usefulness
this exercise presents! It turns the mind away from evil, filling it
with confidence and joy. The soul experiences enlightenment and
humility; it is enflamed.

The medieval reception of Adam's book of threefold contemplation is difficult to determine, since no manuscripts survive. On the
other hand, his subsequent work, a soliloquy *On the Instruction of
the Soul*, was copied many times.[40] Although it has variously been
attributed to Adam of Saint Victor, Adam of Perseigne, and Adam
of Royal-lieu, reading and comparing it with the sermons on the
Order of Prémontré attest that it is the work of Adam Scot. Never
was this writer more completely himself; never did he offer a more
complete and penetrating explanation of the Premonstratensian
formula of profession.

---

[39] *Et hoc modo video in me imaginem tuam ad quam fecisti me: et te secundum aliquem
modum video in hac imagine. Nondum plene te video in ipsa re, hoc est speculum per quod
te video in aenigmate, nondum facie ad faciem. Speculum quidem per quod te video cor
meum est: sit tamen sic extersum, tamque clarificatum et purificatum a te fuerit, ut evidens
in eo vultus perspici possit. Itaque quamdiu sibi vel a dorso vel supra verticem es, in hoc
quidem prout mihi concedere dignaris te intueor speculo, nondum vero in teipso. A dorso
namque et super verticem mihi es, quia et a te aversus et tibi diversus sum. Tu etenim justus
es et ego injustus, et sic sumus aversi. Tu beatus es, ego vero miser, et sic sumus diversi.*
Adam, *De triplici genere*, PL 198, col. 834.

[40] Adam, *De instructione animae*, PL 198, cols. 843–72.

After a dedication to Walter, prior of the regular canons of the cathedral of Saint Andrew, the author presents two books of dialogues between the soul and reason. The first book has as its intent to support the soul in the ordinary temptations of the cloistered life and that boredom which is the great obstacle to contemplation; the second book resumes a detailed commentary on the formula of profession. The work is marked by an insightful religious psychology, deeply steeped in evocative feeling and inspiration. Although life in the world brings many troubles, so too does cloistered life, with its own temptations and sufferings. First among these is the battle to preserve chastity. The phantom of a woman is not shut out by the cloister door. The religious imagines it; he sees the small mouth, the soft lips, the rosy cheeks, the sweet traits, the smiling eyes—flattering, soliciting, speaking, offering, alluring, seizing. Reason must reveal this image to be a silken sack full of filth, a sepulcher made beautiful but filled with putrefaction, over which triumph comes only by the strength of meditation, psalmody, mortification, and vigilance.[41] The chapter of faults is the occasion of many such battles:

Reason: What is it that is still bothering you?

Soul: I find the chapter of faults very burdensome.

Reason: What do you see in chapter?

Soul: Not much charity or love in those present, virtually no kindness or compassion in him who presides, much impatience and unrest in my own part.

Reason: How comes it that you see all this in the chapter? Such things ought not to be found there.

Soul: Those who are present show little charity or love, for however small or negligible the failing they see in me, they accuse me from all sides. As if I were surrounded by savage enemy troops and unable to defend myself, one sets a trap behind me, another attacks from the front, then another tries to strike from the right, another from the left. As they say about me everything they wish, the one presiding

---

[41] Adam, *De instructione animae*, PL, 198, col. 846.

listens eagerly, as if he would rather hear bad things about me than good. He keeps on listening as if happy to have found the chance to reproach me. Then he adds still harsher words to my accusers'. By defining and parsing my error, he exaggerates it, making it huge, enormous. He says that he hardly knows what penance to give me for such a fault. And in the face of all these accusations, these denunciations, I am not allowed to say a single word in my defense. It seems to me that neither those present nor he who presides would be so cruel if they loved me. And since I am treated this way every day, it is no wonder I am so upset and anxious. All this makes me love chapter as though it were a prison—or hell itself.[42]

Reason might easily set these matters straight, but one or another accusation or chapter might indeed be unjust, malicious, or envious. Reason might admit this too but still treat the problem with arrogance.

---

[42] *Ratio: Unde adhuc gravaris?*

   Anima: . . . De capitulo valde gravatus sum.

   R: Quid vides in capitulo!

   A: Modicam in circumsedentibus charitatem et dilectionem, nullam pene in praesidente pietatem et compassionem, magnam vero in me ipsa impatientiam et inquietudinem.

   R: Quomodo haec in capitulo vides? Omnia enim haec a capitulo aliena esse debent.

   A: Modica in circumsedentibus charitas est et dilectio, qui ibi de omni quam in me vident negligentia, etiam licet minima et pene nulla sit, undique accusant. Et sicut aliquis saevissimis hostium suorum vallatus hinc inde catervis a quo se debeat observare ignorat; dum undique insistentes et iste et insidias parat a tergo et ille ei resistit in facie; alius vero a dextris, alius eum etiam ferire a sinistris conatur, sic in capitulo sum. Cumque omnia quae potuerint de me dixerint, inhianter haec praesidens audit et quasi magis mala de me quam bona audire desideret, sic se in auscultando habet ut mihi quodammodo valde laetus videatur, quod aliquam saltem occasionem invenit unde me gravare possit. Tunc verbis eorum amaris amariora superaddit, et definiendo, dividendo culpam exaggerat et eam tamquam immanem et enormem facit et quae mihi pro tali culpa injungi paenitentia possit pene se ignorare asserit. Et in his omnibus nec illorum accusationibus nec istius increpationibus unum saltem verbum excusatorium mihi licet proferre. Ut autem mihi videtur, nec illi nec iste sic umquam in me saevirent si me amarent. Cumque diebus singulis hoc modo me tractari video, mirum non est si magnam in me inquietudinem et impatientiam tolero. Unde etiam compellor sic diligere capitulum quasi profundum ergastulum vel etiam infernum. Adam, *De instructione animae,* PL 198, col. 848.

Reason: Although we say that it is no great sin for the just man to
declare himself blameless, yet we can also say it is no great
merit for the unjust not to excuse himself. While he may
be pardoned and avoid punishment, he merits neither the
grace nor the glory to which the just who do not excuse
themselves are happily raised. The one state is good but
the other is better. You recall that on the day of the Lord's
passion three men were hung on the cross: the blasphemous thief, the penitent thief, and the innocent Lamb
himself. And what do we think the rigor of the chapter
might be except that of the passion and the cross? In this
passion some are blasphemers, some are guilty and confess
it, while still others are innocent. The first are rebels, the
second penitents, the third humble. The first deserve
punishment, the second pardon, and the third glory. The
blasphemous thief represents the first group; the second
thief, the penitent, represents the second group; and the
innocent and humble Jesus represents the third. Although
all suffer the same, singular passion, the first murmurs and
does what he ought not; the second prays and does what
he ought; the third sacrifices himself for us and does more
than he ought. Although all are accused, the first is accused
justly, for by defending himself pridefully he casts himself
into the hell of sin. The second is accused, not unjustly,
but by confessing his fault and making a virtue of necessity
he is reconciled by the absolution of his prelate; although
a thief, he becomes a martyr entering the paradise of the
Church. The third is accused altogether unjustly. Although
he does not protest his innocence, the silent witness of his
clear conscience, his evident disdain for earthly glory and
the triumph he so brings to himself carries him to
heaven.[43]

---

[43] R: *Etsi dicimus non magnum esse peccatum quod se excusat justus, dicere tamen
possumus non magnum esse meritum quod se non excusat injustus. Potest namque et
percipere veniam et evadere poenam; sed illam ad quam feliciter sublimantur qui se non
excusant justi nec gratiam meretur nec gloriam. Illud itaque bonum, hoc vero melius est.
Scis itaque quia tres in die passionis Domini in cruce fuerunt suspensi, videlicet latro
blasphemus, latro confitens et Agnus innocens. Et quid aliud putamus esse capituli rigorem
nisi quamdam crucis passionem? Et in hac passsione quidam sunt blasphemantes, quidam*

Obedience is also costly. The religious sees the weaknesses of his superiors, for they too are men prone to take their own will as reason and themselves to neglect what they ask others to do. Yet here faith helps to recall these superiors' divine mission: that they command in the name of the Church. "Do you not know that prelates command you in place of the High Priest?"[44] He who hears them hears Christ and he who ignores them ignores Christ.

Another very heavy weight to bear is claustration: not to leave the cloister without permission and to go out only in order to go to the dormitory or the church, then to return as soon as one is able. The religious is tempted to say to himself that those brothers required by their duties occasionally to leave the cloister are fortunate because they are revived by variety. Reason then rises up, however, and points out that those are entirely carnal thoughts. The cloister then weighs only upon him who does not know how to keep it, for in the cloister the religious may search the depths of the allegorical explanations of scripture, reads the beautiful lives of the saints, feeds upon the sweet nourishment of the psalms. Meanwhile, the officers of the monastery suffer from hunger and cold, travel at night, face storms, snow, and rain, and they are thereby made vulnerable to many faults.[45]

---

confitentes, quidam etiam innocentes. Primi rebelles, secundi paenitentes, tertii humiles. Primi merentur paenam, secundi veniam, tertii gloriam. Primos designat latro blasphemus, secundos latro quidem alius sed confitens, tertios innocens et humilis Jesus. Et cum in una eademque passione, primus tamen murmurat et facit quod non debet, secundus orat et facit quod debet, tertius semetipsum pro nobis immolat et facit plus quam debet. Cumque omnes accusentur, primus tamen accusatur juste quia suam nequitiam per superbiam defendens ruit in infernum peccati. Secundus vero non injuste qui et culpam per confessionem agnoscens et in voluntatem necessitatem convertens per absolutionem praelati reconciliatus et ex latrone martyr effectus, intrat paradisum Ecclesiae. Tertius vero omnino injuste et suam non excusans innocentiam per tacitum bonae conscientiae testimonium, per plenum mundanae gloriae contemptum, per fortem ipsius triumphum etiam caelum ascendit. Adam, *De instructione animae*, PL 198, col. 850.

The same notion, borrowed from Saint Augustine, evidently inspired Bossuet's magnificent Palm Sunday sermon on suffering.

[44] *Nescis quia vice summi Pontificis praelati tibi praesunt?* Adam, *De instructione animae*, PL 198, col. 851.

[45] *In claustro . . . rimaris profunditates expositionum, narrationes exemplorum legis, dulcem ruminas cibum psalmorum. . . . Quoties ipsi foris jejunant et esuriunt! . . .*

Certainly, however, the brothers do not suffer greatly from their fasting, for the food is healthy and abundant, although perpetual abstinence can also be tiresome. Adam is indignant at this complaint, asking whether they are then like infants or pregnant women who need delicate, carefully seasoned dishes?[46] In short, the office, the work, the vigils, the silence: all these features of regular life take their toll. The abbot of Dryburgh sympathizes, even excuses to degree, but above all he raises up his reader by the love of Christ and draws him to heaven. Thus in this first book of his dialogue on the instruction of the soul, Adam sets forth the very best of his ascetical theology, just as he offered the essence of his mystical theology in *On Threefold Contemplation*.

The second book discusses the soul of the Premonstratensian in relation to his vocation, again explaining the formula of profession but this time in a manner more vigorous and compact than in the sermons. The soul promises the conversion of its moral habits: "If you were stained before, you must now be chaste and pure; if you were proud and envious, you must now be humble and kind; if you were haughty and angry, you must now be lowly and meek."[47] The soul also promises stability of place; here begins a dialogue about which Adam's conscience must have anguished, since his vocation now began to draw him to Chartreuse:

Reason: You vowed stability in this house? As I see it, if at all possible you must then not break that vow before the end of your life.

Soul: But if, inflamed with a desire for a greater perfection and a more austere way of life, I desire to amend my life and better my ways, would you not recommend that I go elsewhere?

---

quoties algent . . . quoties tempestates et nives et imbres et ventos . . . sustinent! Adam, *De instructione animae*, PL 198, col. 854.

[46] *Ad instar infirmantium vel etiam . . . ad similitudinem mulierum praegnantium.* Adam, *De instructione animae*, PL 198, col. 856.

[47] *Si prius inquinata eras, amodo sis casta et munda; et si prius superba et invida, modo humilis et benigna; prius tumida et iracunda, modo mitis et mansueta.* Adam, *De instructione animae*, PL 198, col. 860.

Reason: No. I would not recommend this.

Soul: Why not?

Reason: First, because I suspect that you are weak, that you are
        unable to live in this order, so you will the less be able to
        survive a more rigorous way of life. Second, because I fear
        that your departure will bring harm and scandal to those
        who remain here.[48]

The soul promises poverty, and to fail in this is to be guilty of theft,
lying, sacrilege, and apostasy, as in the crime of Ananias and
Sapphira. The soul promises obedience, but in Christ—that is in
all that is not contrary to moral law.

At this point in Adam's text the author opens a debate in which
his prior conclusions now become insufficient. He wants the guilty
to confess to their prelate, since he has charge of their souls. In his
view such confession was necessary as framing perfect trust and
charity between the prelate and his subjects. Next, Adam discusses
private devotions. Although he states that these are good, common
devotions are preferable. Anything diminishing common religious
practices and anything disturbing the peace of the community must
be avoided. Meanwhile, Adam prefers to abstain from celebrating
Mass and leave the altar to another in charity and humility rather
than to grieve that confrere.[49] In short, Adam counsels striving with
all one's might to please the superiors and all the brethren in order
to please God. Therefore, to avoid all that is injurious and to desire
all that is salutary; to obey superiors; to serve equals; to remain

[48] R: *Vovisti stabilitatem in domo tua? Meo quidem consilio, quantum ad te pertinet,
eam ante vitae terminum non dimittas.*

A: *Quid si majoris perfectionis et rigidioris ordinis desiderio accensa vitam meam
emendare et conversationem meam augere voluero: numquid ad alias, ut id faciam,
transmigrare non consulis?*

R: *Certe, non consulo.*

A: *Quare?*

R: *Primum, quia suspectam habeo infirmitatem tuam, ut quae non potes sufferre ordinem
istum, consequens est quod nec sufferre potes rigidiorem. Secundo quia timeo ne per
discessum tuum eis qui post discessum tuum remanent aliquod damnum inferatur et
scandalum.* Adam, *De instructione animae*, PL 198, col. 861.

[49] *Tunc fortasse missam devotius cantas, quando idcirco non cantas ut fratri tuo qui
desiderat cantare cedas.* Adam, *De instructione animae*, PL 198, col. 870.

upright in manner; to be simple in eating habits, diligent in the cloister, rarely in public, attentive to the psalms, and deaf to useless conversations; to be serious and open in the choir, grave and recollected at the altar, useful and conscientious in work, holy and recollected in the dormitory, reserved and joyful in the refectory. All this constitutes a perfect program but is also deeply human in the noblest sense of the word. Adam's dialogue in no way addresses zeal for souls and apostolic ministry, but in regard to community life, it constitutes a manual for the perfect Premonstratensian.

Adam's final work before his departure for the Carthusians is a collection of sermons in two volumes. The collection includes one hundred discourses.[50] The first volume, embracing forty-seven sermons from Advent to the Second Sunday after Epiphany, was published for the first time in 1699 on the basis of a manuscript once belonging to the Celestines of Mantes.[51] The second volume is known only in part from a manuscript of the Celestines of Paris later belonging to the Abbey of Saint Ouen of Rouen.[52] Sixteen sermons remain unknown: one for Ash Wednesday, one for Holy Thursday, four for Easter, two for a synod, one for the Ascension, seven for Pentecost, and one for the election of an abbot.

Adam's preaching, although its tone is easygoing and fatherly, is nonetheless carefully crafted. Its sentences' meter is particularly polished, although alien to our literary style. To an inattentive reader, Adam as preacher may seem simply to follow the free association of his ideas. In fact, however, each of his sermons is a commentary on a sacred text. His close attention to words leads to discussion of their etymology and in turn to allegory. This is the preacher's goal: to allow his reader or listener to appreciate in the scriptural figures the allegorical meaning filled with Christ's riches. For example, for Christmas [Day], Adam considers the Virgin Mary arriving in Bethlehem. Mary is for him the figure of divine grace visiting souls and representing their mother, "our mother bringing

---

[50] Adam, *Sermones*, PL 198, cols. 91–440.

[51] Bibl. Nat. N. f. 1. 17.154.

[52] Rouen 618. This manuscript was edited by Gray Birch in 1901. The sermons *Ad viros religiosos* published by me in 1943 on the basis of Ms. Mazarin 1003 appear in this codex as well. The missing sermons might be preserved in Mss. 23.995 and 34.749 of the British Museum.

us grace."[53] All the deeds of Mary related in the Gospel then shed light on the precise character of the grace that forms Christ in our souls. Thus Adam helps his readers raise themselves to a level of meditation preliminary to mystical contemplation. Further, because Adam desires nothing so much as contemplation, he is in his preaching an insistent and persuasive apostle. Whenever the least opportunity is offered to him, he returns to the topic of contemplation in order to praise its effects and to develop the dispositions it requires in the soul. The reader whose heart lacks this mystical bent cannot understand and still less can appreciate the sermons of Master Adam, but with this key his enchanted world opens. Several passages demand citation here. Let us listen to the preacher speak about the unction of the Holy Spirit.

> That unction teaching us about all things especially makes us aware of the power of God when it comes. The Holy Spirit, the Paraclete whom the Father sends in the name of the Son, himself teaches us and implies all that the Son then directly says. The Spirit teaches us every truth and announces to us what is to come. He not only enlightens us in order that we may know him but also inflames us in order that we may love him, forming these affections in us in various ways. Sometimes he places before the eyes of our soul the sins we committed, arousing us to corporal penance and so afflicting us with deep sorrow. Sometimes he shows us how complete our weakness is in flesh and spirit; destroying our pride and humbling us in his sight, he sometimes shows us the meaninglessness of temporal things. Before the eyes of our mind he depreciates all that takes place here below and lifts us to a manly contempt for such things. At other times he teaches us how terrible God is to the sons of men. Recalling his secret and fearsome judgments, he strikes us with powerful fear. . . . Often too he presents to our inner vision the horrible pains of hell. . . . Then, in contrast, he recalls to us the feasts of our heavenly homeland, the joys of eternal brightness. . . . And sometimes he rouses us to the heights of perfection.[54]

---

[53] . . . *matrem gratiam nos comitantem.* Adam, *Sermones,* PL 198, col. 230.

[54] *Unctio quae docet de omnibus dat nobis potissimum videre Dei potentiam venientem. Paraclitus namque Spiritus sanctus quem mittet Pater in nomine Filii, ipse nos docet et suggerit omnia quaecumque idem Filius dicit nobis. Ipse nos docet omnem veritatem: ipse*

Now he speaks about the power of grace:

> When grace is absent, as each of you knows and has experienced
> is often the case, the temptation of the flesh rages. The hand-
> maiden tries to take possession of her mistress's inheritance. The
> lazy, evil slave, although he has been meticulously nourished,
> revolts as Solomon predicted. Eve steals and offers her husband
> that ill-gained food. The thorns she planted in the field of our
> body rise up, multiply, and greatly increase as she cultivates and
> waters them; the bramble pricks and its thorns are bloodied. Our
> flesh is covered with decay and filth and dust while the angel of
> Satan does not cease to beat it. . . . This poor man is sick almost
> unto death, so weak that he can scarcely breathe. But then the
> morning light of which we speak appears and day breaks. In the
> brightness of a new morning, that is the coming of interior grace
> into the soul, Israel's spiritual sons will see the glory of God. . . .
> Anticipating this joyful and life-bringing arrival, the weak and
> sickly flesh submits and the strong, prompt spirit regains its
> power, that is, the spirit forcefully mortifies the deeds of the flesh.
> Thus Job, when he hears the evil suggestions of his wife, declares
> manfully that she has spoken as a foolish woman. The spirit
> bridles the beast who bears it, that is its own flesh, lest it be im-
> petuous. The spirit drives the flesh lest it lose its way and spurs
> it lest it be lazy. . . . Fasting becomes a game, vigils are frequent,
> nakedness seems warmth, poverty is embraced as the highest
> pleasure.[55]

---

*etiam quae ventura sunt annuntiat nobis. Ipse nos non modo ad cognitionem illuminat,
sed ad affectionem inflammat. Et variis quidem modo varios in nobis affectus format. Modo
enim peccata quae jam commisimus mentis nostrae oculis opponit et ad paenitentiam
corpora nostra excitans, dolore nos maximo ferit. Modo nobis quantam et in carne et in
mente infirmitatem circumferimus demonstrat et omnem in nobis superbiam perimens, in
suo nos conspectu humilians, aliquando vero quam nullius momenti sunt omnia temporalia
ostendit, et ante mentis nostrae oculos universa quae hic volvuntur vilipendens in eorum
nos contemptum viriliter erigit. Nonnunquam quam sit terribilis Deus super filios hominum
nos erudit et occulta ejus judicia valde formidanda asserens timore nos validissimo concutit.
Plerumque horribiles infernos paenas considerationis nostrae oculis repraesentat. . . . Ipsa
enim festa supernae patriae, ipsa gaudia internae claritatis . . . imprimit; . . . Nonnumquam etiam ad perfectionis culmen . . . excitat.* Adam, *Sermones,* PL 198, col. 126.

[55] *Absente namque gratia, ut unusquisque vestrum multoties sentit et experitur; carnis
statim tentatio saevit. Haereditatem dominae praeoccupare tentat ancilla. Delicate*

Here Adam speaks about the spiritual union between souls and God in reference to the wedding at Cana.

> While maintaining the complex and truthful understanding of the profundity of this miracle handed down from our teachers and fathers, let us here apply the ministry of our language to only the moral level of interpretation, seeking in the text on the wedding that inner, sweet, and pure bond by which God and the soul are joined in the unity of true love as Bridegroom and bride. I speak of this bond with much trepidation because none can discuss it in an appropriate way who has himself not yet experienced it. Therefore I heartily wish that some one of you who has known this union would now continue my work, dipping his pen in the ink of his own experience. He might then proceed to depict for us how a man's spirit—cleansed and purified by that supreme and uncreated Spirit who created all spirits and all bodies—may be united with God in the holy sweetness of true love and, to the extent possible in this earthly exile, in sweet holiness, when this great benefit is fully complete and entirely perfected so that the joy of this true love is pure and untroubled in its purity. But perhaps some one of you might be angry and respond to this, "Why do you make this excuse? How long will you keep us waiting? Tell us straightforwardly, and without any admixture of any useless remarks, what you think about this subject you have raised." So be it. I have said, then, that God is the Bridegroom and the soul the bride. O how great a dignity for the soul

---

aliquando nutritus servus ille malus et piger, contumax, ut promittit Salomon, sentitur. Eva furit; illicitam viro comestionem suggerit. Insurgunt et germinant atque in immensum crescent, ipsa rigante et excolente, quas in agro corporis nostri plantavit spinae. Et tribuli pungunt et cruentant stimuli. Induitur caro putredine et sordibus et pulvere, ipsam denique colaphizare non cessat angelus Satanae. . . . Aegrotat certe iste, imo pene usque ad mortem et est languor ejus fortissimus, ita ut vix remaneat in eo halitus. Sed erumpente hoc lumine de quo loquimur mane, illucescente et hac clara crastina die, illapso scilicet in mentem adventu internae gratiae, viderunt ipsius spirituales filii Israel Dei gloriam. . . . Percepto siquidem laetificante et vivificante ipsius adventu, caro debilis et infirma subjicitur, spiritus facta carnis valenter mortificat. Viriliter Job, cum male suadentem conjugem audit, quasi unam ex stultis mulieribus locutam esse redarguens asserit. Refrenat spiritus jumentum suum; carnem suam, ne sit impetuosa, urget et calcaribus, ne sit pigra, exstimulat. . . . Pro ludo habentur jejunia; pro re quae maxime frequentatur vigiliae; nuditas habetur pro fomento, paupertas possidetur pro summo oblectamento. Adam, *Sermones*, PL 198, cols. 213–14.

to be the bride of God! But not every soul can attain to this dignity, for she who prostitutes herself to every one who walks by, fornicating with her lovers, is rightly called a harlot rather than a bride. And yet God makes the harlot into his bride, effecting that the former harlot may now be married, for he washes and restores her, adapts her and perfects her so that she can truly be called a bride. He washes away her impurity, amends her disarray, rectifies her unsuitability and perfects what was ruined. Finally, he bathes her to make her pure, repairs her to restore her, dresses her to adorn her, and he perfects her to make her whole.[56]

---

[56] *Salvo . . . intellectu illo vario atque veraci quem semper miraculi hujus profunditate a magistris et Patribus nostris percepimus, ad solum sensum moralem linguae nostrae ministerium hic applicemus et in nuptiis istis internam, jucundam et mundam qua invicem in unitate veri amoris copulantur Deus sponsus et anima sponsa conjunctionem requiramus. De qua conjunctione loqui non parum formido quia de ea digne loqui non potest qui eam in semetipso adhuc expertus non est. Quam vellem lubenter ut expertus tractaret modo inde aliquis vestrum: et intingens calamum, in atramento propriae experientiae dirigeretur, depingens coram nobis quid est spiritum hominis defaecatum et purificatum Spiritui illi summo et increato, omnium tam spirituum quam corporum conditori, in sancta veri amoris jucunditate et jucunda (quantum in hoc exsilio possibile est) sanctitate uniri: in tantum hoc bono undique coaptato et perfecte consummato ut nec laetitia mutui hujus amoris immunda, nec munditia in aliquo sit turbulenta. Sed substomachans fortassis ad hoc responde aliquis vestrum et dicit: ut quid haec excusatio tua? quousque nos suspendis? dic nobis in directum sine adjectione aliorum quae sunt praeter rem: quid tibi videatur super his quae proposuisti. Ita fiat. Diximus ergo Deum sponsum et animam sponsam. O quanta dignitas animae esse sponsam Dei! Non autem omnis anima ad hanc potest pertingere dignitatem, nam illa quae divaricat pedes omni transeunti, fornicans post amatores suos magis meretrix quam sponsa dicenda est. Attamen de meretrice facit Deus sponsam suam, talem faciens eam quae aliquando meretrix fuit, ut jam sponsa esse possit. Lavat namque eam et reparat, coaptat et consummat, ut jam ex re sponsa appellari queat. Lavat immundam, reparat discissam, coaptat ineptam, consummat destructam. Denique lavat ad emundationem, reparat ad restitutionem, coaptat ad decorum, consummat vero ad perfectionem.* Adam, *Sermones,* PL 198, cols. 414–15.

This passage might suggest to the careful reader that Adam had never been raised to mystical contemplation. Yet the multiplicity of the degrees of contemplation encourages any truly humble soul to speak as Adam does; then too Adam's contemporaries all regarded him as a notable contemplative. Therefore even a cursory reading of his collected works persuades to the contrary. No one becomes such an apostle of contemplation, with such energy and perserverance, unless he has had at least some experience of it. *Ignoti nulla cupido:* "one who does not know cannot desire."

Adam's sermons provide us many more such examples of his frank-
ness and sensibility, including this delightful passage on the love
of Christ:

> Your whole goal ought to be not only to touch but to anoint
> Jesus, because every fruit of your tranquil, learned, and enlight-
> ened life, o you who are cloistered, ought to be truly to love
> Christ. Love therefore is the unction you offer. Mary's ointment
> was made of nard; the scent is in the nard just as the sweetness
> is in the ointment. What then is the light of reason in us, what
> is the certitude of faith, if not a certain sweet fragrance? It often
> happens, as we said earlier, that we perceive something by its
> odor that we recognize by its appearance. Thus we seek him who
> is absent from us by the odor of reason, with all humility, yet not
> without fear in our investigation, until such time as we can em-
> brace him in our presence. So let us caress him again with the
> sweetness of unction and seek to please him by the gentleness of
> our true love responding to his innumerable gifts to us. That love
> you ought to offer him springs from your full awareness of his
> gifts to you. Perhaps that awareness is the vase in which Mary
> kept the ointment with which she anointed Jesus. According to
> the other evangelists, she kept that perfume in a vase; they called
> it an alabaster jar of unction. This apparently means a vase of a
> type of marble crafted specifically to contain such ointment. What
> more suitable, more transparent a reason can you find to love
> your God than in the consideration of the many great gifts you
> know you have received from him? Diligently consider what he
> has conferred on you, what he still confers on you, which your
> hope rightly trusts he will continue to confer on you. Review
> thoughtfully the benefits of these three periods, looking back to
> the past, forward to the future, and intently examining the
> present. Just as an alabaster jar contains ointment, so this con-
> sideration incites feelings of love. Thus Mark says rightly that
> Mary broke the alabaster jar to pour out the ointment inside. You
> too, in your careful consideration, then crush, stir, turn, press,
> and grind these bits in the pestle of your frequent, oft-renewed
> memory, so discovering there the sincere love which you owe to
> your Jesus. Break your alabaster jar by your consideration of the
> blessings the Lord Jesus has conferred on you in the past and
> what he unceasingly gives you in the present. Do not forget to
> reconsider and rehearse what you hope to receive in the future.

In your threefold consideration—if it is applied with such diligence that you break the alabaster jar containing the perfume
meant for the Lord Jesus—you will find plentiful means and
sufficient reason to love him.[57]

And later:

This love, according to the psalm, is the fire which goes before
the face of Christ toward every soul to which he will come, burning away any rust of the vices in it and establishing a foundation
of virtues. As his enemies are encircled in flames, he then makes
for himself a pure dwelling. When he comes he enters, when he

---

[57] *Omnis itaque intentio non modo ut tangat sed ut ungat Jesum, quia omnis
conversationis vestrae, o claustrales, tranquillae, eruditae et clarificatae fructus est ut ametis
veraciter Christum. Dilectio igitur vestra unctio vestra. Mariae unguentum ex nardo est
compositum et odor in nardo sicut et pinguedo in ungento. Quid in nobis jubar rationis,
quid certitudo fidei nisi quaedam suavis est fragrantia odoris? Solet ut paulo superius
diximus odore deprehendi res quae aspectu non valet apprehendi. Odore igitur rationis cum
humilitate, non sine pavore tamen investigantis; et fidei sine ambiguitate, cum involutione
tamen tenentis; quaerimus per speciem absentem quousque amplecti possimus praesentem.
Et idcirco unguenti eum iterum pinguedine foveamus, verae dilectionis ei suavitate
placeamus, quae dilectio in ejus beneficiis nobis imo innumeris modi collatis consistit. In
plena ergo consideratione beneficiorum ejus illa consistit dilectio qua eum amare debetis.
Et fortasse haec consideratio vas illud est in quo habuit Maria unguentum quo unxit Jesum.
Nam juxta alios evangelistas in vase unguentum illud habuit quo Dominum unxit et
vocaverunt illud alabastrum unguenti. Est autem, ut aiunt, vas ex illo genere marmoris
factum, aptum et optimum ad servandum intus positum unguentum. Et ubi aptius vel
evidentius causam reperire potes qua Deum tuum diligere possis quam in consideratione
tantorum ac talium beneficiorum ejus quae ab ipso te percepisse cognoscis? Considera
diligenter quae contulit et quae adhuc conferre non desinit et ipsum tibi collaturum pia in
te quae non confundit spes confidit. Horum itaque trium temporum beneficia in mente,
prout potes, collige, praeterita respiciens, praesentia prospiciens et quasi in alabastro quo
ungere possis unguentum sic quoque in hac consideratione quo queas diligere illum invenies
affectum. Unde bene dicit Marcus quod fracto alabastro effudit illam quae in eo erat
unctionem, ut tu hac diligenter consideratione apud te quam detrita, voluta et revoluta et
quodammodo fracta atque pistillo crebrae ac multimodae recordationis in quaedam quasi
frusta comminuta sinceram quam tuo Jesu impendas in ea reperies dilectionem, frange ita
alabastrum tuum studiosa consideratione quae tibi contulit Dominus Jesus beneficia in
praeterito, quae adhuc incessanter confert in praesenti, nec illa apud te retractare et
recogitare omittas quae te in futuro accepturum speras. In triplici consideratione tua si
diligenti fuerit recordatione discussa ut frangatur alabastrum in quo unguentum est quo
ungendus est Dominus Jesus, plenam materiam et sufficientem invenies causam ut diligas
eum.* Adam, *Ad viros religiosos*, 230.

enters he lives, and where he lives he possesses the soul without stain or wrinkle. This love pours into the soul itself, filling it not only with rejection but also forgetfulness of all earthly things, such that all other sweetness becomes bitter to it and every other beauty fades away. How far away then can he be, he who is the sweetness that does not deceive and the beauty which does not fade? This love in the soul is sweet and pleasant, savory and captivating, fragrant and burning, glowing and brightening, shining, resplendent. It illumines and clarifies, smites and strikes, finally inflames and sweetens. It elicits a hunger so insatiable that the soul finds delight or satisfaction in nothing less than the Beloved.[58]

In all these passages that we cited on grace, intimacy with Jesus and freedom of the heart, the major themes of the *Imitation of Christ* appear. As the scholar Dom Butler once said: "In order to know the spirituality of the regular canons it is enough to read the *Imitation*."

The writings of Master Adam of Dryburgh after he became a Carthusian have no place in the present work, but this period in his life gave rise only to the well-known *Four Exercises from the Cell*; it offers the reader much of interest and much spiritual joy. Importantly, Master Adam taught among the Carthusians the same doctrine he taught among the Premonstratensians, although this work is nonetheless one of the most significant monuments of Carthusian spirituality. This one example indeed demonstrates that, during the thirteenth century, schools of spirituality were markedly similar.

A glance at the complex whole of Adam's work is then useful. His rich, fresh imagination furnished his work with ingenious

---

[58] *Hic amor ille apud psalmum ignis est qui ante faciem Christi procedit ad omnem animam ad quam ipse est venturus rubiginem si qua ibi est exurens vitiorum et solidamenta fundans virtutum ut, inflammatis in circuitu inimicis ejus, quoddam sibi eam mundum coaptet receptaculum, quatenus ille veniens introeat, introiens inhabitet, inhabitans possideat illam sine macula et ruga. Infundit siquidem amor iste menti cui se infundit omnium visibilium non modo abjectionem sed et oblivionem ut omnis eorum ei dulcedo amarescat et in ea species marcescat, quatenus eis apud eam ipse succedat qui est tam dulcor non decipiens quam decor non marcescens. Hic in ea dulcescit et placet, sapit et rapit, fragrat et flagrat, fulget et lucet, nitet et splendet, illuminat et illustrat, percutit et concutit, accendit denique eam et ungit, internum quoque os ejus gula quadam insatiabili inficiens, ut eam prorsus non delectet nec satiet quidquid ipso qui amatur minus est.* Adam, *Ad viros religiosos*, 233.

allegories, poetic and heavy with doctrine; his sensibility was apt at understanding, appreciating and loving all that he knew; his intellect was clear, logical, and penetrating; his learning was carefully fed by continual reading and meditation. Overall, he was a man of the first rank. Yet he remains relatively unknown in modern times because, as noted above, in that immense intellectual movement of the twelfth century—extending from a prayerful, fervent Augustinianism concerned with the entire man, to a scholasticism aimed principally at the intellect and little concerned with literary craft and sensibility—Adam remained faithful to the Augustinian tradition. Surely he found it more useful for a life of contemplation and this was indeed all that concerned him in this life. Since he found God and helped others find him, he desired no more.

The Spirituality of Adam Scot

This study of Adam concludes with a synoptic view of his rich, complex spirituality. In his asceticism he is continually concerned, like a true Augustinian, with man's final end:

> Is a creature's great happiness not to be like God? Yet to see him is to be like him. *We shall be like him*, as the apostle says, *because we shall see him as he is* [1 John 3:2]. Is God not light, unchanging, eternal? In seeing his light we ourselves become luminous; in seeing his immutability we free ourselves of change; in seeing eternity we ourselves become immortal.[59]

Adam here evinces a nostaligia for heaven, but because one cannot possess God in heaven without an image of him sketched on earth, as he points out, our life's work is increasing union to him. The continuity between this life and the life of heaven is like that between Sunday and the weekdays. The ideal, that is, the sabbath—the rest which comes with mystical contemplation—might come

---

[59] *Deo quoque in regno similem esse nonne magnae . . . felicitatis est? et videre eum similem ei esse est.* Similes, *ait,* illi erimus quoniam videbimus eum sicuti est. . . . *Nonne Deus lux, incommutabilitas et aeternitas est? Videndo autem lucem, erimus et nos lucidi; videndo autem incommutabilitatem, et nos efficiemur immutabiles; videndo aeternum, erimus et nos perennes.* Adam, *Sermones,* PL 198, cols. 120–21.

among the days of work, symbols on the one hand of ascetic labor and on the other of great Sunday joy.[60] For Adam, then, all asceticism is toward this cultivation of mystical life. Man is aided by grace in his journey toward God. Grace is our mother. Nothing helps us know it so much as contemplating the Virgin Mary. Grace accompanies us as Mary accompanied Jesus, for if it did not go before us as aspiring grace, if it did not follow us as helping grace and if it did not accompany us as consoling grace, no progress would be possible. This tender mother smiles upon us and allows us to hope for heaven, but she is invisible; so long as we are on this earth we are not absolutely certain of possessing her.[61]

The journey toward God first presupposes conversion, for the error of our first father wounded each human soul in all its faculties. We must turn back to God. The Father will cure the memory by creating in it a salutary fear; the Son will repair our reason by investing it with wisdom and knowledge; the Holy Spirit will relieve the will by kindly inspiring in it charity.[62] Disgust for sin, fear of death and hell, desire for divine mercy, and joy at the thought of heaven follow one another into the soul in order to divest it of evil. Sacramental confession will obtain pardon for the soul, but absolution does not suppress the attraction of evil. The effort to choke off every evil disposition in the soul, fasts, vigils, manual labor, the maintenance of chastity, a serious expression, the love of silence,

---

[60] *Post hanc dies illucescit septima, et est Sabbatum requietionis, clara videlicet quies et quieta claritas internae contemplationis.* ("After this the seventh day shines, and it is the Sabbath of rest, the bright rest and the quiet brightness of internal contemplation.") Adam, *Sermones*, PL 198, col. 232.

[61] *Arridet nobis mater nostra, gratia interna et pie speramus quod ipsa nobis quae modo sanctitatem confert in via, custodiens et perficiens opera misericordiae, conformiter et felicitatem nobis conferet in patria, et quae coepit in nobis opus bonum perficiet usque in diem Christi Jesu, sed tamen vitam nostram absconditam intuentes et circumdatos atque involutos nos tenebris intelligentes, plene, ut dixi, jam certi non sumus.* ("Our mother smiles upon us; and by internal grace we piously hope that she who confers sanctity on us here along the way, guarding us and performing works of mercy, will likewise confer on us happiness in heaven, and will perfect that good work she began in us until the day of Christ Jesus; but seeing as we do our hidden life and knowing that we are surrounded and wrapped in darkness, we are indeed, as I said, not certain.") Adam, *Sermones*, PL 198, col. 231.

[62] Adam, *De tripartito tabernaculo*, PL 198, col. 770.

poor dress, and gravity of manner then will mortify any remaining disorder.[63]

Religious life supports the organization of all these ascetical practices. In his dialogue Adam shows that he well knew both its crucifying pains and its spiritual advantages. He listens, he shows mercy, but most of all he raises his reader up by the love of Christ and the attraction of heaven. On many occasions Adam speaks of the exercises of the monastic life: reading, work, and prayer. At Witham he would list four: reading, meditation, prayer, and work. He describes them, expounding their advantages for the soul, taking on this subject especially willingly. His comprehensive ascetic program leads to that contemplative life he loved with all his soul and experienced profoundly, despite his humble denials.

For Adam a natural continuity bound faith and contemplation so closely that the juncture between them was sometimes unclear. In meditating on sacred scripture man is ordinarily elevated to God. By the influence of the Holy Spirit sudden illumination uncovers in the letter of the text its profound and mysterious meanings. Then the soul is raised up more, coming instantly to repose and silence where, through the Holy Spirit, it perceives God. It then falls back to the allegorical meditation on the text, whence it may up again, perhaps moments later. Contemplation is a kind of knowledge, like the vision of God's works in creation—like faith, like apparitions, another species of vision by which one sees God while in this world. One sees God, not in himself, yet one indeed sees him. Such contemplation comes to those whom God judges worthy of this grace; their hearts must be purified because such vision cannot be known except by pure hearts. It is occasioned sometimes by imaginative or corporeal representations and sometimes by that unction teaching all things.[64] But contemplation is more than

---

[63] Adam, *Sermones*, PL 198, col. 256.

[64] *Est alia quoque visio qua etiam in praesenti videtur Deus, licet non in se ipso, etsi qui videtur sit ipse. Et videtur quidem ab illis quos haec gratia dignos judicat, quos et ipsos mundos corde esse oportet. Neque enim vel haec visio nisi a mundis cordibus apprehendi potest. Haec est quae per imagines sive mentis sive corporis ostensas oculis aut etiam per unctionem quae docet de omnibus fidei animae confertur qua vel raptim per intellectum vel securitate per fidem videt.* Adam, *Sernones*, PL 198, col. 121. Mystical knowledge is represented specifically by the unction.

knowledge; it is also rest, an end, the relative satisfaction of our
desire to see God. One cannot approach this rest without purifying
preparations. Adam describes these as successive slumbers closing
the soul away from all created things before it passes as through
successive places even to God:[65] through the womb of the Virgin,
through the crèche, and through the cross before arriving at the
sepulcher.[66] These are the spiritual nuptials for which the Bridegroom prepares the bride by the sweet torment of love.[67] Even when
one has arrived at contemplation, only humility and purity of
intention can guard it. The adjectives *pura* and *defaecata*, pure and
cleansed of filth, are integral in Adam's works alongside the term
contemplatio. The author attributes this contemplation to the
unction of the Holy Spirit and its gift of wisdom, which he studies
under the allegory of Abisag, the virgin bride of the aging David.[68]
Her name signifies "the roar of my father," and she thus represents
that unspeakable groaning rising up from the soul in silent clamor
and clamorous silence. She is beautiful in every way and the servants
of David—holiness of life, prayer, purity, and meditation—seek her
everywhere. David himself is the soul about to receive wisdom. He
is an old man; he is cold. Such a soul no longer receives any consolation from the things of this world. But Abisag presents herself.
She stands upright before the king in order to direct the intention
toward God. She sleeps with him, giving his soul complete rest and
his heart tranquillity. She warms him by the ardor of charity and
interior sweetness she lets him taste. But the king does not know
her carnally, for her fertility is only from God. Human activity can
only harm her. This wisdom, then, has wonderful fruits: humility,
mortification, patience, the desire for heaven, justice.[69] Contemplation lends such action as leads it to a new fertility, while it brings
life-giving impulse to sollicitude for one's neighbor. The fertility of
Leah is united to the beauty of Rachel.[70] This contemplation, located

[65] Adam, *Sermones*, PL 198, col. 321.

[66] Adam, *De ordine, habitu et professione canonicorum ordinis Praemonstratensis*, PL
198, col. 474.

[67] Adam, *Sermones*, PL 198, col. 416.

[68] Adam, *Sermones*, PL 198, cols. 231, 825, 311, 312.

[69] Adam, *Sermones*, PL 198, cols. 314–16.

[70] Adam, *De tripartito tabernaculo*, PL 198, col. 774.

by Adam within the normal course of grace, can be reached. Even the laity can attain it.[71] That said, to make known this precious pearl is most useful in the cloister.

This rapid synopsis offers only a pale notion of the spiritual riches in Adam Scot's work. His entire life was an effort to promote mystical experience in the monastic context. To the Premonstratensians he recalled the thousand ways in which the role proper to the regular canons is to rest their care of souls on their contemplative life whose observances are but a framework toward reaching sufficient power of purity, desire, and prayer for their work. Adam then reminded the Carthusians of the grandeurs of the solitary life uniquely occupied with seeking the One. He could not escape the affectation of his time but readers and disciples were drawn to his poetry, his rhetorical abundance, his frank humility, and his moving sincerity.

---

[71] *Fideles laici . . . propter quinque sensuum munditiam cui intendunt ad mentis etiam nonnunquam quietem etiam in praesenti pertingunt.* ("They faithful laity, on account of the purity of the five senses towards which they strive, often attain repose even in this life.") Adam, *De tripartito tabernaculo*, PL 198, 726.

Part 3
Norbertine Life

Despite the accomplishments of Philip of Harvengt and Master Adam of Dryburgh, these authors' respective syntheses of Premonstratensian spirituality are necessarily incomplete because they so closely follow the foundation of the order and they were constructed without mutual awareness. Most important, these authors were perforce unaware of later developments in the spiritual tendencies of their brothers. Therefore the present study here requires an outline of the whole of the life of Saint Norbert and his first sons based in the works that we have now analyzed. What central idea might then shape our observations? This question is useful because prior discussions have yielded diverse opinions. If we ask it of authors outside the order but contemporary with its foundation and early development, they are quick to point out that the foundational tone of Norbertine life is of austerity and mortification. Herman, abbot of Saint Martin of Tournai, tells us how Norbert began to serve God in the solitude of Prémontré under the Rule of Saint Augustine with great rigor and strictness.[1] James of Vitry—bishop of Saint John of Acre and later cardinal bishop of Tusculum, a superb observer of monastic

---

[1] *Multum rigidiori et arctiori.* Herman, qtd. in intro. to *Vita S. Norberti,* PL 170, col. 1245.

customs—also remarks that Saint Norbert made the Rule of Saint Augustine much more severe by adding new observances and modifying old ones.[2] For his part, the author of the hundred sermons edited among the works of Hugh of Saint Victor, himself a regular canon, ranks the Premonstratensians along with the Carthusians, the Cistercians, and the Order of Grandmont as among the glories of the desert life on account of their rigorous penance.[3]

If we return, however, to Premonstratensian spiritual authors— Philip of Harvengt and Adam Scot, as well as the sermon of Saint Norbert—the essence of the order's life appears rather to be contemplation or the care of souls founded on a truly contemplative life. This is their central focus. As we look more closely, however, we note that a similar perspective marked all the other regular canons as well, even among those whose life was the most active. In sum, the role of the spiritual masters is always and everywhere to recall readers to the contemplative life as the foundation of their apostolate, pointing out that too many active pursuits continually risk neglect of contemplation. No preacher, generally speaking, fails to reprimand the sloth of confreres or the negligence of superiors. All struggle to enjoin the cloistered to peaceful devotion to their sacred reading and meditation.

Still again, attention to collections of Premonstratensian sermons or to the lives of certain saints, for example Christine of Christ, suggests that liturgical life was the order's central framework. The author of the annals of Laon, evidently a Premonstratensian, wrote in 1218 that the Premonstratensians sought nothing other than to praise the name of the Lord and to sing him a new song.[4] And indeed all of Norbertine life is ordered by the rhythm of the liturgy: prayer, habitual thoughts, penances, the regime of life; all strictly follows the ecclesiastical calendar, but in a fashion similar to the practice of all the religious communities founded before the modern period.

[2] *Vivendi modum . . . in se et in discipulis suis coarctavit.* James of Vitry, qtd. in intro. to *Vita S. Norberti,* PL 170, col. 1250.

[3] *Speciosa deserti.* Hugh of Saint Victor, *Sermones Centum,* PL 177, col. 1127.

[4] *Annales Laudunenses,* qtd. in intro. to *Vita S. Norberti,* PL 170, col. 1249.

More recent authors, writing in the eighteenth century, listed the central traits of Norbertine life as five: praise of God in the choir, eucharistic devotion, Marian devotion, a spirit of continual penance, and zeal for souls. This enumeration is insightful, suggesting profound experience of the Premonstratensian life, but it points to no singular governing principle. Anselm of Havelberg is much closer to the thought of Saint Norbert himself when he says that the founder gathered a great crowd of religious through his preaching and founded numerous monasteries informed by his word and example for the perfection of the apostolic life.[5] Likewise, the author of the life of Saint Norbert summarizes the intention of the founder with words borrowed from the Augustinian Rule: "He wished to live the apostolic way of life."[6] Later, wherever the order has since rediscovered its original vigor and fervor, this notion has assumed new life.

Here, then, we shall open up the thought of Norbert and his first disciples by addressing the characteristics of their life according to the formula of their profession: to live "according to the Gospel of Jesus Christ, the apostolic institution and the Rule of Saint Augustine." The two latter phrases are practically identical, since the eleventh and twelfth centuries embraced the Augustinian Rule, as discussed above, precisely because they held it to be the most exact prescription for the apostolic life. To see how they understood the Gospel of Christ and the apostolic institution will then be sufficient, yet sometimes we will add to that description observations from personal experience. As demonstrated by the great number of the texts cited here, Norbertines form one family fully united on the most important points of religious life. It is therefore entirely possible to highlight both the great traditions and deep tendencies expressed in the literary inheritance of Premonstratensian ideas and sentiments.

---

[5] Anselm, *Dialogi*, PL 188, col. 1247.

[6] *Apostolica enim vita jam optabat vivere. Vita S. Norberti*, PL 170, col. 1292.

Chapter 1
The Gospel of Christ

The first Premonstratensians, in professing a life according to the Gospel of Christ, clearly did not mean, according to one modern formula, to follow the entire Gospel in every aspect of their life. Of course they lived the Gospel, for no one can otherwise be a Christian at all. Yet for the early followers of Norbert, as for all their contemporaries—for instance Saint Peter Damian—the Gospel life was grounded in that specific passage where Christ counsels his apostles on how they must go forth to proclaim the good news: traveling in pairs without money, without walking stick or change of clothes; working without payment but trusting in Providence to feed them because the worker is worth his wage. Here the Savior wished to guarantee the independence of the Gospel message from the secular state, from riches and from human collectivities; no one has great influence among the poor without embracing their poverty. Saint Norbert was thus joyful, when he first began to preach, at the thought that he was now like the apostles in his renunciation.

At Christmas of 1121 the first professions were made at Prémontré *ad instar dominicae descriptionis*, according to the Lord's own model. No obstacle to the Gospel precept was tolerated. Like Norbert, the first Premonstratensians were Christ's own poor, freely offering their apostolic labor to all, asking for no food or clothing in return and confident in the grace of that God who furnishes his servants

240

with the necessities of daily life.[7] Such was clearly the intention in 1121 of the first members of the community at Prémontré in their profession *secundum evangelium*, according to the Gospel. Perhaps in the course of time this phrase took on a more general sense, especially when missionary preaching became rarer as detailed above. The words "according to the Gospel" then signified imitation of the entire life of Christ in communion with all his mysteries. Adam Scot suggested this when he spoke to his own soul, "You are bound by the practices of humility in the school of Christ." They considered the monastery, as earlier monks had, a *schola Christi*, a school of Jesus Christ[8]—the more so when in the twelfth century the love of the Savior's humanity increasingly won the hearts of the faithful, especially of religious. Thus, in characterizing the Premonstratensians, the monk Herman of Laon said: "They are unceasingly inflamed with only the love of Christ."[9] But the original meaning of the Gospel institution remained essential. Gospel institution and apostolic institution remained distinct yet closely associated. In renewing the life of the early Church the apostolic institution enabled the formation of apostles who were then able to go and preach the Gospel in poverty according to the counsels of the Lord. The monastery was the greenhouse where, like precious flowers, the souls of these preachers might bloom in contemplation and so be renewed. The prayers and penances of the entire community would assure these missioners of the support of divine grace.

Norbert himself was the model of these apostolic preachers. As his contemporaries believed, no one else since the apostles had won so many souls for Jesus Christ. The founder seems nevertheless to have had few imitators within the order. The only widely known Premonstratensian preachers of the twelfth and thirteenth centuries were: Waltman, abbot of Saint Michael of Antwerp; Eberwin, provost of Steinfeld; Almaric, first abbot of Floreffe; Anselm of Havelberg; Zachary of Besançon; Robert of Wimy; Adam Scot; Cain

---

[7] *Erant enim vere pauperes Christi laborem suum aliis gratuito impendentes, nihil a quoquam in victu seu vestitu vel accipientes. Vita S. Norberti*, PL 170, col. 1276.

[8] *Humilitatis disciplinis in schola Christi associata es.* Adam Scot, *Soliloquiae*, PL 198, col. 844.

[9] *Solo Christi jugiter ardent amore.* Herman, PL 156, col. 989.

of Strahov; Sanctius, abbot of Retorta; Henry of Ninoveh; Nicholas of Vicogne; Ermeric; Stephen of Belval; Nicholas of Haguenau; Thierry of Romersdorff. Many more may go unremembered, but clearly no throngs of white-robed preachers traversed the roads of Northern Europe. The preaching of the Premonstratensians was on the whole much more pastoral than itinerant. Still Norbert's first disciples' notions about preaching bear investigation—their conception of preparation for the apostolate and of appropriate fulfillment of their holy ministry. Their example in this regard is more instructive than their theory. Obviously, only learned preaching in Latin is documented. Other preaching, popular preaching in a Germanic or Romance language, was a distant imitation of Latin models.

The primary characteristic of the order's preaching was, unsurprisingly, its grounding in long contemplation. Just as the tabernacle of the Old Law required adornment within and without, so the preacher must enter within himself to meditate on holy truths, then go out to plant seeds toward the good of others; he must go inside to contemplate and be sanctified, outside to imitate what he has contemplated and to take action; inside in order to please God in his heart, outside in order to support the salvation of his neighbor by his own action.[10] Such was the example of both our Lord and his precursor, John the Baptist, who did not begin their preaching until they were thirty years old, so after long preparation in silence. They were thus required to embrace silence as sacrifice made difficult by their natural impatience to act. A man of Norbert's character, fiery and impatient of rest, surely found this waiting painful, but he "mitigated his desire by the hope of bearing a more abundant fruit."[11] Like the apostles, the Premonstratensians thus acquired the beatitude of mercy—*Blessed are the merciful, for they shall obtain mercy* (Matt 5:7)— through their solicitude for their

---

[10] *Intus ut sancta mediteris, foris ut utilia opereris; intus ad contemplationem sanctificationis, foris ad imitationem actionis, intus ut in corde placeas Deo, foris ut in opere prosis proximo.* Adam, *De tripartito tabernaculo,* PL 198, col. 747. These comments of Adam Scot demonstrate that the care of souls and active apostolate were present even among those who emphasized contemplation.

[11] *Demulcebat desiderium suum spe uberioris fructus. Vita S. Norberti,* PL 170, col. 1262.

neighbor in preaching, in caring for the sick, in healing, in evangelizing. They attained this, however, only by devoting themselves to the acquisition of another beatitude: *Blessed are the clean of heart, for they shall see God* (Matt 5:8).[12] In this commitment to preaching and purity, Anselm of Havelberg, in the remote regions of the North, was the trustee of the founder's thought.

The balance between contemplation and apostolic action is delicate, a question of obedience and finally also of charity. "How should the saints be made drunk by God in contemplation? How ought they maintain their sobriety in good works? Our mother charity effects this," said Adam Scot. In the repose of a twofold charity—in the love of God and of neighbor—they learn when they must abandon action for a time in order to embrace contemplation for the sake of God's sweetness, then when they must lay aside contemplation to focus on action for the sake of the needs of a neighbor.[13] When circumstances changed and the needs of souls abated in those countries where the Premonstratensians flourished, excepting Prussia and Palestine, religious of the order soon ceased their itinerant preaching. The spiritual renewal brought to southern Europe by Saint Francis of Assisi and Saint Dominic had thus come a century earlier to the north—to Picardy, Artois, Champagne, Flanders, Bavaria, Saxony, England, and Scotland—in the efflorescence of the regular canons and the apostolic movement. The disciples of Norbert spread widely, founding monasteries in central Europe, although they were unsuccessful in Gascony and Spain, and their zeal found no effect in the crusade against the Albigensians. The name "North-bert" means the prince of the North; our Norbert's followers' temperament evidently did not bring them the ardor, volubility, and frantic action promoted by the eloquence of the Mediterranean countries.

The twofold end of early Premonstratensian preaching was nonetheless clearly to draw souls away from sin and to attract as many as possible to the religious life—in sum to convert souls in the fullest and most precise sense of that term, turning and orienting them toward God with all their faculties and energy. For the

---

[12] Anselm, *Epistola apologetica*, PL 188, col. 1133.
[13] Adam, *Sermones*, PL 198, col. 129.

preacher, then, the first task was to cause the sinner to reenter himself, to move him to reflect on his own state. No doubt this task came relatively easily in the twelfth century, when passions were strong and brutal but when the faith was lively in the Christian masses.[14] First the preacher needed to unveil the shame of the sinner so that, like the prodigal son, he was reduced to wanting the slops set aside for the pigs; he then needed to draw attention to the brevity of life, as indeed Norbert himself came to recognize it at Xanten: that all is transient, fleeting. In Adam Scot's image, the sinner is like Absalom, galloping on his mule through the forest; the mule is a symbol of the world, where an impious man places all his desire so that he passes through it like lightning, then is hung in the woods by his hair: "The rider on the mule dies because the world passes away and he who loves it is punished."[15] Consideration of this reality, at the preacher's urging, spoiled all the joys in which a sinner took delight and snared him in evil.

Next the preacher was required to constrain the sinner to peer into hell, the site of disorder, suffering, and remorse. Saint Norbert's sermon maintains this rhetorical strategy. Notably, Norbert, like Adam Scot, knew no stronger portrayal of the torments of hell than the language of the Church in the rite of exorcism: where no order governs but where eternal horror, *sempiternus horror*, dwells. The sinner will desist when he sees the joys he once loved now flee, unable to promise anything other than eternal suffering. He then gives his assent to that preacher who imposes on him the sweet harshness of recompense even as that harsh sweetness leading to damnation fades before him.

Fear, however, is only the beginning of conversion. It must lead to love and to maintaining from the start such balance that it brings neither despair nor the desire for dissolution. The severe cold of fear must be tempered with the sweet warmth of love and vice versa. This approach to preaching is grounded in a profound psychology. Souls weaned too early in fear later struggle to persevere in love, but love may be aroused by recalling the mercies of God, his com-

---

[14] Adam Scot indicates in his Sermon 9 the entire strategy which the preacher ought to employ. Adam, *Sermones*, PL 198, cols. 149–54.

[15] *Muli moritur sessor, quia transit mundus et mundi punitur amator.* Adam, *Sermones*, PL 198, col. 149.

portment toward Mary Magdalene and toward both the repentant Peter and the good thief. The preacher must show the sinner that God has more power to pardon than he himself has to sin. Then the sinner's eyes may be successfully directed to the examples of the saints, those of the Old Testament in particular. He will see what others have been able to accomplish by God's grace, even though they were disadvantaged by their sex or age. Finally, the preacher should vividly describe heavenly happiness. Norbert did this often in his preaching. He told his listeners of the life of heaven, of the reward and happiness of the elect, of their eternal glory, and of the joy of the good.[16] In a similar manner Adam emphasized heaven's rewards:

> Our state is twofold: our labor in exile and our rest in the kingdom. The one is like the Holy, the other like the Holy of Holies. The first brings punishment, the second consolation. The one brings us affliction but the other offers us our fatherland.[17]

This homiletic approach closely resembles that of the first week of the *Exercises* of Saint Ignatius. Such a progression is demonstrably effective in preaching to those who have already come to faith.

Although Norbert himself willingly addressed how salvation might be sought by secular people, he and his disciples alike wished to draw as many souls as they could to total conversion, that is, to religious life. These were the *conversi* and *conversae*, the converts of both sexes then called lay brothers and sisters. Norbert's success in this preaching on religious life won great admiration among his contemporaries. As the monk Herman of Laon writes:

> If Lord Norbert had done nothing else but attract so many women to divine service with his preaching—not to mention the conversion of so many men—would he not still be worthy of the greatest praise? But indeed, when so many thousands of both sexes serve Christ because of Norbert's teaching, when so many monasteries

---

[16] *Vita S. Norberti*, PL 170, col. 1277.

[17] *Geminus est status noster: unus in labore exsilii, alius in requie regni; unus qui dicitur Sancta, alius qui Sancta sanctorum; unus in merito, alius in praemio; unus in afflictione, alius in consolatione; unus denique in via, alius in patria.* Adam, *De tripartito tabernaculo*, PL 198, col. 755.

of his order shine forth throughout the world, I do not know what others think but, as for me, I believe that what many assert is true, that since the time of the apostles no other has so quickly won so many imitators of the perfect life for Christ by his teaching.[18]

Indeed, Norbert's followers, drawn to religious life by his inspired eloquence, embraced it completely. "We religious are the bowels of the Lord Jesus, the special sons of God, the receptacle of the Holy Spirit," wrote Adam.[19]

Although the first Premonstratensians' preaching in poverty quickly disappeared in some regions as the spiritual needs of the people were satisfied, their evangelical ideal survived, finding there nourishment for a life imitating Christ's own as closely as possible in attentive meditation on the sacred text. Saint Norbert himself foresaw this evolution, saying to the regular canons of Saint Martin of Laon, when Bartholomew of Jur named him provost of that house, that the evangelical institution would move them to the imitation of Christ—to contempt for the world, to voluntary poverty, to the suffering of oppression, insults, mockery, hunger, thirst, and nakedness.[20] As the founder said, "Those truly live who do not live for themselves, rather the poor Christ lives in them."[21] As devotion to Christ's humanity was renewed, the Order of Prémontré developed this evangelical tendency to such an extent that affection for Jesus in the mysteries of his life seemed its central trait.

---

[18] *Si nihil alius domnus Norbertus fecisset sed, omissa conversione virorum, tot feminas servitio divino sua exhortatione attraxisset, nonne maxima laude dignus fuisset? Nunc vero cum utriusque sexus ejus doctrina tot millia Christo famulentur, cum institutionis ejus tot monasteria per orbem refulgeant, nescio quid alii sentiant, mihi videtur verum esse quod plurimi asserunt, a tempore Apostolorum nullum fuisse qui tam brevi temporis spatio sua institutione tot perfectae vitae imitatores Christo acquisierit.* Herman, PL 156, col. 997.

[19] *Nos etenim viscera sumus Domini Jesu, nos speciales filii Dei, nos reclinatorium Spiritus sancti.* Adam, ed. Gray Birch.

[20] *Cum . . . ostenderet modum evangelicae institutionis quomodo imitatores Christi, contemptores mundi esse deberent, quomodo voluntarii pauperes, quomodo ad opprobria, ad contumelias, ad irrisiones, ad famem, ad sitim et nuditatem et caetera hujusmodi patientes. Vita S. Norberti,* PL 170, col. 1285.

[21] *Vere vivunt qui non sibi vivunt sed in quibus Christus pauper vivit. Vita S. Norberti,* PL 170, col. 1296.

Chapter 2
Apostolic Institution

The meaning of attention to the model and teaching of the apostles is sometimes misunderstood in the context of Premonstratensian spirituality. Dom Paul Benoît, in his book on the life of clerics in the Middle Ages, relates that a nineteenth-century author wished to demonstrate that medieval monks as well were obliged to preach. He found a number of medieval texts affirming that monastic life was indeed apostolic, then concluded that the two great patterns of Christian community—monastic and apostolic—might therefore easily be reunited. When this nineteenth-century scholar considered the two models more closely, however, he came to understand that, in the Middle Ages, apostolic life did not connote a life of preaching and active apostolate so much as imitation of the early Church in Jerusalem during the time of the apostles. The phrase typically used by the Premonstratensians, "apostolic institution," was, moreover, more exact, less susceptible to misinterpretation, than the term "apostolic life." The life of the faithful surrounding the apostles, viewed as the ideal of Christian community, remains normative for all common life in the Church. A beautiful retreat preached by Dom Germain Morin at the abbey of Maredsous applies this model to modern monasticism. Nowhere, however, has imitation of the apostolic community been more emphasized than among the regular canons of the eleventh and twelfth centuries.

Texts from the Acts of the Apostles, in their authentic description of the community of Jerusalem, are essential here:

And when they were come in [to Jerusalem], they went up into an upper room, where abode Peter and John, James and Andrew, Philip and Thomas, Bartholomew and Matthew, James of Alpheus, and Simon Zelotes, and Jude the brother of James. All these were persevering with one mind in prayer with the women, and Mary the mother of Jesus, and with his brethren. (Acts 1:13-14)

And they were persevering in the doctrine of the apostles, and in the communication of the breaking of bread, and in prayers. And fear came upon every soul: many wonders also and signs were done by the apostles in Jerusalem, and there was great fear in all. And all they that believed, were together, and had all things in common. Their possessions and goods they sold, and divided them to all, according as every one had need. And continuing daily with one accord in the temple, and breaking bread from house to house, they took their meat with gladness and simplicity of heart; praising God, and having favor with all the people. And the Lord increased daily together such as should be saved. (Acts 2:42-47)

And the multitude of believers had but one heart and one soul: neither did any one say that aught of the things which he possessed, was his own; but all things were common unto them. And with great power did the apostles give testimony of the resurrection of Jesus Christ our Lord; and great grace was in them all. For neither was there any one needy among them. For as many as were owners of lands or houses, sold them, and brought the price of the things they sold. (Acts 4:32-34)

Then the twelve calling together the multitude of the disciples, said: it is not reason that we should leave the word of God, and serve tables. Wherefore, brethren, look ye out among you seven men of good reputation, full of the Holy Ghost and wisdom, whom we may appoint over this business. But we will give ourselves continually to prayer, and to the ministry of the word. (Acts 6:2-3)

These texts provided the paradigm for Saint Augustine's form of religious life. Likewise, they offered Saint Norbert and the first Premonstratensians the model they wished to emulate.

The characteristics of the apostolic life of the early Order of Prémontré then demand our investigation. Its essential traits were six: common life in poverty and work, liturgical prayer, focus on the Mass and the Eucharist, attentiveness to the word of God, deep charity, union with the Virgin Mary. A seventh trait, austerity of life, may appropriately be added. The Church, in its recognition of the order, considered imitation of the life of the apostles its primary characteristic, as its formal approbation in the name of the Holy See in 1124 by the legates Pierleoni and Gregory de Sant'Angelo states:

> You are they who renew the praiseworthy life of the holy Fathers and those institutions, established by the apostles' teaching, flourishing at the beginning of the Church but virtually obliterated in its later growth. You raise up this life and teaching by the direction of the Holy Spirit. . . . To restore the life of the early Church through the Spirit's inspiration and assistance is no less worthy than to maintain vital religious life, as do the monks, by the steadfastness of that same Spirit.[1]

Such had been the view of Saint Norbert when he adopted the Augustinian Rule. "He embraced the apostolic life in his preaching and he wished to live it. As he understood it, this life was ordered and renewed by Saint Augustine after the apostles' model."[2]

The life of the church of Jerusalem was shared by the many Christians gathered around the apostles; their community, framed in charity, suggested the very presence of the Lord Jesus. In the same way the life of the Order of Prémontré was shaped from the beginning by great numbers of men and women gathering around those priests who were the regular canons of the new abbatial churches.

---

[1] *Vos estis qui sanctorum Patrum vitam probabilem renovatis et apostolicae instituta doctrinae, primordiis Ecclesiae sanctae inolita sed et crescente Ecclesia jam pene deleta instinctu sancti Spiritus suscitatis . . . Non minoris itaque est meriti vitam hanc primitivae Ecclesiae, aspirante et prosequente Domini Spiritu suscitare quam florentem monachorum religionem ejusdem Spiritus perseverantia custodire.* Qtd. in the introduction to works of Adam Scot, PL 198, col. 36.

[2] *Apostolica enim vita quam in praedicatione susceperat jam optabat vivere quam siquidem ab eodem beato viro [Augustino] post apostolos audierat ordinatam et renovatam. Vita S. Norberti,* PL 170, col. 1292.

For apostolic life as Norbert and his companions wished to lead it, priesthood is essential, not a species of spiritual luxury, as it was for the monks of the eleventh and twelfth centuries, an addition to monastic life like a worthy or piously acquired ornament. Rather the college of priests is the central element of the Norbertine community. Lay brothers would eventually be diminished in number and sisters nearly suppressed, but clergy living according to a religious rule would remain as almost the only persons leading the life of the apostles. Therefore priesthood centrally concerned the order's spiritual authors, the more so since the movement for clerical reform had been the historical impetus for the development of the apostolic life. The dignity of priests is emphasized in these authors' works as the optimal pathway to sanctity. Those scriptural texts most frequently studied and discussed by Premonstratensian writers are hence not verses from Leviticus or from the epistle to the Hebrews but passages from Ecclesiasticus on Aaron and his sons. These texts were well known not only because of the splendor of their poetry but because they were often repeated in the divine office for the feasts of martyrs and confessor popes.

Among Premonstratensian writers on this subject are, foremost, Philip of Harvengt and Bernard of Fontcaude, both of whom often recur to priestly dignity and the sanctity it requires. As Philip writes, "for those who attain the lofty status of ecclesiastical orders not also to shine with the light of sanctity is inappropriate. Such rank is more a burden than an honor if it is not supported by sanctity." [3] The measure of dignity separating the priest from the Christian laity denotes the difference in sanctity necessarily separating the pastor and his flock.[4] Given the devotion to spiritual life among the lay brothers and sisters of the order, concern for sanctity among its priests must indeed have been intense, morally obliged as they were to surpass the laity of their communities in charity, self-denial, poverty, patience, and labor.

---

[3] *Non decet ut qui dignitatis ecclesiasticae fastigium obtinent, non etiam luce sanctitatis coruscent, cum dignitas oneri potius quam honori habeatur si non sanctitatis adminiculo fulciatur.* Philip, *De institutione,* PL 203, col. 669.

[4] *Quanto populo digniores tanto eisdem sanctiores.* ("Worthier than the people by as much as they are holier.") Philip, *De institutione,* PL 203, col. 670.

Moreover, these clerics were marked not only by sanctity but also by excellence in sacred learning: "He who must instruct the laity through both his words and example must also be eminent in both so that, after striving to be adorned appropriately with virtues, he may be able with equal diligence, without embarrassment, to clothe others similarly."[5] He must not seek such dignity with ambition or frivolity. Philip of Harvengt's insistence on circumstances of vocation is memorable: clerics must avoid choosing before being chosen.[6]

Clergy steeped in such views might then exercise a sanctifying influence, as the mediocre clergy of the tenth and eleventh centuries never could. At the same time, ordinary Christians were willing to place themselves under the direction of priests deeply concerned with the sanctification of the laypersons in their community and, indeed, the entire world.[7]

---

[5] *Qui enim debet laicos tam verbis quam moribus edocere in utrisque procul dubio debet ampliori diligentia praefulgere, ut cum se studuerit condignis virtutum vestibus insigniri, fronte libero aggrediatur diligenter alios investire.* Philip, *De institutione,* PL 203, col. 690.

[6] *Summopere clericis cavendum ne eligant antequam eligantur.* Philip, *De institutione,* PL 203, col. 681.

[7] Whatever degree of sanctity may be required for the exercise of the priesthood, Premonstratensian authors do not forget that the moral dignity of the minister has no effect on the efficacy of the graces for which he is responsible. They were bound to maintain this point of doctrine against the heretics. For instance, Bernard of Fontcaude writes: *Etsi ex sua despicabilis, tamen ex Domini persona venerandus est.* "Although despicable in himself, he must be revered on account of the person of Christ." Bernard of Fontcaude, PL 204, col. 795.

Chapter 3
Community of Life, Poverty, and Work

A mong the six characteristics of apostolic life listed above, community of life in poverty and work were important to the souls of the eleventh and twelfth centuries. Therefore contemporary monks, for whom such community was central but who understood only weakly the other concerns of the apostolic movement, could purport to lead the very life of the apostles. Among Premonstratensian authors even Adam Scot, in his sermons on the Order of Prémontré, shows some hesitation in defining apostolic life. Nevertheless, he finally characterizes the institution of the apostles as absolute rejection of earthly possessions, common possession of all temporal goods, division of these goods according to the needs of each, and harmony in unity alongside unity in harmony.[1] Adam's emphasis lies on this poverty or rather on this common life, for these two apostolic commitments were fused in the beginning. Poverty underlay all other aspects of Premonstratensian life, for the complete abandonment of temporal goods distinguished the regular canons from those who kept the ancient Rule of Aachen. Hearts and minds were thus directed toward the practice of the early Church, where all who believed were united, holding all things in common. They sold their lands and goods, sharing the proceeds according to each one's needs. Clearly this

---

[1] *Plena abjectio terrenorum, socialis communio rerum temporalium, divisio secundum necessitates, concors unitas et una concordia.* Adam, *De ordine*, PL 198, col. 511.

community of life was not complete in Jerusalem; thousands could not live under the same roof. Community denoted frequent gatherings and common access to resources, but even the latter was not absolute. Saint Peter told Ananias and Sapphira that they were perfectly free not to sell their land and to keep their money. Their crime was that they lied to the Holy Spirit by professing a false renunciation. But the whole of the church of Jerusalem worked to imitate what the apostles themselves practiced at the time of our Lord.

The Augustinian Rule, meanwhile, required of regular canons, indeed of all who wished to lead the apostolic life under their direction, complete renunciation of material goods. It is memorialized in the life of Saint Norbert and in his sermon, in the continuation of the chronicle of Gembloux, and in the life of Saint Godfrey of Cappenberg, in the phrases *voluntaria paupertas* and *spontanea paupertas*—voluntary or spontaneous poverty—so earning its adherents the name *pauperes Christi*, poor men of Christ.[2] Originally this life in full community was the same as the poverty practiced by all monks living under the Rule of Saint Benedict, but during the eleventh and twelfth centuries it became more and more evangelical, gradually approaching Franciscan poverty in its loving imitation of the poverty of Christ. This poverty is liberating. As the life of Saint Norbert says:

> The first confreres had little concern for temporal things, but were utterly absorbed in spiritual matters, in following the sacred scriptures and taking Christ as their model. . . . The tendency of those who came together in the beginning was to prefer an old, patched garment to a new, whole one. Thus some who so embraced extraordinary poverty were embarrassed if new clothes were given to them. In order to show their disdain for the world's pomp and to suppress their pride, they would sew old patches onto their new clothes.[3]

___

[2] *Vita Godefridi*, MGH 12, 515. See also *Vita S. Norberti*, PL 170, col. 1293. Anselm of Havelberg signs himself in his letters as *Anselmus pauper Christi, Havelbergensis vocatus episcopus*. Anselm, *Epistola apologetica*, PL 188, col. 1119.

[3] *De corporalibus cura et sollicitudo vix aliqua erat; universum vero stadium ad spiritualia contulerant, Scripturas divinas sequi et Christum ducem habere. . . . Erat ergo*

In the same way the blessed Herman Joseph later beat his new shoes against the wall so that they might appear worn. Such actions enriched the original concept of poverty, forming a spiritual counterweight to the first manifestations of luxury, holding the simplicity of the Gospel before the Christian people at the very moment when material wealth entered Christendom as the prior age of iron ended.

Again, the poverty of this twelfth-century apostle supported his preaching. As long as Norbert retained his rich ecclesiastical benefices, his work of reform failed. On the day he went forth barefoot, contenting himself with a woolen tunic and a cape in imitation of Christ[4]—the day on which the strength of his soul readied and directed him to sustain complete poverty and indigence[5]—then his contemporaries were able fully to credit his preaching that the things of the world are transient,[6] that we are pilgrims and travelers on the earth.[7] Norbert then maintained this conception of poverty as voluntary, motivated by love. As he said to the blessed Hugh, "Your brothers have chosen you to succeed me in the house of our poverty."[8] When the land had been cleared, the various communities found themselves comfortable, no longer living in real poverty, and this was the beginning of the order's decline.[9]

---

mens eorum qui ab initio collecti sunt sic affecta ut potius eligerent veterem clavatam tunicam quam novam et integrum quodlibet vestimentum. Unde et factum est quidam non minimam paupertatem amplectentes cum datas sibi novas vestes erubescerent, ad ostendendum quam sit vilis saeculi pompa, ad reprimendam superbiam pannos veteres novis superconsuerent. Vita S. Norberti, PL 170, col. 1294.

[4] *Pede nudo, tunica lanea ac pallio sibi sufficiente, solo Christo duce. Vita S. Norberti,* PL 170, col. 1272.

[5] *Vigore animi bene jam compositi et praeparati ad paupertatem omnimodam et indigentiam tolerandam. Vita S. Norberti,* PL 170, col. 1272.

[6] *Omnia . . . fluida et caduca. Vita S. Norberti,* PL 170, col. 1263.

[7] *Fixum tenentes quia peregrini et hospites essent super terram. Vita S. Norberti,* PL 170, col. 1276.

[8] *Tu mihi succedes electione fratrum tuorum in domo paupertatis nostrae. Vita S. Norberti,* PL 170, col. 1330.

[9] Jacques de Vitry recounted: *A principio autem ordinis et novellae plantationis, cum adhuc pretioso paupertatis thesauro abundarent, quasi musto novae religionis inebriati.* ("At the order's beginning, when it was newly planted, when the precious treasure of poverty abounded, its members were drunk as on the wine of new religious fervor.") Qtd. in intro. to *Vita S. Norberti,* PL 170, col. 1250.

Community of life presupposes work. According to the Augustinian Rule, the degree of self-effacement in work marks progress in virtue. Each one ought to work not for himself but in the interest of the group of which he is a part.[10] Labor can be manual or intellectual; in the order's early days manual labor was essential. The lay brothers devoted themselves to varied tasks, from prime until noon, then from noon until compline, making the abbeys into huge agricultural enterprises. The canons themselves were not exempt from this agricultural toil. Twice a day, under the leadership of their prior, each reported with tools in hand to the garden or field assigned to him.[11] All worked in silence, as the Trappists still do today. When there was still more work to be done, as during harvest time, the canons were limited to chanting morning Mass without returning for High Mass; the office was said immediately after, in simple form, while vespers was chanted in the field. Manual labor was at once a mortification, a bodily relaxation—since in those days no time was set aside for recreation—and an active exercise of poverty. Saint Norbert had wished that manual labor be the only source of income for Prémontré, but experience quickly showed that this ideal was impractical because it consumed too much of the confreres' time and energy. Prelates themselves wished to take part in the work. Saint Siard, abbot of Mariengarden, went out to the fields with the confreres. While his religious reaped the hay and bound the sheaves, he carried the bundles and loaded them onto the mules. This farm work, so occupying much of the time of a clergy devoted to renewal of the Church, elicited inevitable criticism. The author of the *Book of the Various Orders and Professions in the Church* writes:

> I praise the magnanimity of this religious profession, I proclaim
> their austerity and I love their great humility, but I nonetheless
> assert that moderation is necessary in all things. Indeed, when I

---

[10] *Nullus sibi aliquid operetur, sed omnia opera vestra in unum fiant majori studio et frequentiori alacritate quam si vobis singulis faceretis propria.* ("Let no one do anything for himself, but let all your works be for the community with greater zeal and swiftness than if you did it for yourself.") *Regula S. Augustini,* c. 8.

[11] *Temporibus determinatis et horis certis ad labores manuum egrediuntur.* Qtd. in intro. to *Vita S. Norberti,* PL 170, col. 1250.

hear that the priests and even the abbot in this order of canons are herding their sheep and mucking their stables, I can scarcely believe it. Then when the truth compels me to accept it, I praise and admire their humility. Nonetheless I would rather that those who daily surround the altar, especially priests who daily touch the Body of Christ, not act thus out of reverence for Christ's Body, which we adore in its purity.[12]

Such thoughts sometimes arose even within the order. "Manual labor," Adam Scot posits, "does not seem fitting for priests and learned men." But he then responds: "Yet this physical exercise offers consolation and recreation, great support and a refreshment."[13] None could state this better. And many Sundays and holidays remained, on which clerics might pass all their time in contemplation. Notably, the manual labor of these clerics was generally simple: digging, spreading out hay, cutting grass. Only rarely were they involved in skilled crafts, as were the lay brothers, unless in small occupations like the clock-making of the blessed Herman Joseph. Clerics were thus assigned work that would not hinder their thinking and their reflection on the psalms, so that nothing kept them from continuing their work of contemplation in bodily relaxation.

Intellectual work, although it was not the central task of the community, also occupied a number of confreres: the administration of goods from the numerous richly endowed monasteries; the organization of granges and farms; the development of libraries in

---

[12] *Laudo professionis hujus magnanimitatem, praedico erga corporis austeritatem, amo tantam eorum humilitatem, sed modum in omnibus tenendum esse pronuntio. Cum enim audio sacerdotes et ipsum etiam abbatem in hoc ordine canonicorum, qui longe vita et conversatione a saecularibus se faciunt, in illo etiam ordine monachorum qui similiter secedunt, de quo superius tractavimus, lac de ovibus suis mulgere, stabula mundare, vix possum credere, sed tamen cum hoc vel tandem credo, humilitatem eorum veneror et admiror. Video enim illos haec ideo agere, ut superbia in eis omnino confundatur, et humilitas erigatur. Vellem tamen eos qui circa altare quotidie ministrant, et maxime illos qui quotidie pro officio sacerdotii corpus Christi tractant, ob reverentiam ipsius corporis, quia nihil mundius esse potest, ita non agere. Liber de diversis ordinibus,* PL 213, col. 831.

[13] *Non mihi videtur ad ordinatos et maxime litteratos pertinere. — Multum eos consolatur exercitium corporale et renovat, multum fovet et reficit."* Adam, *Soliloquiae de instructione animae,* PL 198, col. 855.

transcription and illumination of manuscripts, in which the abbey of Cuissy was particularly eminent;[14] the instruction of the younger clerics, which flourished especially in the communities of Frisia; the composition of written works, of which only a small part have come down to us. All these occupations absorbed many people and much time. Yet whatever the work required, complete surrender of oneself, unstinting in time or energy, was enjoined. As Adam Scot wrote: "In giving yourself to the Church of God in all that you are, in all that you know and in all that you can do, know too that you are a debtor to that same Church in every way you may be of use, in complete fidelity."[15]

Although the faithful of Jerusalem did not live under the same roof, their spirit of community was so manifest that *no man durst join himself unto them* (Acts 5:13), as the sacred text says. The same spirit of community, joined with concern for promoting contemplation, led Norbert and the first Premonstratensians to seek out desert places to inhabit. As the founder himself said to Bartholomew of Jur, "I do not want to live in cities; I prefer deserted and uncultivated places."[16] Norbert's ideal was thus realized at Prémontré, but many of the other abbeys were no less secluded. Today, travelers who desire to visit the ruins must still seek them in distant fields, often in wonderful locations. Origen, commenting on Saint John the Baptist's departure for the desert, states it beautifully: "There the air is more pure, the sky more open, and God is closer."[17] Above all, this proximity to God is attractive; but the beauty of a wild place in which a white Romanesque or Gothic abbey rises up, the image of a civilization both noble and rustic, powerfully raises the soul to easy and constant prayer.

Nevertheless, the rule was not absolute; Saint Martin of Laon, Saint Michael of Antwerp, Saint Marien of Auxerre, Our Lady of

---

[14] The abbey of Cuissy was particularly distinguished in this area.

[15] *In eo quod temetipsam (animam) Ecclesiae Dei tradidisti, in omni quod es, in omni quod scis et in omni quod potes, eidem te ecclesiae ad omnem utilitatem et omnem fidelitatem debitricem te agnosce.* Adam, *Soliloquiae*, PL 198, col. 859.

[16] *Non in urbibus volo remanere sed potius in locis desertis et incultis.* Norbert's words are reported by Herman, *De miraculis*, PL 156, col. 991.

[17] *Ibi aer purior, caelum apertius, familiarior Deus.* Origen, trans. Jerome, *Homiliae XXXIX in evangelium Lucae*, PL 26, col. 241.

Magdeburg, Saint Vincent of Breslau, and many other monasteries are proof of this. Norbert and his companions did not refuse churches situated on the outskirts of major cities when the good to be accomplished there was clear, although their preference for places of solitude remained significant. A century later the mendicants would actively seek cities in order to mingle with urban folk to gain influence among them, like the leaven of which the Gospel speaks. The Premonstratensians, however, as contemporaries of a more rural civilization, wished instead to prepare themselves in prolonged solitude both for brief apostolic ventures into the cities and for pastoral ministry among the country folk. Solitude of place is not essential, but solitude of the heart—the spirit of silence and recollection—is paramount. As Adam Scot writes, "In this solitude comes tranquility of heart, serenity of soul, and purity of conscience; clarity of interior light follows, along with sublimity of contemplation, in a foretaste of the happiness of the Bridegroom."[18]

This solitude of the heart comprises four aspects. It first assumes separation from that sin ruining the solitude of the soul by mingling it with inferior creatures. Next, solitude requires abstinence from unnecessary occupations. As Philip of Harvengt noted, religious uninterested in contemplation are clever in finding all sorts of endeavors to distract themselves and inhibit their thought and prayer. Such solitude also supposes that religious life refrains from creating familial feeling that, though good in itself, nonetheless divides the heart. Finally, solitude is not hostility, disdain for men, or rejection of activity, rather the desire and intent to achieve long, deep intimacy with God, while at the same time supporting the peaceful contemplation of the entire community. Within the monastery the spirit of solitude blossoms into what the statutes of the order call *multa quies*, profound repose manifesting in the absence of useless activity. Nothing is more moving to the outside visitor than meeting in their cloisters religious who are both serious and friendly, demonstrating that each one willingly remains in his cell— or in a corner of the cloister before there were individual cells—

---

[18] *In hac solitudine cordis datur tranquillitas, animi serenitas, conscientiae puritas, internae lucis cernitur claritas, contemplationis apprehenditur sublimitas, Sponsi praelibatur felicitas.* Adam, *De tripartito tabernaculo*, PL 198, col. 746.

profoundly attentive to what he is doing. Nothing in the community of religious promotes a pure and lofty life more than such solitude. The insistence authors of the order devote to the practice of solitude suggests that the fiery temperaments of the twelfth century had trouble attaining it. Adam Scot continually returns to this point: "The strength of the cloistered is their repose. Just as no fish can live without water, so no cloistered religious can live without repose. . . . Sit then, you who are cloistered, with Mary at the feet of Jesus."[19] Adam adds four resolutions. The first is not to leave the cloister for no good reason, as Saint Norbert's sermon counsels, for frequent, useless trips outside the monastery admit to it the world's air of dissipation and frivolity. The second is restraint from useless conversation—easily understood, but far more difficult to practice. Next is disengagement from concern for earthly things, for superiors take care of such matters, as they do the work of Martha in service to their brethren. Weighed down with various concerns, suffering in their journeys from cold, heat, snow, darkness, and the attacks of robbers and thieves, they scarcely procure their own needs, while those who are cloistered have only to think about God and spiritual matters. The whole monastic organization functions for them. Thus, reciprocally, the fruits of their contemplative life enrich those who sacrifice themselves for them. Finally, the fourth resolution is the careful custody of the religious' heart, for the sake of all the precautions detailed here.[20]

---

[19] *Vigor claustralium quies eorum, quia sicut nequaquam sine aqua piscis, nec sine quiete vivere possunt claustrales. . . . Sedete ergo, o claustrales, cum Maria ad pedes Jesu.* Adam, *Ad viros religiosos,* 223.

[20] Adam, *Ad viros religiosos,* 224–26.

Chapter 4
Liturgical Prayer

The liturgical gatherings of the Jews took place at the third, sixth, and ninth hours.[1] When the apostles were in Jerusalem, they took part in these assemblies. Thus, for instance, we see Peter and John going up to the temple to pray at the ninth hour. Even when the apostles were away from Jerusalem, they were therefore united with the others in prayer. Peter prayed in this way in the presence of Cornelius' soldier, when he went up to the roof at the sixth hour. Of course these gatherings were not obligatory. The more pious Jews, like the prophetess Anna who never left the temple, participated each day, while others in the Jewish community readily joined them on the Sabbath and feast days. The first Christian ascetics adopted the same custom, so that in the second and third centuries the office had already assumed the general shape it has since preserved, with the various hours of the day and night sanctified by the chanting of psalms and by sacred readings.

Saint Norbert and his first companions were deeply informed by the rhythm of the liturgical life since they had all been canons from their youth. None of their contemporaries would have been able even to imagine a religious order failing to invest the best of its time and its heart in public prayer. All the early Premonstratensians' life was organized around the conventual church called, as in

---

[1] Nine o'clock in the morning, noon, and three in the afternoon, in our calculation.

the first days of Christianity, their temple, *templum.*[2] In the canons'
mind this church existed not for the community's needs, as prior
monks had seen it; rather, their community was created for the
service of the collegiate Church. Bartholomew of Jur thus in the
first instance enabled Norbert to establish a new church of Our
Lady, where he and his confreres could focus on chanting divine
praises.[3] They placed themselves in the service of this church in
their very profession: "I offer and give myself to the church of Our
Lady and Saint John the Baptist of Prémontré." This conventual
church became a place worthy of this laudation in all its architectural development. In the Middle Ages the buildings of the monastery had not yet assumed the monumental appearance they would
take on in the monastic reconstructions of the eighteenth century,
as is easily demonstrated at Laon, Thenailles, Lucerne across the
Sea, and Braine, but the medieval churches of the order were already
immense and splendid. Not only was the conventual church the
heart of the monastery, just as in modern times, but it fully domi-
nated the cloisters and modest dormitories. The church was thus
the all of the abbey of canons.

Meanwhile, the organization of the liturgy was borrowed from
the leading French churches, among which the rite of the Church
of the Holy Sepulcher seems to have been especially influential.
When the melodies this liturgy employed were not from early Gregorian chant, they were chosen from Germanic sources.[4] Norbert
and his companions instinctively remained faithful to this great
joy of their clerical youth, yet Premonstratensian authors speak
little of their office. Modern times' wide availability of spiritual
books explaining the texts of the missal and the breviary might
make ours seem a great liturgical age, but in fact the faithful are

---

[2] *Ante fores templi.* Compare Lefèvre, 55.

[3] *Notum fieri volumus quod ego Bartholomaeus, Laudunensis episcopus, viro reverendo
et spectabilis religionis nostris temporibus Norberto et successoribus ejus in sancto proposito
viventibus dederim locum . . . ad ecclesiam in honorem Dei et sanctae Genitricis
construendam.* ("Let it be known that I, Bartholomew, bishop of Laon, have granted
to the venerable Norbert, an outstanding religious of our day, and to those successors
living according to his holy ideal, that they build a church in honor of God and the
Mother of God.") *S. Norberti chartae,* PL 170, col. 1359.

[4] This was the case especially for the *Hymnarius,* the *toni communes* and the *Kyriale.*

today for the most part ignorant and unconcerned with the intimate life of the Church. Often an act of the papal magisterium or an episcopal letter urges them to abandon this nonchalance so that, relatively speaking, the liturgy is much discussed. In the Middle Ages, however, this problem of lay negligence apparently did not exist. The simple faithful were enthusiasts for the Church's office, while religious were bathed in the liturgy as in the air they breathed—without even noticing it, so obviating any need to speak of it.

Premonstratensian authors point out in passing, however, the felicitousness of the distribution of the canonical hours. Matins, says Adam Scot, reminds us that darkness is sanctified by the birth of the Lord, by his frequent prayer in the course of his public life, by his agony in the garden, and by his appearance before the Sanhedrin. At prime we think of our Lord before Pilate, his Resurrection, and his appearance to the seven apostles on the shores of the sea. Terce moves us to recall Christ's flagellation and crown of thorns; although its office does not directly mention the descent of the Holy Spirit, such is the theme of the hymn for the beginning of this hour. Sext is when Christ was raised up on the cross as our high priest and sacrifice. None is the sacred hour at which the Redeemer died for our salvation. Vespers and compline make holy that time at which the Holy Eucharist was instituted. Similarly, for the Jews, the third hour had been the memorial of the Law given on Mount Sinai, and the sixth hour the remembrance of the elevation of the bronze serpent, and the ninth of the stone struck by Moses in order to bring forth water for the Israelites.[5]

Careful study of the liturgy of the twelfth century reveals further interesting developments. Manuals of instruction like Rupert de Deutz's *On the Ecclesiastical Office* were copied and read, but no evidence survives of analogous works by Premonstratensians. If they existed, we have no direct knowledge. On the other hand, authors of the order clearly emphasized the way in which the psalms ought to be sung. Adam Scot writes:

[5] Adam, *De ordine*, PL 198, cols. 526–27.

The Divine Office in particular is the work of God. In it you stand before God, here you are present to him and here you speak with him. How piously, how devoutly, how faultlessly then you ought to comport yourself in every action when you are in God's presence! What wisdom it requires to consider in your heart the words you address to him![6]

Preaching meanwhile always closely followed the liturgical year, for the texts expounded were regularly taken from the Mass or the office. The life of Christine of Christ suggests how much even Premonstratensian sisters lived the mysteries of the Savior as they were commemorated in public prayer.

The medieval laity were also deeply engaged in the liturgical hours.[7] Premonstratensian lay brothers and the earliest women religious, before there were canonesses, all heard matins each morning; they then heard prime, followed by the morning Mass and later compline. The office, with the various chants and melodies known and associated in memory with their accompanying feasts, was a musical liberation of the spirit to pure and lofty prayer—effectively what we would call the prayer of simplicity. The office was so beloved that it grew continuously richer with new additions: familiar psalms recited before matins for the community, psalms of petition following certain hours—the *Deus misereatur* for times of tribulation, the *Nisi Dominus* within the octave of professions, the *Ad te levavi* in churches mourning for their respective abbots. Further, the office was extended twice, even three times in the cloisters of the Middle Ages by the addition of votive offices among the Premonstratensians, for instance, the Little Office of the Blessed Virgin and the Office of the Dead. Only solemn feasts precluded the chanting of these votive offices.

---

[6] *Hoc specialiter opus Dei est. Hic namque Deo sisteris, hic ei praesentaris, hic etiam cum eo loqueris. O quam sancte, quam devote, quam etiam in omnibus irreprehensibiliter motibus te habere deberes quando coram Deo stas! Quam sapienter nihilominus illa quibus eum alloqueris verba et corde meditari et ore te decet proferre.* Adam, *Soliloquiae*, PL 198, col. 855.

[7] Saint Louis heard the canonical hours every day, and in Orléans Saint Joan of Arc listened to all the hours on the feast of the Holy Cross.

The Little Office of the Blessed Virgin will demand discussion below in our consideration of devotion to the Blessed Virgin, but the Office of the Dead is of interest in the present context. Its almost daily recitation—along with the fact that the majority of private Masses were requiems—promoted great devotion to the souls in purgatory. Communities prayed for the dead abundantly. From time to time a freed soul would show its gratitude. Thus the life of Saint Godfrey of Cappenberg records that a dead brother appeared to one of his confreres and said:

> Thank you, my brother. When my friends and family forgot me, you never ceased to keep my memory. Now I urge you to remain firm and steadfast in your own intention. Do not waver with regard to our order as if you might find a better religious life, for I could show you none better for your soul. I have come to tell you, in your charity, that the prayers of your dead confreres are offered each day on the golden altar before the very face of the Lord. Therefore do not try to shirk your obedience. You can achieve no more sublime or fruitful merit in the sight of God.[8]

This testimony from the afterlife of the efficacy of Premonstratensian prayer emphasizes the importance of the office. Devotion to the souls in purgatory, lively as well among the Cistercians, was resumed by the mendicants of the thirteenth century, who expressed it in their repetition of the psalm *De profundis* throughout the religious' day. This devotion remained so fervent among the Premonstratensians that in the seventeenth century, when the elevation of certain celebrations to the status of double feasts was proposed at the General Chapter, the Abbot General Michel Colbert—a poor administrator but steeped in the traditional spirit of the order—foresaw the suppression of a certain number of offices for the dead

---

[8] *Frater mi, gratias ago quod hactenus, etiam cum caeteri amici mei vel affines immemores essent mei, tu nostri memoriam nullatenus omisisti. Et nunc adhortor ut stabilis et immobilis in tuo persistas proposito, nec de ordine nostro tamquam alium potiorem inventurus fluctues animo, quia nimirum salubriorem animaeque tuae commodiorem demonstrare non valeo. Nam et hoc veni nuntiare tuae caritati quod orationes confratrum tuorum quotidie recitantur super altare aureum quod est ante oculos Domini. Hortor quoque ne unquam obedientiae subterfugias imperium. Nulla enim virtute coram Deo sublimius et fructuosius consequeris meritum.* Vita Godefridi, MGH SS 12, 517.

and requiem Masses. Colbert wrote with indignation: "To elevate these feasts would be to forget the dead."

The liturgical spirit of the Premonstratensians likewise moved them not only to celebrate the office heartfully but also, like all the older orders of the Church, to make extensive use of sacramental handbooks, for they trusted deeply in the prayer of their mother Church. Blessings of places borrowed from the Gregorian Sacramentary, blessings of tombs, and blessings of the reader of the week were all numerous. Yet the blessing of meals and the aspersion of the confreres after compline, among monks always reserved to the abbot, were made by the priest of the week because, by their institution, regular canons form priestly communities in which many have the power to bless.

All the rites of the Premonstratensian day show the influence of Cîteaux. Nevertheless, the suite of the hours was arranged as a long, varied, and expressive liturgy. From profession to burial, even in the smallest actions of daily life, everything copied the fragrance of the Church's maternal prayer and the majesty of her sacred rites. The appropriate response to the question, "Was the spirituality of the Premonstratensians a liturgical spirituality?" is then clear. In modern times liturgical spirituality denotes embrace of the texts of the office as themes of private prayer because those texts are so deeply enjoyed as to elicit the desire to sing them more devotedly, or because the individual recurs to those scriptures for the sake of the savor appreciated during the office. Such private practice of liturgical prayer marks a legitimate reaction against a spirit of individualism—more correctly, egoism—tending to souls' isolation, to their excessive engagement in prayer for individual needs, and adherence to themes of prayer resonating with individuals' feelings.

Norbertine spirituality, simply, was liturgical in the sense that the Premonstratensians drew its inspiration for personal prayer principally from the public prayer of the Church; Saint Norbert thus always carried the psalter and missal in his itinerant preaching. The early canons, however, retained great liberty for themselves, as their contemplative life shows. Emphasis on liturgical prayer did not remove individual affect; all souls are shaped by their education, by the environment in which they live, and by their devotion to sacred psalmody in unison with the heart of the Church.

Chapter 5
The Centrality of Eucharistic Devotion

Saint Luke understood the breaking of the bread as the distinguishing characteristic of the young Christian community. The Eucharist was not, in the Lord's view, a singular act of sublime love, rather a rite to be repeated in his memory until he comes again. The Church always understood it thus; no Christian life can be without the Eucharist. Nevertheless, the first monastic rules did not assign the Mass a prominent place. Saint Benedict provided for some priests in his monasteries in order to celebrate in their oratories. He nonetheless does not mention the daily Mass that later became the central event in all liturgical prayer. The Middle Ages, however, departed markedly from Benedict's reticence about eucharistic practice. The time of the first Premonstratensians saw great eucharistic fervor. No monastery of monks or canons failed to chant the Mass solemnly at least once, often twice, each day. The Mass became the high point of conventual life.

This focus on eucharistic observance was in reaction to the first heresies concerning the sacraments; it was, at the same time, in full harmony with the Gregorian Reform. The eleventh and twelfth centuries' renewal of eucharistic devotion returned to the clergy an awareness of the dignity and sanctity required in their approach to the altar. Closer examination of the specifically Premonstratensian devotion to the Eucharist will nonetheless be useful here. Unsurprisingly, this devotion was different from that of the post-Tridentine Church since its circumstances were different, but this was only a difference in emphasis resulting from two factors. Neither Thomas Aquinas' eucharistic doctrine nor the feast of Corpus Christi would be known until the late thirteenth century;[1] nor, as yet, had Protestant error denied transubstantiation and the Real Presence in the Eucharist.

Traditionally, then, in a manner conforming completely to Christ's intentions, Premonstratensian eucharistic devotion first concerned the actual celebration of the Mass. Saint Norbert himself made it the center of his spiritual life. When he laid aside all his ecclesiastical benefices, all he kept was a portable altar for the celebration of Mass. Each day he approached the altar for Mass: "he daily offered the rich sacrifices," as *Vita A* records.[2] Sometimes Norbert celebrated Mass twice on the same day, as was then permitted. He then loved to preach after he came down from the altar, his heart filled with the love deriving from his contact with Christ. Moreover, he worked his miracles at the altar, delivering the possessed and curing the blind girl in the cathedral of Würzburg. When riots broke out in Magdeburg during the consecration of the cathedral, all the other clerics left the church immediately after, but Norbert alone remained to celebrate the Mass and then calmly returned to his archiepiscopal residence. Historical accounts show that he frequently urged cleanliness and neatness around the altar and the sacred mysteries. "We show our faith and love for God at the altar."[3] Norbert's first disciples devoutly surrounded the altar with splendor and beauty. While the Cistercians, reacting against Cluny, prohibited ornaments of silk, copes, dalmatics, carpets, and stained-glass windows in order to give their liturgy an austerity with its own grandeur, the Premonstratensians in their collegiate churches devoted themselves to offering God the greatest beauty possible. Later sons of Norbert imitated the founder's devotion, remembering as well the slow and rapturous manner in which the blessed Herman Joseph celebrated Mass.

---

[1] The Office of the feast of Corpus Christi was adopted by the order at the General Chapter of 1322.

[2] *Quotidie sacrificia medullata offerens. Vita A*, 673.

[3] *In altari exhibit quisque fidem et dilectionem Dei. Vita S. Norberti*, PL 170, col. 1295.

Spiritual authors of the order often regarded the Eucharist in its sacrificial aspect. Adam Scot said to his confreres: "The Mass, as you consecrate it daily upon the altar, is the single most efficacious remedy for our wounds. There, in that sacrament, you offer the Son to the Father for our salvation as God reconciling the world to himself in Christ. To exhort you concerning this is wholly unnecessary."[4] Richard the Englishman's central idea in his mystical treatise on the canon of the Mass is the great conformity between the power of the cross and that of the sacrament of the altar. The cross and the Eucharist alike produce the renewal and sanctification of the Church. Richard assigns great importance to the different signs of the cross made throughout the canon because these recall that all the effects of the Eucharist are accomplished in the sacrifice of the cross.[5]

From what source, then, did the early Premonstratensians draw their eucharistic devotion? Today a Church without the great hymns *Lauda Sion, Pange lingua,* and *Adoro te* is scarcely imaginable, but Norbert's sons at least had at their disposal precious texts on the Eucharist—all of John 6 and 1 Corinthians 11—which they often cited. In particular they meditated at length on the text of the canon of the Mass, as in the commentary of Richard the Englishman cited above. An early thirteenth-century note is evidence that Adam Scot also composed a work *De canone missae.* Premonstratensian authors thus accorded these scriptural and liturgical texts virtually scholastic speculation, although not yet with the magnificent development of the *Summa Theologiae.* Such dialectical discussion grew from the natural opposition between the ancient heresies and the eloquent declarations of the Fathers, those errors' antagonists. Against the medieval heretics who denied the reality of the presence of Christ in the Eucharist, however, the ancients supplied no arguments, so Premonstratensians responded from fresh reflection delving into

---

[4] *Singularis atque efficacissima illa medicina vulnerum nostrorum quam in altari quotidie conficitis, ubi pro salute nostra in sacramento Patri Filius immolatur. Ubi spiritualiter Deus in Christo, mundum reconcilians sibi. Ex abundanti est super hoc commonere vos.* Adam, *Sermones,* PL 198, col. 115.

[5] *In virtute sanctae Crucis et in sacramento altaris est magna convenientia.* "Great conformity joins the power of the holy Cross and the sacrament of the altar." Richard, PL 177, col. 450.

the very mystery of the Eucharist. The canons of Saint Victor of Paris had meanwhile made substantial progress in the theory of the sacrament.

Adam Scot offers some examples of these speculations:

> The sacrament has three distinct aspects: its visible appearances, the reality of the Body, and the power of its spiritual grace. . . . Its appearance is to the eyes of the flesh, its reality is evident to the purity of faith and its power is manifest in the merit of faith by means of its bodily reception. Its two species constitute both the sacrament itself and its image of the reality of the Body and Blood of Christ; the Body of Christ is the image and the sacrament of the spiritual grace the species communicate.[6]

These principles would eventually underlie the thought of Saint Thomas in *Sacramentum tantum*, the *Res et sacramentum*, and the *Res tantum*.

The Eucharist thus represented to the early Premonstratensians a great source of contemplation leading toward the Holy Trinity. Richard the Englishman noted that a threefold substance is offered at Mass: bread, wine, and water. Bread, comforting mankind according to the scriptures, is the symbol of the Father, source of all strength and omnipotence; wine, the source of joy in the heart of mankind, represents that Son who is the joy never taken from us; water, washing and purifying us, signifies the Holy Spirit, whom scripture represents several times in the form of living water and who is himself the remission of sins.[7] Finally, the culmination of the canon is its elevation, with the solemn doxology proclaiming that in, with, and through Christ all glory is rendered to the Father in the unity of the Holy Spirit.

This specific question preoccupied Premonstratensian authors: why is the Eucharist repeated when baptism is not? Their initial

---

[6] *Tria ibi discreta proponuntur: species visibilis, veritas corporis et virtus gratiae spiritualis. . . . Species oculo carnis videtur, veritas fidei puritate attingitur, virtus ob fidei meritum mediante corporali assumptione percipitur. Quod autem videtur secundum speciem, sacramentum est et imago illius et quod creditur secundum corporis veritatem sacramentum illius est quod percipitur secundum gratiam spiritualem."* Adam, *De tripartito tabernaculo*, PL 198, col. 705.

[7] Richard, PL 177, col. 459.

response is drawn from the Fathers, especially from Saint John Chrysostom: this is, says Richard, because we fall each day and so each day need to be raised up again. Further, just as the tree of life stood in the middle of the earthly paradise, so the Body of Christ is necessarily continuously at the center of the Church. Philip of Harvengt as well takes up this argument when he says:

> While the Church hastens along her journey toward the joys of the divine vision, she crosses over from the desert, as it were, toward the land of promise. In order that she might not tire out from the labor of this journey, she carries with her no small nourishment when she preserves in hiding the salutary sacrament of the Body of Christ. Even while she keeps it within herself, she is preserved by it, so that the ark is not fortified by the tabernacle so much as the tabernacle is fortified by the ark.[8]

Finally, the third reason for the frequency of the Eucharist is that it makes us one with Christ and, by means of Christ, with God. This notion cannot be better or more fully expressed than in Philip's formulation.[9]

Faithful to the spirit of ancient Christianity and, in particular, enlightened by the rite of their profession, in which they presented themselves on the altar in the offertory of the Mass, the first Premonstratensians were fully conscious that in the Eucharist we become sacrifices offered with Jesus: "Hosts with the Host," they might say. The actual formula expressed this understanding closely: "We shall merit after death to be delivered by the Host, since before death we have been a host for God."[10] The early canons also emphasized preparation for Holy Communion "by integral faith, by

---

[8] *Quae nimirum Ecclesia, dum de hac peregrinatione festinat ad gaudia divinae visionis quasi de eremo transit ad terram promissionis. Ne autem hujus itineris labore defatiscat, habet non mediocre munimentum, dum in secretis suis corporis Christi salutare conservat sacramentum; quod dum intra se videtur conservare, ipsa potius ab eo conservatur ut non tam arca per tabernaculum quam per arcam tabernaculum muniatur.* Philip, *De institutione,* PL 203, 669.

[9] *Ut per hoc unum efficiamur cum Christo et, mediante Christo unum efficiamur cum Deo.* Richard, PL 177, col. 461.

[10] *Salutari hostia post mortem liberari merebimur si ante mortem Deo ipsi hostia fuerimus.* Richard, PL 177, col. 470.

pure confession, and by appropriate penance."[11] Confession concerned them above all else: "Perform it with regularity," said Adam Scot, "especially before major feasts, in order that the joy in which your soul delights be as great as the purity achieved in your confession."[12]

Holy Communion brought great fruits, in the Premonstratensians' understanding. Herman of Scheda, writing with all the enthusiasm of his conversion from Judaism, lists these in his biography: "Words cannot fully describe the banquet at the heavenly table, the sweetness of its delights. Only those who by the grace of God have experienced it can know these things. No one, I say, can appreciate how the faithful soul reverently approaching the altar with integral faith, true humility and contrition of the heart, and sincere devotion of the mind, feasts on the flesh of Jesus Christ, the Immaculate Lamb, and becomes drunk on the cup of his most precious Blood. None can understand this except he who already knows it."[13] Richard the Englishman said simply: "Communion wipes away sins, strengthens virtues, and raises us to eternal life."[14]

Among the virtues exercised and strengthened in our contact with the Eucharist, faith holds the first place. The sacrament of the altar is a mystery of faith.[15] It supersedes all sensory perception. From time to time, however, a eucharistic miracle sheds light on the dim regions of faith in order to confirm our adherence to this mystery. For Christians of the twelfth and thirteenth centuries, belief in the presence of Christ distinguished the true Catholic from the heretic, and especially from the Jew and the Saracen.

---

[11] *Fide integra, confessione pura, paenitentia condigna.* Richard, PL 177, col. 461.

[12] *Frequentate eam assidue, exercete indesinenter, et maxime cum praecipua festa instant ut eo mente in eis sitis jucundiores quo per confessionem fueritis puriores.* Adam, *Sermones,* PL 198, col. 205.

[13] *Hujus caelestis mensae quale sit convivium, quam dulces deliciae, digne verbis explicari non potest, sed haec illi soli noverunt qui per gratiam Dei experiri noverunt. Quale inquam, fidelis sit animae convivium ad reverendam altaris mensam cum integra fide, cum vera cordis humilitate et contritione, cum sincera mentis devotione accedere, et in ea Agni immaculati Jesu Christi carne saginari et sacrosancti Sanguinis ejus calice inebriari, nemo, ut dixi, nisi expertus intellegit.* Hermannus Judaeus, PL 170, col. 834.

[14] *Peccata purgat, virtutes roborat, in vitam aeternam suscitat.* Richard, PL 177, col. 470.

[15] *Mysterium fidei.* Canon of the Mass.

Three miracles affirming this presence especially attracted the attention of Saint Norbert's disciples. The first happened to Saint Norbert himself, when he was celebrating Mass in the abbatial church of Floreffe, near Namur. This incident is recounted by the confreres of Cappenberg:

> One day, when the venerable father was celebrating the sacred mysteries with his characteristically profound devotion, he saw immediately before the reception of Communion a large red drop of the Lord's Blood in the middle of the paten. He called for Brother Rudolph, our sacristan, who was then serving as his deacon, saying, "Brother, do you see what I see?" The other responded that he indeed did see, then began to weep profusely because of the magnitude of the event. After this miracle was made known, the venerable father took the opportunity to direct us to wash the paten. So began our observance of this previously unknown custom.[16]

The second miracle took place in the abbatial church of Vivières, outside Soissons, as attested by Richard the Englishman:

> When Mass was being celebrated there, a brother in the choir, who was looking toward the altar, saw upon it a circle of blinding brightness and, in the same shaft of light, a marvelously white dove over the chalice. He began to admire this vision, gazing intently upon it, when suddenly he was struck dumb and terrified. He fell prostrate in the choir, blinded. The brothers then led him by the hand out of the choir and asked him what had happened. They then prayed fervently until God restored to him his sight.[17]

---

[16] *Cum illic memorabilis Pater divina forte celebraret, in quibus nimirum exsequendis se devotissimum exhibere consueverat, vidit repente ante ipsam perceptionem in medio patenae non modicam stillam sanguinis Dominici rubentem. Vocatoque fratre Rodulpho, sacrista nostro, ejus tunc diacono. "Videsne, inquit, frater, quod video?—Video, ait, Domine." Caepitque pro tantae rei magnitudine ubertim flere. Post cujus miraculi declarationem, ex eodem sumpta, ut credimus, occasione, nobis deinceps patenam abluere mandatum est caepitque apud nos hujus observantia consuetudinis, cum a nobis eatenus nesciretur. Analecta Norbertina, PL 170, col. 1347.*

[17] *Miraculum istud contigit in ecclesia Vivariensi, praemonstratensis ordinis. Cum celebraretur missa in praefata ecclesia, quidam frater respiciens de choro ad altare vidit super illud circulum claritatis immensae et columbam miri candoris super calicem in eadem*

The third, much more widely known miracle took place in the church of Saint Yved of Braine on the Wednesday of Pentecost in 1153. The countess of Braine was the granddaughter of Agnes of Baudiment and daughter of Thibaud of Champagne; at the end of her life she had become a Norbertine sister at Fontenille, near Prémontré. This countess had on her estate a young Jewish girl of rare beauty whom she loved dearly and whom she wished to convert. The countess brought the girl to her castle and assigned her with other young people to her personal service. The young Jewess followed the countess to church every day and remained with her at the hours of the office. Despite the countess' exhortations, however, the young girl—whom she called Agnes after her own grandmother—persisted in her unbelief, declaring that she would never accept what her mistress had taught her unless she herself saw Jesus in the hands of the priest. Many prayers were offered for a miracle for this young woman, then on the Wednesday of Pentecost one of the confreres, the venerable Brother Gerard, was celebrating the conventual Mass in the presence of Bishop Henry of Beauvais, Bishop Ansculf of Soissons, and the abbot Master Peter of Braine along with a great crowd of other people, both Jews and Christians. At the consecration the holy Body of Christ visibly appeared to all those present in the form of a child suspended on the cross. The Jews cried out with their wives and children, "We see, we see the very Body of Christ, stretched out physically upon the cross, just as the lady countess has told us many times." They then asked to be baptized. This miracle is attested in a Latin manuscript in the Bibliothèque Nationale[18] and by Jacques de Vitry in his history of the West. It gave rise to a eucharistic pilgrimage to the abbey of Braine lasting until the French Revolution.

Not only does the Eucharist heroically increase and nourish faith, but charity is also its proper fruit, as Philip of Harvengt stresses: "When we consecrate the divine mysteries at the altar, we ourselves

---

claritate. *Caepit igitur admirari, et admirando intueri, et subito stupefactus et territus amisso visu cecidit in choro prostratus. Quem fratres ad manus extra chorum deducentes et eventus veritatem perquirentes, tamdiu precibus institerunt, donec ei Deus visum restitueret.* Richard, PL 177, col. 461.

[18] *Catalogue 8 de l'Hist. de France*, no. 1376 LK 7.

are consecrated to God because we are filled with the Holy Spirit by the merit of this lofty office; the liturgy renders us worthy to give a kiss of peace to those present. We kiss, I say, not to touch lips but in order to pour upon others the grace of the Holy Spirit we have ourselves received. They may then be present at the sacred mystery with faith and attentiveness. By the action of the Holy Spirit, they too may share in the sacrament in this kiss." [19]

Distinctive Premonstratensian observances with regard to the Mass and the Eucharist are then of interest here. First, the earliest statutes suggest that the Mass was celebrated solemnly twice a day. The morning Mass was chanted for the dead, with the entire monastery present—canons, lay brothers, and sisters—between prime and the daily chapter. This Mass was said with a deacon and subdeacon, but without dalmatics or incense unless it was performed by a bishop. All might freely communicate, but how often those religious who were not priests approached the holy table remains unclear. High Mass was then chanted at the end of the morning between the offices of terce and sext. During the week only the canons were present at this celebration, while the lay brothers and the sisters remained at their work. Lavish ceremony marked this Mass: dalmatics, copes for the cantors, sometimes a silk chasuble. Incense and complex chants were offered. A liturgical sequence was chanted on important feasts. At the consecration the ringing of a bell called all who were working in the monastery to come together in this holy sacrifice.

A third conventual Mass eventually was established in honor of the Blessed Virgin. This Mass does not appear in the first manuscripts of the Premonstratensian ordinary and was likely not introduced until the thirteenth century, when this practice was also widespread outside the order; three Masses were regularly said in the chapel of King Louis, for example. These three eucharistic celebrations corresponded to choral observances of the three offices:

---

[19] *Cum altari praesentamur et sacrantes sacra mysteria ipsi quoque Domino consecramur, quia tanti merito officii sancto Spiritu jam replemur, dignum ducit religio ut adstantes pariter osculemur. Osculemur, inquam, non ut labia labiis confundamus, sed acceptam Spiritus gratiam aliis refundamus, et qui sacro eidem mysterio assistant, humiles et intenti, operante Spiritu, osculo designante, fiant participes sacramenti.* Philip, Commentaria, PL 203, col. 195.

of the day, of the Blessed Virgin, and of the Dead. The Mass of the Blessed Virgin was generally celebrated for the novices while the professed confessed their faults in chapter. That celebration must have had some solemnity in at least a few monasteries, for here and there we find bequests for this Mass[20] along with the addition of chants like *Monstra te esse matrem*.[21] Some missals include sequences to be chanted at this daily Mass, yet it was never placed on the same level as the two other conventual Masses.

Private Masses then remain for discussion. These were envisioned in the early Premonstratensian statutes; in principle, for every priest to desire to ascend the altar after the example of Saint Norbert, who celebrated the holy sacrifice every day, was seen as praiseworthy. In fact, however, for all priests to celebrate Mass daily was likely impossible. At Prémontré, where there were some five hundred confreres, the architectural plans of the church indicated only nine altars. At Saint Martin of Laon seven altars were available for a community of almost the same number. Obviously the majority of the religious were lay brothers, while among the canons many others had received only the diaconate or minor orders. Nevertheless, supposing three Masses daily at the most—along with days full of manual labor—the number of Masses at Prémontré must have been only twenty-eight, twenty-two at Saint Martin, with the solemn Mass said later. Some priests therefore lacked the opportunity to say their Mass. Adam Scot suggests this situation when he writes:

> Perhaps you celebrate with more devotion when you abstain from celebrating so that your brother, who especially desires so to do, is able. Perhaps he would not be able to chant his Mass if you chanted yours. . . . A twofold good ensues: first, that you think such humble thoughts about yourself and such lofty ones about your brother that you believe his devotion to be better and holier than your own, second that you demonstrate such concern to preserve unity of spirit in the bond of peace.[22]

---

[20] As, for example, in the unpublished cartulary of the abbey of Mondaye.

[21] As at Saint Martin of Laon. See Hugo, *Monasteriologium*, Vol. 1, "Saint Martin."

[22] *Tunc fortasse devotius cantas quando idcirco non cantas ut fratri tuo qui desiderat cantare cedas! qui forte cantare non posset, si tu cantares. . . . Duplex bonum . . . ut*

Premonstratensian authors counsel great reverence toward the Most Blessed Sacrament and the altar of sacrifice:

> Pious faith recognizes the presence of Christ and the angels at the altar, where the Body and Blood of our God and Redeemer Jesus Christ are made present. Furthermore, to approach such exalted majesty with humility is right and just, accomplishing all of the sacred functions with care and fidelity, showing the heart's devotion in the thoughtful posture of the body. . . . Each time one passes before the altar or alongside the altar requires a profound bow. Each time one reads or sings alone requires a humble bow of thanksgiving both before and after. The altar itself ought always to be covered with clean linens. It should be adorned on feast days with the most beautiful and precious ornaments at hand.[23]

So begins the *Ordinarius* or ceremonial book of the order.

Numerous details about the eucharistic devotion of the first sons of Saint Norbert remain unknown. Clearly, however, the strongly eucharistic emphasis of the Order of Prémontré is not a later development, but goes back to the very beginnings of the institution. The blessed Juliana of Mont Cornillon, a figure important to the origin of the feast of Corpus Christi, may herself have belonged to the Order of Prémontré. Certainly, the white order adopted that feast enthusiastically when Urban IV gave it official status. The blessed Gertrude, prioress of Aldenburg, distinguished herself by the solemnity with which she directed that this feast be celebrated in her monastic church. But that event exceeds this work's chronological boundaries, bringing this discussion to a close. The practice of dedicating the first chapter of the order's statutes to eucharistic observance, notably, goes back to the end of the thirteenth century, to the version of 1290. "The Centrality of Eucharistic Devotion" has then been a fitting title for the present survey of the Premonstratensian founder's thought and his followers' interest.

---

dum de te tam humiliter et de fratre tuo tam sublimiter sentis ut devotionem ejus tua meliorem et sanctiorem credas . . . aliud vero dum . . . tam sollicitus fueris servare unitatem in vinculo pacis. Adam, *Soliloquiae,* PL 198, col. 870.

[23] Lefevre, 5.

Chapter 6
Attentiveness to the Word of God

The entire book of the Acts of the Apostles attests the fidelity of the apostles in preaching the word of God and the attentiveness of the first Christians in listening to them. Since religious life is founded on faith, all Christian ascetics since the beginning have been committed to enriching that life's doctrine, whether in listening to sermons delivered in the cloister, in reading and meditating on sacred scripture, or in contemplating the divine mysteries. The early Premonstratensians were no different. Because various religious institutes' methods of study, the time dedicated to this pursuit, the sources employed, and the weight placed on one source or the other vary widely, giving the respective orders much of their mutually distinctive character, some detail of the study of the word of God in the Premonstratensian context will be useful here. As readers familiar with the history of spirituality will appreciate, this chapter might briefly be summarized in noting that the contemplation of the first Premonstratensians was intermediate between the Benedictines and the Dominicans. This situation reflected their chronological place in the development of spirituality.

Preaching in the Cloister

Premonstratensians are obliged by their very vocation to preach beyond the cloister. The white habit of the order, declared by Saint Norbert to be appropriate to preachers because the angels of the

Resurrection wore it, was a constant reminder of this calling. The symbolism of this white garment was widely understood, not only by the founder himself. When Arno of Reichersberg, for instance, contrasted the black cowl of the monks with the white surplice of clerics, he wrote:

> The monastic order wears a somber habit, showing that it mortifies itself before the world in order to represent for us the death of Christ and the way in which we too ought to die to our vices and desires. Meanwhile the clerical order shines in its white habit like an angel in witness of Christ's Resurrection, suggesting that we ought to rise with Christ and walk in the newness of life.[1]

But preaching must take place inside the cloister as well. The Premonstratensian preacher must first address the religious themselves, who need the word of God in order to nourish and develop their faith.[2] The duty of preaching to the community falls to the abbot and is ordinarily fulfilled in the chapter, but the abbot shares this responsibility with other priests. Clerics of the community must also offer sermons to the lay brothers and sisters who live on its granges or outlying farms.[3] Preaching in cloisters, as Saint Thomas Aquinas would later say, treats of the richness of the mysteries; its end is the perfection of souls.[4] The sermons of Adam Scot and the

---

[1] *Ordo monasticus in habitu lugubri se ipsum mundo mortificans mortem nobis Christi et qualiter ei cum vitiis et concupiscentiis mori debeamus denuntiat. Ordo vero clericalis in habitu candido cum angelo testis resurrectionis Christi praefulget, nimirum qualiter Christo consurgentes in novitate vitae ambulare debeamus insinuans.* Arno, PL 188, col. 1112.

[2] Saint Paul says, *Faith then cometh by hearing; and hearing by the word of Christ* (Rom 10:17).

[3] *Commorabantur sacerdotes ejusdem ordinis et clerici . . . qui . . . eas [sorores] certis temporibus verbis divinarum Scripturarum instruere et informare studebant.* Intro. to *Vita S. Norberti*, PL 170, col. 1251.

[4] *Multiplex est instructio. Una conversiva ad fidem . . . potest competere cuilibet fideli* [Catholic and missionary action]. *. . . Secunda est instructio qua quis eruditur de fidei rudimentis et qualiter se habere debeat in receptione sacramentorum et haec pertinet secundum se ad ministros, principaliter ad sacerdotes. Tertia est instructio de conversatione Christiana et haec pertinet ad patrinos. Quarta est instructio de mysteriis fidei et perfectione Christiana et haec ex officio pertinet ad episcopos.* ("Instruction is manifold. Its first stage is turning toward faith, and is within the competence of any of the faithful.

commentary of Philip of Harvengt on the Canticle of Canticles suggest this very purpose. Surely, however, many abbots and provosts were incapable of shaping their discourse in a sophisticated way. Indeed, homiletic works that have been copied and preserved were often selected for reproduction because of their literary style. Still, all prelates were at least required to be capable of expounding the mystical senses of scripture to teach the dogmas of the faith and to encourage their listeners with thoughts of heaven. Preaching was regarded as prelates' essential function; indeed this role approximates them to bishops, whose most important role in the Church is to perfect souls by the word of God. Abbots chosen for their capacity to govern rather than their homiletic ability were judged inferior to their task because of their incompetence in preaching, as was Odo, abbot elect of Prémontré in 1174, whom the bishop of Laon refused to bless because of the weakness of his writing.

How was this preaching received? To preach to preachers can be difficult, given their knowledge of the craft and their constant practice in it. Adam Scot notes that criticisms of this manner sometimes arise: "Doesn't Saint Augustine, Saint Gregory, or some other doctor of the Church say exactly this? This preacher is offering us as his own a sermon he has stolen from the works of others and memorized, as if we could not find and borrow the same passages."[5] But this grudging spirit cannot have emerged frequently. In any case, the love of preaching was regarded as a sign distinguishing the children of God. "You listen to me," said Adam, "because you are God's."[6] Certainly twelfth-century sermons no longer appeal to us today because of the innumerable allegories of which they

---

Second is that instruction teaching of the basics of the faith and manner of reception of the sacraments; this teaching belongs, in its very nature, to ministers, principally to the priests. Third is instruction about Christian morals and this pertains to godparents. Fourth is instruction about the mysteries of the faith and Christian perfection; this pertains, by their very office, to the bishops.") Thomas Aquinas, *Summa Theologiae* III, q. 971, a. 4 ad 3.

[5] *Nonne Augustinus, nonne Gregorius nonne alii doctores haec eadem dicunt? Quae passim in libris doctorum furatus memoriter retinuit, haec nobis pro sermone recitavit, ac si et nos non possimus ista videre, ut ipse ea vidit atque collegit.* Adam, *Sermones*, PL 198, col. 184.

[6] *Vos ideo auditis quia ex Deo estis.* Adam, *Sermones*, PL 198, col. 157.

are constituted; this is a question of literary taste. Let us not forget, however, that such discussion was, for medieval preachers, theologically correct; they believed that the literal sense was suitable for beginners while the allegorical sense was fitting for more advanced souls.[7] This was the teaching of Saint Gregory and it makes sense. Medieval interpreters did not read scripture for history or for apologetic material. Their aims were edification and dogma, found only with the help of allegory. "Spiritual interpretations are found in the depths of the scriptures," said Adam Scot.[8] Medieval exegesis could not be better described. Adam compares the preacher to the herbalist who plunges into the forest in order to collect medicinal plants. Sometimes, if he finds a great deal, he delays in a particular thicket. Sometimes the preacher seems to stop in one spot entirely when, through the influence of the Holy Spirit and the strength of his intellect, he finds especially profound meanings.[9]

Much more might be said about preaching in the cloister. Its history has not been thoroughly studied and those authors who do address it set it in the context of moral sermons addressed to secular folk, but preaching within the religious community differs profoundly in tone, language, and object. Meanwhile, we know almost nothing about the preaching addressed to the lay brothers. It must have combined elements of the preaching within the cloister and catechism, since its illiterate audience had no other means of religious instruction.

Lectio Divina

The preached word was nevertheless not the only way to relay the divine message. Attentiveness to the word of God presupposes reading as well—*lectio divina* or divine reading, as Saint Benedict called it. To associate this *lectio* with the spiritual reading required

---

[7] *[Scriptura] modo incipientes et teneros lacte quodam potat historiae, modo autem in fide proficientes pane cibat allegoriae.* Adam, *De tripartito tabernaculo*, PL 198, col. 630.

[8] *Sententiae spirituales in profunditate scripturarum.* Adam, *Sermones*, PL 198, col. 96.

[9] *Mediante infusione Spiritus et acumine intellectus profundiores invenit.* Adam, *Sermones*, PL 198, col. 96.

today, no matter how fervent the soul is during those few minutes, would be inappropriate. *Lectio divina* was one of the lengthiest and most important exercises of the medieval cloister. With manual labor and the office, it was a primary enterprise. This sacred reading took place each day, lasting several hours—about six in the winter and three in summer because of that season's more important agricultural work. On Sundays and major feast days *lectio* filled all the canons' free time. Each remained in the cloister or scriptorium, covering his head with his hood for the sake of easier recollection, to read the scriptures or the Fathers of the Church in order to find God. Notably, such reading was a complex exercise. Hugh of Saint Victor and Adam Scot after him analyzed its conduct at length, noting that it consisted in reading strictly speaking, but also in meditation, contemplation, and prayer. Passage among the aspects of *lectio* occurred through grace, in freedom of the spirit, so demonstrating that the spirituality of former times was much more flexible and humane than in our own. Never did medieval authors, for instance, distinguish prayer from thanksgiving, from contact with the Blessed Sacrament, or from spiritual reading; such distinction is useful only to very busy folk able to give a relatively brief time to these exercises. All earlier ascetics were aware of a great current of communication with God outside of the office and lasting all day long, continuing even into manual labor. In this conversation with heaven, listening took place in reading or contemplation, while speech embraced prayer according to the needs of the individual soul and the action of grace. Such *lectio divina*, established by Saint Benedict, remains an important exercise of piety among the Cistercians.

Examination of the practice of *lectio* will here reveal Premonstratensian authors' views on reading, meditation, contemplation, and private prayer. *Lectio* addresses sacred scripture or the Fathers of the Church, yet surviving manuscripts from libraries of the order suggest that the Fathers held a rather limited place. Saint Augustine and Saint Gregory were favorites among pious readers, although the more learned among them were familiar with many more authors, both sacred and secular. Nevertheless, sacred scripture itself was the basis of *lectio divina*. This tradition dated from the first desert monks and was passed down untouched to the monasteries of the Middle Ages. A popular saying affirmed that a monk is the man of the Bible.[10] The canon regular was still more a reader of sacred texts because of his obligation not only to learn about the things of God but to teach others. The early Premonstratensians knew the Bible by heart; they never ceased to read and meditate upon it. Their speech became a long poem made up of biblical quotations. Scripture itself was the context in which their thought unfolded.

The method governing the medieval canons' reading was predicated on intellectual habits unlike our own. Its practitioners continually considered three senses of Scripture, seeking in its historical sense examples of sanctity, in its allegorical sense a right understanding of faith, and in its anagogical sense the happiness of the heavenly joys.[11] Examples of sanctity in the Old Testament offered the reader delight, as Adam Scot writes:

> Let us contemplate the innocence of Abel, the obedience of Noah, the outstanding modesty of Shem and Jephtah, the faith of Abraham, the purity of Isaac, the patience of Jacob, the chastity of Joseph, the meekness of Moses, the courage of Joshua, the simplicity of Samuel, and the humility of David. Let us admire too the different types of sacred rites, some instituted under natural law and some under written law. Let us read all the things written about Christ in the law of Moses and in the prophets and the psalms. Then none will be able to deny that we see the coming of the power of God. Let us also look from afar and see those many nations under heaven that have been enveloped from the beginning of the world in diabolical darkness—existing in this world without knowledge of God, led to worship silent and ephemeral idols, negligent or even unaware of heavenly goods while embracing the goods of this world.[12]

---

[10] The fourth and fifth centuries, in their flowering of the monastic life, also saw intense adherence to biblical models.

[11] *In historia exemplorum sanctitatem, in allegoria rectam fidei credulitatem, in anagogia supernorum gaudiorum felicitatem.* Adam, *De tripartito tabernaculo,* PL 198, col. 697.

[12] *Contemplemur innocentiam Abel, obedientiam Noe, bonam verecundiam Sem et Japhet, fidem Abrahae, munditiam Isaac, tolerantiam Jacob, pudicitiam Joseph, mansuetudinem Moysis, fortitudinem Josue, simplicitatem Samuelis, humilitatem David. Admiremur etiam diversa genera sacramentorum quae partim sub lege naturali, partim*

Here the method of medieval *lectio* is clear. As we have seen above in the case of Anselm of Havelberg, medieval Augustinians drew from scripture a stronger historical sensibility than did the scholastics of the following period. Most of the time, however, the historical sense did not fully satisfy them, so they dug past the literal meaning to find the allegorical sense. Scripture is, like the wheel of Ezekiel, written on the inside and the outside, and one must penetrate into the secrets.[13] The profit drawn from this reading is a wonder for which continual thanks are due to God, for "each day he deigns to refresh us by this spiritual banquet. He admits us into his inner chambers, showing us his hidden treasures and the mysteries of his secrets; he opens our eyes and unveils our faces, allowing us to consider the wonders of his law and contemplate his glory."[14] This sacred nourishment is so flavorful that the more one eats, the more one hungers; the more one returns to it, the more it grows in savor and quantity.[15] Holy reading, says Philip of Harvengt, is the priest's delight.[16]

A well-organized cloister sets aside for *lectio divina* all the time this exercise requires, never stinting it under pretext of lengthening the liturgical office. This reading is as necessary as psalmody. Arno of Reichersberg—not a Premonstratensian but a regular canon nonetheless, also an admirer of Saint Norbert—notes the imperative to preserve the equilibrium among the three monastic occupations:

---

sub scripta lege instituta sunt, legamus etiam omnia quae scripta sunt in lege Moysi et prophetis et psalmis de Christo. Nec dicere jam poterit quis quin videamus potentiam Dei venientem. Aspiciamus etiam a longe et videamus tot nationes sub caelo ab ipso mundi exordio tenebris diabolicis involutos, sine Deo in hoc mundo exsistentes, ad simulacra muta ductos et pereuntes, relictis, imo prorsus ignoratis caelestibus et terrena totis affectibus amplectentes. Adam, *Sermones*, PL 198, col. 132.

[13] Compare Ezek 1:9.

[14] *Epulis nos quotidie spiritualibus magis ac magis reficere dignatur, admittens nos in interioribus suis et ostendens nobis thesaurus absconditos et arcana secretorum suorum, revelans etiam oculos nostros et faciens ut mirabilia de lege sua scrutemur et gloriam ejus speculemur.* Adam, *Sermones*, PL 198, col. 190.

[15] *Quo magis comeditur eo et magis esuritur; quo frequentius editur eo plus augetur.* Adam, *Sermones*, PL 198, col. 190.

[16] *In linea [tunica Aaronis] videtur scientiam Scripturarum signari in qua debet clericus legendo versari et . . . delectabiliter deliciari.* "Knowledge of Scriptures is written in the linen [tunic of Aaron]; here the cleric ought to busy himself with reading and . . . take joyous delight." Philip, *De institutione*, PL 203, col. 690.

the office, *lectio divina*, and work. "The exercise of work and of reading—together with the sacrifice of turtledoves, that is, private
prayer—must not be delimited by the prolongation of common
prayer and psalmody. The one should not diminish the other."[17]
In fact, negligence in *lectio divina* at the end of the Middle Ages led
to laxity in cloistered life. Religious communities rediscovered their
fervor only when, through other means, they reestablished heart-
to-heart conversation with God in the sixteenth and seventeenth
centuries.

Study

Holy reading leads to study in the monastic context. These two
practices sadly were separated during the decadence of scholasticism but were closely joined in the time of the Augustinians and
great scholastics. Therefore early Premonstratensian authors distinguish *lectio divina* from study only slightly. For them, the primary
object of study was Christ. Philip of Harvengt writes:

> When do we find Christ face to face if not when we push from
> our hearts all worldly tumult, so that nothing foreign interrupts
> our reading and nothing stands in the way of our meditation?
> Then we are absorbed into the pages of the sacred writings so
> that through the benefit of our reading we may know that Christ
> better whom our knowledge makes us love and whom our love
> then leads us fully to embrace.[18]

Philip does not suggest that this reading took place without any
method or specific aim, as works such as Vivian's or Zachary's
demonstrate.

---

[17] *Ne operis ac lectionis exercitium vel secretae orationis turtureum sacrificium per
orationis et psalmodiae in communi protelationem excludatur, cum haec oporteat fieri et
ista non omitti.* Arno, PL 188, col. 1090.

[18] *Quando, quaeso vos, fratres mei, Christum invenimus singularem, nisi quando de
cordibus nostris omnem repellimus tumultum saecularem, ut nihil indecens nostrae obstrepat
lectioni, nihil obsistat meditationi; sed eo intuitu sacris paginis insistamus, ut beneficio
lectionis Christum amplius cognoscamus, cognitum diligamus, dilectum teneamus?* Philip,
De institutione, PL 203, col. 704.

For these medieval Premonstratensians, study was principally the work of exegesis. Useful tools like dictionaries, concordances, and atlases were unavailable to them. Rather their memory of texts and reconciliation among them yielded fruitful reflections and interesting discoveries, so unlocking their deep meaning. The book of scripture is sealed, bringing joy only insofar as the seals are broken. If reflection does not suffice to open it, then prayer and tears may.[19] The abbot of Bonne Espérance frequently stresses the need for study: "Our Lord," he says, "chose ignorant and unlettered apostles to confound the wise, but he did not want them to remain ignorant. He strove to raise them up to the loftiest secrets of knowledge in the course of time. . . . So he sweetly invites his apostles and their successors to study."[20] Philip laments that some religious, under the pretext of urgent manual labor, steal away from study. "Work is useful in preserving our physical health, allowing many of us then to return to our reading with more eagerness. But it is useful, I say, only when it serves reading and other spiritual needs, not when it wrongly oppresses them by disturbing proper priorities."[21]

Meditation

Meditation normally follows reading. To put food into one's mouth is not enough; that food must be chewed and digested in order for it to provide nourishment. Adam Scot noted the importance of

[19] Focus on scripture did not exclude the possibility of studying other, even secular, subjects. In the Augustinian way of thinking, all things were useful for a more profound knowledge of scripture, therefore of God. John of Hollyrood thus left works on mathematics and the venerable Odo of Cappenberg wrote a treatise on computation. Others in the order composed chronicles and historical books. Obviously the more secular the subject, the more its risked distraction from God. Obedience and common usefulness—simply, duty—presided over these studies, turning them to the spiritual good of him who took them up.

[20] *Ipse Dominus cum eligeret apostolos idiotas et sine litteris ut confundat sapientes; eos tamen idiotas noluit permanere, sed ad profunda secreta scientiae processu temporis studuit promovere. . . . Apostolos eorumque vicarios ad studium Dominus invitat blandiendo.* Philip, *De institutione*, PL 203, col. 698.

[21] *Utilis quippe plerisque est labor quia per eum nonnunquam salubritas corporis conservatur et ad usum lectionis avidius remeatur; utilis, inquam, cum lectioni caeterisque spiritualibus officiis famulatur, non cum ordine converso et perverso, eisdem pertinaciter dominatur.* Philip, *De institutione*, PL 203, col. 707.

meditation throughout his life, yet at the beginning of his career even he did not consider meditation a special enterprise, instead naming the three exercises of the cloister as reading, prayer, and work. Later, under the influence of Hugh of Saint Victor, Adam extended his analysis to distinguish four exercises of the cell: reading, meditation, prayer, and work. Meditation is sometimes simply an act of the virtue of prudence, considering in advance the difficulties of the spiritual life and the means of avoiding them by hearty resolution and appropriate precautions. Many pious souls, especially at the beginning of their fervor when they first apply themselves to the spiritual life, engage in it. Saint Norbert did so at the time of his conversion when, as his biographer tells us, "in untiring meditation he set aside all the sufferings and battles that might befall him."[22] Usually, however, meditation is a religious act seeking the contemplation of God. Among the early Premonstratensians discussed here, meditation had this clearly contemplative tendency.

In his Sermon 47, Adam Scot compares six major subjects of meditation to the six jars of water at the wedding of Cana, identifying these as the state of the sinner, his conversion, the judgment of God, death, hell, and heaven.[23] Adam finds meditation necessary even in the higher states of the spiritual life. The bride and Bridegroom are mutually present in meditation; only the wine of spiritual joy is lacking. The bride asks for it and Jesus responds: "What is it to me and to thee?"[24] This spiritual joy is not a right; we must await it in humility and patience. During our wait, however, meditative exercise must fill the six jars until the graces of union are granted.[25] Adam elsewhere lists five appropriate subjects of meditation: the life and passion of Christ, the role of preachers, the obedience of listeners, the practice of good-hearted people, and the joys of heaven.[26] Meditation is then the lamp shining so that the house may be swept until the drachma etched with God's image is finally found. It tends toward the mystical, properly speaking.

---

[22] *Quidquid passionum et agonum accidere poterat infatigaili praemeditatione levigabat.* *Vita S. Norberti*, PL 170, col. 1261.

[23] Adam, *Sermones*, PL 198, col. 437–40.

[24] Compare Jn 2:4.

[25] Adam, *Sermones*, PL 198, col. 424–29.

[26] Adam, *De tripartito tabernaculo*, PL 198, col. 757.

The exercise of meditation requires first a general preparation of the soul consisting first in the furthest possible separation from creatures. For Adam Scot, contemplation is the Sabbath preceding the great Sunday of heaven, but it is itself preceded by a week of work: abstinence, habitual silence, rest in withdrawal from external occupations, vigils, attention to holy reading, and the purest of meditation.[27] As Philip of Harvengt stresses: "By concerted effort all that perishes must be forgotten. Contemplation will then be given to the eye undistracted by outside things, instead directing all of its acuity to the secrets of Christ. Such an eye wounds the heart of Christ with love. It is sharper than a sword, penetrating to that place where Christ hides nothing."[28]

Another condition of meditation—serving as the next stage of its preparation—is that bodily rest we mentioned when we spoke of solitude: *multa quies*, deep quiet. This stage is indispensable. The contemplative is often tempted to fidget, to occupy himself with suddenly urgent worldly matters. Although the body struggles to maintain prolonged tranquility, it must be restrained. Manual labor then serves for refreshment and to render meditation attractive, but to enter and strengthen the meditative state requires full rest. "Release from external occupation calms all the soul's unrest."[29] This love of external tranquility is the effect of a grace inhering in the contemplative life. When it is lacking, the soul suddenly grows weak, as though it were dust blown about the surface of the earth. It becomes fickle, talkative with others because it is talkative within itself, flighty because its affections are disordered, intolerant of rest because its dissipation keeps it in motion. It is incapable of remaining within itself.[30] Exterior asceticism in gait, posture, and speech,

[27] *Abstinentia, silentium, quies ab exteriori occupatione, instantia vigilarum, studium sacrae lectionis, pura meditatio, fervor boni desiderii.* See Adam, *Sermones*, PL 198, col. 210.

[28] *Qui nisu praevalido studet omnia quae praetereunt oblivisci.* Philip, *Commentaria*, PL 203, col. 387. *Collecto intuitu Christi secretario se infundit. . . . Cor illius vulnerat dum illic acutior gladio se recondit ubi Christus oculum nisi unum et simplicem non abscondit.* Philip, *Commentaria*, PL 203, col. 388.

[29] *Quies ab exteriori occupatione omnem in mente inquietudinem sedat.* Adam, *Sermones*, PL 198, col. 211.

[30] Adam, *Sermones*, PL 198, col. 214.

on the other hand, allows meditation to enter not only the soul yielding to it but also those others living in the monastery. But this atmosphere of peace and tranquility must be established by sacrifice.[31]

Does a distinctive method mark that meditation amid contemplative recollection sought in the Premonstratensian cloister? Not if method here denotes a preexisting pattern imposed on the soul committed to this practice. Medieval religious had a greater respect for individual souls' freedom than moderns accord them. Nonetheless, some forms of experience are explained by medieval spiritual authors as supporting the beginning stages of the life of contemplation. Five are not necessarily particular to the Premonstratensians but found among all Augustinians: rumination on the psalms, confession, the method of degrees, exploration of allegorical meaning, and the contemplation of Christ. To ruminate on the psalms is to embrace them in private prayer verse by verse, savoring them and appropriating them. This is an ancient method of prayer, a devotion to the psalms called in the earlier Middle Ages simply "devotion." In the Rule of Saint Chrodegang all novices were enjoined to learn the psalter by heart not only to make chanting the office easier and livelier but especially to form their souls for prayer. The same tradition was continued among all the regular canons. When Saint Norbert set out on his itinerant preaching, he took with him a psalter, the universal manual of spirituality. The Rule of Saint Augustine prescribed memorization for chanting the sentiments expressed by psalms or hymns. The sole means of achieving this mastery was slow meditation on their content. A confrere might devote himself to this simple, easy exercise not only during *lectio divina* but also during manual labor, meals, travels and journeys, sleeplessness, and even sickness. The psalter addresses all of life's circumstances with its acts of thanksgiving, lamentations, prayers, and celebrations. Remarkably, Premonstratensian authors nonetheless discuss this type of prayer very little, probably because it was so constant, ubiquitous, loved, and practiced that none felt the need to treat it at length. The ease with which writers of the order

---

[31] Adam, *Liber de ordine*, PL 198, col. 534.

constantly cited the psalms reveals, however, how much they absorbed this book of prayers inspired by the Holy Spirit.

"Confession" is a scriptural term with two meanings: avowal of past sins and praise rendered to God, especially for benefits received from him. Confession is that species of affective meditation of which Saint Augustine's immortal masterpiece is exemplary; it is based chiefly on previous relations between God and the soul. In confession the soul recalls past faults so that it may experience deep sorrow, the punishment these faults have merited in order to destroy the desire for sin. The mercy of the Lord Jesus then bends down toward the sinful soul to pardon it, as he did in former times to Mary Magdalene. Next, the soul recalls at length the benefits of grace. It has been created, redeemed, and justified. It has received the delights of assiduous attentiveness to reading, zeal for meditation, sweetness in speculation, and purity of contemplation. Even the alternations of health and sickness or of temptations and periods of peace establish many graces, the sum of which forms a marvelous passageway between God and the individual soul.

To pause to consider the small merit of this object of divine favors is here useful. Adam Scot gives numerous examples of a specific style of confession, especially in *On Threefold Contemplation*.[32] In the inspired rhetoric of the abbot of Dryburgh, this modality is magnificent, suggesting the futility of asserting that style matters little in private meditation and that delight in the sweetness of God's gifts is more important than its magnification in words.

Another broad and varied meditative process is the method of stages described by Saint Augustine in book 10 of his *Confessions*. This process consists in beginning with the contemplation of the world in order to rise up to God, looking first at lesser creatures in order to discover what they teach about the Creator, then considering superior beings, addressing especially the human soul in order to obtain an idea of the spirituality of God. This method does not

---

[32] *Quem [librum] per confessionem Dominum alloquendo composuimus, quia iste dicendi modus legentium multum excitare solet affectum.* ("Which book we composed by speaking to the Lord through confession, because this type of speaking is accustomed to excite greatly the affections of the reader.") Adam, *De triplici genere*, PL 198, col. 796.

prove God's existence by stages of being but its dialectical process is familiar; its end is not to prove God, but to find God by entering and delighting in him. Description of such ascent of the soul occupies the entire latter part of Adam's *On Threefold Contemplation*, where it is described in splendid verse.

The fourth and most frequent method of meditation described by Premonstratensian preachers—for them much more a model of prayer than an oratorical method—is exploration of allegorical meaning. Experience has shown them that the divine contact of contemplation comes to surprise the soul, especially when it discovers an allegory of faith in a passage of Scripture and when it then delights in identifying the suitability of the passage's details, intensely experiencing its poetry. This spiritual process goes back to Saint Gregory the Great; his *Moral Interpretation of Job* popularized it in the cloisters of the Middle Ages.

Finally, the fifth and best method described by the order's authors is direct contemplation of the mysteries of Christ, especially his infancy and his passion. This method was, as seen above, employed straightforwardly by the blessed Herman Joseph, the blessed Bronislava, and Christine of Christ. It became the most frequently and preferred method, as even those most passionately interested in allegory knew. Adam Scot himself explained in four different allegorical readings why the Child Jesus had been wrapped in swaddling clothes. He ends by saying: "I leave you to judge which is the most correct sense, but whether you approve one or reject all, certainly you realize here that God, the Son of God, born of the Virgin, was wrapped in swaddling-clothes bespeaks extraordinary humility." [33]

Contemplation

Meditation appeals on the soul's behalf for divine favors to raise it to contemplation. While mankind has of his own nature the power to meditate, contemplation is God's gift, not always according to human desire. Saint Norbert described contemplation as the refreshment of the soul. He wished that his dear disciple, Hugh of

[33] Adam, *Sermones*, PL 198, col. 244. This type of meditation is perhaps enjoyed more than can be verbally expressed; sermons offer few examples.

Fosses, "might come gradually to disdain the barrenness and turmoil of the world in order to drink at the fountain of heavenly
refreshment and sweetness."[34] Likewise Norbert said in his sermon
to his confreres: "There [in contemplation] is a health-bringing
fountain, a never-failing well, a sweet torrent of pleasures."[35] Sometimes he used another comparison, describing contemplation as
the flight of the soul toward the heights of heaven. As his biographer
said: "[Norbert] himself soared in thought and word to find a place
of rest; he made his listeners fly with him. They naively asked
whether they had not suddenly grown wings."[36] Moreover, in his
sermon Saint Norbert writes: "Fly in the clouds with the perfect
and contemplate divine things there."[37]

As we have seen, Adam Scot's consideration of contemplation
was especially compelling. All his life was an apostolate for the
contemplative experience, but other early Premonstratensian authors faithfully echoed him. As Philip of Harvengt writes:

> The grace of divine vision snatches you up from the earth and,
> as it were, ravishes you on high . . . when that Sun brighter than
> the sun penetrates you with a ray of his brightness. Then the
> Bridegroom feeds you as his sheep and lovingly rejoices in this
> rest. He embraces you in such a bright afternoon; as Day he loves
> the day and as Light the light.[38]

In his beautiful book on the harmony between grace and free will,
Vivian, the theologian of Prémontré, expressed great feeling in
describing contemplation: "Contemplatives alone, when they are
raised up on wings in the spirit's flight, happily enjoy the freedom

---

[34] *Volens ut ille, paulatim siccitate aestus saecularis postposita, hauriret caelestis refrigerii et dulcedinis fontem.* Vita S. Norberti, PL 170, col. 1278.

[35] *Ibi saluberrimus fons . . . indeficiens puteus, dulcis torrens voluptatum.* See appen-dix below.

[36] *Volabat quidem mente et ore ad requiescendum et suos auditores volare faciebat. . . . Circa se pennas quaerentes invenire [putabant] statim se volare existimantes et requiescere.* Vita S. Norberti, PL 170, col. 1291.

[37] *Cum perfectis volate in nubibus, contemplando divina.* See appendix below.

[38] *A terra suspensos rapit velut in sublime divinae gratia visionis cum. . . . Sol sole lucidior vos perfundit radio suae claritatis; tunc nimirum in vobis Sponsus pascit et amica requie delectatur, tali gaudet meridie, die dies, lumen lumine gratulatur.* Philip, Com-mentaria, PL 203, col. 243.

of this pleasure, even if briefly and rarely."[39] However rare, though, the effects of contemplation given even in passing and without any spiritual experience are extremely powerful:

> The soul dissolves in love, restless for separation from earthly things and attachment to things divine. It is devoted to reading, pure in prayer, filled with sweetness in meditation, clear in contemplation. It bears the One in its thoughts and affections always and everywhere, it kisses him; wounded in love, it rests in him until it eternally possesses him whom it has loved unfailingly here below.[40]

Like all contemplatives, medieval Norbertine souls received illuminations about God as triune and singular—for Trinity was the first object of contemplation—as well as about divine providence, the judgment of the damned, Christ, the angels, and the splendors of the faithful soul.[41] They often returned to two points as if especially enlightened about these—namely the mystery of grace, upon which Adam and Vivian dwelt joyfully, and the joys of heaven. Like Norbert, his sons were heaven-bent, never quietists. Their pilgrimage on this earth seemed to them all too long and they eased it by thinking on the joys which they would soon taste in glory.

Prayer

Among the central concerns of the early Premonstratensians, prayer follows meditation. Certainly the early canons' private prayer of petition was logically related to the divine office, as among prior

---

[39] *Soli contemplativi quand in excessu mentis penna contemplationis sublevantur, utcumque libertate complaciti fruuntur et hoc ex parte satis modica viceque rarissima.* Vivian, PL 166, col. 1327.

[40] *Fit mens prae amore liquefacta, prae desiderio anxia et a terrenis segregata, in supernis fixa, studiosa in lectione, pura in oratione, dulcis in meditatione, suavis in speculatione, defaecata in contemplatione. Unum quidem semper et ubique in cogitatu et affectu circumferens, Unum diligens, Unum amplectens, in Uno requiescens et caritate vulnerata quousque in aeternum possideat quem nunc quoque indeficienter amat.* Adam, *Sermones*, PL 198, col. 215.

[41] Adam, *De tripartito tabernaculo*, PL 198, cols. 778–80.

monks. Saint Benedict ordained that at the end of the psalms all prostrate themselves in silence for brief but fervent prayer. Among authors of the Order of Prémontré, however, prayer is more readily associated with reading and meditation than with the office. "The place of reading and meditation—and most often of prayer—is the cloister."[42] Again, "in the sanctuary of the soul is found the table of reading, the candelabrum of contemplation and the altar of prayer."[43] Private prayer is, of course, related as well to liturgical prayer. Saint Norbert thus prepared for the celebration of Mass by private prayer which the crowd found too long; the blessed Herman Joseph spent the time before matins in prayer. These canons' souls, it seems, were more moved to the prayer of petition by silent meditation than by chant, although Christine of Christ differed in this regard.

When Premonstratensian religious were so permitted, they loved to spend their night vigils in prayer. Norbert was their model in this practice, careful as he was to imitate the conduct of the Savior himself, and in this the founder had great fortitude; "he was patient in vigils," said his biographer. The founder is said to have remarked: "Vigils are fatiguing but yield great fruits." He sometimes passed the entire night in prayer without a moment's sleep.[44] When Judah of Cologne, the later prelate Herman of Scheda, first met the Premonstratensians of Cappenberg before his conversion, he was struck by their prayer: "We know," he said to them, "that the quieter your prayers, the more they are sincere and efficacious before God in obtaining any kind of grace."[45] In its object, prayer is often tied very closely to the reading preceding it. Prayer completes the reader's dialogue with God; Christ spoke through a book and now the soul responds in prayer. Often, however, Christ spoke obscurely in scriptures. As Philip of Harvengt notes, to receive what Christ refuses

---

[42] *Locus lectionis et meditationis, et plerumque orationis, claustrum est.* Adam, *De ordine,* PL 198, col. 603.

[43] *In sancto habemus mensam lectionis, candelabrum contemplationis, altare orationis.* Adam, *De ordine,* col. 603.

[44] *Vita S. Norberti,* PL 170, col. 1277; compare cols. 1279 and 1321.

[45] *Scientes orationes vestras quanto quietiores tanto esse sinceriores, tantoque esse ante Dei conspectum ad impetranda quaelibet efficaciores.* Hermannus Judaeus, PL 170, col. 826.

to bestow upon the negligent reader requires great effort. He counsels that the reader not fear to inquire devoutly and diligently, for Jesus loves to reveal the hidden matters of scripture to those who ask him, if only the soul find him alone after finding silence within itself.[46]

Adam Scot offers a lengthy and precise analysis of the dispositions of the soul in prayer in his treatise on the tabernacle. Just as the priest mounts three steps in order to ascend the altar so he may offer incense as the symbol of prayer, so the soul rising up to God must by recollection avoid three types of distraction. Some souls are beset by concerns for the temporal things for which they are responsible; they experience such fragmentation that they cannot comprehend what they themselves are saying. Others—and Adam bemoans the fact that he is among this group—are bothered by purely idle thoughts buzzing around them like flies and troubling their hearts in their ascent. Still others, more culpably, indulge themselves in remembering past pleasures. All of this must be pushed into oblivion as much as possible.

Among considerations appropriate to prayer are, first, the speaker, then the addressee, then, third, the intention of the request, and, finally, the manner of prayer. The soul at prayer should consider itself in all its wretchedness, how it is carried away by vice and feeble in virtue, sluggish with respect to good and quick to do evil. Let it understand that it has no right to expect anything from God through its own merits. This perspective will lend the soul a humble and eminently favorable disposition. Let it also then consider the clemency and the power of the God whom it implores. God can and indeed wishes to hear his elect who worthily invoke him, for by his mercy he knows their peril and by his power he supplies them the necessary aid. Thus humility and contrition join hope and confidence in prayer.

The soul ought then to ask three things before all else: pardon, grace, and glory. Adam speaks of no other favors. Indeed, grace is complex and rich; at minimum it has the advantage of placing man clearly in the presence of his final end and of making him under-

---

[46] *Est etiam. . . . Christus devota interrogatione pulsandus.* Philip, *De institutione,* PL 203, col. 704.

stand that the principal object of prayer is the union of the soul with God. Prayer should be offered with fervor and perseverance, desiring above all those favors it seeks and never ceasing to request them. The abbot of Dryburgh, however, stresses a final disposition: to obtain God's pardon requires pardoning one's brethren, as at the end of the very text of the Lord's Prayer.[47] In his *Fourfold Exercise of the Cell*, Adam—now a Carthusian—emphasizes Christ's mediation. Prayer demands our thinking of Jesus as the altar of gold for our petitions, that advocate to whom we ought to attach ourselves in order that the Father look upon him and so be propitious in turning to us.[48]

Although *lectio divina*, with its process of meditation, prayer, and contemplation, constitutes the chief exercise of piety outside of the office, private devotions also have their place. As Adam says, such devotions are good, but common devotions are preferable. It is often salutary, for the good of peace, to renounce one or another individual good in order to do the will of one's brethren.[49]

The present chapter on attentiveness to the word of God has been lengthy because of the importance of its topic, but also because the order's medieval spiritual writers frequently and eagerly returned to those vital issues ensuring the fervor of their monasteries.

---

[47] Adam, *De tripartito tabernaculo*, PL 198, cols. 763–65.

[48] Adam [recte], *De quadripertito exercitio*, PL 153, cols. 862–78.

[49] *Devotiones bonas privatas quidem judico sed eis communes ubique praepono. . . . Saepius bonum salubrius exercetur cum ab eo pro pace et voluntate fraterna ad tempus cessatur.* Adam, *Soliloquae*, PL 198, col. 870. Private devotions obviously have an important place in saints' biographies. In this regard pious personages have generally been eminent in their respective communities.

Chapter 7
Profound Charity

Charity was the Lord's supreme command: *Little children
. . . a new commandment I give unto you: that you love one
another, as I have loved you, that you also love another. By
this shall all men know you are my disciples, if you have love one for
another* (John 13:33-34). The apostles continually returned to this
subject: *Love the brotherhood* (1 Pet 2:17), said Saint Peter and Saint
Paul added, *every one members one of another* (Rom 12:5). Saint John
repeated, *We know that we have passed from death to life, because we
love the brethren. He that loveth not, abideth in death* (1 John 3:14).
In his old age John then had but one exhortation: "My children,
love each other well." In the early Church mutual charity marked
the presence of Christ. The Augustinian Rule stresses this point in
particular: "Love God above all things, beloved brethren, and then
our neighbor. These are the chief precepts established for you who
live in the monastery."[1] Saint Thomas would later teach similarly,
saying that "the perfection of the religious life—as of all Christian
life—consists in charity."[2] Adam Scot as well had understood completely that what he calls "unity of heart and common feeling" was

---

[1] *Ante omnia, fratres carissimi, diligatur Deus, deinde proximus quia haec praecepta
sunt principaliter nobis data.* Augustine, *Regula*, Prologue.

[2] *Omnis christianae vitae perfectio secundum caritatem attendenda est.* Thomas,
Summa Theologiae, II-IIae, q. 184.

an essential part of the apostolic life;[3] he was thus an apostle of fraternal charity almost as much as of contemplation. Hence his beautiful saying: "All our order's aim is toward charity."[4] Love for one's brothers in religion might then never fail, given their eminent place in the mystical body of Christ and the special regard reserved for them by God. "In your closeness to him you exceed—and by far—a great many among the body of Christ. They are members but you are bowels. You are more beloved than they, for he holds you in more fervent charity and in greater proximity to himself."[5]

The great delight of religious life is of course contemplation, as we have seen. Nothing is more favorable to the full flowering of mystical gifts, however, than fraternal charity. "Woe to those who delay the absent Christ in his return or who distance the present Christ. Who are these but disturbers of peace and breakers of unity? In their own disruption they disrupt others, sowing discord among the brethren."[6] Prompt obedience, as our authors term it, toward superiors is clearly important to unity of hearts. From superiors' perspective, direction is gentler, more amiable, and more gracious when he who is in charge is confident that obedience will follow his least sign. The first companions of Saint Norbert would have thrown themselves into water or fire upon a sign from their father. As for subjects, their promptness of obedience establishes a pattern of good will lending the community an odor of fervor, the sweetest of fragrances in a religious house.

Another indispensable element of fraternal charity is refined politeness, a sensitive urbanity in relations with one's neighbor. The early Premonstratensians did not have the opportunity to speak with each other very often, since silence was perpetual and recreation

---

[3] *Unitas concors et una concordia.* Adam, *Liber de ordine,* PL 198, col. 511.

[4] *Ad hoc ordo noster totam intentionem suam dirigit ut caritati militare possit.* Adam, *De tripartito tabernaculo,* PL 198, col. 615.

[5] *Nonnullos etiam illorum qui intus in corpore Christi sunt et ejus per fidem membra fiunt in hac ergo eum familiaritate praeceditis et longe exceditis, quia cum ipsi membra sint, vos ejus viscera estis. Prae ipsis estis dilecti et in ferventiore vos habet caritate et in majore apud seipsum familiaritate.* Adam, *Sermones,* PL 198, col. 204.

[6] *Vae illis per quos Christus et cum absens sit ne veniat moratur, et cum praesens est ne maneat fugatur. Qui sunt hi nisi perturbatores pacis, unitatis divisores, turbati et alios turbantes, seminantes inter fratres zizania?* Adam, *Sermones,* PL 198, col. 221.

absent. Nevertheless, as we see in the lives of saints like the blessed Herman Joseph, religious occasionally had access to the *auditorium*, the room for conversation, when communication was necessary. Gentleness of language and sweetness in the manner of speaking, accompanied by careful mutual respect, promoted the union of hearts.[7] As is true in all human associations, the precaution of never speaking about others in their absence was useful. Saint Augustine defended this prohibition at his own table by posting a memorable couplet on the wall; Adam Scot says: "To keep peace, sow no evil in malice in your neighbor's absence."[8] All of these prescriptions are negative, but charity requires more: the religious must constantly be ready to render every good service to his brothers. Such charity consists not only in frame of mind; rather, it must be translated into multiple acts.[9] Next, that great rule must remain fast to which the author of the *Imitation* would return: "Charity requires that always and everywhere it be permitted and found suitable that each learn to break his own will in everything, deferring willingly to the will of another."[10] Nothing is more contrary to life in community than caprice and stubbornness. Finally, integral to the charity of Saint Norbert's sons was their joyfulness of expression— as they called it, *hilaritas*—after the example of their beloved father.[11] Adam Scot described by a play on words difficult to translate: roughly, "goodly joyfulness and joyous good."[12] This joy nonetheless did not impede the compunction of heart enjoined by Saint Gregory the Great and sought by all the ascetics of the Middle Ages; it was rather present among all the order's saints as an indication of peace, as the sign that they were doing the will of God: "As seasoning is to food, so joyfulness is to the virtues. Everything we do lacks flavor unless it is graced with joyfulness."[13]

---

[7] *Dulcedo verbi, suavis locutio in ore.* Adam, *Ad viros*, 158–61.

[8] *Nil semines mali per malitiam in absentia ejus.* Adam, *Ad viros*, 158–61.

[9] *Ut devotum fratri tuo obsequium praestes.* Adam, *Ad viros*, 158–61.

[10] *Semper et ubique, quantum fas est et decens, propriam discas in omnibus voluntatem frangere eamdemque voluntati alienae libenter inclinare.* Adam, *Ad viros*, 158–61.

[11] *Aspectu hilaris, vultu serenus, sermone jucundus. Vita S. Norberti,* PL 170, col. 1259.

[12] *Jucunditas bona et bonitas jucunda.* Adam, *Sermones,* PL 198, col. 315.

[13] *Quasi condimentum inter cibos hilaritas est inter virtutes. Nam insipidum mihi videtur quod agis nisi gratia illud commendet hilaritatis.* Adam, *Sermones,* PL 198, col. 262.

The joyful peace of the cloister often reached beyond its walls, as in Norbert's apostolate to warring feudal families. Significantly, he carried an olive branch with him in appearances after his death. In life he always held in his heart the words he had heard at the time of his conversion: "Seek peace and pursue it." Later, when Saint Gertrude, prioress of Altenberg, learned that irreconcilable enemies were near her monastery, she made them come to her parlor and showed them a tame lion sitting meekly at her feet. She thus had the joy of bringing concord to many antagonists; many in the order were like her. Adam Scot, for instance, recognized in the charity surrounding him the sweetness of an earthly paradise rediscovered. He cried out, "O sweet delight, o delightful sweetness!" Although authors of the order gladly repeat the words of the psalm, *Behold how good and how pleasant it is for brethren to dwell together* (Ps 132:1)—words that, according to Saint Augustine, drew people to monasteries—they did not have an idyllic image of religious life; they knew well the hazards from which charity must be protected.

The first danger was in allowing injuries to endure; the Rule of Saint Augustine ordains that disputes be remedied by ending them quickly and asking immediate pardon from those offended, lest anger turn into hatred. Failing this, the offended brother later recalls the injury done to him; he ponders the circumstances and thinks about the offending brother in the darkest terms. When he is in the latter's presence, he looks at him with fiery eyes, wrinkled brow, eyebrows raised, and countenance menacing. He maintains superficial quiet but within engages in a stormy dialogue; he asks questions, makes up responses, himself is questioned and responds. Such tumult leaves place for no spiritual exercise, no true prayer, no studious reading, no pure meditation. Even work, meals, and repose become impossible. The offender has caused a true scandal by not reconciling himself as quickly as possible.[14]

Another hazard to be avoided with equal care is natural affections. Love among you, says the Rule of Saint Augustine, must be spiritual rather than carnal. The remedy is always to see God in

---

[14] Adam, *De ordine*, PL 198, col. 561.

one's brethren. Loving them for God and loving God in them discourages those particular affections that might divide the heart, returning then to the very beginning of the rule—that the love of God requires the love of neighbor.[15]

---

[15] Adam, *De ordine,* PL 198, col. 566.

Chapter 8
Union with the Virgin Mary

T he last time scripture speaks of our Lady is to record the union of the entire apostolic Church in prayer around the mother of the Savior. This instance was important to an epoch in which Marian devotion took on a particular freshness and intensity. All discussion above of Premonstratensian saints and teachers amply demonstrates that the early order had a deeply filial relationship with the Blessed Virgin. Here a more analytical perspective on the devotion of the sons of Saint Norbert to their august patroness will nevertheless be useful.

The founder himself set the example the early order would follow, although the well-known vision in which he saw Mary giving him the white vestment is not attested in the twelfth- and thirteenth-century sources, therefore not at issue here. Instead, Saint Norbert's Marian devotion would emerge in the testimony of his contemporaries. The founder seems, first, to have faithfully celebrated the Saturday Mass in Mary's honor—at that time a practice of only some forty years' standing established at the Council of Clermont under Pope Urban II.[1] Norbert even seems to have preferred Saturday as a day for reconciling enemies. Next, he wished that all churches of his order be dedicated to Our Lady. Thus the charter of Bartholomew of Jur for the foundation of Prémontré had been given to construct a new church in honor of God and his holy

---

[1] *Sacris vestibus praeparatus primo missam beatae Virginis Mariae, ut in sabbatis fieri solet, celebrat. Vita S. Norberti, PL 170, col. 1279.*

Mother.[2] This specific mention of the Virgin is the more remarkable because Prémontré already had a patron, Saint John the Baptist, and this priestly precursor himself lived in the desert as an ascetic and preacher; the Baptist thus seemed completely appropriate to take the new order under his powerful protection, yet he was eclipsed by the Blessed Virgin. All the new monasteries bore the title of our Lady: Our Lady of Floreffe, Our Lady of Cuissy, Our Lady of Tongerloo, or the similarly Marian names already mentioned like Mariengaarde, Sepulcher of Mary, and Bethlehem. Even the older churches, although they had already been otherwise dedicated, would add the name of our Lady to precede that of their original patron: Our Lady and Saint Yved of Braine, for example. In practice the faithful did not fully accept this substitution but the intention of Saint Norbert was nonetheless clear. Again, on one of his return visits to Prémontré, the founder, hearing about the number of the poor whom the abbey fed, was concerned lest there be waste. When he learned more of the misery in the countryside, however, he wished instead to increase the liberality of the monasteries and so left a charter to institute the exercise of that charity. The three feasts of Mary celebrated in that period—the Purification, the Annunciation, and the Assumption—were among the most solemn of celebrations and so became the occasions of abundant almsgiving.[3]

Saint Norbert was known as a fierce fighter against demonic influence; many times in the course of his life as a preacher he delivered the possessed after the example of his divine Master. The Holy Eucharist was for Norbert a powerful aid in this work and he worked his greatest miracles during the Mass, but the Virgin Mary was for him an ally upon whom he greatly depended. At Vivières, in the diocese of Soissons, Saint Norbert prostrated himself in the abbatial church dedicated to the Blessed Virgin, persistently begging her for deliverance.[4] Finally, when he was archbishop of Magdeburg and wanted to have religious of his order around him, he chose to

---

[2] *Ad ecclesiam in honorem Dei et sanctae Dei Genitricis construendam. S. Norberti Chartae*, PL 170, col. 1359.

[3] *S. Norberti Chartae*, PL 170, col. 1360.

[4] *Rogabat siquidem orando sanctam Dei Genetricem in cujus honore ecclesia erat consecrata ut ejus misereretur. Vita S. Norberti*, PL 170, col. 1310.

establish them in the church of Our Lady; he was buried in this sanctuary.[5] Although Norbert's Marian devotion did not attract as much attention as Garembert's or Herman Joseph's, his sons thus followed the founder closely in reserving for the Virgin Mary the best of their heart's affection. In the seventeenth century one religious of the abbey of Tongerloo, Augustine Wichmans, wrote aptly of his confreres that they were "Norbertines and therefore Marian." This phrase expresses in simple form a truth fully accepted by history and tradition.

The central focus of the Premonstratensians' Marian devotion was of course her divine maternity, but they also stressed her long-standing and ongoing role as mediatrix. Adam Scot wrote: "Christ himself first came to the Virgin in the fullness of his grace, then called his faithful and elect to participate in it."[6] The role of Mary is so much a function of grace that Adam presents the characteristics of the Blessed Virgin as a long, magnificent allegory of divine grace's present effect. Like grace, our Lady is God's smile.[7] Her role as mediatrix enables her to be for us "a singular delight among all delights, singular sweetness among all sweetnesses, singular beauty among all beauties. She is the advocate of Christians, mediatrix of the human race, nurse of the God-Man, the world's refuge, consolation of the orphans, strength of the weak, courage of the faint-hearted, health of the sick, relief of sinners, affirmation of the just, pardon of penitents, and mistress of all creation."[8] Philip of Harvengt's Marian doctrine did not fully express the maternity of the Blessed Virgin with regard to all mankind—nor did other Premonstratensian theologians—but they approached this teaching. Meanwhile, their meditation on the Canticle of Canticles led them to see in Mary most of all the Bride of Christ, his helper in the world's redemption and the spiritual birth of souls.

Among Mary's privileges, the perpetual virginity linked to her maternity is always exalted by writers of the order. In this discussion our Lady is likened to the fleece of Gideon, remaining dry while

---

[5] *S. Norberti Chartae*, PL 170, col. 1358.

[6] *Primum Christus ad Virginem cum gratiae plenitudine venit, deinde fideles et electos suos ad participandum vocavit.* Adam, *Sermones*, PL 198, col. 181.

[7] Adam, *Sermones*, PL 198, col. 231.

[8] Adam, *Sermones*, ed. Gray Birch, 32.

the entire earth around it was wet. For Adam Scot this scriptural
image gives rise to a beautiful exclamation: "O glorious and beautiful fleece, cover us, for we grow numb for lack of divine love."[9] In
regard to the Immaculate Conception, however, Premonstratensian
authors present the reserve characteristic of their period; Saint
Bernard had dire influence on them. Adam never mentions the
Immaculate Conception in his sermons on Mary's nativity and
Philip of Harvengt explicitly denies it.[10] Only at the end of the
thirteenth century, around 1269, does the canon Robert of Wimy
clearly teach this doctrine in his sermons: the Virgin was safe from
every sin, original and actual.[11] At the General Chapter of 1322, the
Order of Prémontré accepted the feast of the Conception of Mary,
fixed on December 8; the Premonstratensians henceforth showed
themselves ardent defenders of this privilege.[12] A number of Benedictine abbeys already celebrated the feast of the Virgin's conception, but the Order of Prémontré was the third religious order to
solemnize it officially and collectively. The Friars Minor embraced
this feast of the Virgin in 1263 and the Carmelites in 1306. The
Carthusians did not adopt it until later, in 1333. The development
of office propers from this feast among Premonstratensian cloisters
is, however, outside the chronological scope of the present work.

The sources from which the sons of Saint Norbert drew their
Marian devotion are then of interest and easily found in sacred
scripture, first in meditation on the mysteries of the Savior, especially the Annunciation. Next are allegories on the important types
of the Blessed Virgin in the Old Testament: Eve, Rebecca, the mother
of Moses, the rod of Aaron, the burning bush, the fleece of Gideon,
Solomon's throne. Sentence-by-sentence meditation on the Canticle
of Canticles—the true manual of Marian devotion from which all
the antiphons of the Marian feasts were taken—was especially important. Applied to the Blessed Virgin by these contemplatives of

---

[9] *O vellus gloriosissimum et speciosissimum, cooperi nos, frigore . . . torpescimus divini amoris."* Adam, *Sermones,* ed. Gray Birch, 130.

[10] Philip, *Commentaria,* PL 203, col. 459.

[11] *Caruit enim culpa et orginali et actuali.* Robert of Wimy, Laon Ms. fol. 33, chap. 2. See *Histoire littéraire de la France,* Vol. 21, 164–74.

[12] Lefèvre, xxiii.

the twelfth century, this ancient love poem from the East became as "virginal as the peaks of the Alps"[13] to which one might never return. The liturgy also offered abundant sources. Adam Scot cites and comments on the preface of the Mass *Beata*, revived from the early Gregorian sacramentary by the Council of Clermont, and on the *Salve Regina*, as well as on sequences such as *Mundi domina* and *Regina caeli*. A religious from Vicoigne named James asked his master of novices to sing to him on his deathbed the *Ave mundi spes Maria*; he breathed his last to the notes of this magnificent lullaby. Authors of the order meanwhile searched the texts of the Fathers, especially Saint Augustine, although they rarely cited the Greek Fathers. They also studied carefully the tract on the Assumption of the Blessed Virgin by a pseudo-Augustinian author. They copied and widely distributed the homilies of Saint Bernard on the *Missus est*, and many monasteries had local traditions yielding an abundance of miracles and apparitions still remembered. Among these was the story of a blind man who, prostrated before the altar of Mary, received from the Mother of God the command to go to the tomb of Milo, Premonstratensian bishop of Thérouanne; the blind man did so and there recovered his sight. Albert, first provost of Steinfeld, composed a little book on the joys of the Blessed Virgin, there praising the blessed Herman Joseph. And angels came to hold a lamp for the venerable Adam, second abbot of Saint Josse in the Woods, so that he might be able to finish reading the Little Office of the Blessed Virgin. Overall, Marian devotion within the order revealed a ferment of unique spiritual development. Commenting on the text *Draw me: I will run after thee* (Song 1:3), Philip of Harvengt wrote: "The apostles and their successors believed that they had found grace through the example and merit of the Virgin, who ran more swiftly and perfectly."[14] Innumerable further texts show the progress of the soul in holiness through the influence of the Blessed Virgin.

---

[13] Renan.

[14] *Exemplo quidem et merito Virginis quae prius et perfectius invenitur cucurrisse, apostoli et eorum successores credunt se gratiam invenisse.* Philip, *Commentaria*, PL 203, col. 215.

Manifestations of devotion toward that most holy Virgin are next of interest. In an order of regular canons this devotion was naturally expressed liturgically, as was shown first in the joy with which the Premonstratensians always celebrated the Mass of the Blessed Virgin, so honoring her best. Saint Norbert himself, again, performed this Saturday work of piety. The blessed Frederick and the blessed Herman Joseph were alike faithful to this obligation. According to legend, after Herman had been deprived for some time of his accustomed apparitions of the Queen of Heaven, he celebrated a requiem Mass for her, saying: "If she were not dead, she would not forget me this way." After the Gospel, Our Lady deigned to appear to her faithful chaplain, who immediately prayed the offertory *Felix es, sacra Virgo* and finished the Mass *De beata*. The twelfth and thirteenth centuries, however, saw no official Mass in honor of Mary except the one on Saturdays. The first statutes of the order include a chapter on two conventual masses, the morning Mass for the Dead and the High Mass. Little by little—fully by the beginning of the fourteenth century—the custom arose to celebrate each day a third conventual Mass in honor of Mary. This practice is attested in manuscripts of the Premonstratensian ordinary. With respect to the Little Office of the Blessed Virgin Mary, the first statutes say nothing but that the sisters too may practice the hours of Our Lady. A text of Luke of Mont Cornillon meanwhile indicates that this office was already called a "daily" office; this usage was widespread after the Council of Clermont made it the official prayer for the crusade.

Another Marian custom, likewise accepted by all the churches of France, was to end the Sunday procession with a motet in honor of the Blessed Virgin. Rupert of Deutz explained that it was fitting to celebrate the joy of the Blessed Virgin at the resurrection of the Savior and the appearance of Jesus to his mother.[15] For this same reason, he adds, the Roman Church celebrates the Mass of Easter at Santa Maria Maggiore. The Premonstratensians adopted for this

---

[15] Rupert of Deutz, *De divinis officiis*, PL 170, col. 205. Herman Joseph's prayer of thanksgiving alluded to this appearance of Christ to his mother. Although the event was not reported in the Gospel, it was so influential that the choir for Latin religious at the Holy Sepulcher is today dedicated to this appearance.

rite the great antiphons taken from the Canticle of Canticles then in use at the Holy Sepulcher. The life of the blessed Bronislava recounts the Virgin's own chanting of one of these antiphons, *Ibo ad montem myrrhae*, at the moment of Saint Hyacinth's death. Many private prayers were added to these liturgical observances, as the above examples have demonstrated. The majority of such prayers suggested meditation on the joys of the Blessed Virgin but some recall her sufferings. The broad tendency in medieval prayer to focus on the Virgin's experience eventually resulted in the devotion of the Holy Rosary.

The smile of Mary then cast a ray of grace, gentleness, sincere warmth, and poetry on the austere cloisters of the early Premonstratensians, tempering the harshness of penance and the canons' absorption in apostolic work. To relive the joys of the Virgin was to enter deeply into the mysteries of Christ; to imagine her contemplation was optimal stimulus for contemplative life; to recall her sufferings was comfort in times of trial. Without Mary the atmosphere of the abbeys of the order would have been gloomy and joyless, but with her its cloisters become the vestibule of heaven.

The Virgin Mary was not, however, the only saint to attract devotion. Norbert and his sons entered into friendship with a number of the blessed. Nevertheless, profound differences separated their Marian devotion and their devotion to other saints—in both their frequency and intensity of reference to their practices. The angels appeared here and there; the abbey of Steinfeld dedicated a chapel placed on the top of their bell tower to Saint Michael. Luke of Mont Cornillon's love for his guardian angel has been noted above and various miracles were attributed to angelic assistance. Saint John the Baptist, whose austerity was admired along with his role as the attendant who presents the bride to Christ, receives frequent mention.[16] Naturally, Saint Peter and the other apostles—as heads and models of the apostolic movement—received frequent notice, as in the apparition of Saint Peter to Frederick Feikone and the frequency with which Philip of Harvengt calls attention to the Church of Jerusalem. Among the apostles one is preeminent: Saint John

---

[16] Adam, *Sermones*, PL 198, col. 107–8.

the Evangelist, the beloved disciple and guardian of the Virgin Mary. To him was dedicated the church of Parc at Louvain. Adam Scot honored Saint John with two entire sermons marked with tender familiarity.[17] Philip of Harvengt frequently recalls when the apostle leaned on the breast of the Master.[18] In sum, Premonstratensian authors recognized John as the brother of Christ and the son of Mary.

Some further saints especially favored by the liturgy attracted attention: Saint Stephen, Saint Cecilia especially, Saint Lawrence, Saint Nicholas, Saints Cyr and Julitta, Saint Lucy. Occasional mention was made of Saint Cassian, after whom a number of churches and altars were named. Saint Norbert himself introduced the cults of Saint Mary Magdalene and Saint Catherine at Xanten; these were propagated later by the first Premonstratensians in the other regions of Germany.[19] Local devotion at Cologne and relics translated to Prémontré encouraged a special love for Saint Gereon, Saint Victor, the Theban Legion, and especially for Saint Ursula and her companions—those "beautiful doves" of Herman Joseph whose feast had been celebrated in a double rite with an octave, the highest celebration of that time. Saint Thomas of Canterbury was also an object of a contemporary cult, in that time when the freedom of the Church was on the minds of so many.[20] Saint Augustine was honored with a magnificent office and constant recourse to his authority; the early Premonstratensians, according to their statutes, made their profession simply as the canons of Saint Augustine. Finally, the order favored local saints of Belgium and the Low Country: Saint Amand, Saint Sauve, Saint Feuillen, Saint Ghislain, Saint Waudru, and the blessed Landelin.[21]

---

[17] Adam, *Sermones*, PL 198, cols. 299–309 and ed. Gray Birch, May 5.

[18] On the Premonstratensian cult of the beloved disciple, see Herman, *Opusculum*, PL 170, col. 806. See also Schreiber, "Die Praemonstratenser und der Kult des Heiligen Joannes Evangelist," *Zellschrift für katholische Theologie* 65 (1941): 1031.

[19] Wilhem Stüwert, *Die Patrozinien im Kölner Grossarchidiaconat, Xanten* (Bonn: Röhrscheid, 1938). See *Analecta Praemonstratensia* (1944), 205.

[20] See Adam Scot's sermon on Saint Thomas of Canterbury (ed. Gray Birch, December 29). In 1871, William, a canon of Dammartin, brought the surplice stained with the blood of the martyr from England to his abbey.

[21] See the biographies of saints by Philip of Harvengt.

The present survey of the Premonstratensian cult of the Virgin and other saints is only brief. The sanctoral cycle for the office was not yet well developed and the Bible was read much more than the passions of the martyrs. On the other hand, many religious of whom no record survives must have been fervently devoted to one or another saint of their special choice. In general, however, Premonstratensian confreres were guided by the Church and the liturgy as they thought about heaven and its saints, but the order maintained an admirable reserve from imposing personal preferences or devotion.

Chapter 9
Rigor of Life

Here, the rigor of early Premonstratensian life is treated separately from the order's apostolic program because medieval authors did not connect these two features and because Norbert and his sons saw their penance as regular religious as expiation for the sins of their prior lives. Even in the cloisters of other orders in Norbert's time, the words of our Savior were recalled: *Can the children of the Bridegroom mourn, as long as the bridegroom is with them? But the days will come, when the bridegroom shall be taken away from them, and then they shall fast?* (Matt 9:15). As Rupert of Deutz wrote: "The first apostles, sons of the Bridegroom taken away from them, loved fasting and tears throughout their entire life. Their souls were inconsolable; they found joy only in the memory of Jesus."[1] In fact, the penitential system of the Order of Prémontré is borrowed from the monastic life. Austerity of life was willingly emphasized. As the biographer of the blessed Godfrey of Cappenberg states: "The confreres make their profession according to the Rule of Saint Augustine, but with this provision—that they observe it more strictly than it has heretofore been."[2] Again, Philip of Harvengt said of the valley of Prémontré, with its four paths in the form of a cross: "This valley is cruciform not through the work of men but in its nature. Its shape shows that those who

---

[1] Rupert, *De divinis officiis*, PL 170, col. 97.
[2] Qtd. in intro. to *Vita S. Norberti*, PL 170, col. 1250.

come into it must no longer live for the world, but must crucify themselves in that valley or, better, be configured to Christ by this crucifixion."[3] They were indeed so crucified. Critics of the earlier regular canons had assaulted them for the laxity of their life relative to monastic severity, so eliciting the foundation of a canonical life rivaling the austerity of the Cistercians. Hence Norbert's desire to see his sons fast perpetually, to draw their material support from their own manual labor, to use horses only as necessary for long-distance travel, and to maintain all previously lapsed strict observances.

The early order had a system of extremely harsh penance known to us from its first statutes. As Adam Scot notes, "These practices are no less harsh than they are novel. Your austerity is demonstrated in the frequent fasts you maintain, the poverty of the clothing you wear, the frugality in which you live, and in the economy of your speech."[4] Elsewhere he notes as well the gravity of the confreres' manner and the reserve of their deportment.[5] Finally, Adam addresses the cloister, the chapter, and the civility requisite among the brothers. The statutes include, as well, a list of penances proportionate to different possible errors. All this begs explanation: presentation of Premonstratensian spirituality would be incomplete without attention to such dispositions as thus freed their hearts, allowing them to ascend toward God.

Fasting is the first practice of monastic penance, exercised from September 14 to Easter and consisting in a single meal at the end of the morning. In the evening confreres had only a drink before going to chapter for the reading of a conference or collation of Cassian.[6] Only the elderly and children had breakfast; this supplementary meal, called a *mixtum*, was a difficult mortification for

---

[3] *Quae vallis non humano molimine sed naturali opere quodammodo crucifixa, quid monet vel praemonet nisi ut eam confluentes mundo vivere jam non curent, sed se illi, imo Christo crucifixione congrua configurent?* Philip, *Commentaria*, PL 203, col. 238.

[4] *Hac in re testimonium ferunt . . . crebra quae exercetis jejunia, continuae quas ducitis vigiliae, haec quam circumfertis vilitas in habitu, haec quam sustinetis asperitas in victu, haec quam exercetis parcitas in affectu.* Adam, *Sermones*, PL 198, col. 116.

[5] *In gravitate vultus . . . in maturitate incessus.* Adam, *De tripartito tabernaculo*, PL 198, col. 754.

[6] The small evening meal was thus called "collation."

Herman Joseph when imposed upon him in his old age. Abstinence from meat and, during Lent, from dairy products was added to this perpetual fast. Vegetables, fruits, and sometimes a little fish—almost all the monasteries were equipped with fishponds—made up most of the diet. Meat was eaten only in the infirmary.

Vigils were a form of penance at first hard to tolerate. In conformity with the custom of regular canons, matins was chanted at midnight, then followed by the matins of the Little Office of the Virgin. Only in the seventeenth century did those houses with study centers receive permission to recite matins and lauds without chant. Many saints performed still longer vigils. Remarkably, the devil sought frequently to divert Norbert himself from the exercise of harsh vigils. Immediately after his conversion, when he passed the night in prayer, he occasionally dozed. The devil then appeared to Norbert, mocking him: "Hah! You have ambitious intentions, but what will you achieve? You cannot keep your resolution even for one night." The saint forcefully responded: "Who could believe you? Divine truth names you a liar from the beginning, the very father of lies!"[7] On another occasion, as the saint kept vigil in the earliest chapel at Prémontré, the devil appeared to him as a ferocious bear, threatening him with his teeth and claws. The saint, noticing at once that the door of the holy place was shut and that the bear must be an apparition of the devil, sternly sent him away.[8] The blessed Herman Joseph, as noted above, remained each evening in his choir stall from compline until matins. He slept only for a few minutes while his confreres were getting dressed between the first and third bells for matins, after which his nightly rest lasted only a few hours between matins and prime. Many more examples might be given of the early confreres' love of prolonged prayer in the silence of the night, after the example of that Savior whom the Gospels show passing the night in divine prayer. Sleep was short and under uncomfortable conditions. In addition to sleeping in a common dormitory—the Premonstratensians did not have individual cells before the end of the thirteenth century—the confreres rested on hard beds wearing only their undergarments, cinctures,

---

[7] *Vita S. Norberti*, PL 170, col. 1271.

[8] *Vita S. Norberti*, PL 170, col. 1321.

and stockings. Many added their own further penitential practices. The blessed Siard had for a mattress only a horsehide; Saint Gertrude of Altenberg slept on a plank during Holy Week. Since in the twelfth century the secular custom was to sleep entirely naked on featherbeds, these mortifications were indeed severe.

Early Premonstratensians' clothing was all of wool, except for the undergarments Norbert required that they always wear along with a linen neckerchief.[9] Their dress consisted in an under-tunic of wool, serving as a shirt, along with a woolen or goatskin coat and an outer tunic; the latter was replaced for the most solemn offices with a floor-length alb or a surplice. Over this outer tunic the canons wore a cape, which they set aside only for manual labor. A few texts suggest that the perspiration caused by the heaviness of this attire made the constant wearing of wool not only a symbol of penance but an actual opportunity for prolonged suffering.[10]

This strictly disciplined life was not relieved with recreations, as in the modern orders. Each abbey had an *auditorium* for necessary conversations, but all other time was spent in silence. The first companions of Norbert, completely given to contemplation, kept perpetual silence all the time, everywhere and in every situation.[11] Even when they accompanied the founder to town and mingled among dense crowds, they scarcely said a word. According to Adam Scot, this practice reflected their broad ascetic commitment. "The key, the wall, and the rampart of the entire religious life is silence, without which religious life is not maintained and without which religious can neither practice virtue, nor maintain peace, nor maintain themselves securely."[12] To these austere practices was added

---

[9] *Vita S. Norberti,* PL 170, col. 1294.

[10] For example, the prior of Sainte-Barbe-en-Auge, who became a Premonstratensian of Ardenne, wrote: "The greatest difficulty is that the habit, soaked in the sweat of day and night, swarms with vermin unless it is frequently shaken." Edmond Martène, *Veterum scriptorum et monumentorum, collectio nova, miscellanea epistolorum et diplomatorum,* vol. 1 (Reims, 1700), col. 780.

[11] *Juge silentium in omni tempore, in omni loco, in omni statu. Vita S. Norberti,* PL 170, col. 1294.

[12] *Totius namque religionis clavis et murus quodammodo et custodia est silentium sine quo religio non potest esse munita, sine quo viri religiosi nec justitiam colere nec pacem tenere nec securitatem habere possunt.* Adam, *Soliloquiae,* PL 198, col. 858.

seriousness of expression—a willingness to smile but never in an undisciplined way—and slowness of pace. Such comportment showed respect to the recollection of others, supported mastery of self, and obviated such anxiety as might strain the confreres' life of prayer.

These practices were not easy. Although they might seem so on certain days, as when the day was broken up by manual labor—then again when several feasts followed upon one another spent in the divine office and in *lectio*—the carefully restrained need for relaxation became a painful mortification. Rigorous claustration and the daily chapter of faults were sometimes difficult to sustain, as the sorrowful complaints of the soul in Adam Scot's dialogue suggest. Completing the range of rigorous practices was the list of penances appropriate to various faults—psalms, flagellations, and food deprivations—borrowed in Premonstratensian legislation from the customs of Cluny. This system was fully developed; under their white woolen vestments the early Premonstratensians were indeed both priests and penitents.

Some courageous souls added to the community's practice of these mortifications and disciplines, in order to seek out further opportunities for sacrifice, the wearing of a hair shirt, sleeping on the ground, multiple genuflections, rigorous fasts, and travel only on foot. Such additional self-imposed rigor was encouraged within the limits of discretion, the mother-virtue of monastic observance. "You violate the boundaries of sobriety no less when you deny necessity than when you overfill them with excess. The body is a beast of burden, so its rider, the spirit, must be discreet in its care for it. Just as it needs to be reined in, so it should be put to pasture so it does not collapse exhausted."[13] Meanwhile lukewarmness must in all ways be avoided because it kills religious life; this requires continual vigilance: "Whether in manual labor, at the ecclesiastical offices or in any service pertaining to God, we must reject

---

[13] *Non minus sobrietatis modum excedis, cum a corpore tuo necessaria excludis quam cum superflua impendis. Jumentum namque est, et ideo curet necesse est ut discretus sessor ejus spiritus, sicut ei imponere frenum ne recalcitret, ita apponere foenum nec deficiat.* Adam, *Sermones*, PL 198, col. 256.

all harmful tepidity, utterly renounce every sluggishness of the body, even—insofar as is possible—mental instability."[14]

The rigor of the Premonstratensian way of life was conducive to lofty perfection and required such great courage as the service of the Lord Jesus required. Adam Scot counsels his confreres about the heroism of the people of the feudal world in the service of their earthly lords:

> We continually see with what care some men serve other men. The poor serve the rich, striving to please them with diligent service. Neither pains of the heart, bodily toil, travel-weariness, bitter cold, stifling heat, sorrow, embarrassment, the torments of hunger and thirst, perils on land and sea, even the fear of bodily death can stand in the way of their total devotion to the service of their lords. Many never know the nature, the magnitude of the temporal scope of the recompense they are due.[15]

No less was the care and gift of self required of medieval Premonstratensians in the service of God. The thought of heaven helped to sustain their courage and lighten for them the cross of Christ they carried each day in their unceasingly penitential life. When after this life of toil and suffering a white canon was laid on a bed of ashes in a cell in the infirmary, surrounded by the prayers and love of his confreres, and rendered his soul to God, his great reward was to have spent all his strength and his heart. Then he might hear Christ approaching, gentle and rejoicing,[16] and perhaps receive a visit from the Virgin. A milk-white cross was seen on the breast of Tancred, prior of Lucerne-across the Sea, as he lay dying. He had borne the cross in his heart and it went before him into eternal life.

---

[14] *Sive in opere manuum, sive in officiis ecclesiasticis, seu in aliquo quod ad Deum pertinet negotio fueritis, abjecto corpore noxio, renuntia ex toto levitati corporis et pro posse etiam instabilitati mentis.* Adam, *Sermones*, PL 198, col. 99.

[15] Adam, *De ordine*, PL 198, col. 497.

[16] *Mitis atque festivus.* Prayers for the dying.

Conclusion

D om Ursmer Berlière, in his beautiful book on monastic asceticism from its origins to the end of the twelfth century, writes of the regular canons that they differed from monks in their liturgy and customs, but that the spirit of the two groups of religious houses was nonetheless the same. The reader of the present work may now judge whether Berlière is correct or whether this assessment is inadequate—at least with respect to the Premonstratensians but also, for example, to the Victorines. In their practices of asceticism and spiritual doctrine, monks and canons—the two great patterns of religious life—appear closely similar in the Middle Ages. Regular canons, notably, have always pursued priestly perfection through monastic asceticism. This trait is distinctive in them, consistently maintained in their communities. Emphasis on the similarity of monks and canons acknowledges that, whenever monks are also priests, the monastic order embraces what Huysmans in his *L'Oblat* calls "the priestly role."[1] The congruence of priesthood and monastic vocation is then inevitable. Priesthood is in its very nature a social charism calling for the care of souls. The Benedictines of England are, in this regard, in fact regular canons. The responsibility of the superiors of the monastic order is to ensure that this tendency to the care of souls does not therefore diminish the recollection and solitude of their cloisters.

Correspondingly, among the regular canons, what might be called "the monastic role" also always exists. Hugh of Fosses and

---

[1] *[Le] parti curé.*

Walter of Saint Maurice exemplify this tendency. Without it, cloisters of regular canons would soon become little different from communities of secular priests where the religious life would lose its vigor. Yet, although all the elements of the apostolic life addressed here are indeed found in the monastic order, emphasis on them among monks is not the same as among the regular canons, who assign a more important role to the Eucharist, Marian devotion, pastoral engagement, and sustained missionary effort, and who practice a poverty closer to later Franciscan deprivation than the ancient monastic renunciation, along with active welcome of laypersons to their larger churches. These characteristics gave the canons' new monasteries, in the twelfth century, an appearance mirroring the community of the apostles themselves.

Without due acknowledgment of the distinctiveness of the regular canons, the institution of the mendicant orders at the close of the twelfth century appears a rupture in the history of Christian asceticism. If we recall, however, that the canonical order had already demonstrated that new forms of religious life might have as their proper object the care of souls and advancement of Christianity, then the new preachers appear in intelligible context. They do not lose their originality, but they seem less the result of spontaneous innovation than a mature flowering of an old tree still—and ever since—continuing to flower and bear fruit. The general development of religious life in the Church thus tends from contemplation to apostolic action and works of mercy, not because the latter is more perfect than contemplation but rather because of the needs of the Church and of individual souls.

First were the anchorites, ascetics leading a secluded life away from the world. Next were the monks, living in community in monasteries and making of these monasteries models of Christian life. Then were the regular canons, who maintained the entire ancient system of monastic life: liturgical prayer in all its solemnity, the silence of the cloister with fasting, abstinence, and peaceful abbatial government; but the canons added tenderness of religious feeling, affective meditation on the sufferings of Christ and his Mother, concern for study, pastoral zeal, and the obligation to preach—all traits that modern practice would eventually embrace. After them came the mendicants, organized in smaller convents, living in towns rather than in the country, more engaged with the world like yeast in dough, but still maintaining a choral liturgy, the solemnity of community life, and regular mortifications. Next appear clerics in regular religious orders, strengthened by solid and deep personal formation but with a freedom of ministry so extensive as to greatly loosen the constraints of their common life. The addition of new types of religious life does not, however, suppress older longstanding forms—not because of any burdensome conservatism, but because there are always some souls who are more moved toward the contemplative life, which remains the better part. To wish to reduce all souls to contemplative or active types, so eliding intermediate modalities, would be unjust, even absurd. The souls of priests find in a religious life closely modeled on early monasticism an impulse to ministry perhaps less extensive and fast-paced than that of secular priests, but more fortified in study, more steeped in prayer, more supported by penance, and closer to the vision of God in its habit of contemplation. This charism preserves the distinctive role of the canonical order, demonstrating the interest in exploring its historical spirituality as a transition between the early Benedictine spirit and the modernity of the mendicant orders corresponding to the aspirations of a large family of priestly and religious souls.

The primary goal of this work has been to help Premonstratensian brothers in religion, the Norbertine sisters, and the members of the third order of Prémontré to be penetrated with the spirit of Saint Norbert. It proposes further to shed light on the spiritual history of the Middle Ages, an exciting period filled with wonderful developments still undiscovered. The further unavoidable question arises here, however, of the legacy of the spirituality whose history is outlined here. The end of the Middle Ages was darkened by wars, devastation, and epidemics; it was overrun as well by arid academic study and an impoverished scholasticism rendering the life of the cloisters precarious and enervated. The practice of commendam appeared and gradually spread, depriving monasteries of their abbots, so of their proper masters and guides to perfection. Meanwhile, the Great Schism detached hearts from the pontifical see. Then the Reformation destroyed the monasteries of northern Germany, England, Scotland, Frisia, and the Scandinavian countries. Nonetheless, the flowers of sanctity bloomed here and there in the cloisters; the Reformation crowned some among the sons of Saint Norbert with glorious martyrdom. Two, Saint James Lacoupe and Saint Adrian Peckam, canons of Our Lady of Middleburg, were canonized among the martyrs of Gorkum, but a powerful wind of spiritual revival would not appear in the Church until the end of the sixteenth century. Here, the Order of Prémontré would have an important role, experiencing two further centuries of splendor.

The spiritual traditions of the Order of Prémontré have nonetheless been only imperfectly preserved because the order suffered many abuses at the end of the Middle Ages and great damage from the Protestant Reformation. On the other hand, its pastoral solicitude was sufficiently lively to carry it into the current of the Catholic Counter-Reformation. Nowhere else within the Church were the decisions of the Council of Trent accepted with more fervor. Furthermore, the friendship uniting Saint Ignatius of Loyola and one of the most influential of the Premonstratensians, Nicholas Psaume, abbot of Saint Paul of Verdun and later bishop of that same city, gave the Society of Jesus important influence over the monasteries of the white canons. Indeed, the magnificent Premonstratensian reform of Lorraine was begun in a series of spiritual exercises preached in the abbeys of that province. Unsurprisingly then, distinct, almost ritual, exercises of piety—meditation, thanksgiving, visits to the Blessed Sacrament, spiritual reading, and examination of conscience—took the place of the early *lectio divina*, that unique and wonderfully varied exercise of the medieval cloisters. Much liberty of spirit was lost, yet great generosity and fervent desire to realize the views of the founder were realized.

Lively devotion to Saint Norbert marked this new spirituality in general. In 1582, Pope Gregory XIII authorized the liturgical cult of Norbert, inciting an explosion of enthusiasm within the order. Abbot General Jean des Pruets, a Premonstratensian to the depths of his soul and a storehouse of the best Norbertine traditions, composed the office of the new feast. In 1626, the prelate of Saint Michael of Antwerp, Van der Sterre, published the text of the early biography of the founder, so allowing all religious to read it and be permeated by its text. Other writers like J.-P. Camus, bishop of Belley, and the Premonstratensian Maurice du Pré made the story of the patriarch of the Premonstratensians even more widely available in new biographies. Finally in 1627, the body of the great archbishop was removed from the Protestants holding Magdeburg and translated to the monastery of Strahov in Prague. This event was the occasion for new publications and unforgettable celebrations. Norbert, but a name in the Middle Ages, became a beloved master and father.

The early modern Order of Prémontré witnessed a widespread movement of reform in Spain, in Mont Saint-Martin, and in Lorraine. The principal force behind the reform in Lorraine was the abbot of Pont-à-Mousson, Servais de Layruels, author of a *Catechism for Novices* and a commentary on the Rule of Saint Augustine titled *Optica regularium*, a vision for regular religious. This austere man loved to collect the principles of the spiritual life into short maxims, as was conventional in the seventeenth century. His phrases are memorable: "He who lives in religion fruitlessly commits a theft. The negligent religious is the delight of demons. No friend of God is the enemy of prayer."[2] Layruels summarizes the ideal of Saint Norbert in the following twenty points:

1. To bear each day the cross of Christ, that is, to lead a penitential life.

2. To preserve the canonical, that is, the apostolic life.

3. To serve as a soldier under the Rule of Saint Augustine.

4. To wear a completely white habit.

5. To wear clothes of wool, even next to the skin.

6. To abstain from meat perpetually, except when sick.

7. To keep the fast all throughout the year.

8. To chant the office day and night.

9. To add to the office the Little Office of the Blessed Virgin.

10. To celebrate each day the morning Mass, the Mass of the Blessed Virgin Mary, and the High Mass.

---

[2] *Furtum facit qui sine fructu in religione vivit. . . . Religiosus negligens laetitia daemonis. . . . Non est familiaris Deo qui non est amicus orationis.*

11. To observe meticulous cleanliness around the altar and in the holy mysteries.

12. To correct abuses each day in the chapter and elsewhere.

13. To care for the poor and practice hospitality.

14. To keep silence always and everywhere, especially in the church, refectory, dormitory, and in the cloister.

15. To live in solitude.

16. To be attached to one's abbey by the vow of stability.

17. To give oneself to manual labor.

18. To be called *Frater*, brother, not *Dom*, master.

19. For abbots to eat in the refectory and to sleep in the common dormitory.

20. To hold the general chapter each year at Prémontré.

Layruels' careful reading of Saint Norbert's biography is evident here. Regrettably, however, under the influence of the Carmelite reform by Saint Teresa, traditions essential to our order—among them abbatial authority, stability in the monastery, and attachment to the liturgy—were violated during successive reforms. The common observance would, however, also be reformed, leading to publication in 1630 of new statutes. The famous Drusius, abbot of Parc-les-Louvain, redacted this legislation, later offering a study of the spirituality of the Order of Prémontré for use in the formation of novices.

The Premonstratensian, according to Drusius' descriptions, must courageously adapt his will to the discipline of the Rule; he must be humble, meek, modest, flexible, and obedient. He must avoid being rude and harsh, peevish and hot-headed, or obstinate in his will. All this is not the work of one day. The master of novices should have a motherly affection, pleasant and respectfully warm. He should watch for two dangers to his charges: lack of mortification and lassitude compromising work. The new Premonstratensian should first of all purify his soul and change his worldly ways into religious habits, according to God's will. Good confession should be accompanied by tears; the practice of penance is a good starting point. Next, the novice should mortify his own judgment and will for the good of obedience. He should embrace humble jobs and accept whatever work is given him. At the same time he will learn to use sacramental confession for his soul's progress, to prepare himself for Holy Communion and to offer thanksgiving. He should practice spiritual exercises morning, noon, and evening. He should learn meditation and mental prayer, to mortify himself in order to acquire virtue, and especially to remain in God's presence in order that he may direct all his acts to their ultimate end. He should develop the habit of participating in the office day and night with fervent spirits and joyful hearts, for to be called to fulfill the office of the angels while here on earth is a great mercy. Modesty of speech and gaze is important, as is recollection, while the *lectio divina* of the early order retains, in Drusius' program for novices, an important role:

> Let the novices show themselves diligent in reading and rereading the scriptures. They should be shown those passages arousing love of God and disdain for the things of earth, then leading to the practice of virtues and offering the heart a taste of divine sweetness. Let them read these passages frequently, with much care, so that their texts are imprinted on their hearts and in their memory; then they may fully receive the evangelical and apostolic spirit. However, so that novices may profit from studying sacred works, let their master teach them never to begin without first having prayed and assumed an attitude of ardent love, profound humility, great respect and desire to make progress. And especially let them begin only in purity of heart. Only thus does one see God, penetrating the secrets of his wisdom and understanding his teaching.[3]

Drusius' remarks evince concern for uniting the best of early Premonstratensian spirituality with necessary innovations. This program of formation indeed bore fruit. Fervor returned to the monasteries—nor did it diminish here and there until the end of the eighteenth century, when ideas of tolerance, progress, and hu-

---

[3] *Statutes* of 1630. Dist. 1, c. 20, no. 19.

manity sought to impose on Catholicism an ideology governing religion itself.

Premonstratensian spiritual authors continued to emphasize eucharistic and Marian devotions. Gregorian Reform had led to the appearance of the regular canons and its practices flourished in the Premonstratensian cloisters of the Middle Ages, but the same devotional practices marked the Catholic Counter-Reformation in its reaction to Protestantism. Their revival increased their luster. The Immaculate Conception found zealous defenders among the Spanish Premonstratensians, such that it was said that Saint Norbert founded his order in honor of this mystery. The churches became more magnificent and the tabernacles more ornate; the divine office was celebrated with heretofore unknown splendor. At the same time the influence of canonical spirituality was revived by concern for outreach beyond the cloister. The ancient institution of the *fratres ad succurrendum*, of brotherhood or community in the merits and prayers of the order, became a third order properly speaking when it was approved by Pope Benedict XIV in 1751.

The distinguished spiritual author Epiphanius Louis, abbot of Étival, wrote several books deriving from the French school of the Oratory, on the works of Fr. de Condren in particular. These were effectively marginal with respect to the Premonstratensian order because they were written for the Benedictines of the Blessed Sacrament rather than for Louis' own confreres, but they were nonetheless read and enjoyed by the white canons. This author is sometimes reproached for quietism, but comprehensive attention to his thought corrects this impression.

The major spiritual event of the nineteenth century, after the reestablishment of the Premonstratensians in 1830, was the consecration of the Order of Prémontré to the Sacred Heart of Jesus by the General Chapter of 1890. Devotion to the Sacred Heart is the crowning devotion to the sacred humanity of the Savior, as this observance had developed during the Middle Ages.

Despite the increasingly formal system of spiritual exercises characterizing recent centuries, deep Premonstratensian traditions have remained vital in the order; it continues to present itself usefully to souls wishing to ground their apostolic ministry in authentic contemplation. Although the Order of Prémontré has not experienced the thunderous revivals known to other orders, it indeed rose from ruins after the French Revolution through to the love of Belgian religious who, after forty years outside the cloister, valiantly recovered their community life as soon as they had the freedom so to do. Since then the order has continued to make progress slowly but surely. Contemporary aspirations of clergy for community life and the urgency of a well-suited and ongoing rural apostolate favor this development.

Appendix

A Précis of Premonstratensian Spirituality: The "Sermon of Saint Norbert"[1]

When Van der Sterre, abbot of Saint Michael's, Antwerp, first published *Vita B* of Saint Norbert in 1622, he added to this twelfth-century account of the founder's life a further text titled "Sermon of the Most Holy Father Norbert, Established according to Different Manuscripts."[2] This text has subsequently held special authority in the Order of Prémontré. Like the Rule of Saint Augustine, it is read each week in the refectory. Nevertheless, the sermon has apparently, as of this writing, been the object of no careful study.

---

[1] Editor's note: For the late twentieth-century scholarly consensus on the authenticity and date of this sermon, see introduction above. The text of the sermon is included here, despite recent wide agreement that it is not the work of the founder-saint Norbert himself, because it is nonetheless an important document in Premonstratensian spirituality. The critical apparatus reproduced by Petit from Van der Sterre's edition is, however, omitted in this translation because those interested in comparing manuscript variants of this central, if spurious, text will have recourse to both Petit's and the seventeenth-century editions. Van der Sterre used three manuscript exemplars, from the abbey of Knechtstadt, from a Saxon monastery, and from France respectively; variants are indicated in Petit's edition, after Van der Sterre's, by the sigla K, S, and F. As in PL quotations above, Petit's adoption of prior editors' conventions in capitalization and punctuation are unaltered below.

Because more recent textual and stylistic criticism has largely obviated the usefulness of Petit's commentary on this text, the final pages of his appendix are omitted here, as is a second appendix listing the Premonstratensian houses of his day.

[2] "Sermo SS. P. Norberti ad varia exemplaria recensitus," ed. Jean Chysosotome Van der Sterre, *Vita sancti Norberti* (Antwerp, 1662), 261–70.

Latin Text of the Sermon

Sermo Sancti Patris nostri Norberti Magdeburgensis archiepiscopi necnon fundatoris candidi ordinis praemonstratensis, ad fratres suos

Hortamur vos, Fratres dilectissimi, ad sedulam Dei, cui specialium votorum professione vos obligastis, servitutem. Tenemini enim, vobismetipsis et cunctis vestris sponte abnegatis, et pure propter Deum derelictis, in humeris vestris quotidie portare crucem Christi,[3] hoc est: crebris diversarum passionum angustiis patienter ducere vitam totam in poenitentia. Haec est enim arcta via coeli, quae in ea perfecte ambulantes ad veram perducit Patriam; quam Christus moriendo et vivendo, opere et verbo vobis strenue praemonstravit. Quam nisi cum fiducia aggrediamini, et pro modulo vestrae possibilitatis in ea ambuletis, non potestis ad Christum venire, sicut dicit Apostolus; nullus coronabitur, nisi qui legitime certaverit [1 Tim 2:5]. Et iterum: qui voluerit Christo commanere, debet, sicut ipse ambulavit, ambulare.[4] Ambuletis ergo in via Dei caute, ne morte comprehendemini improvise, promptam observantes obedientiam, voluntariam paupertatem, et famosam castitatem. Sine his omnis substantialis virtus Ordinis penitus desolatur.

Vos etiam, qui stabilitatem promisistis in hoc sacro loco, sitis sine fastidio suscepti oneris in Dei servitude continui, nisi interdum necessitate exteriorum actionum praepediti, ne dissolutio inutilium divagationum suavitatem virtutum interna dulcedine divinorum mysteriorum gustatam auferat, et labentis mundi, qui nullum locum a sordibus habet tutum, fallaciter amorem inducat. Quia sicut piscis extra aquam penitus alimentis naturalibus carens, cito moritur, sic instabilis Religiosus munitione et custodia claustri exutus, exemplis et doctrinis boroum alienus, mundo, cujus status in maligno positus est,[5] pluries conversatus, cito ad vitia labitur et nexibus perpetuae mortis detinetur. Fugite igitur saecularium hominum frequentiam, sicut piscis siccitatem; ne obliviscamini interioris custodiae diligentiam, quae mentis generat puritatem.

---

[3] Compare Matt 10:38.
[4] Compare 1 John 2:26.
[5] Compare 1 John 5:19.

Illud enim gloriosum nomen sanctae religiositatis vobis indigne usurpatis, si in desideriis vestris non soli Deo, sed plus mundo religati estis. Debetis igitur esse stabiles, charitate concordes, maxime linguas vestras refraenantes, ut sine murmuratione, detractatione, et absque invidia in domo Domini unanimes habitetis.[6] Lingua enim maliloqua et dolosa inquietum malum est,[7] plena veneno mortifero, non desinens laedere, bonum pacis conturbans, et religionis devotionem enervans; idcirco de talibus scribitur: qui litigiosus vel querulosus est, verus monachus non est.[8]

Quapropter refraenate linguas vestras, figentes vel erigentes corda vestra ad supernorum regna, ubi vera sunt gaudia,[9] et desiderio devotionis vestrae cum perfectis volate in nubibus contemplando divina, et cum moerore portate pondus carnis vestrae, ut possitis dicere cum beato Apostolo: cupio dissolvi et esse cum Christo [Phil 1:23]. Et cum Psalmista: educ de carceribus corporum nostrorum animas nostras [Ps 141:8], ut valeatis conregnare Christo in aeternum. Si qui autem habitu religioso sub specie columbinae simplicitatis et lactis innocentiae exterius nitide amicti, a devotione perfectae religionis coram Deo, cui cogitationes omnium nudae et apertae sunt, interius misere nudati salutaris doctrinae monita monitoremque contumaci corde spernunt, sanctum regularis disciplinae ordinem non observantes: procul dubio ad illum deterrimum aeternorum tormentorum locum, nisi se prius emendaverint perducentur, ubi nullus ordo, sed sempiternus horror inhabitat.[10] Praecaveatis igitur horrenda divinae Majestatis judicia, illi devote servientes in timore et justitia, ut vos conservet in religiosa vita, et a poenis praedictis vos custodiat ejus clementia; qui sibi fideliter servientes affluenter ditabit, pie dans pro parvis magna, pro temporalibus aeterna, sicut ille discipulis suis de contemptu rerum suarum et de labore bonorum operum suorum mercedem inquirentibus dicebat: Centuplum accipietis et vitam aeternam possidebitis [Matt 19:29]. Ad quam vos perducat Christus. Amen.

---

[6] Compare *Regula S. Augustini*.

[7] Compare Jas 2:8.

[8] Cited by Drexelius, who attributes this saying to Abbé Pastor.

[9] *Missale Romanum*, Fourth Sunday after Easter.

[10] Compare Job 10:21.

Nullum taedeat vel molestet hanc chartam saepius inspicere, in qua brevis exhortatio ad cultum Dei reperitur. Verbum Dei ignitum est,[11] secundum Prophetam, ardore sancti Spiritus inflammatum, urens vitia, acuens virtutes, benevolas animas ditans sapientia, ministrans illis coelestia alimenta. Et ideo voce Salvatoris dicitur: Beati, qui audiunt verbum Dei, et custodiunt illud [Luke 11:18]. Sic beata Maria Magdalena intenta aure perfectae devotionis et ardenti desiderio divinae contemplationis verbum Dei fideliter audiendo,[12] optimam partem discitur elegisse, quam beata Martha sedulo cultu laboriosae ministrationis Salvatori nostro, in suis humanis fragilitatibus impenso, nequaquam potuit consequi, nec valuit obtinere.

Audite ergo illud libenter, custodite sapienter et adimplete semper, ut in fine saeculorum illud mellifluum verbum Dei hilariter possitis audire: Venite benedicti Patris mei, percipite regnum aeternum [Matt 25:34]. In quo tunc tranquilitate perpetuae pacis, glorificata facie visionis perfectae et cognitionis Dei aeternaliter gaudebitis; ubi Deus absterget omnes lacrimas oculorum vestrorum.[13] Nec erit ultra mors, neque ullus dolor quia momentanea tormenta priorum passionum vestrarum omnia breviter transierunt. Ibi manifestabitur multitudo dulcedinis Dei quam abscondit vobis et omnibus timentibus se.[14] Ibi apparebunt delectationes infinitae mirabilium dexterae Dei, quibus consolabitur vos, et omnes electos suos usque in finem. Ibi saluberimus fons hortorum Dei,[15] quo vos foecundabit; ibi indeficiens puteus aquarum viventium quo vos inundabit; ibi inaestimabilis ubertas deliciarum domus Dei, qua vos inebriabit; ibi dulcis torrens voluptatum ejus, quo vos potabit; ibi Deus praecinget se virtute et potentia et candore lucis aeternae vestitus[16] ministrabit vobis, dans se ipsum in mercedem magnam et in omnium desiderabilium vestrorum superfluentem immensae largitatis effectum; sicut quondam beato Abrahae Patriarchae ipsi

---

[11] Compare Ps 118:140.
[12] Compare Luke 10:42.
[13] Compare Rev 7:17; 12:4.
[14] Compare Ps 30:21.
[15] Compare Song 4:15.
[16] Compare Ps 112:2.

credenti et obedienti promisit dicens: Ego ero merces tua nimis valde [Gen 15:1]. Haec merces est illa sola una pretiosissima margarita[17] jam praedicta, pro qua debetis omnia vestra vendere et incessanter laborare,[18] ut comparetis eam. Cujus nobilitatis suavitatem prae multitudine magnitudinis suae, indagatio sensus humani, secundum Apostolum, non valet ad plenum cognoscere,[19] nec intima cordis suarum subtilium acie cogitationum metam scientiae illius attingere, neque scire, quam etiam propter magnitudinem virtutum et excellentiam dignitatum nec suppliciis passionum, nec exercitiis bonorum operum potestis ad plenum promereri nisi Deus vobis illam dederit gratiose. Quia secundum Apostolum: non sunt condignae passiones hujus temporis, ad futuram gloriam [Rom 8:18], quae post hanc vitam revelabitur in vobis.

Rogetis ergo devote omnipotentem Deum, qui pro vobis homo factus est, qui fragilitatem humanae conditionis in se ipso expertus cognoscit figmentum vestrum [Ps 88:48], quoniam vane constituti sunt omnes filii hominum [Gen 8:21], et quod sensus hominum proni sunt ad malum, ut sua vos pietate custodiat et bonitate adjuvet quatenus peracto cursu sine delectatione carnalis amoris, sic transeatis per bona temporalia, ut non amittatis, sed obtineatis aeterna.[20] Hoc vobis pie tribuat, qui cum Deo Patre et Spiritu sancto, vivit et regnat Deus per infinita saecula saeculorum. Amen.

English Translation[21]

I exhort you, dearly beloved brothers, to observe carefully the commandments of God, to which you are bound by profession of special vows. You are obliged to renounce yourselves, to detach yourselves, and divest yourselves freely and completely of all that

---

[17] Compare Matt 13:46.

[18] Compare Luke 18:22.

[19] Compare 1 Cor 2:9.

[20] *Missale Romanum*, Third Sunday after Pentecost.

[21] Editor's note: Petit offered no French version of this text, assuming as he did that his readers might easily understand the Latin of the original. Here, translation into English is supplied, since the present volume assumes no such linguistic facility, although the inclusion here of the Latin text invites those who are able to consider it alongside this interpretation.

is yours for the sake of God, so to bear the cross of Jesus Christ on your shoulders each day[22]—in other words, each day to lead a penitential life, patiently suffering the repeated trials that come to you from all sides. This is the narrow way that leads to heaven, our true homeland, for those who walk it perfectly. Jesus Christ, by his death and by his life, has gone before us courageously on this way, pointing it out to us[23] by his words and works. If you do not set out on it with determination and if you do not walk on it according to your strength, you will not be able to reach Jesus Christ. As the Apostle says: *No one will be crowned who does not strive lawfully* [1 Tim 2:5]. And again: Whosoever wishes to belong to Jesus Christ must walk in the way in which he walked.[24] Set out, then on the way of God and be careful as you walk that death not catch you by surprise. Therefore, your obedience must be prompt, your poverty voluntary, and your chastity above all suspicion. These three things are the very essence of our Order; if they are lacking it cannot stand.

You who have promised stability in this holy place, serve God each day without growing weary of the burden you have taken upon yourselves. Do not let yourselves be drawn outside except rarely and in cases of necessity, lest in the dissipation of useless running about you lose that heavenly sweetness tasted with all its delights in meditation on the divine mysteries, lest you open the door to love of this deceitful and passing world, with all its danger and defilement. A fish out of water, deprived of its natural element, soon dies. In the same way, a religious who lacks stability, no longer protected by the walls and shelter of the cloister, no longer having before him the good that his brothers preach by their word and example, will soon find that too-frequent contact with the world— totally immersed as it is in evil[25]—will cause him to fall into vice and be caught in the net of eternal death. If you wish to maintain that internal vigilance leading to purity of soul, avoid contact with

[22] Compare Matt 10:38.

[23] Editor's note: Here the author of the sermon uses the verbal form *praemonstravit* as a wordplay reminding his reader or listener of the connection between Christ's "ponting out" of the narrow way to the "pointing out" or "showing forth," *praemonstratum*, to Saint Norbert of the site for his first religious foundation.

[24] Compare 1 John 2:6.

[25] Compare 1 John 5:19.

people of the world as carefully as a fish avoids dry land. For you would be unworthy to be called a religious if, despite this sacred bond, your desires kept you attached to the world rather than to God alone.[26] Preserve stability, love, and harmony by curbing your tongue. Avoid murmuring, malicious gossip, and jealousy, so that all of you may be of one heart and one soul in the house of God.[27] The tongue that loves to speak ill and to deceive is a wound that grows ever larger and spreads its deadly poison everywhere. It constantly injures, disturbs the peace that religious ought to preserve among themselves, and inhibits all devotion. The common saying goes: "An argumentative and querulous monk is not truly a monk."[28]

Curb your tongue, therefore; set or raise your heart to the kingdom of heaven where true joys are found[29] and, inspired by a desire for perfection, follow those who are perfect beyond the heavens on the wings of the contemplation of divine things. Grieve that you must bear the weight of your flesh so that you may be able to exclaim with the Apostle, *I desire the dissolution of my body that I may be with Jesus Christ* [Phil 1:23], and with the psalmist, *Bring our souls out of this prison of our bodies* [Ps 141:8], that we may reign eternally with Jesus Christ. As for those who wear this dazzling white habit of religion, externally feigning the innocence and apparent simplicity of doves, yet in the eyes of God, who sees our inmost thoughts, sadly lack that devotion which makes for a perfect religious; as for those who from the bottom of their rebellious hearts despise salutary counsel and those who give it to them, thus refusing to obey the holy prescriptions of regular discipline—if they do not amend their ways, they will surely be condemned to the pains of hell, that most terrible place where confusion and great chaos reign forever.[30]

Be on your guard then, that you may avoid the terrible judgment of the divine majesty. Serve God devoutly in fear and righteousness,

---

[26] Editor's note: Here again Latin worldplay on the part of the author enriches his text's meaning. He reminded his hearer that to be named a religious, *nomen sanctae religiositatis*, means to be bound, *religati estis*, emphasizing the etymology of the term *religio* in the Latin root for tying or binding.

[27] Compare Rule of Saint Augustine.

[28] Cited by Drexelius, who attributes this saying to Abba Pastor.

[29] *Missale Romanum*, Fourth Sunday after Easter.

[30] Compare Job 10:21.

that he may preserve you in the practices of religious life, and that in his mercy he may keep you from such punishments. This God can show himself generous and rich in mercy toward those who have served him faithfully. He will give them great riches in exchange for small effort, eternal goods for temporal work, as he himself said one day to his disciples when they asked: *What will be our reward for having despised and left all things, and for the good works we have done?* He replied: *You will receive a hundredfold in this life and you will have eternal life* [Matt 19:20].

May Jesus Christ lead us to it. Amen.

No religious should find it difficult or burdensome to reread frequently the short exhortation to serve God contained on this page. The word of God, according to the prophet, is a fire[31] whose flames grow stronger at the breath of the Holy Spirit; it consumes vice, it is an incentive to virtue, it opens the treasures of wisdom to people of good will and obtains for them heavenly nourishment. That is why our Savior said: *Blessed are they who hear the word of God and keep it* [Luke 11:18]. Mary Magdalene, because she faithfully listened with attentive ears to the word of God,[32] totally absorbed as she was by her devotion and burning desire for divine contemplation, was praised because she had chosen the better part, which Martha could not obtain or merit by the laborious occupations and attentive care to which she was devoting herself in order to serve our Savior and provide for his human needs.

Listen to this word eagerly; in wisdom, keep it and fulfill it always, so that at the end of the world you may joyfully hear this sentence, sweet as honey, from the Sovereign Judge: *Come, blessed of my Father, receive the eternal kingdom* [Matt 25:34]. Then, enjoying the tranquility of unchanging peace, you will rejoice eternally in glory, where you will see God face to face and where you will know his infinite perfection. God will wipe away every tear from your eyes,[33] and there will be no more death or sadness; all the momentary pain of temporal sufferings will pass in an instant. There the

---

[31] Compare Ps 118:140.
[32] Compare Luke 10:42.
[33] Compare Rev 7:17; 12:4.

abundant sweetness that God has reserved for you and for those who fear him will be revealed.[34] There God will console you eternally with all his elect as you fully contemplate the infinite delights of the marvels of his omnipotence. There you will draw unfailing fruitfulness from the fountain that waters the garden of God;[35] there you will be flooded by living waters whose source will not grow dry; there you will be inebriated by the abundance of the delights of the house of God, delights that surpass all experience; there you will be satisfied at the sweet torrent of his ineffable pleasures. There God will surround himself with power and strength, and shining with the brightness of eternal life with which he will be robed,[36] he will become your servant and give himself to you, a magnificent reward by which his immense generosity will fulfill all your desires. This is the promise he once made to the holy patriarch Abraham, that he would reward his faith and obedience, when he said to him, *I will be your very great reward* [Gen 15:1]. Behold this unique pearl of infinite worth that is offered to you; to obtain it you must sell all your goods and work unceasingly.[37] Its beauty and soft sparkle are such that, according to the Apostle, they cannot be perceived by human senses.[38] Even the human heart itself, whose sentiments are so penetrating and profound, cannot rise to such sublime knowledge. Finally, because of the virtues and excellence of its merits, unless God in his utterly gratuitous generosity gave you this reward, you would not have a full and complete right to it, neither through the sufferings you endure, nor through the practice of good works. As the Apostle says: *The sufferings of this life cannot be compared with the glory that will be revealed in you in the life to come* [Rom 8:18].

The almighty God became man for you; having experienced in himself the frailty of the human condition, he knows the clay of which you are made[39] and knows too that all people are given to vanity and led to evil by each of their senses.[40] Fervently ask him

---

[34] Compare Ps 30:21.
[35] Compare Song 4:15.
[36] Compare Ps 112:2.
[37] Compare Luke 18:22.
[38] Compare 1 Cor 2:9.
[39] Compare Ps 88:48.
[40] Compare Gen 8:21.

to protect you in his mercy and in his goodness help you to complete your course without allowing you to yield to the pleasures of the flesh. Thus you will use temporal goods in such a way as not to lose, but to obtain, those that are eternal.[41] May he grant you this grace, he who lives and reigns with the Father and the Holy Spirit, forever and ever. Amen.

[41] *Missale Romanum*, Third Sunday after Pentecost.

Index

Ricverde

Ɏ Sikornik Hill

(now a district of Krakow)